Monitoring Detention, Custody, Torture, and Ill-Treatment

A Practical Approach to Prevention and Documentation

Edited by

Jason Payne-James
Jonathan Beynon
Duarte Nuno Vieira

CRC Press
Taylor & Francis Group
Boca Raton London New York

CRC Press is an imprint of the
Taylor & Francis Group, an **informa** business

CRC Press
Taylor & Francis Group
6000 Broken Sound Parkway NW, Suite 300
Boca Raton, FL 33487-2742

International Standard Book Number-13: 978-1-4441-6732-0 (Paperback)

Library of Congress Cataloging-in-Publication Data

Names: Payne-James, Jason, editor. | Vieira, Duarte Nuno, editor. | Beynon, Jonathan, 1964- editor.
Title: Monitoring detention, custody, torture and ill-treatment : a practical approach to prevention and documentation / [edited by] Jason Payne-James, Duarte Nuno Vieira, Jonathan Beynon.
Description: Boca Raton, FL : CRC Press, 2018. | Includes bibliographical references and index.
Identifiers: LCCN 2016053246| ISBN 9781444167320 (paperback : alk. paper) | ISBN 9781138632929 (hardback : alk. paper) | ISBN 9781315211459 (eBook)
Subjects: | MESH: Physical Abuse--prevention & control | Custodial Care--standards | Patient Harm--prevention & control | Human Rights Abuses | Torture--legislation & jurisprudence | Custodial Care--legislation & jurisprudence
Classification: LCC HV713 | NLM W 860 | DDC 362.76--dc23
LC record available at https://lccn.loc.gov/2016053246

Visit the Taylor & Francis Web site at
http://www.taylorandfrancis.com

and the CRC Press Web site at
http://www.crcpress.com

Contents

Monitoring Detention, Custody, Torture, and Ill-Treatment

A Practical Approach to Prevention and Documentation

Companion Website

In *Monitoring Detention, Custody, Torture, and Ill-Treatment: A Practical Approach to Prevention and Documentation*, the author team identify the medical, legal, and professional frameworks and international instruments applicable to those detained, and highlight how torture or other cruel and inhuman or degrading treatments or punishments are identified, investigated, and should be prevented.

The companion website, https://www.crcpress.com/cw/paynejames, comprises links to the many key documents, guidelines, and legal frameworks to assist in the documentation and prevention of torture and ill-treatment referenced throughout the text. Also included in the bank of resources are links to relevant publications and societies.

Foreword

Torture—arguably one of the most brutal and devastating human rights violations—is still practiced in most countries. This fact remains in spite of numerous tools and mechanisms available in the fight against torture and other cruel, inhuman, or degrading treatment or punishment (ill-treatment). These measures include *inter alia* the UN Convention against Torture, the Optional Protocol to the Convention against Torture (OPCAT), the UN Nelson Mandela Rules on standard minimum rules for the treatment of prisoners, the Istanbul Protocol, and many others.

Despite the availability of such important instruments and tools, the international community has not yet succeeded in eradicating the practice of torture. One part of the explanation may be that the absolute prohibition of torture and the means to fight torture are not known to those at risk of committing torture and ill-treatment. The uniformed staff involved with the treatment of detainees and prisoners are mostly those who have the legitimate authority to apply force. This places them at risk of excessive use of such force, and often with little knowledge of how to prevent torture or to react to torture once encountered. Other professions in criminal justice institutions include medical doctors, judges and prosecutors, social workers, psychologists and teachers. Such professions are at risk of active or passive complicity in torture if alleged cases of torture encountered are not handled correctly.

For these reasons, knowledge of how to prevent torture from being committed and of how to report and document cases of alleged torture is crucial for those professions involved with any aspect of the interrogation, custody and treatment of detainees. The UN Convention against Torture, as stated in the first chapter of this book, puts an obligation on State parties to the Convention to ensure that training in such topics is provided to these professions.

The adoption of the OPCAT and the current ratification process further increases the need for key knowledge on torture among those involved with preventive monitoring of places of detention. As the National Preventive Mechanisms (NPM) mandated to undertake such monitoring emerge, the need to build the skills and knowledge on torture prevention and documentation further grows.

This book makes a strong contribution to the dissemination of knowledge of how to document and prevent torture. It is edited and authored by prominent experts in the field, and it addresses the key topics at both theoretical and practical levels.

I sincerely hope that this book will be read and used extensively and thus release its potential as a strong tool in the fight against torture.

Jens Modvig, MD, PhD
Director, Health Department DIGNITY
Chair, UN Committee against Torture

Preface

This is a book that really should not have to be written. It might be expected that states and governments should always protect the interests of those detained by their law enforcement, security, and military agencies, but that is not the case. This book is intended as a practical guide to assist all those individuals and organizations who may be tasked to monitor detention conditions and investigate and prevent torture, and other cruel and inhuman degrading treatments or punishments. Often, they themselves are working in coercive and oppressive settings. The current geopolitical state of the world means that knowledge about the national and international frameworks for monitoring and assessing those in detention is needed more than ever. There appear to be few locations worldwide where abuses of some kind do not occur.

A group of very experienced authors from a wide range of backgrounds and jurisdiction in relevant fields have provided the legal and professional framework of international standards for the treatment of those detained in any form of custody. Others with clinical and medical backgrounds explore how to determine and assess whether these standards are being properly applied and how specific aspects of detention may impact on the detained individual. The settings referred to are extensive and include police stations, prisons (civilian and military), detention centers (e.g., pretrial detention centers, immigration detention centers, juvenile justice establishments), mental health and social care institutions, and any other places where people are or may be deprived of their liberty. The editors and authors aim to provide guidelines on how these standards can be monitored, assessed, and documented both by individual practitioners and national and international monitoring bodies and non- or quasi-governmental organizations. The authors identify existing national and international reporting mechanisms for the findings of these monitoring visits, and identify sanctions or penalties that may be imposed on those countries, bodies, or individuals that breach acceptable standards.

We hope that the book will have a multinational and multiprofessional readership including doctors and other healthcare workers, lawyers, those working within refugee and asylum seekers, and any individual who may form part of a visiting team, including law-enforcement professionals and laypersons. Perhaps most importantly we hope it will be read by politicians, policy makers, and those authorities tasked with the care of those deprived of their liberty, so that over time the existence of torture and cruel, inhuman, and degrading treatment will be reduced, and when it does take place, those responsible, whether individuals, organizations, or governments, can be properly made accountable and brought to justice.

J. Jason Payne-James
Southminster, UK
Jonathan Beynon
Geneva, Switzerland
Duarte Nuno Vieira
Coimbra, Portugal

Contributors

Jonathan Beynon
Independent Expert
Prevention of Torture, Monitoring
    Conditions of Detention and Health
    in Detention
Geneva, Switzerland

Marc Bollmann
University Center of Legal Medicine
    Lausanne-Geneva
Lausanne, Switzerland

Bernice Elger
University Center of Legal Medicine
    Lausanne-Geneva
Lausanne, Switzerland

Peter Glenser
Barrister
9 Bedford Row Chambers
London, United Kingdom

Peter Green
St Georges University
London, United Kingdom

Vincent Iacopino
Senior Medical Advisor
Physicians for Human Rights
New York, New York

and

Adjunct Professor of Medicine
University of Minnesota Medical School
Minneapolis, Minnesota

and

Senior Research Fellow
Human Rights Center
University of California, Berkeley
Berkely, California

Michael Levy
Medical School
College of Medicine, Biology
    & Environment
Australian National University
Canberra, Australia

Patrice Mangin
University Center of Legal Medicine
    Lausanne-Geneva
Lausanne, Switzerland

Juan E. Méndez
Professor of Human Rights in Residence
UN Special Rapporteur on Torture
    (2010-2016)
Washington College of Law American
    University
Washington, DC

and

Commissioner of the International
    Commission of Jurists
Geneva, Switzerland

Nimisha Patel
International Centre for Health Human
    Rights & Reader in Clinical Psychology
University of East London
London, United Kingdom

Jason Payne-James
Consultant Forensic Physician & Specialist
    in Forensic & Legal Medicine
Faculty of Forensic & Legal Medicine
    of the Royal College of Physicians

and

Honorary Clinical Senior Lecturer
Centre for Clinical Pharmacology
William Harvey Research Institute
Barts & the London School of Medicine
    & Dentistry
Charterhouse Square

and

Honorary Consultant
Emergency Medicine
St George's Hospital
London, United Kingdom

and

Director
Forensic Healthcare Services Ltd
Essex, United Kingdom

Máximo Alberto Duque Piedrahíta
MD Forensic Consultants S.A.
Bogotá D.C., Colombia
and
Member of the American Academy
    of Forensic Sciences
Colorado Springs, Colorado

and

Member of the International Association
    of Legal Medicine
Lausanne, Switzerland

Hernán Reyes
Human Rights Center
University of California, Berkeley
Berkeley, California

Sharon Shalev
Centre for Criminology
University of Oxford
Oxford, United Kingdom

and

International Centre for Prison Studies
London, United Kingdom

Kirsty Sutherland
Barrister
9 Bedford Row Chambers
London, United Kingdom

Jørgen L. Thomsen
Institute of Forensic Medicine
University of Southern Denmark
Odense, Denmark

Morris Tidball-Binz
Forensic Coordinator
International Committee of the Red Cross
Geneva, Switzerland

Duarte Nuno Vieira
Faculty of Medicine
University of Coimbra
Coimbra, Portugal

H. Vogel
Institute of Legal Medicine
University-Hospital Eppendorf
University of Hamburg
Hamburg, Germany

1

International Legal Framework on Torture

Juan E. Méndez

CONTENTS

Introduction

Of all protections against attacks on human dignity that are included in the canon of international human rights law, the prohibition on torture and other cruel, inhumane, or degrading treatment (CIDT) or punishment enjoys the broadest consensus among nations and societies. There is universal condemnation of the brutality involved in the deliberate infliction of pain and suffering on other human beings. Countries where torture is practiced despite this condemnation tend to deny the facts or to deny that "enhanced interrogation techniques" amount to torture. Cynical as such denials may be, they ratify the existence of a moral, legal, and political condemnation that is truly universal. That is why the right to physical and mental integrity—or the right to be free from torture—has been at the center of the development of international law on human rights that began after the end of World War II. In fact, one can trace the prohibition of torture even further, to the so-called Martens clause in the Hague Convention of 1899 that established that "… populations and belligerents remain under the protection and empire of the principles of the laws of humanity and the requirements of the public conscience" (Preamble, Hague II 1899; Preamble, Hague IV 1907). The prohibition of torture is one of a handful of international laws that are jus cogens, an imperative norm of international law from which no nation can depart because it is a *constitutional* provision of the international community, similar to the prohibition of the use of force between nations, the mandatory peaceful resolution of disputes, and the principle of nonintervention in internal affairs of other nations. In addition, the prohibition of torture is unanimously recognized as a customary international law norm. For these two reasons, it applies to all states and societies, regardless of whether or not they have ratified the relevant treaties. In that sense, the treaty norms to follow are considered to have codified obligations that exist beyond and before them; there is no sense, therefore, in a state claiming to be bound by them only from the date of ratification.

The right to personal integrity is established in the Universal Declaration of Human Rights (UDHR) of December 10, 1948 (UDHR 1948). It is also clearly spelled out in the first comprehensive treaty intended to make the UDHR legally binding, the International Covenant on Civil and Political Rights (ICCPR) (1966). More recently, these norms were elaborated upon by the Convention against Torture and other Cruel, Inhuman or Degrading Treatment or Punishment (CAT [Convention against Torture] 1984). The CAT distills specific legal consequences and binding obligations that derive from and apply to the prohibition of torture, all of which are also considered to codify customary international law (Office of High Commissioner for Human Rights 1992). Later, the United Nations (UN) adopted an Optional Protocol to CAT (OPCAT) directed toward the prevention of torture by means of regular and ad hoc visits to facilities that hold persons deprived of freedom (OPCAT 2006). In terms of universal standards, it is worth mentioning that the prohibition of torture and ill-treatment applies also in wartime, both because in such circumstances international human rights law and the laws of armed conflict apply coextensively (*Prosecutor v. Dragolijub Kunarca* et al. 2001) and because the Geneva Conventions of August 12, 1949 includes a specific prohibition on "outrages against personal dignity" of detained enemy combatants and similar protections for the civilian population (The Geneva Conventions of August 12, 1949).* A common feature of all those provisions is that the prohibition of torture is absolute. International law extends that absolute nature to the comparatively lesser offense of CIDT. The differences between torture and CIDT are (1) the severity of the pain and suffering inflicted, CIDT being less severe than torture; (2) that torture requires specific intent to inflict pain and suffering, whereas CIDT can be committed by negligence, as, for example, in inhumane prison conditions; (3) the legal obligations triggered by one and the other, as discussed later in the text (CAT 1984, Article 16). The absolute prohibition means that no state of war or national emergency can be invoked to justify any departure from it. Even in states of emergency that are publicly declared, the right to personal integrity is one of the fundamental rights that are nonderogable, meaning that they cannot be suspended, even temporarily, due to such circumstances (ICCPR 1966; CAT 1984 [Articles 2.2 and 4.2, respectively]).

Both torture and CIDT must be committed by state agents, meaning public officials or other agents acting at "… the instigation of or with the consent or acquiescence of a public official or a person acting in an official capacity" (CAT 1984, Articles 1.1 and 16.1). Members of paramilitary groups or of gangs that do dirty work for a government certainly qualify as perpetrators of torture for the purposes of these provisions. In keeping

---

* See also Protocols I and II Additional to the Geneva Conventions of 1977.

with the evolution of international human rights law, states have also been held responsible for torture and ill-treatment in the hands of private parties in circumstances where the state knew or ought to have known of the risk and neglected to protect the victim. For that reason, some cases of domestic violence or abhorrent practices in healthcare, under appropriate circumstances, come under the definition (SRT [Special Rapporteur on Torture] 2013).

The definition requires a certain severity (different for torture from that for CIDT), but is not limited to custodial situations. For example, CIDT, and even torture, can take place in cases of excessive use of force in repressing street demonstrations, provided that the physical or mental pain and suffering is severe enough to qualify (UN News Centre 2014). International law defines *torture* as an "international crime," in the sense of an offense that is so injurious to the conscience of humanity that it compels the interests of every state and of the international community to prevent and punish it. In this sense, torture stands alongside such other human rights violations as genocide, crimes against humanity, war crimes, slavery, and the slave trade. Even in comparison to those mass atrocities, torture is unique in that its nature as an international crime means that even a single episode of torture gives rise to the international community's insistence on its investigation, prosecution, and punishment (Cassese 2005). In addition, when committed as part of a pattern of "widespread or systematic" violations, torture is a crime against humanity that triggers the jurisdiction of the International Criminal Court (ICC) (in cases where such jurisdiction is applicable on geographic or other grounds) (Rome Statute 1998).

For purposes of the subject-matter jurisdiction of the ICC, "widespread" torture necessitates a certain number of similar episodes. The "systematic" character is arguably satisfied by a smaller number of cases or an approach that applies torture only to suspects of certain crimes, as long as it can be shown that perpetrators implement a deliberate plan or that those officials charged with preventing and punishing it deliberately refuse to do so. In other words, acquiescence in or tolerance of torture is enough to make it systematic.

The jurisdiction of the ICC is premised on the territorial state being "unwilling or unable" to investigate, prosecute, and punish the crime of torture, a principle known as complementarity (Rome Statute 1998, Article 1.7). It must be noted that the rule does not apply to the ad hoc tribunals created by the UN Security Council to try war crimes and other offenses in the former Yugoslavia and Rwanda, courts that actually enjoy primacy over domestic jurisdictions. Whether or not organs of international criminal justice have jurisdiction in cases of torture, it is also clear that torture gives rise to the exercise of *universal jurisdiction* in states that choose to allow their own courts to hear cases despite the offense happening elsewhere and not involving nationals of the forum state, either as victims or perpetrators. This principle is codified in the CAT and is sometimes referred to under the Latin aphorism *aut dedere aut judicare* or *aut dedere aut punire* (CAT 1984, Articles 5.2 and 6.4). It means that the state that has or can obtain custody of a torture suspect must either extradite him/her to a state with legitimate jurisdiction, or transfer him to an international court. If it chooses not to extradite, the state must prosecute him. The clear language in CAT indicates that even a single case of torture that is not part of a widespread or systematic pattern can give rise to universal jurisdiction in the custodial state, or else to the obligation to extradite (*R v. Bartle ex parte Pinochet* 1999). In practice, all cases of universal jurisdiction to date have involved systematic patterns, and since universal jurisdiction is a permissive norm, not an obligation, it is unlikely that we will see such jurisdiction applied in isolated cases. But even then, the obligation to extradite would still be present.

State Obligations

The international law framework imposes the following obligations on states party to the CAT (as mentioned earlier, all of them are also customary international law obligations, so they apply to signatories and nonsignatories of CAT):

Obligation to Investigate, Prosecute, and Punish Torture

The obligation to investigate cases of torture is established in Article 12 of the CAT, and significantly, it also applies to acts that are not torture but amount to CIDT (CAT 1984, Article 16). The investigation has to be surrounded by guarantees that prevent it from being an exercise in futility or tokenism. It has to be "prompt and impartial" according to Article 12. By its terms, this norm would suggest that an internal investigation by the same law enforcement body whose agents are suspect could satisfy the requirement, as long as the body conducting it is given early access to all evidence (prompt) and conducts its inquiries without interference (impartial). In practice, international organs of protection against torture and CIDT also require the investigation to be "independent" in the sense that the body itself is not subordinate to authorities who may have an interest in the outcome. In several instances, international courts and organs have required the inquiry to be judicial in nature, as the only guarantee of independence and impartiality (e.g., *Gutiérrez Soler v. Colombia* [2005]) The inquiry must have the specific objective of identifying perpetrators and gathering evidence for purposes of prosecution and not simply as a truth-telling endeavor (*Barrios Altos v. Peru* 2001). Most importantly, it cannot be conducted in a pro forma fashion, as a series of steps destined to fail. Indeed, if such were the case, international law requires that the outcome of such a bad-faith inquiry can never achieve the status of res judicata for purposes of precluding serious investigations (*Velásquez-Rodríguez v. Honduras* 1987; *Almonacid-Arellano et al. v. Chile* 2006). The obligations to prosecute and punish must be regarded as the good-faith interpretation of the obligation to investigate. In addition, they also emanate from other provisions in CAT (Articles 4–8), namely, those that make torture punishable in the domestic jurisdiction, assert jurisdiction over cases of torture, consider torture a nonpolitical crime for purposes of extradition, and the already cited *aut dedere aut judicare* standard (which applies to the territorial state as well as to all possible custodial states). Furthermore, as indicated in CAT, Articles 2 and 16, the obligation to prosecute and punish is an offshoot of the overarching obligation to *prevent* torture and CIDT, because failure to investigate, prosecute, and punish invites repetition of this insidious practice.

As a consequence of this affirmative obligation, amnesties and pardons that stand in the way of fulfilling the obligation are violations of the state's international obligations. For this reason, the state is obliged to strip such legal obstacles of any effectiveness in domestic law (*Barrios Altos v. Peru* 2001) Indeed, the state is obliged to remove other legal obstacles that may be invoked to refuse investigation, prosecution, and punishment, such as statutes of limitation, military court jurisdiction, fraudulent res judicata, and even de facto impunity factors, such as lack of political will, undue interference with the ordinary course of justice (*Almonacid-Arellano et al. v. Chile* 2006). Finally, and in keeping with the principle established at the Nuremberg trials of Nazi-era crimes, obedience to superior orders is not a valid defense (CAT 1984, Article 2.3) unless the order was not manifestly illegal under the circumstances or, even if manifestly illegal, the accused did not have a moral choice (Rome Statute 1998, Article 33). It is difficult to envision a situation in which the order to torture is not manifestly illegal.

Some states that have signed and ratified CAT view their obligations quite narrowly, specifically regarding whether the obligation to investigate, prosecute, and punish applies not only to torture (here, there is no discussion), but equally to CIDT. That is the reason for the now infamous torture memos, secretly elaborated by the US Justice Department of the George W. Bush administration (Office of Legal Counsel 2002). Those and other secret memos, eventually withdrawn by then President Bush, purported to advise intelligence officials as to what techniques to use without being subject to prosecution, supposedly because those techniques would not reach the level of severity required for torture. Aside from the fact that they did not consider that, used in conjunction, those methods would amount to torture even if individually they might not; the memos were wrong on the law in other aspects. They did not, for example, warn that CIDT is also prohibited and therefore illegal even if it does not lead to prosecution. The point is that US legislation implementing CAT does indeed contemplate criminal prosecution for torture, but not for CIDT. This may be consistent with a narrow reading of CAT, and at the time of the promulgation of the implemented legislation, it was not foreseen that it would give grounds for the gross mischaracterization of state obligations involved in the torture memos. But it is regrettable that, despite the withdrawal and disavowing of those memos, they continue to have lingering effects; today, the US government refuses to prosecute torture in the so-called war on terror on grounds that all suspects would have acted under the impression that they were acting legally (Mayer 2005, 2010).

Nonrefoulement

No state may expel, return (refouler), extradite, deport, or transfer any person to a jurisdiction where there are substantial grounds to believe that he or she is in danger of being subjected to torture (CAT 1984, Article 3). This provision is reminiscent of the customary law obligation of nonrefoulement in refugee law (Convention Relating to the Status of Refugees, 1951, Article 33). It is different, however, in several significant ways. In the first place, it does not depend on the person having the status of refugee or being entitled to asylum. Second, the 1951 Convention prohibits giving refugee or asylee status to persons who have persecuted others; such restriction is not present in CAT, so even the worst criminal cannot be sent to a place where he or she could be tortured. Third, the CAT nonrefoulement provision protects persons only from torture (and arguably from CIDT), but not from other forms of persecution such as denial of political rights. CAT also establishes that, in evaluating the risk of torture, states are entitled to analyze if the receiving country exhibits a pattern of gross and consistent violations of human rights. Of course, the inquiry cannot end there; even without such a demonstrated pattern, the person could still face the risk of being subjected to torture or CIDT; and if so, the sending state is under an obligation to prevent it by refusing to send him/her there (SRT 2014). The analysis of patterns of gross and consistent violations opens the door to the use of medical evidence in support of such practices, in the context of preventing refoulement. The sending state is under an affirmative obligation to allow such assessment to be argued and invoked in appropriate proceedings.

The remedy for an illegal refoulement could include a variety of diplomatic initiatives. In a recent case, the SRT and other mandates urged the Italian government not to send back to Kazakhstan a woman, the wife of a former president who is currently in exile in Europe. Despite our urgent actions, Italy sent the woman and her young daughter back to Kazakhstan. The clamor in Italy for the illegal action was such that the Italian government requested and obtained their return to Italy (UN News Center 2013).

Exclusionary Rule

An important preventive provision is the Exclusionary Rule, which prohibits states from using statements or confessions established to have been obtained under torture in any proceeding against the victim. The only exception is in cases against those accused of torture (CAT 1984, Article 15), to show that the statement was made/or obtained under torture. The treaty does not expressly apply this principle to CIDT, but the proper interpretation is that statements obtained through CIDT, likewise, must be excluded. The obligation to investigate CIDT (Article 16) does not expressly mention that statements obtained through CIDT can only be used in prosecutions of the perpertrators, but the language in Article 15, preceded by the words *in particular* shows that the list of articles that comes next is not meant to be exhaustive. In any event, since the state's absolute obligation is to prevent CIDT as well as torture, it would be absurd to allow statements obtained under CIDT to enter the record; this would only encourage more ill-treatment. The purpose of this exclusionary rule is to ensure fair trials of persons accused of crime, but more importantly, it serves the objective of prevention by providing a disincentive to mistreat in interrogations. If the police officer knows that the success of an investigation is put in jeopardy by his/ her behavior, he or she is more likely than not to refrain from abusive or coercive practices (SRT 2014).

In practice, this rule is frequently violated with impunity. Judges and prosecutors refuse to investigate torture ex officio, and even when the victim files a complaint, it remains in the record until it "is established" that it was coerced. In practice, if not in law, this is effectively an unwarranted shift in the burden of proof, and the victim—generally emerging from several days of incommunicado or pretrial detention and still in custody—is in the worst possible situation to meet that burden. Judges and prosecutors are complicit in the practice by allowing the police to let some days pass before bringing the detainee to the first hearing, so that physical signs of torture are no longer visible. Medical examinations are rarely ordered, and when they are, they are practiced after another long delay and by professionals who are beholden to the police, the prosecutors, or the judiciary. Needless to say, the state should carry the burden of showing that statements have *not* been so obtained; for example, by requiring corroboration or reaffirmation of any statement extrajudicially obtained and by giving the detainee a chance to recant the extrajudicial statement without prejudice to the presumption of innocence. Not only the statement, but also any other evidence obtained as a result of it must be excluded as well, even if that other evidence was gathered by formally following rules of procedure. This "fruit of the poisonous tree doctrine" is domestic law in several jurisdictions (*Mapp v. Ohio* 1961). The SRT believes that it is also the proper, good-faith interpretation of CAT Articles 15 and 16, as well as the one that reflects the preventive purpose of the treaty.

Another reason to deplore the limitations of the exclusionary rule, as spelled out in CAT, is the recent tendency of some governments to interpret the words "in any proceeding" very narrowly. Especially as a result of the global war on terror, governments have sometimes used torture-tainted evidence for intelligence purposes, for covert operations, to support decisions to maintain detainees in prolonged detention without trial, and to refuse protection from nonrefoulement. All this is compounded by the fact that the same governments refuse to disclose crucial elements of these practices on protection of state secret grounds. Unfortunately, some domestic courts have let the executive branches get away with this practice, which undermines the preventive purpose of the exclusionary clause (SRT 2014).

Right to a Remedy and Reparations and Rehabilitation

The victim of torture or CIDT has both a right to a remedy and a right to reparations for the harm suffered, the latter including the right to as full a rehabilitation as possible (CAT 1984, Articles 13 and 14). Although often treated together, these rights are conceptually different and rightly established separately in CAT (1984). The right to a remedy reflects and complements the State's obligation to prevent torture by means of establishing procedures and structures through which a victim's complaint may be heard on a timely basis and impartially acted upon by the competent authorities. To the extent that the impartial nature of the inquiry requires evidence of mistreatment, the intervention of medical professionals to ascertain the physical or psychological traces of such treatment acquires enormous importance. The right to a remedy also requires that the state establish and implement arrangements, so that judicial authorities can immediately inquire about the conditions of the detention of a person recently arrested (CAT 1984, Articles 2.12 and 12; ICCPR 1966, Article 9.4). In this fashion, international law incorporates the ancient common law writ of habeas corpus, a quick remedy to examine the lawfulness of any deprivation of freedom that long before had also been adopted by virtually all legal cultures. In international law, the writ does protect not only against unlawful arrests, but also against unacceptable conditions of detention—including ill-treatment—even in cases of lawful arrest (Inter-American Commission on Human Rights 1987).

The right to reparations and rehabilitation reflect the well-established rule in international law that every violation of an obligation gives rise to the obligation to restore the status quo ante, if possible, and to compensate for harms suffered (International Court of Justice 1970). The scope, modality, and *quantum* of compensation to be paid or of rehabilitation services to be offered have to be proportionate to the harm suffered. It goes without saying that objective scientific evidence, especially medical, which includes psychiatric, as well as psychological evidence, is crucial to make such an assessment. The state must afford the opportunity and medical personnel with the highest scientific competency to facilitate it; in addition, its laws must make room for the possibility of private medical experts that may be available to a claimant, with no other restriction or requirement regarding its scientific persuasiveness.

Adaptation of Legislation and Regulation to Bring It into Conformity with CAT

On becoming parties to international human rights treaties, states acquire general obligations to respect and ensure the enumerated rights and adapt domestic legislation to them (ACHR [American Convention on Human Rights] 1969). In the case of torture, those obligations are further specified: the state must adopt legislative, judicial, and administrative measures to fulfill the obligation to prevent torture (CAT 1984, Article 2.1). In addition, the state must ensure that torture is criminalized in the domestic jurisdiction and accompanied by penalties proportionate to its seriousness (CAT 1984, Article 4, paras. 1 and 2) That obligation also extends to torture attempts and to complicity in torture. In terms of jurisdictional and procedural norms, the state must also organize its court system and codes so as to establish its ability to bring perpetrators to justice and to afford victims access to justice, meaning their participation in criminal proceedings as well as ability to bring civil actions for damages (CAT 1984, Article 5).

Even though more than 140 states have become parties to the CAT, the fulfillment of this obligation to adapt the domestic legal order to its provisions lags far behind. This is also true of the OPCAT; many states sign and ratify it, but then take a long time to create, organize, and put in motion the national preventive mechanism (NPM) that OPCAT calls for (Article 3). The NPM is designed to maintain the system of periodic and unannounced visits to sites of deprivation of liberty to complement the visits by the Subcommittee on Prevention of Torture (SPT), also created by OPCAT. To be effective as a preventive mechanism, visits to detention centers must include competent medical experts, including experts in forensic medicine, trained in the Istanbul Protocol for the documentation of torture. For that reason, it is imperative that states live up to their obligations by creating NPMs, but more importantly, by providing them with the means to conduct serious, scientifically competent, independent, impartial, and transparent visits.

Other Obligations

The CAT also refers (in Articles 10, 11, and 16 [1984]) to other state obligations that are germane to the subject of this book, especially on the training of law enforcement and judicial personnel and on the periodic review of practices and policies of governmental agencies with a view to ensure compliance with the prohibition of torture and CIDT in the interrogation, custody, and treatment of detainees. Article 10 specifically includes medical personnel among the public officials that must be adequately trained. It is imperative that doctors and other healthcare professionals employed by police, corrections departments, and courts become proficient in the Istanbul Protocol and other internationally recognized standards for the documentation of torture and the treatment of its *sequelae*.

International Mechanisms for the Protection of All Persons against Torture

Human rights obligations and their violations are monitored by a variety of supranational mechanisms established at the universal level (under the umbrella of the UN) and by other organs set up by regional organizations.

The Universal Protection System

The universal system consists of two large branches: the treaty-based and the charter-based organs. Some human rights treaties include provisions to create an organ of implementation and interpretation of rights and obligations, generally called committees. The UN treaty bodies with specific responsibility for torture and related matters are the Human Rights Committee (the organ of protection of the ICCPR); the Committee on Torture, the implementing body of CAT (sometimes itself referred to as CAT); and the SPT, which monitors the application of the OPCAT. Other treaties deal with torture or CIDT within the specific realm of their subject matter, such as the Committee on the Rights of the Child, the Committee on Elimination of Discrimination against Women, or the Committee on the Rights of Persons with Disabilities.

A common thread among all treaty bodies is that they do their work by way of three main procedures: (1) general commentaries issued from time to time on aspects of the treaties they monitor, which are considered highly authoritative interpretations of such instruments; (2) periodic reviews of the general state of treaty implementation in a specific country, conducted every 4 or 5 years. States appear at a hearing and produce a self-report; the observations and conclusions of the committee related to this review are contained in a public report; and (3) case specific examinations of allegations and the views issued by the committee as to where a violation has taken place and recommendations for state redress. For this, each committee has jurisdiction to hear complaints only if the state party to the treaty has made a separate declaration in its ratification (for an example, see CAT Article 22 [1984]) or signed an additional optional protocol agreeing to subject its practices to this scrutiny. The views of the committee issued at the end of each proceeding also constitute an authoritative source of interpretation of rights and duties. In exceptional circumstances, a committee seeks an invitation to visit a country to conduct an on-site investigation. CAT and OPCAT avail themselves of the advice of forensic experts for all these functions, and medical and other healthcare professionals are sometimes selected to be commissioners themselves.

The charter-based mechanisms are also called special procedures. They were originally created by the now-defunct Commission on Human Rights of the Economic and Social Council and, since 2006, have been transferred to the authority of the Human Rights Council, a principal organ of the UN that replaced that commission. The council has created new procedures since then, now totaling nearly 50. Ten of those are country specific as of 2014, although the council decides to continue or terminate them from time to time by a vote of its state members. Nearly 40 at the present are thematic in nature, including the Special Rapporteurship on Torture, created in 1985. Most mandates are assigned to a single person (the Special Rapporteur) selected by the president of the council for a term of 3 years, renewable once. Some, however, called working groups, are composed of five members appointed from the five geographic voting blocs of the UN. The Special Procedures are designed to act under the UN Charter and not under a specific treaty, so they conduct their work with regards to all 194 member states of the UN. They act in three major ways: (1) by publishing thematic reports on areas of their mandate that require special attention or dialogue to foster new standards. Most mandates have two opportunities a year to present thematic reports: once before the Human Rights Council and once before the General Assembly; (2) by conducting country visits at the invitation of the relevant state. The visits are comprehensive and intensive on-site inquiries with opportunities for dialogue with authorities, civil society organizations, and other experts, including in the case of the SRT visits to detention centers and other sites where persons are deprived of freedom. At the end of the visit, a country report is prepared and submitted to the Human Rights Council for discussion, together with the state's response; and (3) communications sent to states on the basis of allegations received from the public about specific cases. Once a year, the SRT chooses to submit to the council a summary of each case, with his/her observations or conclusions on the facts and law applicable. The Special Procedures have the advantage of not being limited to act only on signatories of treaties, and their work is not subject to procedural requirements for the exhaustion of domestic remedies or exclusive jurisdiction norms. They apply treaty norms as well as customary international law standards. On the other hand, Special Procedures' observations and comments are specifically stated to be nonbinding.

In addition to the SRT, the Working Groups on Enforced or Involuntary Disappearances and the Working Group on Arbitrary Detention (WGAD) have mandates that bring them in contact with the prohibition of torture and CIDT. The area of CIDT that results from inhumane conditions of detention has been traditionally covered by the SRT, although the WGAD also claims some mandate over them. In practice, Special Procedures work together and join forces, especially in the mechanism of communications on specific cases, as they generally present complex fact patterns. The SRT has long had the practice of seeking and obtaining expert medicolegal advice, particularly in the conduct of country visits. A forensic expert is essential not only to determine the veracity of allegations of mistreatment where physical or mental signs are present, but also to analyze the sufficiency of medical services in detention centers. In addition, forensic doctors provide essential advice on whether domestic practices in the investigation of torture comply with internationally recognized standards such as the Istanbul Protocol.

Regional Protection

The Council of Europe, the Organization of American States (OAS), and the African Union have in place systems of protection that apply similar mechanisms to states under their jurisdiction and within their geographic area. Those systems also include substantive state obligations contained in region-specific treaties, and such treaties create organs of protection that combine a series of promotional, standard-setting, and supervisory activities. More so than the organs of the universal system, the regional mechanisms tend toward emphasis on the case-complaint procedure and, within that, favor a judicial approach rather than a quasi-judicial or an informal exchange between the organs, the petitioners, and the state. In addition to their courts, the inter-American and African systems retain commissions which are responsible for case-complaint procedure and have a wider spectrum of functions such as the ability to conduct on-site visits and follow-up visits, produce country reports, establish thematic rapporteurships, and develop standard setting initiatives. The judicial approach to case complaints presents clear advantages over the quasi-judicial procedures of the UN treaty bodies, not only because it gives victims and state representatives a fuller opportunity to air grievances and present evidence at public hearings, but also because decisions on the merits tend to explain and develop the content of state obligations emanating from treaties in a more systematic way.

Europe

The European Court of Human Rights operates under the aegis of the Council of Europe and is based in Strasbourg, France. After the incorporation of many Eastern European countries, the European Court now has jurisdiction to hear allegations of violations of the European Convention on Human Rights by 47 countries (European Convention on Human Rights 1950). It consists of 47 judges, each one appointed by a member state of the European Convention; although for different stages, it operates with single judges, chambers, and grand chambers. This court is, of all the organs of supranational protection of rights, by far the most well-established and with the largest body of jurisprudence produced so far. It has also enjoyed the highest degree of compliance with its judgments; although some recently incorporated states repeatedly ignore them. At the same time, the European Court suffers from an increasing backlog of cases. The Council of Europe has also elaborated a Convention on the Prevention of Torture, which in turn creates a Committee on the Prevention of Torture (CPT) that conducts visits to detention centers in all member states, both regular and periodic, as well as unannounced visits (European Convention for the Prevention of Torture and Inhuman and Degrading Treatment or Punishment 1987). The CPT also has 47 members, one from each country, as all member states of the Council of Europe have ratified the convention. As in the case of the SPT, several members are themselves healthcare professionals or forensic experts, and the CPT organizes itself in areas of expertise, including a medical sector.

In 1999, the Council of Europe created the office of a Commissioner for Human Rights, whose task is to promote reforms in all 47 countries so that domestic policies and practices afford better protection of human rights to all persons under their jurisdiction. The commissioner does not have the capacity to hear individual cases.

The Inter-American System

The OAS was founded in 1948 and immediately enacted the American Declaration on the Rights and Duties of Man (1948). This instrument was later incorporated into the Charter of the OAS and thus obtained treaty status. In later years, the OAS developed a more complete system for the promotion and protection of human rights. In 1959, it created an Inter-American Commission on Human Rights, which in 1967 became a principal organ of the OAS by its incorporation into the Charter (Protocol of Buenos Aires 1967). In 1969, the OAS drafted an ACHR, also known as the Pact of San José de Costa Rica, which in turn incorporates the commission and creates a separate organ, the Inter-American Court of Human Rights, which was adopted on November 22, 1969 and entered into force on July 18, 1978. In subsequent years, the substantive norms of the American Declaration and Convention have been supplemented by other treaties, such as the Protocol of San Salvador on Economic, Social and Cultural Rights (in 1988), the Protocol to the ACHR to Abolish the Death Penalty (in 1990), the Inter-American Convention to Prevent and Punish Torture (in 1985), the Inter-American Convention on Forced Disappearance of Persons (in 1994), the Inter-American Convention on Prevention, Punishment and Eradication of Violence against Women (Convention of Belem do Para 1994), and the Inter-American Convention on the Elimination of all Forms of Discrimination against Persons with Disabilities (1999). As can be seen, virtually all these instruments contain norms that can apply to cases of torture or CIDT.

The Inter-American Commission receives complaints under most of these instruments and applies them to signatories or, in the case of the declaration, to all member states of the OAS. This procedure is quasi-judicial in nature. At its end, the commission issues a report that may find that the state has violated the rights of a person or persons and transmits its report with recommendations to the state. If the state does not accept or does not comply with the report, the commission usually sends the case to the Inter-American Court. At that stage the procedure becomes fully judicial, with participation of the commission, the state, and representatives of the petitioner or victim. The trial includes open hearings and witnesses, including expert witnesses. The Court has frequently heard expert testimony from forensic doctors and anthropologists, as well as other experts.

In its other functions, the commission appoints special rapporteurs. A special rapporteur on persons deprived of liberty has made important contributions to the advancement of principles and standards applicable to conditions of detention and treatment of detainees.

African System

The African Commission on Human and Peoples' Rights was created in 1986 under the aegis of the then-called Organization of African Unity, now replaced by the African Union (AU). Its main substantive treaty, the African Charter on Human and Peoples' Rights, combines civil, political, economic, social, and cultural rights in a single instrument and without differentiated treatment. Since its creation, the system has promulgated other human rights instruments, such as a Protocol on the Rights of Women (in 2003, entered into force 2005), the African Children's Charter (in 1990/1999), the African Charter on Democracy, Elections and Government (in 2007, not yet in force), and the AU Convention for the Protection and Assistance of Internally Displaced Persons (in 2009, not yet in force).

The commission conducts studies, on-site visits, country reports, and case complaint proceedings in much the same way as the Inter-American Commission. It also has appointed special rapporteurs, including one on persons deprived of freedom. A Protocol to the African Charter (in 1998/2004) created the African Court on Human and Peoples' Rights. Until 2013, when the court issued its first substantive decision dealing with the exercise of political and civil rights in Tanzania, the court had declared all cases inadmissible (*Tanganyika Law Society & Legal and Human Rights Centre v. The United Republic of Tanzania* 2013).

Other Regions

There have been failed (and misguided) attempts to develop regional systems of human rights under the League of Arab States and under the Organization of Islamic States (Shelton and Carozza 2013). Article 45 of the Revised Arab Charter on Human Rights (adopted on May 22, 2004, e.i.f. March 15, 2008) creates an Arab Human Rights Committee whose function is exclusively to receive periodic self-reports from states and comment on them. The only other subregion that, after a long and arduous process, has created the rudiments of human rights protection system is the Association of Southeast Asian Nations (ASEAN), whose charter announces the creation of a Human Rights Body (in 2007). That body is now called the ASEAN Inter-Governmental Human Rights Commission, composed of representatives of all 10 member states of ASEAN and "accountable to the appointing Government" (ASEAN Intergovernmental Commission on Human Rights 2009). Its functions are exclusively to provide advice to states, to develop strategies, and to promote awareness of human rights; it cannot hear complaints.

As can be seen, the geographic and population coverage of the existing regional systems of protection leaves wide areas and peoples of the world without significant supranational protection. In this context, strengthening the universal system, and particularly the Special Procedures, acquires great significance.

Conclusions

Throughout the previous sections, this chapter has attempted to show the importance that scientific evidence has in the struggle to combat and eventually to abolish torture in our time. Torture must be combated in a comprehensive and holistic way. We definitely need to refine definitions and strengthen procedural guarantees. We also need to build institutions dedicated to oversight and control, with adequate powers and binding force. We definitely need to increase public awareness and especially prop up the moral condemnation of torture, which, in some countries falters, at times because of a perception that without torture, our societies are vulnerable to terrorism, organized crime, and more generally to societal violence.

Very significantly, however, we have an imperative need to develop and apply scientific proof of torture, in order to address the cynical and self-serving denial that many authorities engage in. Forensic evidence allows us to close the loopholes that states are inclined to use to evade their international and domestic responsibilities for this human rights crime. It is also crucial to stress that medical evidence of torture may be confined only to psychological/psychiatric evidence since, increasingly, states are using supposedly purely psychological methods of torture or CIDT in the misguided belief that only physical methods actually amount to torture and that the latter can be more easily documented. In addition, it can be shown that scientific evidence is a much more effective way to solve crime and punish wrongdoers compared to the brutality of interrogation methods that rely on torture or CIDT.

For medical expertise to play this role, it is important to insist that forensics be surrounded by guarantees of effectiveness, so that examinations and reports are provided on a timely basis and are rendered to authorities that respect the integrity of medical practitioners and the soundness of their scientific findings. At the same time, forensic evidence is credible and will attract the appropriate judicial decisions if practitioners and experts are protected by guarantees of independence and impartiality. These guarantees rely on the method of appointment, the comparison of credentials, their insertion in a chain of supervision, and control that does not make them beholden to law enforcement or prosecutorial bodies whose interest in the outcome of scientific expertise could very well be determinant in the results. Even with all the external safeguards of independence, it will be necessary for forensic experts to defend the integrity of their analysis by demonstrating a subjective sense of impartiality and a devotion to the truth that is revealed through scientific methods, without consideration given to a false esprit de corps or to institutional loyalties.

In conjunction with other disciplines, physicians, psychiatrists, and psychologists have developed protocols and standards of excellence that provide guidance to human rights advocates and organs of protection to determine whether State practices of investigation of torture are acceptable. Those standards, such as the law, will always be in constant progressive development. As the science of detection advances, our struggle to end torture will become more effective.

References

ACHR (*American Convention on Human Rights*) 1969, ACHR, Washington, DC, adopted on November 22, 1969, entered into force on July 18, 1978.

African charter on human and peoples' rights 1981, Articles 30 et seq. African Union, Addis Ababa, adopted June 27, 1981, entered into force on October 21, 1986.

Almonacid-Arellano et al. v. Chile, Preliminary objections, merits, reparations and costs, IACtHR (September 26, 2006).

ASEAN Intergovernmental Commission on Human Rights 2009, *Terms of reference of AICHR*, ASEAN Intergovernmental Commission on Human Rights, Jakarta.

Barrios Altos v. Peru, Merits, Inter-American Court of Human Rights (IACtHR) (March 14, 2001).

Cassese, A. 2005, *International law*, University of Oxford, Oxford.

CAT (Convention against Torture) 1984, CAT, New York, adopted by the UN General Assembly Res. 39/46 of December 10, 1984, entered into force on June 26, 1987.

Charter of the Organization of American States as amended by Protocol of Buenos Aires, 1967, in Inter-American Commission on Human Rights, *Basic Documents Pertaining to Human Rights in the Inter-American System* (Updated to January 2007), Washington: OAS, 2007; p. 1.

Convention Against Torture and Other Cruel, Inhuman or Degrading Treatment or Punishment, December 10, 1984, 23 ILM 1027 (1984) as modified 24 ILM 535 (1985), UNTS 85, entered into force June 29, 1987.

Convention on the Status of Refugees, 1951, in Damrosch, Lori, Henkin, L., Murphy, S. and Smit, H., *Basic Documents Supplement to International Law Cases and Materials*, 5th. Ed.; New York: West, 2009.

European Convention for the Prevention of Torture and Inhuman or Degrading Treatment or Punishment, 1987, in Shelton, D. and Carozza, P., *Basic Documents, Regional Protection of Human Rights*, 2nd. ed.; Oxford: OUP, 2013; p. 128.

European Convention on Human Rights, 1950, ETS No. 5, in Shelton, D. and Carozza, P., *Basic Documents, Regional Protection of Human Rights*, 2nd. ed.; Oxford: OUP, 2013; p. 9.

Gutiérrez Soler v. Colombia, Judgment, IACtHR (September 12, 2005).

Inter-American Commission on Human Rights 1987, *Habeas Corpus in Emergency Situations*, Advisory Opinion OC-8/87, IACtHR, San Jose.

Inter-American Convention on the Prevention, Punishment and Eradication of Violence Against Women, June 9, 1994, No. A-61, entered into force March 5, 1995.

International Court of Justice, 1970, *Case concerning The Barcelona Traction, Light and Power Co.*, Judgment, ICJ (February 5, 1970).

International Covenant on Civil and Political Rights, in Carter, B., *International Law Selected Documents*, 2011–2012 edition, New York: Wolters Kluwer Law and Business, 2011; p. 392.

Mapp v. Ohio, 367 US 643 (1961).

Mayer, J. 2005, Outsourcing torture: The secret history of America's "extraordinary rendition" program, *The New Yorker,* February 14, 2005.

Mayer, J. 2010, Counterfactual: A curious history of the C.I.A.'s secret interrogation program, *The New Yorker,* March 29, 2010.

OAS (Organization of American States) 1948, *American Declaration on the Rights and Duties of Man*, adopted by the Ninth International Conference of American States, Bogotá, Colombia.

Office of High Commissioner for Human Rights, 1992, *General comment no. 20*, Office of High Commissioner for Human Rights, Geneva.

Office of Legal Counsel 2002, *Memorandum for Alberto R. Gonzalez, Counsel to the President, U.S. Department of Justice*, US Department of Justice, Washington, DC.

Optional Protocol to the Convention Against Torture and Other Cruel, Inhuman or Degrading Treatment or Punishment, December 18, 2002, G.A. Resolution A/Res/57/199, entered into force June 22, 2006, available at http://www.ohchr.org/EN/ProfessionalInterest/Pages /OPCAT.aspx

Prosecutor v. Dragoljub Kunarca et al. 2001, Judgment, International Criminal Tribunal for the Former Yugoslavia (February 22, 2001).

Preamble, Hague II Convention on Laws and Customs of War on Land, 29 July 1899; and Preamble, Hague IV Convention on Laws and Customs of War on Land, 18 October 1907.

R v. Bartle ex parte Pinochet, Judgment, United Kingdom House of Lords (March 24, 1999).

Rome Statute for the International Criminal Court, A/Conf.183/9, 1998 in M. Cherif Bassiouni, comp., *The Statute of the International Criminal Court: A Documentary History*, Ardsley and New York: Transnational Publishers, 1998; pp. 39 et seq.

SRT 2013, Report of the Special Rapporteur on Torture in Health-Care Settings, UN G.A., A/ HRC/22/53, February 1, 2013, in *Torture in Health Care Settings: Reflections on the Special Rapporteur on Torture's 2013 Thematic Report*, Washington: Center of Human Rights and Humanitarian Law, 2014.

SRT 2014, *Thematic Report: Exclusionary Rule and the Use of Torture Tainted Evidence and Information*, A/HRC/25/60, available at: http//:documents-dds-ny.un.org/doc/UNDOC/GEN/G14/134/68 /PDF/G1413468.pdf.

Shelton, D., and Carozza, P. 2013, *Regional Protection of Human Rights,* 2nd. ed., Oxford: OUP.

Tanganyika Law Society & Legal and Human Rights Centre v. The United Republic of Tanzania, Applications No 09/2011 and 11/2011, African Court of Human Rights, Judgment of June 14, 2013.

"The Geneva Conventions of August 12, 1949," (Conventions I through IV), Geneva: International Committee of the Red Cross.

Universal Declaration of Human Rights, G.A. Res. 217 (III) U.N. Doc. A/77, December 10, 1948, in Barry Carter, *International Law Selected Documents*, 2011–2012 edition, New York: Wolters Kluwer Law and Business, 2011; pp. 386 et seq.

UN News Center 2013, UN experts urge Italy to facilitate return of illegally deported Kazakh mother, daughter, July 18.

UN News Centre 2014, Egypt: Top UN human rights official urges investigations amid escalating violence, January 27, 2014.

Velásquez-Rodríguez v. Honduras, Preliminary Objections, IACtHR (June 26, 1987).

2

Role and Responsibilities of Health Professionals Involved in the Care of Those in Detention

Jørgen L. Thomsen

CONTENTS

Introduction

Work as a prison physician (or in any other setting where individuals are detained) may be full time or part time. It can be a difficult role as the physician has a dual obligation toward the detainee (prisoner, inmate) and the prison authorities. It is a classical controversy, and when training medical doctors, obligations and duties toward the individual must be emphasized. It must, however, not be forgotten that the physician has an obligation toward the society as he/she should report any shortcomings or systematic abuse that he/she may find in his/her work as a prison physician. This should become a benefit for those detained in prisons and the society, as improvements will benefit both parties. As for physicians not working in prison or detention settings, the prison physician must have good awareness of the prevention, treatment, and care of communicable diseases as they may pose a threat to the prison community.

Detainees are always vulnerable as it may be difficult to raise concerns to the administration or other authorities both inside and outside the prison. The subjected detainee may be subject to unfair, random treatment and physical or mental ill-treatment or torture. This may take place in inaccessible places of detention with limited or no access of family or higher authorities. Therefore, the visit of a physician as part of a visiting team may be the only means of monitoring and improving the treatment and conditions of detention, as well as the prevention and treatment of physical and mental illnesses.

In the following, the term *prison* will be used as a general term for a range of detention facilities, including prisons (military and civilian), police stations, detention centers, immigration detention centers, and juvenile justice establishments as defined in the *Optional Protocol to the Convention against Torture (OPCAT): Subcommittee on Prevention of Torture* (United Nations [UN] Office of the United Nations High Commissioner for Human Rights 2006).

No distinction in this chapter is made between pretrial (remand) and posttrial (sentenced) detention.

Medical Ethics in General

To a physician, a prisoner is a patient, and he/she should not be seen as another category of individual even though he/she has been deprived of his/her freedom and irrespective of his/her background and the reason for his/her detention. The physician must recognize that the principles and practice of medical ethics apply in the detention situation in the same way they do in a nondetention setting. Specifically, prisoners have the right to confidentiality, to informed consent, and to the same treatment that they would receive in a nondetention setting. It should be a common aim of both the prison authorities and the physician to protect and promote the physical and mental health of the prisoners. The physician's duties to all inmates are the same, but some categories (e.g., political detainees or those detained on security grounds) may need more attention with reference to increased risks of ill-treatment and torture. The role of prisons as punishment institutions is over, and the aim of prison is resocialization and rehabilitation and reintegration into the community.

The World Medical Association (WMA) Declaration of Geneva (1948) states the following:

> The health of my patients will be my first consideration.
> The doctor must not permit considerations of religion, nationality, race, party,
>   politics or social standing to intervene between my duty and my patient.

It is an accepted ethical principle that a patient has the right to privacy and confidentiality when consulting a physician. The author was once requested by Amnesty International to enter a prison in Mexico City in order to examine one of the prisoners, as there was an allegation of physical ill-treatment by the authorities. Reclusorio Norte is an enormous prison with hundreds of prisoners in the prison yard at the same time. The author found the prisoner but was not given the opportunity to examine him in a private room. The examination took place in a foul-smelling common bathroom with constant movement of other prisoners at the same time. Obviously, such conditions are not ideal, but the examination was undertaken for two reasons: (1) although documentation would not be ideal, no harm would be done and (2) it provided an opportunity to raise awareness of the existence of torture (see Figure 2.1).

Rarely, the occasional prisoner may have acute behavioral disorder and be unpredictable and potentially violent, for a variety of reasons for example just pure aggression or sometimes because of mental health issues. In such exceptional cases where there is perceived risk, it may be necessary for the doctor to have a guard with him/her for protection during the consultation, but for the most part, such consultations must take place without the presence of authorities (Rule 31, UN Standard Minimum Rules for the Treatment of Prisoners or Mandela Rules 2015 [UN 1955]). The physician must enter into an agreement with the prison authorities to

FIGURE 2.1   Torture in the inmates. Visitors from Amnesty International demonstrate that some of the prisoners in a Mexican prison have been tortured.

have a prisoner comply with rules that are against his/her conviction and his/her well-being. Identifying the specific risks of prison physicians being instrumental in the ill-treatment of prisoners, the UN Standard Minimum Rules now explicitly state that the physician must not engage, actively or passively, in any act of torture or other CIDT or punishment, which would be understood to include acts of corporal punishment (UN 1955, Rule 32.(d)).

The UN Principles of Medical Ethics (UN General Assembly 1982) state that

> health personnel, particularly physicians, charged with the medical care of prisoners and detainees have the duty to provide them with protection of their physical and mental health and treatment of disease of the same quality and standard as is offered to those who are not imprisoned or detained.

The recently updated UN Standard Minimum Rules reaffirm that prisoners should enjoy the same standards of healthcare that are available in the community and should have access to necessary healthcare services free of charge. This is referred to as equity of care.

The lack of resources in a prison must not justify the infringement of prisoners' human rights. As the prisoner is deprived of one important human right, namely, the right to freedom, the utmost must be done to uphold other human rights. The physician may have an important role to play in that respect (Council of Europe 2006, Part I/4).

> Every prison shall have the services of at least one qualified general medical practitioner (Council of Europe 2006, Part III/41.1).

In some countries, this rule is difficult to fulfill. There are countries with few doctors, and although the health of prisoners should be given high priority (which is usually not the case), it may be difficult to have the necessary medical prison visits. In many places, medical work for the prisons is a part-time occupation. The work of a prison physician has not always been highly valued in the hierarchy of physicians, and such work is often undertaken by generalists with no specific training or experience in the custodial setting. Remuneration may be less than other established medical specialties. It may therefore be difficult or impossible to achieve the intended target of high-quality medical service let alone equity of care—which is of major concern bearing in mind the complexity and vulnerability of many detainees. In some countries, nurses are replacing physicians, which can be an acceptable solution under the circumstances, when there is a poor supply of physicians and if those nurses are appropriately trained and have access to physicians when they encounter issues beyond their competence. The aim that prisoners should have the right to their own choice of doctor is in practice unrealistic and unachievable, as in many countries, it may not even be possible to access a doctor. Detainees thus have to trust the available physician, but they do have the right to refuse to be examined by him/her, leaving them with an impossible option. Either they may suffer from their disease, or even die, or they may undergo examination and treatment by a medical person that they do not trust.

In 2000 the author visited a prison in Tuxtla Gutierrez, in the southern part of Mexico, Chiapas, and was told that the prisoners had access to competent medical service. Having asked to see the medical clinic, the director showed a totally empty room that had obviously not been used for a long time with no medical facilities (see Figure 2.2), and this is not an unusual situation.

Ideally, a prison physician should also have experience in the examination and treatment of psychiatric patients as mental health issues are a substantial problem in the detention

FIGURE 2.2   Medical room in a prison in Chiapas, Mexico. There was no indication that the room had ever been used.

setting. This goal is far from being achieved in a worldwide perspective. The physician should be able to conduct mental state examinations and competent in identifying self-harm and suicidal ideations with the aim of preventing suicide in prison.

> The services of qualified dentists and opticians shall be available to every prisoner (Council of Europe 2006, Part III/41.4).

Poor countries in remote parts of the world will often lack trained medical personnel as these are few and may be used for treatment of the sick in the society outside of the prisons.

Other examples of poor general healthcare involve simple activities of daily living, such as the opportunity to clean teeth. The author has previously examined prisoners from Kosovo who had been held in prison for about 6 months. Prison conditions had been poor with no opportunities for oral hygiene. There was no opportunity to see a dentist. The prisoners gradually lost their teeth due to caries and gum disease with loosening and then loss of dentition. Some also had their teeth damaged by violence such as beating or kicking (see Figure 2.3). All detainees with oral hygiene or trauma issues should have the opportunity to be reviewed by dental practitioners.

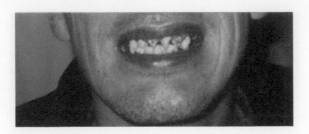

FIGURE 2.3   Traumatic lesions of the teeth due to physical abuse in a Kosovo prison.

Dual Obligation

It is easy to understand that a prisoner who may feel lonely and vulnerable is suspicious toward a physician who is employed by the prison authorities. It is the duty of the physician to establish confidentiality and trust. In many places, this is not easy as the prison authorities, typically the prison governor, may have the view that they are responsible for security and must be aware of everything that happens in the prison. The prisoner does not see the doctor as independent, and the prisoner may be convinced that any information to the doctor will go directly to the prison director. In some prisons, the medical staff must be strong and persistent in order to keep their neutrality and act according to the ethical rules. The prisoner may (sometimes correctly) suspect that the physician will take his/her salary and employment into consideration more than the interests of the prisoner when he/she is facing a conflict with the prison director.

Prisoners should be able to request for a physician whenever they need it. This may give rise to conflict, as the prisoner may not be believed as far as his/her symptoms are concerned, it may be too difficult to request for a physician at short notice, and there may be financial restrictions. In 1984, the author examined suspected Irish Republican Army prisoners who had been incarcerated in the interrogation centers of Northern Ireland. He was informed by them that after the first report on torture in the interrogation centers, they stopped using physical abuse, but used psychological methods instead. One of these was the denial of medical assistance. There were reports that the prisoners would request for a physician and the guard would accept that, but in fact, he/she never called a physician and, when faced with this, he/she denied everything, and it was word against word.

Confidentiality

Confidentiality is an important aspect of the physician–patient relationship. It is important that the patient at any time may ask a physician for help without risking to be reported to the authorities. This is especially important in prison conditions, as the prisoner does not have much confidence in the prison authorities. It may be with good reason as the prison authorities would generally like to control any aspect of life in prison. The physician must be aware of this attitude. He/she must of course keep records, and if he/she is a permanently employed prison physician, he/she will often have his/her records. If not, or if it is a new prisoner, he/she should start making records and ask the prisoner for permission to obtain any previous records or information that may be of relevance from hospitals or other physicians. If the prisoner does not want to be examined by one particular physician, then the physician must withdraw from the examination. As the rules are the same in prison and outside a prison, any prisoner who has mental capacity can refuse medical help. The physician must keep the confidence of the prisoner and assure that no information will go to the prison authorities. This applies to any consultation. If the prisoner suffers from a communicable disease (e.g., tuberculosis, acquired immune deficiency syndrome [AIDS], hepatitis B or C), there may be an exceptional necessity for disclosure of this information (for example, if there are specific health risks to others). Specific rules and regulations differ in various countries and jurisdictions. In some countries, it may not be possible to inform the prison authorities of the identity of the patient with the disease, but the physician must be prepared to find other ways to limit the risk of the spreading of the disease. In those cases of serious communicable diseases, he/she may go to the prison authorities, not mentioning the name of the prisoner(s), but presenting the problem in general, introducing precautions to keep the prisoners safe from acquiring the disease. This is not an easy task, and the rumors will quickly spread in the prison so it is difficult to keep the anonymity of a person of whom the other prisoners know that he/she recently had a visit from the physician.

The prevention, treatment, and care of communicable diseases in a prison is of course much easier if the inmates cooperate. This calls for a high degree of confidence as any prisoner will suspect that suffering from a disease would make him a target by the authorities, and he/she will run the risk of isolation.

In noncommunicable diseases, such as cancer, diabetes, cardiac diseases, the physician will find it easier to maintain confidentiality. In cases of sexually transmitted diseases, the patient must be urged to inform his/her partners, as they may also need treatment, and the disease must be prevented from spreading further. In case of investigations in a prison of serious crimes, the physician may be questioned by the police or by the courts and may be left with the ethical dilemma of under which circumstances medical confidentiality can be broken.

With reference to a forensic medical examination (one where there may be legal process requirements above and beyond general healthcare), practices may differ. The physician carrying out legal (forensic) functions is also bound by all medical ethical principles. Any victim of, for instance, violence in a prison may refuse to be examined by a physician. However, depending on the rules and laws of the country and the physician's regulatory body, suspects may be compelled by law or statute to accept forensic documentary examinations. In the United Kingdom, the physician cannot undertake any intervention on a detainee (e.g., taking a blood sample, undertaking a physical examination) without the patient's consent. In Denmark, anyone who is accused of a serious crime (prison sentence of more than 18 months) must allow the physician to take samples, even if physical restraint is needed. It is however very rare that medical health officers or forensic practioners colaborate, as it is also said in the law that you can refuse this obligation for "medical reasons."

It cannot be emphasized enough that if a physician/forensic physician comes across cases of physical or mental abuse in an institution, it must be reported to relevant authorities (for example, the police and/or the prison authorities). Great care must be taken to protect the confidentiality of the complainant, especially to avoid further ill-treatment or retribution. Recent changes in UN rules give standard minimum rules for the confidential reporting, and management of allegations of torture and other ill-treatment must be put in place (UN 1955, Rule 34). In some countries with gross violations of human rights, it may not be possible to find an authority that will take proper measures, be it prison authorities, police, administrative authorities, politicians, or government. In such cases, it is advised that the healthcare professional report their concerns to the local medical association or even to the World Medical Association (1997).

Body Search

The misuse of illicit drugs is a problem in many prisons. Prison authorities may be cautious, and extensive restrictions may be put on a prison in order to keep drugs out. This is in practice not feasible, and the attitude toward body search differs. In some places, searches are performed as a routine when a prisoner has been outside of the prison for a longer or shorter time. This will in many instances be seen as an assault on the prisoner's dignity. There must, however, be a possibility for these investigations as the existence of drugs, as well as weapons and other contraband, in a prison is a security risk. But the prisoner is also in this respect a patient with patients' rights. In some countries, a person cannot resist a body search performed with due suspicion. In other countries (e.g., the United Kingdom), a physician cannot perform any intimate examination (e.g., of the vagina and rectum) without the individual's consent, unless there are exceptional circumstances in which case the physician should act in the patient's best interests (e.g., a collapsed patient who is believed to have concealed drugs in the rectum). In Denmark (where the author practices), a body search may be performed against consent but only after a court order that is given only in case of a serious crime. Even in cases of vaginal or rectal explorations in search of concealed drugs, a person may be subdued by the police while the physician is performing the examination. In practice, this never happens. The author sees this as a very remote possibility even if the argument is that it is for the benefit of the accused, as a container with cocaine or heroin may rupture in the gastrointestinal canal and cause immediate death. The rules should of course be followed, and it may be necessary to isolate a prisoner if there is a strong suspicion of the presence of drugs in his/her body cavities, until such time as the contraband is evacuated naturally.

An examination performed with a screaming and fighting prisoner held down by five guards is not dignified, neither for the prisoner nor for the physician who is performing it. In the United Kingdom and some other jurisdictions, this would not be acceptable without the consent of the detainee. Usually, the only alternative is to isolate a prisoner if there is a strong suspicion of the presence of drugs in his/her body cavities, until such time as the contraband is evacuated naturally. Where readily available, X-rays may also reveal packages of contraband that have been ingested. In women, it may be more difficult as the drugs may stay in the vagina for very long. In such cases, a forced gynecological examination with retrieval of the drugs may be necessary. Again, this would not be acceptable in the United Kingdom and some other jurisdictions in the absence of consent. It should always be remembered to look in other body orifices and cavities, including the nose, the oral cavity, the ears, and under the foreskin.

It must be emphasized (World Medical Association 1993) that this type of examination must be performed by a healthcare professional other than the prison health staff, to avoid compromising the relationship between the prisoners and the prison health staff. At a minimum, the body cavity searches could be conducted by prison staff who have been trained by the health staff.

Drug/Alcohol Abuse

The misuse of drugs is a major problem in many prisons. It is not only a problem to keep the drugs out, but also a problem that the prisoners may suffer from withdrawal symptoms. Withdrawal due to the intake of opiates is not lethal in itself. Alcohol withdrawal may also become a problem, and if untreated, it has the potential for fatality. Physicians need to be aware of and understand not only the effects of intoxication with drugs and alcohol but also the assessment and management of the assorted withdrawal states.

Many, if not most, prisoners will have access to drugs, including opiates, and new psychoactive drugs (e.g., spice) (Public Health England 2015). Much energy is spent smuggling drugs into the prisons, constituting a big market. This may be via other prisoners, guards, or relatives. This may affect the prison community and disturb it in many ways. It is almost impossible to stop the flow of drugs into a prison. Therefore, other ways must be applied, and the prison physician may play a major role. Harm reduction whereby the use of drugs is accepted, but there are attempts to minimize the complications of drug use, by strategies such as making clean needles available, is an important aspect of care but may not be possible in many countries with strict laws on drugs. The physician may introduce drug rehabilitation treatment, and this may prove efficient, especially in prisoners with long sentences. Many countries have strategies and guidelines for treatment of drug misuse in prison (Department of Health 2009). The inmates may be motivated for treatment as their prison sentence is often related to the misuse of drugs. In some prisons, the inmate may voluntarily choose to become isolated or isolated together with other motivated prisoners in parts of the prison that are kept free of drugs and with no access of the other inmates.

Sick Prisoner

As the prisoner has the same rights to physical and mental health, it is the duty of the physician to diagnose any disease, give the proper treatment, and admit to a hospital if necessary. Especially in contagious diseases, such as sexually transmitted diseases, tuberculosis, human immunodeficiency virus (HIV)/AIDS, and hepatitis, it is in the interest of the society, including the fellow prisoners, that proper precautions are taken. It may not be easy in a poor country to prescribe drugs, and of course, the treatment may be modified accordingly. It is the experience in many places that the prison authorities may resist admittance to a hospital. If necessary, the prisoner may be accompanied by a guard into a hospital, but the prison authorities may find this too cost consuming, and discussion of priorities may arise. It is the duty of the physician to give priority to the health of the prisoner.

The problem is even faced in forensic examinations, for instance, in cases of fights or homicide attempts between inmates. As the forensic medical examiner is also a physician with medical ethical duties, he/she has an obligation to refer a prisoner to treatment should his/her examination reveal a disease that needs admission to a hospital or drug therapy. Infrequently, the police or prison authorities may agree to the medical suggestion, but in reality, in many cases, they will ignore it. In such cases, the physician should follow up on his/her recommendations and insist on the medical necessity of proper follow-up and care in the appropriate setting.

The authority of the physician is mainly based on international declarations and conventions, the medical oath, and the medical ethical obligations which are internationally respected and uniform. It is not easy in a remote area of a poor country to stand up against prison authorities and/or police, and in those cases, the national medical society may be contacted for support. If that is of no help, then the WMA can also be approached to gather international support (World Medical Association 1997).

Prison Conditions

It may be argued that the physician must stay only within his/her own professional territory, examining and treating prisoners. There are, however, so many factors that may influence the health in a prison. The hygienic conditions are poor in many places, with dirty, overcrowded cells and limited access to washing, tooth brushing, and toilet facilities. The prisoners must have access to outdoor facilities and be able to exercise in the free air. The physician may also intervene with respect to food in order to ensure that the prisoner is having enough food and food of sufficient quality, including proteins, vitamins, and food without bacterial contamination.

Prevention and Pregnancy

Women may deliver babies in prison, or they may bring babies into prison. This calls for special measures, and the ideal situation is the creation of a special ward for women with children.

Pregnancy prevention is also relevant, and the prison doctor should make sure that the inmates have access to condoms. This is a problem not only in mixed-gender prisons, but also in prisons with only males, as they should have access to the prevention of HIV and other sexually transmitted diseases. In most prisons, the inmates may have a private visit from their partners, and in those cases, access to condoms is necessary and should be mediated by the prison physician.

Corporal Punishment, Bodily Harm, and Sanctions

The Council of Europe (2006) states that "collective punishments and corporal punishment by placing in a dark cell and other forms of inhuman or degrading punishment shall be prohibited." This aim has not been reached yet as corporal punishment is still practiced in many places. Prisons must have rules, and if these rules are not followed, then there must be sanctions. These sanctions, however, should be restrictions in everyday life and not amount to torture or inhumane or degrading treatment or punishment. The physician must never be part of the punishment. He/she should never be asked to support any form of punishment being more human than others or any form of punishment that will be more effective to achieve a goal of repression. In some countries, it has been known that prison physicians were inspecting parades of prisoners in order to estimate if these were "fit for flogging" in order to abbreviate their stay in prison. The author became aware of this practice from Danish physicians who were sent out to developing countries to work and were asked to make this estimation. When it became known, the Danish Foreign Ministry issued a declaration to all physicians that they were not allowed to participate in this practice. No physicians should ever take part in such considerations and should report any such abuses to the appropriate authorities. Some countries and jurisdictions may have inhumane forms of sanctions such as amputations, and in these cases, the physician should report to the proper authorities.

Education

In many settings, prison physicians lack support and ongoing medical education from the community health system. The work as a prison doctor may be a small part of the occupation, and there may be few educational or learning opportunities to improve practice. Prison work is seen as just another type of medical work. This is of course true so long as prisoners are seen as ordinary civilian patients. There are, however, many aspects of the medical work in prisons that are not obvious to the outsider. First of all is the cooperation with the authorities and the obligation to advocate the prisoners' needs as far as physical and mental health are concerned. There are specific demographic features for detained prisoners (e.g., an overrepresentation of drug and alcohol issues, mental health issues, and learning difficulties) (Payne-James et al. 2010). The prison physician must know of the national and international rules and should know his/her rights to refuse, for instance, to assist in corporal punishment. He/she should also know his/her possibilities of appeal to national and international medical associations. Prison physicians do not necessarily constitute a medical specialty in most countries, and it should be considered whether such a specialty should be created, possibly in the form of a subspecialty to internal medicine. It would give more respect to the work of the prison doctors, and they may find it easier to cooperate with the authorities.

Medical Research

In the Council of Europe (1993), Committee of Ministers, it is stated that "persons deprived of their liberty may not undergo medical research unless it is expected to produce a direct and significant benefit to their health." This is a conditioned prohibition as it is difficult to foresee if medical research will produce a direct benefit. It is obvious that the prisoners are in a position making it easier to exploit their health and to achieve a confirmed consent to medical research. Therefore, the physician should be very careful to uphold the rules of medical ethics and make sure that an informed consent is not the result of the prisoner's hope of a better life in prison. Invasive procedures and projects involving danger to the prisoners should be avoided. The updated UN Standard Minimum Rules also permit participation in clinical trials if these are also taking part in the outside community but

reiterate the prohibition on scientific experimentation and expressly forbid the harvest-
ing of cells, tissues, or organs for transplantation to third parties, except for donation to
immediate relatives (UN 1955, Rules 32.1.(d) and 32.2). It is of course not prohibited to make
sociological research in a prison population with descriptive and preventive aims and
with appropriate research and ethics committee approval.

Conclusions

It should always be remembered that prison inmates represent a vulnerable and marginalized population. Prisoners are deprived of their freedom but hold other rights in the
society. Thus, they are entitled to mental and physical health and should receive the necessary treatment against diseases. The inmate must be seen as any other patient. The prison
physician primarily has a duty toward the inmate. He/she has the possibility to improve
prison conditions by recommending ways to improve factors such as sanitation, nutrition,
and hygiene to the prison authorities. The physician must pay particular attention to any
suspicion or allegations of torture and ill-treatment and properly document and report
any cases. The prison physician must not approve nor participate in any form of corporal
punishment and must report any such activity to higher authorities.

Duties of consent and confidentiality for physicians are equally applicable in prison.
The doctor must uphold confidentiality as in the society outside. The inmate must give
informed consent before examination or treatment.

Examinations of body cavities for drugs or other contraband pose a special problem,
as in some countries, forced examinations are lawful. The prison physician should not be
involved in what is essentially a security procedure, but instead an independent healthcare worker, or a properly trained member of the prison staff, should perform such tasks.

All in all, the work of the prison physician and those working in other places of detention is a difficult balance between the demands of the prison management and the health
needs of the prisoners. The physician must always have as their primary focus the health
and physical and mental well-being of their patients.

References

Council of Europe 1993, *Prison and criminological aspects of the control of transmissible diseases including
AIDS and related health problems in prison*, Recommendation R (93) 6, Council of Europe, Strasbourg.
Council of Europe 2006, *Committee of Ministers recommendation Rec (2006) of the Committee of Ministers
to the Member States of the European Prison Rules*, Council of Europe, Strasbourg.
Department of Health 2009, *Clinical management of drug dependence in the adult prison setting*, Public
Health England, London.
Payne-James, J. J., Green, P. G., Green, N., McLachlan, G. M., Munro, M. H., and Moore, T. C. 2010,
Healthcare issues of detainees in police custody in London, UK. *Journal of Forensic and Legal
Medicine*, vol. 17, no. 1, pp. 11–17.
Public Health England 2015, *New psychoactive substances (NPS) in prisons: A toolkit for prison staff*,
Public Health England, London.

United Nations (UN) 1955, *The United Nations standard minimum rules for the treatment of prisoners*, UN, New York.

UN General Assembly 1982, Resolution 37/194, *Principles of medical ethics*, UN, New York.

UN Office of the United Nations High Commissioner for Human Rights 2006, *Optional Protocol to the Convention against Torture (OPCAT)*. Subcommittee on Prevention of Torture, UN, New York. Available from: http://www2.ohchr.org/English/bodies/cat/opcat/index.htm.

World Medical Association (WMA) 1948, *Declaration of Geneva 1948*, WMA, Ferney-Voltaire, France; amended by the 22nd World Medical Assembly, Sydney, August 1968, and the 35th World Medical Assembly, Venice, October 1983; last revised 2006.

World Medical Association 1993, *Statement on body searches of prisoners*, WMA, Ferney-Voltaire, France, revised by the 170th WMA Council Session, Divonne-les-Bains, France, May 2005.

World Medical Association 1997, *Declaration of Hamburg concerning support for medical doctors refusing to participate in, or to condone, the use of torture or other forms of cruel, inhuman or degrading treatment*, WMA, Ferney-Voltaire, France.

3

Standards Applicable in the Prevention of Torture in Places of Detention

Jonathan Beynon

CONTENTS

Concept of Prevention

It is now an established practice that the prevention of torture and other forms of cruel, inhumane or degrading treatment (CIDT) or punishment (torture and other ill-treatment) goes well beyond the consideration of individual complaints of physical or psychological ill-treatment. It encompasses every aspect of the detention from the legal and judicial guarantees protecting against arbitrary arrest and detention and ensuring due process, to the classification and separation of categories of prisoner, to the basic conditions of detention including overcrowding; access to food, water, and medical care; the maintenance of hygiene; the particular treatment of vulnerable groups such as women, children, and those with disabilities. It also embraces issues such as the use of restraints and discipline.

As a cornerstone to prevention, states must of course sign or ratify the various international and regional instruments on the prevention of torture, but these laws must then be put into practice (Subcommittee on the Prevention of Torture [SPT] 2010a). The practice of prevention of torture is not a static one, but one that requires the updating and oversight of national laws, policies, and procedures governing places of detention. States are assisted in this task by reference to and the implementation of universal and regional standards on detention, the protection of detainees, and the prevention of torture in general. The task of national, regional, and international monitoring bodies is to ensure compliance with these standards. While monitoring bodies must conduct routine visits to all places of detention, they should also assess whether national laws, policies, regulations, and practices are in conformity with international laws and standards. This includes protections against arbitrary arrest and detention such as judicial review of detention and due process procedures. They should also assess whether national oversight bodies and complaints mechanisms function since these should also provide protections against ill-treatment.

Monitoring bodies should develop an understanding of the social, economic, and political contexts since all these can have an impact on the management of places of detention and the treatment of detainees. As an example, when assessing the levels of and access to healthcare in places of detention, it is crucial to form an understanding of the national and local healthcare systems. Thus, the healthcare professionals on the monitoring body should visit health clinics and hospitals as well as the ministry of health in order to learn about national healthcare policies and standards for the community as a whole and whether the same standards and practices are applied within places of detention (Association for the Prevention of Torture [APT] 2008). However, it has long been established that prisoners must be treated humanely and with dignity whatever the available material resources of a state (UN 1992).

The definition of a place of detention has also expanded beyond the obvious police stations and prisons, to any public or private place where people may be held against their will, which may include juvenile homes, homes for the elderly, immigration, and asylum centers and psychiatric institutions. Thus, the SPT and the National Preventive Mechanisms (NPMs), both under the Optional Protocol to the Convention Against Torture (OPCAT), the UN Special Rapporteur (UNSR) on torture (UNSRT), and at a regional level, the European Committee for the Prevention of Torture, all include visits to this spectrum of places of detention in their mandate.

As well as having a broad experience in human rights, the composition of the visiting team should reflect the broad range of social, legal, and health issues covered by the prevention of torture and other ill-treatment. As such, the team should include, among others, both legal and health professionals, as well as those with experience in the management of detention systems (APT 2004). The healthcare professional should have knowledge of public health so as to be able to assess the impact of hygiene, nutrition, accommodation, and the healthcare service on the health of the detainees.

While the aim of monitoring visits is the prevention of torture, it is probable that the team will encounter detainees who allege that they are victims of physical or mental abuse that may amount to torture or other ill-treatment, or whom they suspect may have been subjected to such treatment (APT 2013). In order to assess such allegations and in order to submit objective and factual reports to the concerned authorities, the visiting team should ideally include a physician with expertise in the documentation of torture according to the UN Manual on Effective Investigation and Documentation of Torture and Other Cruel, Inhuman or Degrading Treatment or Punishment, commonly known as the Istanbul Protocol (UN 2004).

The visiting physician should also ascertain the level of competence of the detention healthcare staff in documenting torture, their level of awareness and training in the Istanbul Protocol, and the internal mechanisms that exist for reporting allegations of torture, including protection of the victim and any witnesses. In his 2014 report, the UN SRT stressed the vital nature of adequate forensic medical expertise in the documentation of both physical and psychological aspects of torture and on the need for more states to train health professionals on, and to implement, the Istanbul Protocol (UN Special Rapporteur on Torture 2014).

Standards in Detention

Places of detention in each state should be governed by national laws, regulations, and standards of practice. While these national standards are one of the first references for monitoring bodies, it is paramount that their conformity with international standards is assessed and, if necessary, recommendations for revisions made. In international law, as well as the overarching obligations and protections provided by international human rights and humanitarian law such as the right to life, the right to health, and the right to freedom from torture, there are both regional and universal instruments that provide minimum standards for the treatment of prisoners.

Regional Standards

Regional standards and mechanisms that protect the human rights of people deprived of their liberty can be found in Africa, the Americas, and in Europe. In each of these regions, there are mechanisms for the inspection of, and reporting on, places of detention and the treatment of prisoners.

Regional Standards in Africa

In 2002, in order to provide clear guidance to African states, as well as non-state actors, on the prohibition of torture contained in Article 5 of the African Charter on Human and Peoples' Rights, the African Commission on Human and Peoples' Rights (ACHPR or African Commission) adopted the Guidelines and Measures for the Prohibition and Prevention of Torture, Cruel, Inhuman or Degrading Treatment or Punishment in Africa, known as the *Robben Island Guidelines* (Robben Island Guidelines 2002). The Robben Island Guidelines promote the ratification of and cooperation between regional and universal human rights treaties and bodies for the protection of prisoners in Africa from torture and encourages the fight against impunity for perpetrators. Although they do not themselves establish any monitoring bodies, the guidelines encourage the ratification of the UN OPCAT and the establishment of both international and national monitoring mechanisms.

The Robben Island Guidelines further outline basic safeguards for the protection of prisoners, such as access to legal counsel, to judicial review of their detention, and to a medical examination and the maintenance of accurate detention records. While provisions on the conditions of detention are only a summary and focus on the separation of categories of prisoners and the reduction of overcrowding, the guidelines state that the treatment of prisoners should be in conformity with the UN Standard Minimum Rules (SMR).

The Follow-Up Committee, which was initially established as a special mechanism to follow up on the promotion and implementation of the Robben Island Guidelines, later changed its name to the Committee for the Prevention of Torture in Africa (CPTA). The CPTA however does not have any mandate for routine monitoring of visits to places of detention, but is more charged with disseminating the Robben Island Guidelines through training, information sharing, and promotion of best practices. In 2008, the ACHPR, UN High Commissioner for Human Rights, and the APT published a practical guide for the implementation of the Robben Island Guidelines (African Commission 2008) with a commentary on the provisions and recommendations to states, civil society, and the CPTA (formerly the Follow-up Committee).

The only regional body that is empowered to conduct country visits is the Special Rapporteur on Prisons, Conditions of Detention and Policing in Africa, which is a special mechanism established by the African Commission. The detailed reports provide descriptions of many aspects of the places of detention and provide general recommendations to the state. However, the last country visits published are from 2004 to Ethiopia (African Commission 2004a) in which nine prisons, two police stations, and two prison farms were visited and to South Africa (African Commission 2004b) during which prisons, juvenile centers, immigration centers, and a psychiatric hospital were visited. The mandate of the special Rapporteur and other reports, including the recent Guidelines on the Conditions of Arrest, Police Custody and Pre-Trial Detention in Africa (the Luanda Guidelines) can be found on the website of the African Commision (African Commission 2016).

The ACHPR can also receive individual complaints concerning violation of the rights contained in the African Charter on Human and People's Rights and, if the case is admitted, can rule on the merits of those cases. The decisions of the ACHPR in relation to the deprivation of liberty, in particular, Article 5 of the African Charter, the right to be free from torture and other ill-treatment; Article 6, the right to liberty and security; Article 7, the right to a fair trial; and Article 16, the right to health, can be found on the website of the African Commission. For example, most recently in 2014, the African Commission found a violation of the right to be free from torture and ill-treatment, against arbitrary arrest and detention and against the right to health of individuals detained in Sudan in 2008 (African Commission 2014).

Regional Standards in Latin America

Regional standards for the protection of people deprived of liberty in the Americas are enacted and promulgated by the Organization of American States, the OAS, and its main human rights bodies, the Inter-American Commission and the Inter-American Court on Human Rights. In reaction to states' often-repeated claims that poor conditions of detention are due to lack of funds, the Inter-American Court of Human Rights first ruled in 2006 that "the States cannot invoke economic hardships to justify imprisonment conditions that do not respect the inherent dignity of human beings" (Inter-American Court 2006).

The Inter-American Commission on Human Rights had concerned itself with detention for many years, and in 2004, it formally created the Rapporteurship on the Rights of Persons Deprived of Liberty with a mandate to visit and report on places of detention in OAS member states and to consider petitions from individuals deprived of liberty (OAS 2016a). The Rapporteur's most recent working visits to places of detention were to Honduras in 2012, Uruguay in 2011, and El Salvador in 2010. Press releases and observations and recommendations on the conditions of detention following such visits are released on the OAS website.

While both the American Convention on Human Rights of 1969 and the Inter-American Convention to Prevent and Punish Torture of 1985 prohibit torture and other ill-treatment, it was only in 2008 that the Inter-American Commission adopted the Principles and Best Practices on the Protection of Persons Deprived of Liberty in the Americas (Principles in the Americas) that lays down far-reaching and progressive protections (Inter-American

Commission 2008). The scope of deprivation of liberty is very broadly defined, and as well as prisons and police stations, includes any public or private institutions where people may not be free to leave when they wish, such as homes for juveniles and the elderly, asylum and immigration centers, and psychiatric facilities. The principles specifically provide that all places of deprivation of liberty should be open to national and international inspections that should have full access to places and information and to interviews in private with prisoners and staff (Principle XXIV).

As in other regional as well as universal standards, the Principles in the Americas sets out fundamental standards of humane treatment, including equality before the law, non-discrimination including of sexual orientation, due process, and judicial review while at the same time stressing that deprivation of liberty should be a last resort. The principles include provisions on accommodation, nutrition, hygiene, and measures to prevent overcrowding. The principles state that any human rights violations resulting from overcrowding may be considered as CIDT or punishment (Inter-American Commission 2008, Principle XVII). The Principles in the Americas also sets out special protections for people with disabilities, women, and juveniles.

Several years before the UN SMR were updated, the Principles in the Americas clearly set out the principles protecting the patient–physician relationship such as medical confidentiality, patient autonomy, and informed consent. In relation to disciplinary sanctions, the principles are progressive in prohibiting solitary confinement in punishment cells in general (Principle XXII.3) and prohibiting it completely for children, pregnant women, and women imprisoned with their children.

The Inter-American Commission itself also produces country reports from time to time, usually following specific concerns relating to the deprivation of liberty in member states. Thus, following devastating fires in prisons of Honduras that killed hundreds of prisoners, the commission published a report on prison conditions in Honduras, based on a working visit of the Rapporteur on Persons Deprived of Liberty (Inter-American Commission 2013). Other country reports of the commission, which cover human rights issues, may more broadly contain small sections on the deprivation of liberty (e.g., report of the Inter-American Commission on Bolivia in 2009 and Haiti in 2008). The Inter-American Commission has also published several thematic reports which provide detailed background on conditions, standards, as well as regional and international jurisprudences on the deprivation of liberty (e.g., *Report of the Human Rights of Persons Deprived of Liberty in the Americas* 2011 [Inter-American Commission 2011]).

Lastly, jurisprudence of the Inter-American Commission and of the Inter-American Court on Human Rights can be referred to for interpretation and decisions on specific aspects of human rights law relevant to those deprived of their liberty (OAS 2016b).

Regional Standards in Europe

Regional standards for European prisons are detailed in the European Prison Rules (EPRs), which are applicable in all Council of Europe countries. The EPRs were first adopted in 1987 and were updated in 2006 to reflect the evolution in penology, sentencing, and prison management (Council of Europe 2006a). The EPRs contain provisions for detailed record keeping on the admission and processing of new detainees, including medical examinations; the separation of categories of prisoner, the conditions of lighting, ventilation, bedding and hygiene, food and nutrition, contact with family and legal counsel; and the prison regime (including exercise, recreation, work, education). There are also specific provisions for the protection of women, juveniles, foreign nationals, and ethnic minorities.

Particular attention is given to the organization and duties of the healthcare services and staff and to the management of the prison in respect to organization, safety, security, and discipline and the recruitment and training of staff. Detailed provisions on disciplinary sanctions and the use of force and restraints are provided. For a more thorough explanation and discussion of each rule, the Council of Europe also published a commentary on the EPR (Council of Europe 2006b).

The Council of Europe also elaborated standards for juveniles who were subjected to sanctions in the community or who were deprived of liberty (Council of Europe 2008a) and produced a detailed commentary on these standards (Council of Europe 2008b). These include specific provisions on protecting and promoting the physical and mental health of juveniles, in particular, the prevention of suicide and self-harm, and developing their education and training. Due to their particular vulnerabilities, the provisions on discipline, use of force, and restraints are especially adapted to juveniles, including, for example, the prohibition of the use of solitary confinement. Also, particular attention is given to an interdisciplinary approach between prison services and specialized community services in preparation for their release. The through-care of juveniles (the individual attention and planning of the time in detention and the eventual release) should start from the time of admission to a place of detention, by involving the specialized community services at the outset.

In addition to the general prison rules, the Council of Europe has adopted more detailed recommendations on specific aspects of detention policy and practice, including the spread of infectious diseases (HIV, in particular), disciplinary sanctions, healthcare services, overcrowding, the management of life and long-term prisoners, and ethics for prison staff. They can be found, along with other documents relating to detention in Europe, in a compendium of documents on prisons (Council of Europe 2014).

In 1989, shortly after the adoption of the first EPRs, the European Convention for the Prevention of Torture and Inhuman or Degrading Treatment or Punishment came into force. The convention set up the European Committee for the Prevention of Torture and Inhuman or Degrading Treatment or Punishment (CPT), which has the power of access to any place of detention in Europe with the aim of preventing ill-treatment and generally improving conditions of detention. The places of detention to which the CPT has access are broadly defined so as to include not just police stations and prisons, but also other places where people may be detained involuntarily such as psychiatric institutions, juvenile detention centers, immigration centers, and social care homes.

The CPT monitors all aspects of detention, including, for example, access to legal counsel, medical examination and medical care, food, nutrition and hygiene, discipline, and maintenance of records, since many of them may amount to or contribute to inhumane or degrading treatment, as well as torture (CPT 2011a). The CPT visits are unannounced and can take place at any time of the day or night, can be repeated, and include the right to interview any detainee in private. It has become a custom for almost all countries to allow the publication of the CPT country visit reports, as well as the replies of the states to specific findings and recommendations of the CPT, and these documents are very useful background for any monitoring body that intends to visit those states.

In what are known as the CPT Standards, the CPT has used its 25 years of experience, and country and general reports, to contribute to the evolution of international law and the prevention of torture through its examination of specific issues related to detention. The CPT Standards provide detailed analysis and recommendations on specific issues that are relevant, not only to detaining authorities, but also to monitoring bodies since they provide interpretation and lead to the evolution of human rights law and practice. The CPT has looked at issues such as police detention, healthcare in detention, detention in psychiatric institutions, the use of restraints in psychiatric institutions, and vulnerable groups such as women in detention (CPT Standards 2015). More recently, in their Annual General Reports the CPT has looked in detail at the use of solitary confinement (CPT 2011b), documenting and reporting medical evidence of ill-treatment (CPT 2013) and juveniles deprived of liberty (CPT 2014) and life sentenced prisoners (CPT 2015c).

In late 2015, in an effort to assist authorities, nongovernmental organizations, the courts and monitoring bodies and, in particular, the NPMs under the OPCAT, the CPT compiled a standard on the minimum living space for prisoners to be 6 m^2 for a single cell and 4 m^2 per person for multiple occupancy cells, although it should be recalled that it is only strictly applicable in the 47 Member States of the Council of Europe (CPT 2015a).

In 2015, the CPT also published a checklist for visits to social care institutions (CPT 2015b) which will be a useful aid to other monitoring bodies as it covers procedures for initial placement in the institution and review of this decision, the deprivation of legal capacity as well as the use of restraints, ill-treatment, and access to healthcare, including consent or refusal of treatment.

Universal Standards

International Human Rights Law and International Humanitarian Law

UN conventions, optional protocols, minimum rules, codes of conduct, principles, and declarations collectively form universal standards that apply to the protection of people deprived of liberty. A complete list of universal standards relating to detention can be found on the website of the UN High Commissioner for Human Rights (High Commissioner for Human Rights 2016). International Humanitarian Law (IHL), which among others includes the four Geneva Conventions and their Optional Protocols, are laws that apply only in times of armed conflict and which among other aspects protect the sick and injured, civilians, and prisoners. However, in relation to prisoners, the current provisions of IHL provide detailed regulations only for true prisoners of war. The treatment of detainees in all other situations of armed conflict is still covered by the far more detailed provisions of international human rights law. The International Committee of the Red Cross (ICRC) has begun a process with states and other concerned actors for strengthening the protection of detainees in non-international armed conflicts (ICRC 2011). For a general discussion of the differences and overlap between IHL and human rights law, see ICRC (2015).

United Nations Principles

Although the UN Convention Against Torture of 1984 prohibits and obliges states to prevent torture and other ill-treatment, there are no provisions on the more general treatment and conditions for detainees. But other UN universal standards exist that contain overarching rules for all prisoners and more detailed protections for vulnerable groups, such as juveniles, women, people with disabilities, foreign nationals, etc. The 1990 UN Basic Principles for the Treatment of Prisoners (UN 1990a) provide just 11 essential principles. Whereas most of the principles cover general topics related to prisoners such as nondiscrimination, religious freedom, access to healthcare without discrimination, and access to work, this standard is noteworthy since it specifically calls for the abolition of solitary confinement (Principle 7).

The UN Body of Principles for the Protection of All Persons under Any Form of Detention or Imprisonment (UN 1988) broadens the coverage of the standards beyond prisons to anyone who is detained in any way. Thus, in addition to legal safeguards and judicial guarantees, the Body of Principles includes some safeguards relating to interrogation (Principles 21 and 23) and the need for a medical examination upon arrival in order to document any pre-existing injuries or health problems (Principle 24). The Body of Principles is also of note since in reiterating the prohibition of torture and other ill-treatment (Principle 6), a footnote gives some interpretation of the phrases *cruel, inhumane,* or *degrading punishment* as providing the widest protection possible against any form of mental or physical abuse including forms of sensory deprivation. Also reflecting the epidemic of enforced disappearances in the decades around which it was drafted, the principles contain provisions for the investigation of deaths and disappearance during, or immediately after, detention (Principle 34).

Further universal standards whose objective is the prevention of torture or other ill-treatment as well as the prevention of the use of excessive or deadly force have also been agreed by states. See, for example, the Code of Conduct for Law Enforcement Officials, Basic Principles on the Use of Force and Firearms by Law Enforcement Officials, Basic Principles on the Independence of the Judiciary, and Basic Principles on the Role of Lawyers (High Commissioner for Human Rights 2016).

United Nations Standard Minimum Rules

Perhaps paramount among the universal standards are the UN Standard Minimum Rules for the Treatment of Prisoners (SMR). The SMR, being first adopted in 1955 and having only undergone minor amendment in 1977, were in real need of modernizing. After several years of discussions and negotiations, the SMR were recently updated to bring them into line with developments in penology and best practices in the human rights of detainees (UN 2015). The negotiations between states were informed and to an important extent driven by a very active civil society (including by Penal Reform International [PRI] and with the assistance of the University of Essex, United Kingdom) since some states claimed that either there was no need to open the SMR for renegotiation or the global economic downturn meant that extra burdens should not be placed upon them.

The updated SMR includes express prohibitions of torture and other ill-treatment, which was surprisingly absent in the earlier versions, as well as nondiscrimination. Since they are central to the good management of any place of detention, there are also detailed provisions on prisoner file management, including records on discipline, allegations of torture or ill-treatment, and information on injury of death of a prisoner. In relation to healthcare, the SMR now reflects the contemporary concept of equivalence of care in which the healthcare services in the prison should be the same as those in the community and thus allow for continuity of care, particularly for HIV, tuberculosis, and drug dependence (Rule 24). The rules further clearly indicate that the principles of patient confidentiality, autonomy, and informed consent apply to prisoners (Rule 32). There is an express obligation on healthcare staff to document and report any suspicion or allegation of torture or ill-treatment (Rule 34).

Disciplinary offenses must be subject to due process and review, and it is now clearly stated that the fundamental provisions of the UN SMR, such as those relating to food, hygiene, sanitation, space, and light and to exercise and healthcare, apply to all prisoners at all times, thus including during the imposition of sanctions (Rule 42). Clearer provisions on the use of solitary confinement (Rules 44 and 45) indicate that it should be used only in exceptional circumstances; should not be used for women, children or those with mental or physical disabilities that could be worsened by such treatment; and can never be indefinite or prolonged (greater than 15 days) (see also Chapter 16). Clearer provisions on the use of restraints are given, including the prohibition of the use of restraints on women during labor and during and just after childbirth (Rule 48), as well as directions on the use of searches, including intimate body searches (Rules 50–52). Access to conjugal visits is now expressly to be applied for women as well as male prisoners (Rule 58). Clearer rules governing the documentation and reporting of allegations of torture or other ill-treatment, as well as the investigation of deaths in custody, are given (Rules 57, 71, and 72).

Optional Protocol to the UN Convention Against Torture

The OPCAT established both international and national monitoring mechanisms for the prevention of torture. The international visiting mechanism, the UN Sub-Committee for the Prevention of Torture (SPT) conducts periodic and follow-up visits to states who have ratified the OPCAT. Each state party to the OPCAT must also set up an NPM that is charged with the prevention of torture through regular visits to all places of detention in that country.

As of October 2016 the Protocol had 75 Signatories and 83 parties have ratified the OPCAT, of which 40 are in Europe and Central Asia, 15 in Africa, 15 in Latin America, 6 in Asia Pacific, and 4 in the Middle East and North Africa (APT 2016). As of the end of January 2016, the SPT had conducted 27 country visits and four follow-up visits. As an example of the 15 states in Africa that have ratified the OPCAT, five among them (Benin, Gabon, Mali, Liberia, and Togo) have received visits from the UN SPT. The SPT reports on Benin, Gabon, and Mali are public and can be found on the OPCAT website (OPCAT 2016). Seven of the 15 states in Africa have also established an NPM. The states should also publish an annual report of the NPM, but to date, from Africa, only that of Nigeria can be found on the OPCAT website. Of the 15 states in Latin America, 13 have established an NPM and seven have received a visit from the SPT, of which five reports have been published (OPCAT 2016).

In their country reports, the SPT provides recommendations aimed at the prevention and reporting of torture and other ill-treatment. In doing so, the SPT is further interpreting and developing specific universal standards of detention. For example, in the SPT country visit to Mexico (SPT 2010b), they recommend among other things, the content of records for newly admitted prisoners and the specific content of medical examinations on arrival in a place of detention. The SPT also makes specific remarks on the minimum standards of detention in respect to hygiene, light, ventilation, bedding, food, etc., as well as measures for the protection of vulnerable groups such as children and women. In their country visit to New Zealand, the SPT, among other topics, addresses the need to adopt clear and simple systems for the classification of detainees, to protect the mental health of detainees through the introduction of national policies on mental health in prisons, and to provide proper training to staff on health risk assessments (SPT 2014a). The SPT also comments on whether particular forms of detention may amount to torture or inhumane or degrading treatment, such as some small disciplinary cells in so-called management units in New Zealand (SPT 2014a) or small, dark, humid, and unhygienic disciplinary cells in SIZOs (pre-trial detention facilities) and colonies and the inhumane conditions of cells holding life-sentenced prisoners in Kyrgyzstan (SPT 2014b).

The SPT has also started to publish some guidance documents on specific topics, for example, on the rights of persons institutionalized and medically treated without informed consent (SPT 2015a), which discusses protections against involuntary confinement in healthcare settings, the principle of informed consent, forced treatment, and limits and protections in the use of chemical or physical restraints and of solitary confinement. The SPT has also published a document on the situation of women deprived of liberty

(SPT 2015b) focusing on specific issues such as exposure to sexual violence (including that from intrusive body searches of women by prison staff) (see also Chapter 10), access to specialized healthcare (including the prevention of self-harm and suicide), and the situation of mothers deprived of their liberty with children. The guidance also covers issues of discrimination against women in relation to education, work, and recreation. In addition, the protection of judicial review and due process in the prevention of torture has been addressed by the SPT (2012).

While the SPT can only conduct periodic visits to states, the dual mechanism of preventive visits established by the OPCAT means that routine visits to all places of detention in a state should be carried out more regularly by the NPMs. Of the 80 states to have ratified the OPCAT by the end of 2015, 64 have nominated an NPM. Of the 64 NPMs, 39 have made their annual report public in at least 1 year since being established (OPCAT 2016). As part of its role in providing international support to NPMs, the SPT has also conducted some advisory visits to NPMs. During such visits, the SPT may participate in visits of the NPM in order to build capacity and provide technical advice on issues such as the composition, functions, and funding of the NPMs, as well as addressing problems of access to all places of detention (see, for example, the advisory visit to Armenia [SPT 2015c] and Honduras [SPT 2013]).

Examples of Standards Specific to Issues or Groups

Healthcare

Healthcare services in, or provided to, places of detention form a key part of a human rights-based approach to the deprivation of liberty. Prisoners retain the right to health and thereby to the same programs of prevention, treatment, and care of disease as those in the surrounding community (World Health Organization [WHO] 2014). This can be facilitated by ensuring that, as a minimum, the healthcare service is run in close coordination with the community healthcare service (UN SMR), but ideally, as detailed in a policy brief by the WHO and United Nations Office on Drugs and Crime (UNODC), the service should be directly under the responsibility of the Ministry of Health (WHO 2013).

A detention healthcare service that reports to the ministry of health is a means to ensure the clinical and ethical independence of the health staff. In those jurisdictions where the health staff is under the same ministry as those responsible for the place of detention, they are subject to dual loyalties, that is, they have a responsibility to the health and well-being of their patients but, simultaneously, are subordinate to the dictates and aims of security. Healthcare staff in places of detention are subject to the same ethical obligations as those in the community. The SMR stipulates that there must be clinical independence in the treatment of prisoners (Rule 25) and that prisoners have the right to medical confidentiality, autonomy, and informed consent in decisions relating to their health (Rules 31 and 32). Due to the inherent risks for doctors working in places of detention, the UN Principles of Medical Ethics (UN 1982) and the Declaration of Tokyo of the World Medical Association (World Medical Association 2006) categorically forbid the participation of physicians in the interrogation of detainees and in any active or passive participation in torture or other forms of ill-treatment. For further details, a comprehensive analysis and explication of the ethical challenges and duties of physicians and other health staff in places of detention has been published by the Council of Europe (Lehtmets and Pont 2014).

A medical examination upon arrival in a place of detention provides an essential baseline for the health service. It is an early opportunity to assess the overall health of the person and to screen in particular for physical and mental health problems for which treatment or rehabilitation programs exist. The healthcare needs of particularly vulnerable groups such as juveniles, women, and those with mental and physical disabilities should also be assessed, protected, and promoted. Mental illness, especially the risk of self-harm or suicide, should be screened for and addressed.

Due to the increased prevalence of HIV, hepatitis C, and tuberculosis in prison populations, it is of utmost importance that prisoners have access to national programs of prevention, treatment, and care for these infections (UNODC 2013). A tool has been developed for monitoring bodies to assess the prison health systems' response to these diseases and to the availability of harm-reduction strategies and thereby assessing compliance with human rights standards in relation to health issues in detention (Sander 2016). The healthcare staff also has a role in ensuring that the conditions of detention are in conformity with basic standards. In both the EPRs and the UN SMR, the health staff are charged with regular inspection of the food, hygiene, sanitation, clothing, and bedding and reporting of any deficiencies to the higher authorities.

The health staff are obliged to document and report to an independent and impartial body any allegation, or suspicion, of torture or ill-treatment that may have occurred prior to arrival or subsequently, while at the same time safeguarding the victim and any witnesses (UN 2015; UN Special Rapporteur on Torture 2014).

Vulnerable Groups

As well as being protected by rules within the SMR, vulnerable groups of prisoners, particularly children, women, and those with mental health problems or disabilities, have more specific protections detailed in additional texts.

Women

The particular vulnerabilities of women in detention go far beyond the common attention that is given only to pre- and postnatal care. Women and girls make up around 6.8% of the estimated total world prison population of 10.35 million people, and since the year 2000, the total women population has increased by around 50% (World Prison Brief 2015). Women often arrive in a place of detention with a myriad of physical and mental health problems and in a state of neglected healthcare. Women in detention have often experienced various forms of abuse while in the community, including child abuse, sexual abuse, and domestic violence. Rates of drug and alcohol misuse are higher among women prior to their detention (WHO 2009).

In women prisoners, there is often a higher prevalence of sexually transmitted infections, including HIV, than in male prisoners. In some cases, this is related to sexual violence and, in others, to sex work. Women in detention have higher rates of mental health problems, including post-traumatic stress, and are at a higher risk of suicide and self-harm (WHO 2009). Once in detention, women are also at high risk of intimidation, threats, and gender-based violence, especially rape and other ill-treatment (APT/PRI 2015a) which may be used as part of interrogations or as a means of submission and control. Rape may also take place in return for the provisions of goods or services to the women.

Prison policies in general, but also healthcare policies, often do not take women and girls into account. Since there are fewer prisons for women, women are often held far from family and social support. In 2011, the WHO produced a checklist and guidance on prison policies and practices to assess gender inequalities, including health services for women

(WHO 2011). The guidance is aimed at policy makers, prison managers, and prison health staff. In addition to limiting the use of detention for women, who are often imprisoned for nonviolent crimes and drug offenses, the WHO recommends that a comprehensive screening of the social, physical, psychological, and healthcare needs of women must be put in place from the outset of detention. Gender-specific health policies should be put in place to address the high rates of mental illness, drug and alcohol dependence, and sexually transmitted infections. Sections of prisons for women should be staffed by female guards, and if male guards are present, they should always be accompanied by female staff (Rule 81, UN SMR).

The United Nations Rules for the Treatment of Women Prisoners of 2010 (the Bangkok Rules) provide gender-specific protections that are supplementary to the UN SMR (UN 2010). Together, these two standards provide for the separation not only of women from men, but also of girls (under 18 years of age) from adult women. For women with children, the best interests of the child should be the key factor in deciding on the imprisonment of the mother and whether the child should remain with the mother.

Detailed attention is given to admission procedures, particularly the screening for torture and other ill-treatment as well as other physical, psychological, or sexual violence prior to admission. Additionally, other mental health issues, particularly the risk of self-harm or suicide, drug and alcohol misuse, and physical health problems, particularly HIV and sexually transmitted infections, should be screened for. Gender-specific healthcare should be provided by regular visits of gynecologists who should also conduct screening for breast and cervical cancers. Gender-specific treatment programs for mental health, HIV and sexually transmitted infections, and drug and alcohol problems should be put in place (PRI/TIU 2013).

The Bangkok Rules and the SMR together provide for increased protection of women in other aspects of prison life. Limitations are placed on intimate body searches, and safeguards against harassment or intimidation are included (UN 2010). Solitary confinement is expressly forbidden for pregnant or breastfeeding women and those with children and in all cases is forbidden for greater than 15 days. While some forms of restraint, such as irons or chains, are prohibited for any prisoners, no form of restraint should be used on pregnant women or during labor or just after delivery of the baby.

Children

Children are defined by the UN Convention on the Rights of the Child (CRC) as those under 18 years of age (UN 1989). In addition to prohibiting torture, and arbitrary arrest and detention, and providing for basic legal safeguards, the CRC stresses, as do the UN Standard Minimum Rules for the Administration of Juvenile Justice (UN 1985), that the arrest and detention of children should be used as a last resort. Once in detention, children should be held separately from adults and provided with the necessary means for their social, physical, and psychological well-being and educational and vocational development (UN 1985).

While the UN SMR for the Treatment of Prisoners contains some provisions relating to the treatment of children in detention, more exhaustive protections are provided by the UN Rules for the Protection of Juveniles Deprived of their Liberty (UN 1990b). These rules detail not only the need for specially recruited and trained staff (Rules 81–87) and the separation of children from adults, but also the need for different levels of security and rehabilitation among the children. The rights to education, development, and health of children are specifically protected and promoted, and these are reinforced by promoting contact with family (Rules 59–61). The use of restraints or force on children is generally prohibited other than in exceptional circumstances as a last resort (Rules 63 and 64), and corporal punishment or solitary confinement are expressly prohibited as disciplinary measures. The main vulnerabilities of children in detention and how to address them are considered in a report of a symposium held by the Association for the Prevention of Torture in 2014 (APT 2014) and in a training manual on children in the criminal justice system by PRI (2013). A more in-depth discussion of children in detention can be found in Chapter 11.

People with Disabilities

Highlighting the risks of discrimination, the UN Convention on the Rights of Persons with Disabilities 2006 provides an express prohibition on the detention of people solely based on their disability and further stresses the obligation of the state to prevent torture, in particular, of people with disabilities (UN 2006). Both the convention (Article 13) and the SMR stress the need for the training of judiciary, police, and prison staff on the rights of people with disabilities. Also, recognizing that detention may not be an appropriate response to some people with disabilities, the updated SMR provide for their diversion to mental healthcare facilities (Rule 109).

If people with disabilities are detained, the authorities must ensure that the facilities are adapted in such ways that allow them full and equitable access to prison life (SMR Rule 5). In the management of the prison, the administration must also take into account whether mental illness or developmental disability may be a causal factor of any disciplinary offenses and, where this is the case, should not punish the individual (SMR Rule 39). The updated SMR expressly forbids the placement of those with mental or physical disabilities in solitary confinement if their condition would be exacerbated by this form of isolation (Rule 45).

LGBTI

Particular vulnerabilities of lesbian, gay, bisexual, transgender, and intersex (LGBTI) persons deprived of freedom such as being subject to arbitrary arrest and ill-treatment during interrogation should be considered (APT/PRI 2015b). Caution should also be used in the allocation of LGBTI prisoners since, for example, placing a transgender woman in a male prison exposes them to the very real danger of rape. Body searches should be conducted with consideration to the perceived gender of the individual and with regard to nondiscrimination and the prevention of humiliation. Measures must be taken to protect LGBTI from the risk of all forms of violence, but especially sexual violence from other prisoners and from staff. The use of solitary confinement as a form of protective custody for LGBTI prisoners exposes them to the inherent risks of this form of isolation and so must be used judiciously and where feasible with the agreement of the individual and with appropriate safeguards in place.

Conclusions

Standards for the protection of people deprived of liberty have been developed over the last 60 years, but have evolved and progressed steadily since the adoption of the UN

Convention Against Torture in 1984. Standards specific to Europe, Latin America, and Africa have, to varying degrees, provided enhanced protections for the treatment of prisoners in those regions. Although the revision in 2015 of the UN SMR for the Treatment of Prisoners targeted only certain key areas of the rules, there was a significant progression in universal protections surrounding healthcare, vulnerable groups, discipline, the investigation of deaths and torture, and access to legal representation, among other areas. Whereas three decades ago, places of detention were largely closed settings with little or no independent oversight, the acceptance of outside monitoring is slowly but steadily taking hold. Firstly, in Europe the CPT has made important strides in monitoring the conditions and individual treatment in places of detention and in developing extensive standards for the protection of detainees. More recently, the adoption of the OPCAT has led not only to a universal, international system of monitoring of places of detention, but perhaps more significantly has established NPMs with the authority to routinely access and monitor places of detention. The increasing transparency of places of detention can only widen the implementation of standards for the prevention of torture and other ill-treatment, although it remains a painstakingly slow process.

References

African Commission 2004a, *Reports of the visits of the Special Rapporteur on Prisons, Conditions of Detention and Policing in Africa to Ethiopia 2004*. Available from: http://www.achpr.org/files/sessions/37th/mission-reports/ethiopia/misrep_specmec_priso_ethopia_2004_eng.pdf.

African Commission 2004b, *Reports of the Special Rapporteur on Prisons and Conditions of Detention in Africa* Mission to the Republic of South Africa. Available from: http://www.achpr.org/files/sessions/37th/mission-reports/prisons-2004/misrep_specmec_priso_southafrica_2004_eng.pdf. [June 14–30, 2004].

African Commission 2008, Robben Island guidelines for the prohibition and prevention of torture in Africa, in *Practical guide for implementation*, African Commission on Human and People's Rights, UN Office of the High Commissioner for Human Rights, Association for the Prevention of Torture. Geneva, Switzerland.

African Commission 2014, Communication 379/09—Monim Elgak, Osman Hummeida and Amir Suliman (represented by FIDH and OMCT) v Sudan. Banjul, The Gambia at the 15th Extra Ordinary Session of the African Commission on Human and Peoples' Rights held from March 7–14, 2014, African Commission, Addis Ababa.

African Commission 2016, *For the mandate of the Special Rapporteur and more mission reports*. Available from: http://www.achpr.org/mechanisms/prisons-and-conditions-of-detention.

Association for the Prevention of Torture (APT) 2004, *Monitoring places of detention: A practical guide*, APT, Geneva.

APT 2008, *Visiting places of detention: What role for physicians and other health professionals?* APT, Geneva.

APT 2013, *Monitoring police custody: A practical guide*, APT, Geneva.

APT 2014, Addressing children's vulnerabilities in detention: Outcome report. *Jean-Jacques Gautier NPM Symposium 2014*, APT, Geneva. Available from: http://apt.ch/content/files_res/report-jjg-symposium-2014-en.pdf. [February 16, 2016].

APT 2016, Global status, *Association for the Prevention of Torture Opcat database*, APT, Geneva. Available from: http://apt.ch/en/global-status/. [February 10, 2016].

APT/PRI 2015a, *Women in detention: A guide to gender-sensitive monitoring*, Association for the Prevention of Torture and Penal Reform International, London.

APT/PRI 2015b, *LGBTI persons deprived of their liberty: A framework for preventive monitoring*. Association for the Prevention of Torture and Penal Reform International. Available from: http://www.apt .ch/content/files_res/thematic-paper-3_lgbti-persons-deprived-of-their-liberty-en.pdf.

Council of Europe 2006a, *Committee of Ministers recommendation Rec(2006)2 of the Committee of Ministers to Member States on the European Prison Rules adopted by the Committee of Ministers on 11 January 2006 at the 952nd meeting of the Ministers' Deputies*, Council of Europe, Strasbourg.

Council of Europe 2006b, *Commentary to recommendation Rec(2006)2 of the Committee of Ministers to Member States on the European Prison Rules*, Council of Europe, Strasbourg. Available from: http://www.coe.int/t/dghl/standardsetting/prisons/E%20commentary%20to%20the%20 EPR.pdf. [February 10, 2016].

Council of Europe 2008a, *Recommendation CM/Rec(2008)11 of the Committee of Ministers to member states on the European Rules for juvenile offenders subject to sanctions or measures (adopted by the Committee of Ministers on 5 November 2008 at the 1040th meeting of the Ministers' Deputies)*, Council of Europe, Strasbourg.

Council of Europe 2008b, *Commentary on the European Rules for juvenile offenders subject to sanctions or measures*, Council of Europe, Strasbourg. Available from: http://www.coe.int/t/dghl/standardsetting /prisons/Commentary_Rec_2008_11E.pdf. [January 2016].

Council of Europe 2014, *Compendium of conventions, recommendations and resolutions relating to penitentiary questions*, Council of Europe, Strasbourg. Available from: http://www.coe.int/t/DGHL /STANDARDSETTING/PRISONS/PCCP%20documents%202014/COMPENDIUM%20E%20 2014.pdf. [February 10, 2016].

Committee for the Prevention of Torture and Inhuman or Degrading Treatment or Punishment (CPT) 2011a, *CPT in Brief 2011*, Council of Europe, Strasbourg. Available from: http://www.cpt .coe.int/en/documents/eng-leaflet.pdf. [February 2, 2016].

CPT 2011b, *21st General Report of the CPT. European Committee for the Prevention of Torture and Inhuman or Degrading Treatment or Punishment 2011*. Available from: http://www.cpt.coe.int/en/annual /rep-21.pdf.

CPT 2013, *23rd General Report of the CPT. European Committee for the Prevention of Torture and Inhuman or Degrading Treatment or Punishment 2013*. Available from: http://www.cpt.coe.int/en/annual /rep-23.pdf.

CPT 2014, *24th General Report of the CPT. European Committee for the Prevention of Torture and Inhuman or Degrading Treatment or Punishment 2014*. Available from: http://www.cpt.coe.int/en/annual /CPT-Report-2013-2014.pdf.

CPT 2015a, Living space per prisoner in prison establishments: CPT standards, *CPT/Inf (2015) 44*. Available from: http://www.cpt.coe.int./en/working-documents/cpt-inf-2015-44-eng.pdf.

CPT 2015b, Checklist for CPT visits to social care institutions where persons may be deprived of their liberty. *CPT/Inf (2015) 23*. Available from: http://www.cpt.coe.int/en/working-documents/CPT -Inf-2015-23-eng.pdf.

CPT 2015c, *25th General Report of the CPT. European Committee for the Prevention of Torture and Inhuman or Degrading Treatment or Punishment 2015*. Available from: http://www.cpt.coe.int/en/annual /CPT-Report-2015.pdf.

High Commissioner for Human Rights 2016, Universal human rights instruments, in *Human rights in the administration of justice: Protection of Persons subjected to detention or imprisonment*. Office of the High Commissioner for Human Rights, Geneva. Available from: http://ohchr .org/EN/ProfessionalInterest/Pages/UniversalHumanRightsInstruments.aspx. [February 16, 2016].

International Committee of the Red Cross (ICRC) 2011, *ICRC-led process aimed at strengthening IHL as it applies to people detained in connection with non-international armed conflict*, ICRC, Geneva. Available from: https://www.icrc.org/eng/resources/documents/feature/2012/12-07-detention-law .htm. [February 5, 2016].

ICRC 2015, *What is the difference between IHL and Human Rights Law?* ICRC, Geneva. Available from: https://www.icrc.org/en/document/what-difference-between-ihl-and-human-rights-law. [February 16, 2016].

Inter-American Commission 2008, *Principles and best practices on the protection of persons deprived of liberty in the Americas*, Inter-American Commission on Human Rights, March 3–14, 2008, Washington, DC. Available from: http://www.oas.org/en/iachr/mandate/Basics/principles deprived.asp.

Inter-American Commission 2011, *Report of the Human Rights of persons deprived of liberty in the Americas 2011*. Available from: http://www.oas.org/en/iachr/pdl/docs/pdf/PPL2011eng.pdf.

Inter-American Commission 2013, *Report of the Inter-American Commission on Human Rights on the situation of persons deprived of liberty in Honduras*, Washington, DC. Available from: http://www .oas.org/en/iachr/pdl/docs/pdf/HONDURAS-PPL-2013ENG.pdf.

Inter-American Court 2006, Case of Montero-Aranguren et al. (Detention Center of Catia), Judgment of July 5, 2006. Series C No. 150, para. 85, Inter-American Court of Human Rights, San José, Costa Rica.

Lehtmets, A., and Pont, J. 2014, *Prison health care and medical ethics: A manual for health-care workers and other prison staff with responsibility for prisoners' well-being*, Council of Europe, Strasbourg. Available from: https//rm.coe.int/CoERMPublicCommonSearchServices/Display DCTMContent?

Organization of American States (OAS) 2016a, *OAS Home page*, OAS, Washington, DC. Available from: http://www.oas.org/en/iachr/pdl/default.asp. [16 February 2016].

OAS 2016b, *Reports on petitions and cases*, OAS, Washington, DC. Available from: http://www.oas .org/en/iachr/pdl/decisions/iachr.asp. [February 16, 2016].

Optional Protocol to the Convention against Torture (OPCAT) 2016, *Optional Protocol to the Convention against Torture (OPCAT) website—SPT country visits*, Office of the High Commissioner for Human Rights, Geneva. Available from: http://tbinternet.ohchr.org/_layouts/TreatyBodyExternal /CountryVisits.aspx. [February 10, 2016].

Penal Reform International (PRI) 2013, *Protecting children's rights in criminal justice systems: A training manual and reference point for professionals and policymakers*, PRI, London.

PRI/Thailand Institute of Justice [TIU] 2013, *Guidance document on the United Nations rules on the treatment of women prisoners and non-custodial measures for women offenders (the Bangkok Rules)*. PRI, London; TIU, Bangkok.

Robben Island Guidelines 2002, Guidelines and Measures for the Prohibition and Prevention of Torture, Cruel, Inhuman or Degrading Treatment or Punishment in Africa) (Robben Island Guidelines 2002) Resolution of the African Commission on Human and Peoples' Rights, 32nd ordinary session, October 2002, Banjul, Gambia.

Sander, G. 2016, *Monitoring HIV, HCV, TB and harm reduction in prisons: A human rights-based tool to prevent ill treatment*, Harm Reduction International, London. Available from: http://www.ihra .net/files/2016/02/10/HRI_MonitoringTool.pdf. [February 22, 2016].

Subcommittee on the Prevention of Torture (SPT) 2010a, *The approach of the Subcommittee on Prevention of Torture to the concept of prevention of torture and other cruel, inhuman or degrading treatment or punishment under the Optional Protocol to the Convention against Torture and Other Cruel, Inhuman or Degrading Treatment or Punishment*, CAT/OP/12/6, SPT, Office of the High Commissioner for Human Rights, Geneva.

SPT 2010b, *Report on the visit of the Subcommittee on Prevention of Torture and Other Cruel, Inhuman or Degrading Treatment or Punishment to Mexico*, CAT/OP/MEX/1, SPT, Office of the High Commissioner for Human Rights, Geneva.

SPT 2012, *Provisional statement on the role of judicial review and due process in the prevention of torture in prisons, adopted by the Subcommittee on Prevention of Torture and Other Cruel, Inhuman or Degrading Treatment or Punishment at its sixteenth session*, February 20–24, 2012, CAT/OP2, SPT, Office of the High Commissioner for Human Rights, Geneva.

SPT 2013, *Report on the visit made by the Subcommittee on Prevention of Torture and other Cruel, Inhuman or Degrading Treatment or Punishment for the purpose of providing advisory assistance to the national preventive mechanism of Honduras*, SPT, Office of the High Commissioner for Human Rights, Geneva. Subcommittee on Prevention of Torture and Other Cruel, Inhuman or Degrading Treatment or Punishment. January 25, 2013. CAT/OP/HND/3.

SPT 2014a, *Report on the visit of the Subcommittee on Prevention of Torture and Other Cruel, Inhuman or Degrading Treatment or Punishment to New Zealand. Subcommittee on Prevention of Torture*, July 28, 2014, CAT/OP/NZL/1, SPT, Office of the High Commissioner for Human Rights, Geneva.

SPT 2014b, *Report on the visit of the Subcommittee on Prevention of Torture and Other Cruel, Inhuman or Degrading Treatment or Punishment to Kyrgyzstan. Subcommittee on Prevention of Torture*, February 28, 2014, CAT/OP/KGZ/1, SPT, Office of the High Commissioner for Human Rights, Geneva.

SPT 2015a, *SPT Approach of the Subcommittee on Prevention of Torture and Other Cruel, Inhuman or Degrading Treatment or Punishment on the rights of persons institutionalized and medically treated without informed consent*, SPT, Office of the High Commissioner for Human Rights, Geneva. Available from: http://www.ohchr.org/Documents/HRBodies/OPCAT/CAT .OP.26.R.7_PrevencionTorturaMalosTratoscontraMujeres.doc. [February 10, 2016].

SPT 2015b, *Prevención de la tortura y los malos tratos contra mujeres privadas de la libertad*, SPT, Office of the High Commissioner for Human Rights, Geneva. Available from: http://www.ohchr.org /Documents/HRBodies/OPCAT/CAT.OP.26.R.7_PrevencionTorturaMalosTratoscontraMujeres .doc. [February 10, 2016].

SPT 2015c, *Report on the visit made by the Subcommittee on Prevention of Torture and other Cruel, Inhuman or Degrading Treatment or Punishment for the purpose of providing advisory assistance to the national preventive mechanism of the Republic of Armenia*, SPT, Office of the High Commissioner for Human Rights, Geneva. Subcommittee on Prevention of Torture and Other Cruel, Inhuman or Degrading Treatment or Punishment, May 22, 2015. CAT/OP/ARM/1.

UN 1982, *Principles of medical ethics relevant to the role of health personnel, particularly physicians, in the protection of prisoners and detainees against torture and other cruel, inhuman or degrading treatment or punishment adopted by General Assembly Resolution 37/194 of December 18, 1982*, UN, Geneva.

UN 1985, *United Nations Standard Minimum Rules for the administration of juvenile justice ("the Beijing Rules") adopted by General Assembly Resolution 40/33 of November 29, 1985*, UN, Geneva.

UN 1988, *Body of principles for the protection of all persons under any form of detention or imprisonment adoption adopted by the UN General Assembly December 9, 1988 Res. 43/173*, UN, Geneva.

UN 1989, *Convention on the rights of the child adopted and opened for signature, ratification and accession by General Assembly Resolution 44/25 of November 20, 1989*, Entry into force September 2, 1990, UN, Geneva.

UN 1990a, *Basic principles for the treatment of prisoners adopted and proclaimed by General Assembly Resolution 45/111 of December 14, 1990*, UN, Geneva.

UN 1990b, *United Nations rules for the protection of juveniles deprived of their liberty. Adopted by General Assembly Resolution 45/113 of December 14, 1990*, UN, Geneva.

UN 1992, *Human Rights Committee general comment no. 21: Humane treatment of persons deprived of liberty, adopted at the 44th session (1992)*, UN, Geneva.

UN 2004, *Manual on effective investigation and documentation of torture and other cruel, inhuman or degrading treatment or punishment (the Istanbul Protocol)*, Professional Training Series No. 8/Rev.1 2004, Office of the United Nations High Commissioner for Human Rights, Geneva.

UN 2006, *Convention on the rights of persons with disabilities*, A/RES 61/106. 24 January 2007, UN, Geneva.

UN 2010, *United Nations rules for the treatment of women prisoners and non-custodial measures for women offenders (the Bangkok Rules)*. UN General Assembly A/C.3/65/L.5 2010, UN, Geneva.

UN 2015, *United Nations standard minimum rules for the treatment of prisoners adopted by the General Assembly*, December 17, 2015, A/RES/70/175 Resolution, UN, Geneva. Available from: http:// ohchr.org/Documents/ProfessionalInterest/NelsonMandelaRules.pdf. [February 16, 2016].

UN Office on Drugs and Crime (UNODC) 2013, *HIV prevention, treatment and care in prisons and other closed settings: A comprehensive package of interventions*, UNODC, Vienna.

UN Special Rapporteur on Torture 2014, *Interim report of the Special Rapporteur on torture and other cruel, inhuman or degrading treatment or punishment*, A/69/387 23 September 2014, Office of the United Nations High Commissioner for Human Rights, Geneva.

World Health Organization (WHO) 2009, *Women's health in prison: Correcting gender inequity in prison health*, WHO, Geneva.

WHO 2011, *Women's health in prison action guidance and checklists to review current policies and practices*, WHO, Geneva.

WHO 2013, *Good governance for prison health in the 21st century: A policy brief on the organization of prison health*, WHO, Geneva; UNODC, Vienna.

WHO 2014, *Prisons and health*, WHO, Geneva.

World Medical Association 2006, *Declaration of Tokyo—Guidelines for physicians concerning torture and other cruel, inhuman or degrading treatment or punishment in relation to detention and imprisonment adopted by the 29th World Medical Assembly, Tokyo, Japan, October 1975, and editorially revised by the 170th WMA Council Session, Divonne-les-Bains, France, May 2005, and the 173rd WMA Council Session, Divonne-les-Bains, France, May 2006*, World Medical Association, Ferney-Voltaire.

World Prison Brief 2015, *World prison population list*, 11th edn. Available from: http://www.pris onstudies.org/sites/default/files/resources/downloads/world_prison_population_list_11th _edition.pdf.

4

Healthcare for Those in Detention

Michael Levy

CONTENTS

Introduction

The right to health is dependent on, and contributes to, the realization of many other human rights (Office of the United Nations High Commissioner for Human Rights 2008). The interdependence of human rights is tested in the custodial environment. The dignity of the individual and the role of the health professional are but two contested principles, which require constant and independent review. The enduring principle related to the health service to prisoners is all of the following (Elger 2011):

- Independence.
- Health-based.
- The authority to deliver and advocate for the previous two principles.

A separate principle related to health services provided to persons in detention is that of *equivalence*—a guarantee that at a minimum, services provided are equal to those offered in the general community. However, given the growing body of evidence that the health of persons in detention is far worse than that of community counterparts, a principle of *equity* could be explored.* However, the assessment of equal outcomes has not yet entered into the principles of minimum standards (Charles and Draper 2012; Exworthy et al. 2012).

Each of these guiding principles can be assessed independently, but importantly, the competence of the assessment is best done by health professionals who are themselves independent and persons of authority within the assessment team.

---

* While the principle of equivalence offers prisoners the prospect of the same resources as civilian patients, given the increased needs of prisoner–patients, additional resources should be offered to prison health service, so that the same outcomes can be achieved for prisoners, as are achieved in the community.

Right(s) to Health

The right to health is an inclusive right which embraces the underlying determinants of health, including safe drinking water, adequate sanitation, safe food, adequate nutrition, adequate accommodation, healthy working conditions, healthy environmental conditions, health education, and gender equality.

The right to health includes freedom from nonconsensual medical treatment; protection from unethical research (and the right to participate in ethical research) (Elger 2008); and freedom from torture and other cruel, inhumane or degrading treatment (CIDT) or punishment.

The right to health also comprises entitlements, including the protection of equality of opportunity for all to attain the highest level of health; the right to the prevention, treatment, and control of diseases; access to essential medicines; equal and timely access to basic health services; provision of health education/information; and participation of the population in health-related decision making.

In order to analyze the functioning of a place of detention, it is necessary to conduct interviews with the following:

1. Authorities (custodial and health staff).

2. Detainees (current and recently released).

3. Visitors (family members [adults and children], legal officers, non-government organizations, oversight officers [ombudsman, tribunal members]).

The analysis of the functioning of a place of detention involves examining compliance with international and national norms and standards regarding conditions of detention. Health professionals can uniquely contribute to the content and application of norms and standards on the provision of, and access to, healthcare and on codes of ethical practice for other health professionals working in places of detention, as well as documenting alleged cases of ill-treatment. The health professionals can then take part in a constructive dialogue between the monitoring team and the authorities, based on their findings, the visit report, and its recommendations.

The Association for the Prevention of Torture (APT) (2012) states that

> A physician, or other health professional, can provide an invaluable contribution to the drafting of the report and recommendations, to the dialogue with the authorities, as well as to the follow-up of the implementation of recommendations. A medical perspective is vital in all reflections on preventing torture and improving the system and conditions of detention, including observations on legislative aspects.

There is a long history of health professionals visiting places of detention. The English parliament passed the Madhouses Act 1774 establishing a commission of the Royal College of Physicians to license and visit private madhouses in the London area. The commissions continued until 1827—at least once a year, the commissioners visited each madhouse; any keeper refusing admission forfeited his/her license (Roberts 1981)!

The European Committee for the Prevention of Torture and Inhuman or Degrading Treatment or Punishment (CPT) was founded on the basis of the European Convention for the Prevention of Torture and Inhuman or Degrading Treatment or Punishment (1987), which came into force in February 1989. The CPT conducts visits to all places of detention in all the member states of the Council of Europe (COE) and, other than in exceptional cases, would also include a physician as a part of the visiting team (CPT 2002).

More recently, the United Nations (UN) has developed a global process of multilateral review of places of detention. The UN adopted the Optional Protocol to the Convention Against Torture (OPCAT), which entered into force on June 22, 2006. A double system of visits is envisaged:

- An international body, the Subcommittee on Prevention of Torture and other Cruel, Inhuman or Degrading Treatment or Punishment (SPT), of the UN was established to conduct periodic visits.
- National mechanisms, known as National Preventative Mechanisms (NPMs), were established to provide an independent national body that can visit places of detention more frequently.

Article 18.2 of the OPCAT states that "the States Parties shall take the necessary measures to ensure that the experts of the national preventive mechanism have the required capabilities and professional knowledge."

It has been an established practice that a health professional is an integral member of every assessment team, as only they can adequately assess the contents of a medical record, assess the health system (including the state of health and access to treatment of the people in detention), and medically document alleged cases of ill-treatment. There are also concerns about consent and an assumption that only a health professional could competently seek consent to inspect a medical record. However, this practice is avoided in the inspection process, as visiting teams assert that they cannot be denied access to any document, and therefore, consent from individual prisoners is not actually sought.

The health professional must operate independently within the delegation. It is appropriate for other delegation members to alert the medical expert to sentinel events, but then to leave the specialist/professional (nonlegal) expert to conduct inquiries without further prompting.

The APT (2012) asserts that

> Only a qualified health professional can fully assess all aspects of a place of detention that impact upon health; discuss specific health issues with detainees and with the authorities; assess the adequacy and appropriateness of health services in the place of detention and of the quality of care being provided, provide essential medical expertise in the prevention of torture and ill-treatment.

An important function of the health professional in a visiting team is to liaise on a professional basis with the physicians and nurses working in the place of detention.

It is recognized that health professionals working in a place of detention are often isolated and work with insufficient resources. The presence of a physician on the visiting team provides the possibility to have a dialogue on an equal level between professionals, which can build the foundations for a relationship of trust.

The physician working in the place of detention can be a source of invaluable information, such as the existence of potential ill-treatment, the standard of medical care, challenges faced by the medical service in accomplishing its mission, pressures to disclose information from the clinical records, and system responses to previous reviews of the service.

In addition to assessing the conditions of detention and the health system, the role of the visiting health professional is to assess the standards of ethical practice among healthcare staff in the place of detention. Healthcare staff working in such environments are often confronted with conflicting responsibilities. On the one hand, they have a duty to provide impartial healthcare to the detainee-patient, and on the other hand, they are working in an institution in which the primary concern of the authorities is the security and safety of the place of detention. This conflict has been termed *dual loyalty* (Allen et al. 2010; Pont et al. 2012). There are specific situations in which healthcare staff may be confronted, including the following:

- The role of physicians in disciplinary sanctions (in particular the use of solitary confinement in any form and the use of restraints).
- Body searches (intimate or body cavity searches).
- Any participation in administering the death penalty.
- Refusal of treatment.
- Hunger strikes.

Health professionals in the visiting team should pay particular attention to the way these situations are dealt with and whether international ethical standards are being respected. They should also assess the procedures in place in case of conflict between the director of the institution and the healthcare staff.

The overarching principle when considering the prevention of torture is that the physician shall never participate in, either actively or passively, or condone torture or any other form of ill-treatment.

All types of places, where people are deprived of their liberty, should be subjected to visits by independent bodies—prisons, police stations, migrant detention centers, mental health institutions, juvenile justice centers, and military detention facilities (even, especially, those under security service control). In some jurisdictions (e.g., New Zealand), the possibility of extending the mandate to aged care facilities has also been raised.

The specific role of the health professional, indeed whether they lead the delegation, should match the degree of clinical function of the institution being reviewed—e.g., a mental health institution should be visited by a psychiatrist-led team.

A comprehensive approach to visits to places of detention requires the monitoring and documentation of all possible forms of ill-treatment, including the following:

- The assessment of conditions of detention (including infrastructure, nutrition, water, sanitation, and hygiene).
- The adequacy, appropriateness, and access to healthcare.
- The protection of human rights.
- The protection of judicial guarantees.

Another body that has developed routine inspections of places of detention is Her Majesty's Inspectorate of Prisons for England and Wales. Their principles of review (called *Expectations*) are referenced against international human rights standards (Her Majesty's Chief Inspector of Prisons 2012):

- Improvement in services.
- Focus on outcomes.
- Ensuring a user perspective.

- Proportionate to risk.
- Encouraging self-assessment.
- Providing impartial evidence.
- Clear and disclosed criteria.
- Open and transparent processes.
- Value for money.
- Continuing to learn.

Expectations are based on the four tests of a healthy prison. The four tests are as follows:

- Safety—Prisoners, particularly the most vulnerable, are held safely.
- Respect—Prisoners are treated with respect for their human dignity.
- Purposeful activity—Prisoners are able, and expected, to engage in activity that is likely to benefit them.
- Resettlement—Prisoners are prepared for their release into the community and helped to reduce the likelihood of reoffending (Inspectorate of Prisons for England and Wales 1999).

Health of Prisoners

In 2016, the International Centre for Prison Studies reported that there were more than 10,750,000 million people held in penal institutions throughout the world, mostly as pretrial detainees, or as sentenced prisoners. Almost half of these were in China (over 2.3 million), the United States (2.29 million) (Dumont et al. 2012), and Russia (810,000) (Walmsley 2016).

Males account for over 90% of prisoners. Accordingly, women form a significant minority within prisoner populations, but with special health needs (van den Bergh et al. 2011). Access to screening from community public health programs, such as breast and cervical screening; pregnancy care, and termination of pregnancy if requested; access to trauma services, especially domestic violence and sexual assault.

The most common age range of prisoners is 18–35 years, with few prisoners over the age of 50 years, making health service provision to elderly prisoners an issue of special concern (because the health services are not geared up to attend to an aging prison population, can you expand on this?) (Hayes et al. 2012). The punishment "deprivation of liberty" implies severe social dislocation—with all the adverse health consequences that that brings with it. Low educational achievement, high unemployment, and unstable accommodation are common.

Alcoholism, illicit drug use, and benzodiazepine dependency are common examples of drug use present in the histories of inmates. Indeed, in most western countries ~75% of female inmates and ~50% of male inmates are imprisoned for offenses which are drug related. A lifestyle of drug dependency lends itself to increased risk of infectious disease and other illnesses (Herbert et al. 2012). The impact of HIV on prisoners, and the response of prisoner health services to HIV, is of particular concern (United Nations Office on Drugs and Crime 2007a, 2007b). Similar concerns related to hepatitis C infection will increasingly become an issue of concern for prison health services, as testing for the virus becomes more common (Boonwaat et al. 2010).

While it is true that old patterns of drug use are likely to resume after leaving prison, the time in prison can potentially be a time of stabilization and rehabilitation (Chandler et al. 2009). Drug use tends to be an ongoing problem even after release from custody (Pelissier et al. 2007). Intravenous drug use is especially hazardous given the lack of clean injecting equipment in prisons and the consequent poor habits that may have been reinforced during incarceration (Kinner et al. 2012a). More generally, the interaction between the prisoner and the health service can sometimes be difficult—the health-seeking behaviors (also referred to as *health literacy*) can be perceived as aberrant, by community standards (Nesset et al. 2011).

Because the average period in custody is short—about 6 months, the number of ex-prisoners returning to the community in any year is even higher—perhaps by a factor of 2 (Cuellar and Cheema 2012; Martire and Larney 2012). Ex-prisoners die at rates far higher than their community peers, most often due to drug overdose or suicide, and particularly in the weeks immediately following release (Lim et al. 2012). Rates of hospitalization for physical and mental health problems are similarly elevated (Leukefeld et al. 2006; Kinner et al. 2012b).

The summary of a comprehensive surveillance system for Australian prisoners reported for 2010 the following alarming results:

- 83% of prisoners were tobacco smokers.
- 66% had used illicit drugs in the previous 12 months.
- 35% were antibody positive to hepatitis C.
- 58% consumed alcohol at risky levels.
- 39% reported having had a head injury that had resulted in unconsciousness.
- 31% had a history of mental illness (this is 2.5 times higher than the general population [Australian Institute of Health and Welfare 2012]).
- 21% reported a history of self-harm.
- 26% had at least one chronic health condition, such as asthma, arthritis, cardiovascular disease, diabetes, or cancer (Australian Institute of Health and Welfare 2011).

Assessment of a Competent Health Service

The overall conditions of detention can have direct and indirect effects on the health of the detained population, and in certain circumstances, the conditions themselves can amount to ill-treatment, or even torture. Therefore, during the visit, the health professional should analyze the public health aspects of the place of detention, including environmental factors (such as protection from the climate, ventilation, access to the open air), overcrowding, water and sanitation, general hygiene, food and nutrition, and outbreaks of disease. While these health-related aspects should also be examined by other members of the visiting team, the medical perspective provides a comprehensive analysis of the health dimension.

Due to their expertise, health professionals on the visiting team are especially qualified to provide a credible evaluation of the overall functioning of the healthcare services in places of detention. The relevance of such an evaluation can be seen from comments of the European visiting body, the CPT, which has stated that "an inadequate level of healthcare can lead rapidly to situations falling within the scope of the term 'inhuman and degrading treatment.'" This evaluation should therefore look at the individual care provided to detainees as well as the overall organization of the health services. It should be stressed that while some individual cases will need to be assessed, the purpose is not for the visiting physician to provide a second opinion, nor indeed to provide treatment, but to use such examples in order to understand and advise on how to improve the system. This particular role of the visiting physician must be made clear to both the detainees and to the authorities.

As well as assessing the infrastructure and level of healthcare provision within the place of detention, the physician must assess how, in cases where the detainee requires a level of care which cannot be provided within the institution itself, they can access healthcare in community health facilities. In addition to the provision of general healthcare, the assessment should include facilities or programs available for people with drug and alcohol dependencies, for women, for the elderly, and for those with any form of disability. As psychosocial problems are often widespread in places of detention, particular attention should be paid to the management of people with such conditions.

The review of a health service offered to persons in detention should follow the standards expected of a community-based health service. This tests the services' success, or otherwise, of achieving "equivalence"—if not the higher principle of equity.

Points of assessment include the following:

Patients are provided with high-quality care throughout the care delivery process.
- Assessment ensures current and ongoing needs of the patient are identified.
- Care is planned and delivered in collaboration with the patient and, when relevant, the carer, to achieve the best possible outcomes.
- Patients are informed of the consent process, and they understand and provide consent for their healthcare.
- Outcomes of clinical care are evaluated by healthcare providers and, where appropriate, are communicated to the patient and the carer.
- Processes for clinical handover, transfer of care, and discharge address the needs of the patient for ongoing care. This is particularly important at the time of entry into detention and the transition period back to the community.
- Systems for ongoing care of the patient are coordinated and effective. This is particularly important at the time of entry into detention and the transition period back to the community.
- The care of dying and deceased patients is managed with dignity and comfort, and family and carers are supported.
- The health record ensures comprehensive and accurate information is collaboratively gathered, recorded, and used in care delivery.

Patients have access to health services and care appropriate to their needs.
- The population has information on health services appropriate to its needs.
- Access and admission/entry to the system of care is prioritized according to healthcare needs.

Appropriate care and services are provided to patients.
- Healthcare and services are appropriate and delivered in the most appropriate setting.
- The organization provides care and services that achieve effective outcomes.
- Care and services are planned, developed, and delivered based on the best available evidence and in the most effective way.

The organization provides safe care and services.
- Medications are managed to ensure safe and effective patient outcomes.
- The infection control system supports safe practice and ensures a safe environment for patients and healthcare workers.
- The incidence and impact of breaks in skin integrity, pressure ulcers, and other nonsurgical wounds are minimized through wound prevention and management programs. (This particular point may have limited application to the prison setting.)
- The incidence of violence is minimized.
- The system to manage sample collection, blood, blood components/blood products, and patient blood management ensures safe and appropriate practice.
- The organization ensures that the nutritional needs of patients are met.

The organization is committed to patient participation.
- Patients, carers, and the community participate in the planning, delivery, and evaluation of the health service.
- Patients are informed of their rights and responsibilities.
- The organization meets the needs of patients and carers with diverse needs and from diverse backgrounds.
- Healthcare incidents are managed to ensure improvements to the systems of care.
- Healthcare complaints and feedback are managed to ensure improvements to the systems of care.

Information management systems enable the organization's goals to be met.
- Health records management systems support the collection of information and meet the patient's and organization's needs.
- Corporate records management systems support the collection of information and meet the organization's needs.
- Data and information are collected, stored, and used for strategic, operational, and service improvement purposes.
- The organization has an integrated approach to the planning, use, and management of information and communication technology.

The organization promotes the health of the population.
- Better health and well-being is promoted by the organization for patients, staff, carers, and the wider community (Akesson et al. 2012).

An evaluation of the overall healthcare services requires the examination of medical records, be they records of individual patients or a representative sample of records for more general analysis. Once again, it is essential that a physician take part, not only to access the records, but also to read and analyze their technical content.

In most national jurisdictions, access to individual medical records is governed by strict rules of confidentiality so as to protect the specific nature of the physician–patient relationship. Under normal circumstances, access to a person's medical records can only be obtained with that person's specific consent. Thus, during a private interview with a detainee, the visiting physician should expressly request for consent to consult their medical records.

As already stated, when the visiting mechanism wants to conduct an overall evaluation of the functioning of the healthcare services in a place of detention, it will be necessary for the physician to review a cross-section, or sample, of medical files in order to understand whether care is provided impartially and on the basis of needs, that is, without any form of discrimination. In such cases, the visiting physician has an audit-type function. Thus, provided the patients' personal data are anonymized (e.g., name, address, date of birth) and are not disclosed, their express consent may not be required.

Conclusions

The responses to the health of prisoners are a critical element of the humane custody of individuals deprived of their liberty. Ultimately, standards of care provided in the general community will be the standards expected of prison authorities. Monitoring agencies recognize this as a general principle and will always make assessments of the current health of detainees and the responses of the authorities to this challenge. Importantly, the monitoring agencies acknowledge the professional sensitivities around this aspect of reviewing places of detention, by requiring that a health professional lead the investigation into health status and health service provision. In acknowledging the unique responsibilities of health professionals, the broader monitoring enterprise requires that these specialists contribute meaningfully not just within their discipline, but also to the broader aims of any review.

References

Akesson, B., Smyth, J. M., Mandell, D. J., Doan, T., Donina, K., and Hoven, C. W. 2012, Parental involvement with the criminal justice system and the effects on their children: A collaborative model for researching vulnerable families. *Social Work in Public Health*, vol. 27, pp. 148–164.

Allen, S. A., Wakeman, S. E., Cohen, R. L., and Rich, J. D. 2010, Physicians in US prisons in the era of mass incarceration, *International Journal of Prisoner Health*, vol. 6, pp. 100–106.

Association for the Prevention of Torture (APT) 2012, *Visiting places of detention: What role for physicians and other health professionals?* APT, Geneva. Available from: http://www.hrea.org/erc/Library/display_doc.php?url=http%3A%2F%2Fwww.apt.ch%2Findex.php%3Foption%3Dcom_docman%26task%3Ddoc_download%26gid%3D302%26Itemid%3D259%26lang%3Den&external=N. [July 29, 2012].

Australian Institute of Health and Welfare 2011, *The health of Australia's prisoners 2010*, Australian Institute of Health and Welfare, Canberra. Available from: http://www.aihw.gov.au/publication-detail/?id=10737420111. [August 3, 2012].

Australian Institute of Health and Welfare 2012, *The mental health of prison entrants in Australia 2010*, Australian Institute of Health and Welfare, Canberra. Available from: http://www.aihw.gov .au/publication-detail/?id=10737422201. [August 3, 2012].

Boonwaat, L., Haber, P. S., Levy, M. H., and Lloyd, A. R. 2010, Establishment of a successful assessment and treatment service for Australian prison inmates with chronic hepatitis C, *Medical Journal of Australia*, vol. 192, pp. 496–500.

Chandler, R. K., Fletcher, B. W., and Volkow, N. D. 2009, Treating drug abuse and addiction in the criminal justice system: Improving public health and safety, *Journal of the American Medical Association*, vol. 301, pp. 183–190.

Charles, A., and Draper, H. 2012, "Equivalence of care" in prison medicine: Is equivalence of process the right measure of equity? *Journal of Medical Ethics*, vol. 38, pp. 215–218.

Committee for the Prevention of Torture and Inhuman or Degrading Treatment or Punishment (CPT) 2002, *The CPT Standards*, revised 2006, Council of Europe, Strasbourg. Available from: http://www.cpt.coe.int/en/documents/eng-standards-prn.pdf. [July 29, 2012].

Cuellar, A. E., and Cheema, J. 2012, As roughly 700,000 prisoners are released annually, about half will gain health coverage and care under federal laws, *Health Affairs (Millwood)*, vol. 31, pp. 931–938.

Dumont, D. M., Brockmann, B., Dickman, S., Alexander, N., and Rich, J. D. 2012, Public health and the epidemic of incarceration, *Annual Review Public Health*, vol. 33, pp. 325–339.

Elger, B. S. 2008, Research involving prisoners: Consensus and controversies in international and European regulations, *Bioethics*, vol. 22, pp. 224–238.

Elger, B. S. 2011, Prison medicine, public health policy and ethics: The Geneva experience, *Swiss Medical Weekly*, vol. 141, pp. w13273.

Exworthy, T., Samele, C., Urquía, N., and Forrester, A. 2012, Asserting prisoners' right to health: Progressing beyond equivalence, *Psychiatry Services*, vol. 63, pp. 270–275.

Hayes, A. J., Burns, A., Turnbull, P., and Shaw, J. J. 2012, The health and social needs of older male prisoners, *International Journal of Geriatric Psychiatry*, vol. 27, pp. 1155–1163.

Herbert, K., Plugge, E., Foster, C., and Doll, H. 2012, Prevalence of risk factors for non-communicable diseases in prison populations worldwide: A systematic review, *Lancet*, vol. 379, pp. 1975–1982.

Her Majesty's Chief Inspector of Prisons 2012, *Annual report 2010–2011*, Her Majesty's Chief Inspector of Prisons, Kingsway, London. Available from: http://www.justice.gov.uk/downloads/publications /corporate-reports/hmi-prisons/hmip-annual-report-2010-11.pdf. [July 15, 2012].

Inspectorate of Prisons for England and Wales 1999, *Suicide is everyone's concern: A thematic review by Her Majesty's Chief Inspector of Prisons for England and Wales*, Her Majesty's Chief Inspector of Prisons, Kingsway, London. Available from: http://www.justice.gov.uk/downloads/publications /inspectorate-reports/hmipris/thematic-reports-and-research-publications/suicide-is-everyones -concern-1999-rps.pdf. [July 30, 2012].

Kinner, S. A., Jenkinson, R., Gouillou, M., and Milloy, M. J. 2012a, High-risk drug-use practices among a large sample of Australian prisoners, *Drug and Alcohol Dependence*, vol. 126, pp. 156–160.

Kinner, S. A., Streitberg, L., Butler, T., and Levy, M. 2012b, Prisoner and ex-prisoner health— Improving access to primary care, *Australian Family Physician*, vol. 41, pp. 535–537.

Leukefeld, C. G., Hiller, M. L., Webster, J. M., Tindall, M. S., Martin, S. S., Duvall, J., Tolbert, V. E., and Garrity, T. F. 2006, A prospective examination of high-cost health services utilization among drug using prisoners re-entering the community, *Journal of Behavioral Health Services and Research*, vol. 33, pp. 73–85.

Lim, S., Seligson, A. L., Parvez, F. M., Luther, C. W., Mavinkurve, M. P., Binswanger, I. A., and Kerker, B. D. 2012, Risks of drug-related death, suicide, and homicide during the immediate post-release period among people released from New York City jails, 2001–2005, *American Journal of Epidemiology*, vol. 175, pp. 519–526.

Martire, K. A., and Larney, S. 2012, Increasing numbers of inmate separations from Australian prisons, *Medical Journal of Australia*, vol. 196, p. 110.

Nesset, M. B., Rustad, A. B., Kjelsberg, E., Almvik, R., and Bjørngaard, J. H. 2011, Health care help seeking behaviour among prisoners in Norway, *BMC Health Service Research*, vol. 11, p. 301.

Office of the United Nations High Commissioner for Human Rights 2008, *The right to health*, Office of the United Nations High Commissioner for Human Rights, Geneva. Available from: http://www.ohchr.org/Documents/Publications/Factsheet31.pdf. [July 15, 2012].

Pelissier, B., Jones, N., and Cadigan, T. 2007, Drug treatment aftercare in the criminal justice system: A systematic review, *Journal of Substance Abuse Treatment*, vol. 32, pp. 311–320.

Pont, J., Stöver, H., and Wolff, H. 2012, Dual loyalty in prison health care, *American Journal of Public Health*, vol. 102, pp. 475–480.

Roberts, A. 1981, *The physician commission*. Available from: http://studymore.org.uk/2s.htm. [Accessed January 13, 2017].

United Nations Office on Drugs and Crime 2007a, *Interventions to address HIV in prisons: Drug dependence treatments*, United Nations Office on Drugs and Crime, Geneva. Available from: http://www.unodc.org/documents/hiv-aids/EVIDENCE%20FOR%20ACTION%202007%20drug_treatment.pdf. [August 3, 2012].

United Nations Office on Drugs and Crime 2007b, *Interventions to address HIV in prisons: HIV care, treatment and support*. United Nations Office on Drugs and Crime, Geneva. Available from http://www.unodc.org/documents/hiv-aids/EVIDENCE%20FOR%20ACTION%202007%20hiv_treatment.pdf. [August 3, 2012].

van den Bergh, B. J., Gatherer, A., Fraser, A., and Moller, L. 2011, Imprisonment and women's health: Concerns about gender sensitivity, human rights and public health, *Bulletin World Health Organization*, vol. 89, pp. 689–694.

Walmsley, R. 2016, *World prison population list*, 11th edn. Available from: http://prisonstudies.org/sites/default/files/resources/downloads/world_prison_population_list_11th_edition_0.pdf. [Accessed January 13, 2017].

5

Psychological Assessment and Documentation of Torture in Detention

Nimisha Patel

CONTENTS

Introduction

Detention of individuals can be in a variety of custodial settings, including civil, military, or other settings within the context of armed conflict as well as in refugee camps or detention centers. Detention of individuals can also be in psychiatric settings, such as secure mental health units, ostensibly for the provision of compulsory mental health care, or in medical settings, psychiatric wards, and psychiatric institutions. The conditions of detention and the treatment in detention, including torture or other cruel, inhumane or degrading treatment (CIDT) or punishment, can have devastating psychological consequences, which will be considered here, specifically with a focus on civil, military, or other armed conflict places of detention. Specifically, guidance drawing on international standards established in the UN Istanbul Protocol (IP) (UN 2004) and clinical experience will be provided on conducting psychological assessments and documentation, whether by physicians or clinical psychologists or other mental health professionals.

Need for Psychological Assessments in Detention

The imperative for psychological assessment of detainees arises essentially from three key obligations: (1) to prevent torture and the legal requirement to ensure the investigation of any allegation of torture or other ill-treatment, (2) to ensure legal protection from further harm or refoulement, and (3) to ensure health protection and access to appropriate, timely, and effective rehabilitation, both as a professional obligation to provide healthcare to those in need and as an obligation under the right to rehabilitation, as a form of reparation. It is also a principle of medical ethics that health professionals have a duty to provide detainees with the protection of their physical and mental health and treatment of the same quality and standard as is provided to non-detainees (UN 1982).

Psychological assessments should be conducted by health professionals qualified and competent to undertake such assessments (e.g., clinical psychologists), although all medical investigations should also include a component assessing the psychological state. The justifications for a psychological assessment include the following: First, the impact of detention itself; the conditions of detention and of torture can manifest psychologically, and indeed, sometimes this is only discernible in a psychological assessment, since the impact of torture is not always visible and may not leave physical signs (IP, para. 260 [UN 2004]). Second, all conditions of detention and torture methods have psychological features, both in the methods used and in their impact. Third, psychological difficulties can become severe and chronic and lead to other health complications, as well as heightening the vulnerability of the detainee and the risk of harm to self or others. Fourth, a psychological assessment can contribute to the early identification of those detainees who are vulnerable and those who are currently suffering from harm, including torture, and for whom the impact of detention is having an adverse impact on their health. Detainees are often too afraid to disclose or give details of torture while they remain in detention and under threat of further harm and repercussions if they do speak to a health professional. In the case of health professionals employed or in the service of detention sites, detainees may fear the absence of independence and confidentiality on the part of the health professional, minimizing the likelihood of them seeking, fully engaging in an assessment, or disclosing torture or other ill-treatment. On the other hand, even with apparently independent health professionals, the detainee may fear that they lack independence and that they are helpless to effect any change or to offer protection from further harm or repercussions for disclosing experiences of torture.

Torture

Torture is deliberate and systematic violence, an extreme manifestation of discrimination, against those already marginalized people on such grounds of gender, sexuality, religion, political beliefs and activities, ethnicity. Many practices and conditions of detention may amount to torture, although they may be considered, including by detainees, as routine practice and indeed seen as "normal" in particular contexts. Whatever the circumstances and context, torture is by definition an intentional act, inflicted for a range of reasons, including for the broad purposes of silencing, punishing, terrorizing, and oppressing individuals and their communities, and endorsed by the state or state organs, either explicitly or by failure to protect individuals from such harm from others.

In international law, Article 1 of the UN Convention Against Torture and Other Cruel, Inhuman or Degrading Treatment of Punishment defines torture as the

> act by which severe pain or suffering, whether physical or mental, is intentionally inflicted on a person for such purposes as obtaining from him or a third person information or a confession, punishing him for an act he or a third person has committed or is suspected of having committed, or intimidating or coercing him or a third person, or for any reason based on discrimination of any kind, when such pain or suffering is inflicted by or at the instigation of or with the consent or acquiescence of a public official or other person acting in an official capacity. It does not include pain or suffering arising only from, inherent in or incidental to lawful sanctions.

Psychological Impact of Detention and Torture

The combined regime of detention and torture cannot be easily separated in understanding their psychological impact. Overall, it is important to understand that torture seeks and functions to shatter any trust, and the capacity to trust again, another human being. In doing so, it destroys intimate relationships and social bonds within families and communities, while simultaneously creating, for some, a perverse dependency on the captors, where the captors can be experienced by detainees as if they are in total control of the fate of detainees. Torture also aims to destroy a sense of agency and autonomy, seeking to immobilize the capacity to resist.

While not all detainees respond in the same way to conditions of detention and to torture, it is widely recognized that the impact is not always visible (Jacobs 2000) but can be profound, long term, and severe. For those detained for long periods, the psychological impact and suffering may not be easily assessed since some may develop a range of ways of coping, or rather, surviving detention and repeated experiences of torture and may appear to be functioning.

Given the complex and multifaceted nature and different types of torture and detention conditions, the impact can be both physical and psychological (Burnett and Peel 2001). The absence of visible lesions makes a psychological assessment essential, not least because of the psychological aspects of physical injury or debility. For example, physical injury may heal, although the experience of persistent pain, with its psychological aspects (Williams and Amris 2007) can lead to information about the possible causes of the pain. Psychological assessments will differ in depth and quality according to the professional background of the interviewer, although at the very least, there should be an understanding by all health professionals of the factors which influence psychological presentations of detainees.

Factors Influencing Psychological Impact

The psychological impact of detention and torture is complicated by one significant factor—that direct causal links cannot be established, since the psychological responses to any event, situation, or setting depend on the cognitive appraisal of those experiences by the individual in question. In other words, the way a person makes sense of what happened to them (a process referred to here as *meaning-making*), or of the conditions in which they are held, can shape the way they respond psychologically. Thus, no act of torture, or an event, behavior, or conditions of detention, will necessarily have the same impact on each individual, and not all forms of torture have the same outcome (IP, para. 234 [UN 2004]).

Numerous factors influence the meaning-making process and, therefore, the psychological responses and outcomes for each person. These include factors related to the person's early and developmental history; their family history; their health history; their political history and activities; the social, cultural, and political context of the detention; the nature of torture or other ill-treatment during detention; the conditions of detention; the person's own belief systems, personal resources, social support, and resilience; and the wider cultural context with its related gendered norms. Psychological assessments should take into consideration these factors, detailed in the following, in the assessment and in providing an opinion for documentation purposes.

Pre-Detention Context

Practices in detention, including torture, exist in a specific social, economic, and political context and cannot be treated in isolation, or the context excluded from the psychological assessment and documentation. The experience of historical subjugation, marginalization, and persecution, for example, for detainees from particular ethnic backgrounds, mediate the psychological appraisal and meaning given to the experiences of torture and harsh conditions of detention. For example, detainees from particular persecuted minority groups may see detention as to be expected as part of oppressive and intimidating practices by the authorities, and torture as routine practice, for which they feel they have grown up, since childhood, to expect. This is not to say the impact is any less, but the psychological consequences may be mitigated to some extent (e.g., where the detainee holds a strong belief that the ill-treatment is part of a regime of group persecution, rather than directed at particular individuals). Whereas for some, the detention and torture may be seen as totally unexpected (e.g., for a detainee who feels they were in the wrong place at the wrong time and arrested unjustly or that their arrest and detention was a case of mistaken identity). For some, fleeing war and atrocities in their own countries, arriving in another country under perilous conditions, only to be detained as illegal immigrants or for not having appropriate documents, the detention and torture can be experienced as intensely unjust, cruel, and bewildering. For women, a context of historical injustices, pervasive sexual discrimination, domestic violence, and subjugation can also mediate the impact of detention and of gender-specific torture (e.g., rape, burns or cuts on breasts, sexual insults, sexual taunts, and threats) against women.

Pre-Torture History

Some detainees may have experienced previous detentions and torture. Some may have experienced traumatic events in their early childhood, such as the loss of or separation from a parent, sexual abuse, or other violence, or later in life, including traumatic losses of loved ones, injury, accidents, abuse, intimate partner violence, etc. Their resilience and capacity to manage those experiences, or the extent to which they were current at the time of detention, is significant psychologically, since this may mediate the psychological impact of detention and torture. The previous psychological, psychiatric, medical, and obstetric (for women) histories are important in a psychological assessment, since they can have a bearing on the psychological responses (or seeming absence of) to detention and possible torture.

A detainee's personal (e.g., significant others), internal (coping capacity and resilience), and social (e.g., family, community, peers) resources can also mitigate against the potentially harmful impact of detention and torture. Their previous ways of coping, including religious, political, cultural, or other beliefs they held, may be helpful, or on the other hand, inaccessible to the detainee in their current detention, hence potentially hindering their ability to cope.

In an assessment, a detainee who visibly appears to not be suffering, or expressing psychological symptomatology, may be a person who has the capacity to cope and the resources to mitigate against the adverse impacts of detention and torture. However, the absence of psychological symptomatology cannot be assumed to indicate that torture did not take place. Furthermore, the presence of psychological difficulties may indicate possible torture, but this may also be mediated by other current or previous traumatic experiences triggered and intensified by the current detention. A full psychological assessment would consider the range of factors in a detainee's history and consider their significance to the current psychological presentation of the detainee.

Nature of Torture Methods

Despite the common use of the term *torture methods*, there is no definitive list or description of torture as the definition of torture requires a legal interpretation of an act or range of acts, behaviors, and events, according to the legal definition afforded in international law, specifically in the Convention Against Torture.

The distinctions between what are sometimes described as physical and psychological torture methods are also considered outdated and artificial (IP, para. 145 [UN 2004]), since they are not always so distinct, and acts of torture can have both physical and psychological aspects and impacts. Torture can also be a combination of acts, including verbal, physical, and sexual, and compounded by conditions of detention (IP, para. 145 [UN 2004]). Examples of torture are given in the following purely for illustrative purposes and should not be used as a checklist in any assessment with a detainee:

- Suspension/hanging, prolonged constraint of movement, enforced positioning
- Beatings (punches, kicks, slaps, use of blunt instruments, boot, rifle butts, etc.)
- Falaka (beating to soles of feet)
- Stabs, cuts, gunshots
- Whipping
- Electric shocks
- Crushing of limbs, removal of digits
- Medical amputation
- Avulsion of nails
- Burning, branding, cutting
- Cold water/pressurized hosing
- Immersion in water/urine/feces

- Suffocation (wet and dry methods, use of chemicals)
- Pharmacological toxicity
- Fluid or food deprivation
- Denial of toilet facilities
- Solitary confinement/isolation
- Sleep deprivation (blindfolding, hooding, etc.)
- Sensory deprivation
- Loud/white noise
- Enforced prolonged standing
- Restricted positioning
- Pharmacological torture—forced injection of drugs
- Mock executions
- Rape: penile, truncheons, bottles, other objects
- Forced to receive or to perform oral sex
- Forced masturbation
- Sexual assault, touching, biting, burnt or cut on breasts/vagina
- Forced nakedness
- Denial of privacy
- Forced to witness others being tortured (including family members)
- Forced rape by a relative, by other prisoners
- Verbal threats of torture, verbal insults and humiliation
- Violations of religious or other beliefs and taboos

Detainees may have experienced repeated torture, over different periods, with the use of a range of methods of varied duration, intensity, circumstances, and combination. The psychological impact may be cumulative and present as a complex picture reflecting the combination of these abuses, as well as other factors (outlined subsequently).

The psychological impact of torture can manifest in many ways, including physical, emotional, social, interpersonal, daily functioning, and existential. It can also have an impact on not only the individual, but also their family and more widely on communities and on society (see the studies by Gurr and Quiroga [2001] and Quiroga and Jaranson [2005] for reviews). While psychological effects can be immediate, in detention, these may not be identified unless a person is assessed soon after the experiences of torture. For detainees who have been in custody for longer periods, the impact may be long term, while in detention, and extend beyond detention, for many years.

Although some types of torture are related to particular psychological responses, given the complexity of the combination of torture and detention conditions and the overlap of psychological responses, it is difficult to ascertain which psychological indications are clearly responses to particular acts or detention conditions. Thus, a psychological assessment needs to consider the nature of torture the detainee has been subjected to and how the detainee describes these experiences and their own thoughts, beliefs, and feelings in relation to those acts. For example, a detainee may describe being subjected to repeated threats and beatings, and verbal insults, but the nature of the insults may be central to how the person thinks of and experiences the beatings and the mediated psychological response they have: "they beat you all the time, with everything, everywhere, but they say I will never leave here alive, that they have my sister and my mother … that thought is killing me, it's my fault, I can't help them, it's because of me… ."

A careful assessment needs to be made of the nature of the torture and other relevant details the person may share, about their immediate and later thoughts, feelings, and concerns. Details of what happened; the duration, frequency, intensity of torture; who else was there; what was said to them; where this took place; and other relevant details can all be important in exploring, wherever possible, the meaning of these experiences for the detainee, and their psychological responses and difficulties. For example, being told that they will never be released and will face the death penalty for alleged possession of illegal substances, where the detainee adamantly holds this is false, can be experienced as a double injury, the torture endured and the false accusation, which may mean that they are killed. Another example can be of a father forced to witness his daughter being raped may experience this as more traumatic and annihilating than being subjected to brutal physical torture and kept in solitary confinement themselves, particularly because of the meaning this may hold and related beliefs that he had failed in his ultimate duty to protect his daughter and the honor of his family.

The gender, age, culture, mental capacity, and wider background of the detainee at the time of detention and assessment are also important to understand the nature of the psychological impact, and the capacity of the detainee to express what happened or is happening to them in detention. For example, minors may not be able to articulate, partly from fear and partly depending on their age and emotional, cognitive, and linguistic capabilities. Age may also mediate how a person makes sense of what happened to them, or not, and their capability to emotionally and cognitively process their experiences, and this may manifest in the nature of the psychological problems they experience and their ability to express these problems in language or behavior.

Conditions of Detention

The conditions of detention can constitute a regime and environment amounting to cruel, inhumane, degrading treatment or punishment and even torture. Conditions of crowdedness, poor sanitation, poor ventilation, absence of daylight, and lack of adequate opportunity for exercise and movement can all have a range of psychological consequences. Detainees can suffer from acute anxiety, lethargy, helplessness, hopelessness, irritability, intense anger, depression, and feelings of suicidality and self-harm. They can also experience flashbacks, heightened arousal, sleep disturbance, and visual or auditory hallucinations (e.g., the studies by Sultan and O'Sullivan [2001], Steel et al. [2006], and Fazel and Silove [2006]). Overcrowding is common in many detention facilities and known to lead to uncontrollable rage and aggression (Haney 2003). Overcrowding can mean that detainees have to take turns to lie down, or crouch to be able to sleep, sometimes on concrete floors covered in urine, excrement, and blood and in unbearable heat or cold conditions without ventilation. Not only does overcrowding heighten the risk of contagious diseases, it can lead to intense helplessness, prolonged stress, and violence (Gaes 1985), with threats to personal security, lack of personal space, and unwanted social interaction leading to pervasive fear, vigilance, guardedness, aloofness, withdrawal, and heightened irritability and violence. Overcrowding can mean sleep is broken, short, and not restorative, leading to chronic exhaustion, irritability, aggression, depression, hallucinations, and poor cognitive functioning. The lack of opportunity for exercise, where detainees are kept in solitary confinement or in cells or other detention facilities for long periods without being allowed to go outside, or to engage in any physical movement, can also have a psychological impact and and lead to poor health (Haney 2003). These conditions, in combination, described by detainees as being treated "like cattle," or "like animals," or "like rats," also further strip detainees of dignity and humanity, often intended by the authorities as the aim of the detention regime.

In some detention settings, for example, in the "War of Terror" in Guantanamo, the conditions have been described as explicitly based on psychological–behavioral principles of reward and punishment (Bloche and Marks 2005; Patel 2007). Detention regimes can also be deliberately unpredictable, thereby intensifying fear, anticipatory and generalized anxiety, dependency on the captors, and a sense of loss of control and of helplessness in detainees.

Context of Torture

The wider social context in which detainees are held and subjected to torture is essential to consider in a psychological assessment. Historical persecution, devaluation, oppression, degradation and discrimination, a context of civil conflict, religious and political divides, and widespread state terrorism against its own population all provide a context which shapes the way a detainee understands and makes meaning of their detention (e.g., if they were arrested during civil protest), of the experiences of torture (e.g., if they are from a persecuted minority), and of the possibility of any justice or reparation (e.g., if they live in a country context where such treatment is routine practice, there is corruption and impunity for perpetrators). The wider cultural and religious context also requires the consideration of factors which influence the psychological appraisal, meaning-making, and impact of torture (e.g., when torture involves the deliberate breach of religious taboos—being forced to eat beef as a Hindu; sodomy with accompanied threats that the man is now homosexual as a result; smearing of menstrual blood on religious texts).

Post-Torture History

Often, there is no sense of post-torture when detainees are assessed in detention. However, detainees' accounts of what happened immediately after a particular event or period of detention are important to understand, for example, whether they were concussed, for how long, who else was there, or if there was any access to medical, psychiatric, or psychological care, whether they were left in poor conditions deprived of fluids or food, etc. These factors cannot only contribute to the overall psychological presentation, but they may also influence the meaning-making by the detainee, of what they endured, and of the psychological impact. For example, left alone concussed and lying naked in their urine, only to regain consciousness and find that they are in solitary confinement may be experienced as not only brutal, but also abandonment and a feeling of "being left to die, like an animal in a small cage."

Current Recovery Context

For detainees, while detained, there can be no context where psychological recovery can take place in a meaningful way. The current context is an important consideration in a psychological assessment, for example, where there is no hope for reprieve from a death penalty, or no likelihood of imminent release, a detainee cannot be expected to easily disclose torture nor exhibit signs of psychological problems, for fear that after an assessment, they may still face further torture and further threats and incarceration. The belief that they will never be released, or survive detention, may manifest in apparent withdrawal, lethargy, passivity, helplessness, and reluctance to engage in any health assessment.

Impact of Torture on the Individual

As intended, harsh conditions of detention and torture attack the integrity, dignity, security, and well-being of detainees. As noted earlier, many factors mediate the psychological impact of torture and detention conditions on a detainee. These include factors related to the detainee themselves (e.g., their age; gender; background; cultural and religious beliefs; their family and personal history; personal, internal, and social resources), factors related to the nature of torture and conditions of detention, and factors related to the wider social context. There is no one clinical picture presented by detainees, or specifically by detainees who have been subjected to torture and other ill-treatment. There is no torture syndrome, no psychiatric disorder, no one psychological problem always associated with torture. As such, the identification of those who may have suffered torture is complex and requires a skilled psychological assessment, rather than a checklist approach of noting particular symptoms or particular diagnoses and thereafter inferring torture. Psychological responses to torture vary widely and cover a vast range of psychological signs and difficulties (for examples, see the studies by Alayarian [2009], Basoglu et al. [2001], and Quiroga and Jaranson [2005]), many overlapping and related to each other in mutually enforcing and complex ways.

Common psychological responses (see also UN 2004, paras. 241–249) include the following:

Psychological (emotional, behavioral, cognitive) responses
- Aggression: Irritability, anger, aggressive behavior
- Anxiety: Acute and chronic anxieties and fearfulness, commonly presented as nervousness, excessive worrying, restlessness, fidgeting, tension headaches, inability to relax, light-headedness, palpitations, dizziness, panic attacks
- Hypersensitivity to noise, exaggerated startle response to an external stimulus, commonly acoustic, such as a door slamming or a bell ringing
- Hypervigilance: A state of extreme psychological arousal in which the sufferer is constantly on the alert for and anticipates further danger or harm
- Numbness: Emotional blunting, restricted affect
- Dissociation, detachment from others, detachment from oneself/one's body (depersonalization)
- Loss of control with a profound sense of being helpless and powerless—to not have any control over their environment, the impact on their health and body, leading to learned helplessness and hopelessness
- Loss of trust in others (including family members, friends, physician, authority figures)
- Withdrawal: Diminished or no communication, withdrawal and isolating self from others or any social contact

- Guilt: At not being able to stop torture or to protect family members or others, having survived, escaped, etc.
- Shame, self-disgust, humiliation: As a result of nature of torture (e.g., sexual torture), scars, burns, disability, etc.
- Sleep difficulties: Insomnia, hypersomnia, frequent wakening, disturbed sleep with nightmares, etc.
- Pain: General pain, aches, headaches, musculoskeletal or pain specific to physical torture and injuries or disability
- Poor memory or memory disturbance
- Depression or depressive functioning (where the diagnosis of depression is not appropriate): Sadness, low mood, insomnia or hypersomnia, lethargy, despair, hopelessness, worthlessness, helplessness, poor appetite and weight loss, anhedonia, poor concentration, suicidal ideation, history of self-harm, guilt, and a variety of similar complaints such as headaches, general aches and pains, fatigue and apathy; often coexists with post-trauma reactions and persistent pain.
- Post-trauma stress responses: Even where a formal diagnosis of post-traumatic stress disorder is not appropriate, many will present with trauma responses. These include intrusive phenomena (flashbacks, nightmares), numbness (emotional numbing or blunting, dissociation), avoidance behavior (avoiding people, places, or situations which remind them of what happened), hyperarousal (can manifest in agitation, general anxiety, restlessness, startled response, irritability, including aggressive outbursts, insomnia, and frequent wakening), inability to function in everyday life (e.g., work, study, cook, clean, take care of the home or children, go shopping, attend to paying bills, taking children to school).
- Grief reactions: Shock, numbness, despair, anger, withdrawal, guilt, searching behavior, depressive functioning
- Ruminative thoughts, obsessive compulsive behaviors (e.g., washing, checking rituals)
- Sexual difficulties: Fear of intimacy and of sexual relationships, inability to trust partner, no or diminished sexual arousal, loss of desire, loss of sexual enjoyment, pain during sex and avoidance of any sexual contact, self-disgust and shame, fear of disgust and rejection by sexual partner, fear of permanent damage to sexual organs, erectile dysfunction, vaginismus, premature ejaculation
- Substance misuse: Misuse of illegal substances, alcohol, or prescribed medication as a way of coping with the impact of torture, pain, sleep disturbance, anxiety, fear, and despair
- Neuropsychological difficulties: Brain injury as a result of torture (e.g., suffocation, blows to head), may be related to injury, disease, malnutrition, psychological trauma response, or depressive functioning
- Hearing voices, unusual auditory, visual or tactile experiences, as part of psychoses or not

Psychological aspects of physical injury, illness, debility from torture

- Acute and persistent pain specific to injury, debility, disease
- Grief and despair at debility, loss of function and chronic pain

- Poor self-esteem, poor body image, shame and self-disgust at scars and injuries
- Helplessness, hopelessness, depressive functioning, anger, irritability, despair at illness, or diseases as a result of torture (e.g., HIV+)

Spiritual/existential

- Loss of faith and despair where spiritual beliefs and faith were previously central and had a support function in their life
- Loss of sense of self/identity (e.g., cultural, sexual, religious)
- Sense of worthlessness and despair at not being able to make sense of torture and its impact
- Loss of sense of future, purpose, and meaning of life

Interpersonal

- Inability to trust significant others, partners, spouse
- Isolation, withdrawal
- Interpersonal conflict, verbal and physical aggression
- Shame (e.g., when raped, sexual torture) and intense fear of rejection or harm by others
- Difficulties forming or maintaining intimate relationships
- Difficulties establishing new relationships, friends, social networks, friends due to heightened suspiciousness and lack of trust

Psychological Assessment of Detainees: Aims

As noted earlier ("Need for Psychological Assessments in Detention" section), the need for the psychological assessment of detainees arises from key obligations to ensure legal protection against harm, including torture and other ill-treatment, and to ensure health protection with appropriate, timely healthcare. The legal framework, which has established standards related to these obligations, include the Convention Against Torture and the IP (United Nations 2004). Also highly relevant are the legal standards for the right to rehabilitation for torture survivors, as established in the UN's General Comment 3 on the UN Convention Against Torture (United Nations 2012). Psychological assessments of detainees and documentation should be compliant with these international standards.

Overall Aims of Psychological Assessments

Psychological assessments of detainees should have several overarching aims:

1. Health needs: To identify psychological health needs, coping, health risks, and vulnerability.
2. Early identification: To identify detainees who are being/have been subjected to torture or to CIDT or punishment.
3. History of torture: To establish what the detainee has been subjected to and details of by whom, when, how, etc., wherever possible.
4. Consequences of torture and/or other ill-treatment: To establish the relationship and consistency between what the detainee reports being subjected to and the

presenting and reported psychological difficulties (IP, paras. 261, 288–289 [UN 2004]). Psychological assessments can inform asylum determination processes and legal proceedings to ensure justice and reparation for the person and, in some cases, their family members too.

5. Healthcare: To ensure where there is a need for immediate action (e.g., in the case of the high risk of self-harm) or for follow-up health investigation or healthcare, that appropriate action is taken in terms of what is available and possible within the given context. Psychological assessments can facilitate appropriate healthcare, which can alleviate distress as well as diminish the risk of further deterioration.

Aims in Conducting a Psychological Assessment

The aims (Table 5.1) in conducting a psychological assessment apply to those brief assessments conducted by medical professionals, as well as to those fuller assessments conducted by clinical psychologists.

TABLE 5.1

Aims in Conducting a Psychological Assessment

Establish trust	• Establishing trust and rapport with the detainee, however brief the time available, in order to facilitate the assessment and information gathering
Informed consent	• Involves providing the detainee with sufficient information to ensure they understand (1) the purpose of your visit and assessment; (2) what will happen to the information; (3) how and where it will be stored; (4) the parameters and limitations of privacy and professional confidentiality; (5) who will have access to the information; (6) what may likely be the outcomes of the assessment findings or limitations; and (7) limitations to the interviewer's ability to protect the detainee or their family members
	• Enables valid, informed consent to be taken and reduces the unpredictability and fear detainees may have about your role and independence and the threat of further harm to them if they speak to you
	• Provides some control to detainees about how much they feel safe disclosing and when and to whom
	• Where there is an apparent pattern of torture or ill-treatment in a particular detention facility, for example, sexual or psychological forms of torture, several follow-up assessment visits may be required (IP, para. 131 [UN 2004]); detainees should be informed if a follow-up visit is possible, or not, to give them some choice and control over disclosure of torture
	• Where a detainee discloses torture, they should be asked if the information can be used and how to prevent further harm and reprisals against them (IP, para. 129 [UN 2004])
Gather information	• Gathering relevant and the most important information (see Table 5.5, Section 7.1), particularly where time is lacking
	• Ensuring duty of care to the detainee and gathering information without compromising the safety of the detainee
Recordkeeping	• Ensuring that there are adequate notes kept of the assessment, including any areas of assessment not completed (for example, due to time pressures, interruptions, lack of privacy) to highlight the provisional nature of opinion given
Documentation	• Ensuring that there is appropriate, prompt, and accurate documentation of the psychological assessment and of details of any disclosures of torture or other ill-treatment

Preparation: Interview Setting

By their very nature, detention settings are coercive and strip detainees of their autonomy and ability to feel safe. As such, a place of detention is never the ideal setting for conducting a psychological assessment, nor is it conducive to enabling trust and rapport to be established between the interviewer and the detainee. As such, any psychological assessment can only be considered interim and provisional, until a full assessment can be conducted in a setting and context where the person feels safe.

Interview settings are often constrained by strict regimes for visiting, strict time limits, and sometimes conducted without a room, or chairs, or privacy, in crowded facilities, or where there are guards, police, or other detainees nearby who can hear what is being discussed. Discussions during assessments may be recorded by the authorities, without the knowledge of the interviewer or the detainee. Sometimes, the detainee may be aware and told that they are being watched and listened to and that they are not to say anything about what they are subjected to or punishment will follow.

The nature of the detention setting is then not only important to establish, as far as possible, before a psychological assessment is conducted. It is essential that the interviewer remains alert to and records the nature and details of the detention setting, interview setting, constraints (including the presence or proximity of prison guards, police, soldiers, or others) and the reaction of the detainee to the setting (e.g., the presence of others, interruptions, noises, voices of others), during the interview. Where detainees are brought to the assessment in restraints or blindfolded, this should be noted in the clinical records, and the authorities should be asked to remove them, as such restraints are contrary to health professional ethics and deny detainees dignity (Peel et al. 2005) and prevent the establishment of trust and emotional safety with the interviewer. Documentation should note the impact of the interview setting and conditions and any restraints on the detainee and on the quality of the assessment.

An ideal setting for conducting a psychological assessment is one where

- The detainee is not in restraints, hooded, or blindfolded
- There is a privacy and the interview cannot be overheard
- There are no guards, police, or other law enforcement officials present in the assessment room
- The door is closed; windows are adjusted for sound, light, temperature, and ventilation
- Chairs are arranged, ideally, at the same level and positioned at an angle, not directly opposite the detainee, not too close to be intrusive (take lead from interviewee and allow them to adjust their chair if they wish)
- Seating/positioning of interviewer allows easy access to exits or alarms to ensure the interviewer's own safety
- Obstructive furniture is removed to enable eye contact and view of the face and demeanor of the interviewee
- Potentially threatening medical or other instruments are out of sight
- There is access to toilet facilities
- Water and tissues are provided, within reach of interviewee, where possible
- There are no interruptions/disturbances by others

Psychological Assessment of Torture: Content

The content of a psychological assessment of detainees depends on (1) the professional background, knowledge, and skill of the health practitioner; (2) sources and availability of background information; (3) urgency and nature of health risks; (4) time available; and (5) constraints of the setting. These factors interact in determining what the interviewer may choose to prioritize in the psychological assessment.

Professional Background and Competency of the Interviewer and Key Content

Medical and psychological health professionals should be appropriately qualified and competent in conducting a psychological assessment of detainees, although the nature, breadth, depth, and analysis of the assessment will inevitably be determined by their professional background and skills.

Medical professionals should include at the very least a brief psychological assessment covering key content (see Table 5.2), including a full or mini mental state assessment (Table 5.3). Clinical psychologists should conduct full psychological assessments, covering various content areas (see Table 5.4). Where limited time, lack of privacy, or other features of the detention setting preclude a full psychological assessment, this should be noted and taken into consideration in the evaluation of the assessment and the final opinion.

Where time is severely restricted, a clinical judgment has to be made as to which areas to prioritize and whether further visits are necessary. The essential content to be addressed in time-limited and other constrained settings is summarized in Table 5.5, and key indications of vulnerability which warrant further assessment are outlined in Table 5.6.

As noted earlier, there are many factors which mediate the impact of torture and the presentation of psychological distress and many factors which hinder the disclosure of torture (Table 5.7). Therefore, sometimes, psychological distress is not visible, or easily identifiable. Where there are no indications from the detainee of psychological difficulties

TABLE 5.2

Content of a Psychological Assessment by Medical Practitioners

- Current psychological difficulties and cultural context
- Mental state assessment and cultural context (see Table 5.3)
- Conditions of detention and psychological impact
- History and context of torture and other ill-treatment (see IP, Chapter 4, Section E [UN 2004])
- Personal history (developmental history, cultural, religious context, educational and/or employment history as relevant, etc.)
- History of past trauma, torture, or significant events in a person's life
- Family history (impact of torture of individual on other family members, other family members who have been tortured)
- Psychological impact of physical injury, debility, pain, or illness as a result of torture
- Coping (methods of coping, availability of and contact with social support networks)
- History of substance use/misuse, including as a way of coping
- Medical, surgical, and obstetric history and psychological impact
- Physical health and psychological impact (e.g., pain, debility, injury, illness)
- Medication and side effects
- Assessments or examinations by health professionals (medical, psychiatric, psychological) during detention
- Everyday functioning in detention
- Risk assessment (risk of suicide, self-harm, harm to others, child-protection concerns where the detainee is a minor or cares for a minor with them in detention)

TABLE 5.3

Summary of a Mental State Assessment

Area	Prompts
Appearance	Self-care, neglect, general psychological presentation
Behavior	Manner, posture and gait, eye contact, rapport and engagement, psychomotor agitation or retardation, suspiciousness, withdrawal
Speech	Rate, fluency, volume, quantity, accents, impediments
Mood	Subjective/objective, range (flattening), appropriateness (incongruence) Biological indications of mood disturbance: Sleep, appetite, and weight
Thought form and content	Thought processes accelerated or slowed, logical or tangential, unusual ideas or beliefs, themes of worthlessness and/or hopelessness
Perceptions	Unusual sensory perceptions, visions, hearing voices, depersonalization
Cognitive function	Orientation, memory, attention, concentration
Person's views on their symptoms/difficulties	Beliefs and explanations about their symptoms or difficulties
Risk	Suicidal, homicidal, or violent ideation, intent, impulse control, plans

TABLE 5.4

Content of a Psychological Assessment by Clinical Psychologists

- Current psychological presentation
- Current psychological difficulties (emotional, behavioral, interpersonal, cognitive, social functioning, including unusual thoughts, beliefs, or sensations which cause emotional distress), cultural context, and meaning given by the detainee to these difficulties, including details on onset, triggers, duration, frequency, severity, etc.
- Coping (patterns and methods of coping, internal, personal, and social resources, social support network availability and use)
- Past psychiatric/psychological history
- History of substance use/misuse
- Personal history (developmental history, cultural, religious context)
- Educational history: Brief account of number of years at school, relevant experiences at school, literacy
- Employment history: Brief account of paid or other employment, previous functioning, skills, etc.
- Current detention: Detainee's detailed account of experiences of torture and other ill-treatment, including verbal insults and threats, of detainee's beliefs about why they were detained and subjected to torture or other ill-treatment
- Nature and conditions of current detention (type of detention facility, location, size of cell, ventilation, light, temperature, bedding, access to food, water, toilet, overcrowding, etc.)
- History and context of previous detention(s), including circumstances of detention, dates, location, type of detention facility, conditions of detention, duration, and psychological impact
- Experiences of past torture and ill-treatment (nature, frequency, duration) (see also IP, Chapter 4, Section E [UN 2004]; IP, p. 276 [UN 2004])
- History of past trauma and other significant events in a person's life
- Family history (family structure, relationships, difficulties, whereabouts, losses, impact of torture of individual on other family members, other family members who have been tortured, and social functioning and how they manage their roles in the family)
- Current physical health (main complaints, illness, disease, injuries, disability, functioning, pregnancy, sexual health, etc.) and psychological impact
- Beliefs about physical health (beliefs about causes of symptoms and health difficulties, including relation to experiences of ill-treatment, beliefs about how best to manage the problem)
- Past medical, surgical, and obstetric history and psychological impact
- Assessments or examinations by other health professionals (medical, psychiatric, psychological) during detention
- Current medication and side effects
- Risk assessment (risk of suicide, self-harm, harm to others, child-protection concerns), priority, and mitigating factors
- Any health risks impacting the psychological health (e.g., pregnancy by rape, HIV+, epilepsy)
- Everyday social functioning in detention

TABLE 5.5

Essential Content of a Psychological Assessment

- Current psychological presentation
- Current detention: Detainee's detailed account of experiences of torture and other ill-treatment, including verbal insults and threats, of detainee's beliefs about why they were detained and subjected to torture or other ill-treatment
- Coping (patterns of coping, internal, personal, and social resources, social support network availability and use, use of substances)
- Nature and conditions of detention (type of detention facility, location, size of cell, ventilation, light, temperature, bedding, access to food, water, toilet, overcrowding, etc.)
- History and context of current detention and experiences of torture and other ill-treatment
- Current physical health (main complaints, illness, disease, injuries, disability, functioning, pregnancy, etc.) and psychological impact
- Risk assessment (risk of suicide, self-harm, harm to others, child-protection concerns), priority, and mitigating factors
- Everyday social functioning in detention
- Assessments or examinations by other health professionals (medical, psychiatric, psychological) during detention

TABLE 5.6

Common Signs Indicating Psychological Vulnerability and Possible Torture

- Psychological signs of distress
- Distracted, poor concentration, agitated
- Uncommunicative, poor or no eye contact
- Flattened affect, numbness, distant/cut off
- Tearfulness, incoherence when speaks, disoriented/confused
- Unable to elaborate on certain aspects of their story or experiences/or provide details
- Poor memory/poor or no recall of certain events or dates/incoherent account
- Anxiety about who else may know, or see health records, or which family members will be told of details of the assessment
- Indifference, detachment, anger, or intense ambivalence about being pregnant
- Uncomfortable and fearful in the presence of someone from the opposite sex
- Inability to relate to others, including family members, close, significant others
- Complaints related to sexual health
- Physically agitated, in pain or discomfort
- Visible injuries, poor mobility, pain, bruising
- Content of nightmares and intrusive recall (flashbacks) related to themes of coercion, loss of control or being attacked or running away from men or torturers
- Unusual thoughts, beliefs, or auditory or visual sensations which cause emotional distress

or reports of any specific symptoms, this does not mean that the detainee is not suffering, or that they have not been subjected to torture (see IP, paras. 236, 289, [UN 2004] and Peel et al. [2000]).

Psychological assessments should not focus on or over-rely on psychiatric diagnoses since psychological manifestations of distress are mediated by context, culture, and other factors, and psychiatric diagnoses are often a crude representation of these complex psychological difficulties. They also do not provide understanding of what, how, and why particular acts or conditions of detention are related to and consistent with psychological problems, nor do they consider the significance of historical persecution and repeated detentions, torture, and other traumatic experiences. Further, psychiatric diagnoses are

TABLE 5.7

Factors Which Can Impede Psychological Assessment and Disclosure of Torture

Safety	A detention setting always has the potential to be experienced as unsafe by detainees, even if objectively it might be "safe." In the absence of safety, a psychological assessment is likely to be compromised, limited, and, at best, provisional. Many factors can contribute to the assessment not feeling safe for the detainee: being overheard, watched, or monitored by the authorities; being threatened before or during the interview by the authorities; a rushed interview; too many closed questions; not feeling listened to or feeling judged or disbelieved by the interviewer; and feeling that the interviewer is not independent, disinterested, indifferent, or resentful of having to conduct an assessment.
Trust	An absence of trust and rapport with the interviewer can be related to poor listening; a lack of empathy; rushed questions; poor nonverbal communication; aggressive, intrusive, judgmental, cynical, or disinterested style of interviewing; the interviewer's background (age, culture, ethnicity, gender, nationality, professional background, etc.); and poor context setting by the interviewer (no introduction, no explanation of their role, affiliations, confidentiality, purpose and context of the interview, possible outcomes, etc.).
Confidentiality and privacy	The absence of privacy and lack of confidence in the confidentiality of the interview can hinder trust, rapport, and the interview process. The presence of a third party, such as a guard, nurse, or interpreter, can also hinder trust (particularly when there are concerns about the lack of independence, the gender, age, ethnic background, etc.).
Arousal	Heightened arousal can manifest in anxiety, irritability, and restlessness, which can affect concentration, attention, listening to and comprehension of questions, as well as impairing the detainee's ability to recall relevant information—all adversely impacting the interview process. Not rushing an interview and showing a genuine interest and empathy can help, as can breaks or pauses for the detainee, wherever possible.
Memory impairments	Memory impairments related to beatings to the head, suffocation, near drowning and starvation, psychological distress (anxiety, post-trauma stress, depression), fatigue, and pain can hinder an interview. Psychological trauma can have an impact on cognitive functioning, including the ability to recall and to provide detailed, coherent and complete accounts of what the detainee has experienced or been subjected to. Specific torture methods (e.g., hooding; drugging; alternations of sensory stimulation, such as total darkness with bright lights; intentionally disrupting sleep and inducing confusion; disorientation; and prolonged fatigue) can also have an impact on recall of certain details of torture. Ensuring breaks, where possible, the use of short sentences and simple questions and of free narrative, followed by prompts, clarification questions, and questions asked in reverse order (e.g., "What happened then?" "What happened before that and before that . . .?") can be useful.
Avoidance	Detainees subjected to torture and other ill-treatment may have also experienced other traumatic events, including loss or witnessing loved ones being tortured or killed. Avoidance behavior is a protective and defense mechanism to avert intense psychological distress, and detainees may actively avoid recalling traumatic memories, including avoiding talking about anything that reminds them of these events, even if asked sensitively during the interview. Going at the pace of the detainee, even where time is pressured, is important, while conveying an understanding of why they may feel the need to avoid talking about distressing events.
Guilt, shame, and stigma	Detainees may say nothing or avoid providing any details of what they have experienced to avoid exacerbating their feelings of guilt, shame, self-blame, self-disgust. They may also fear further harm, taunts, threats which may intensify their shame, guilt, and fear of being ostracized by their family or community if the nature of the torture or ill-treatment (e.g., sexual torture, rape) was disclosed (for details of interviewing and assessment of women survivors of rape or other sexual torture, see Patel and Cohen [2015]). Awareness and acknowledgment of culture or gender norms, which also influence these anxieties, may facilitate the assessment process.

(Continued)

TABLE 5.7 (CONTINUED)

Factors Which Can Impede Psychological Assessment and Disclosure of Torture

Time	Inadequate time can cause pressure and give rise to anxiety for both the detainee and the interviewer, contributing to mistrust, fear, and rapport. Acknowledging this to the detainee at the outset is important, explaining that there are key areas that you would like to explore and understand, but also making contingency plans, if possible, to complete the assessment if necessary, at another visit.
Risk of harm	Detainees who are at risk of harm to themselves or others may appear noncommunicative, withdrawn, disengaged, or intermittently extremely distressed. Pursuing a broader psychological assessment can elevate their distress and make the detainee feel unheard. Prioritize a risk assessment and establish priority and urgency and nature of action required, explaining to the detainee why you are asking questions related to risk.
Interpreters	Where interpreters are required to conduct the assessment, key considerations and standards must be adhered to (see IP, paras. 150–153 [UN 2004]). Attention to differences in gender, ethnicity, political, religious, etc., between the detainee, the interpreter, and the interviewer is important as they can all give rise to anxiety, fear, suspicion, and mistrust, which can adversely have an impact on the quality of an assessment. Where possible, ensure careful selection of interpreters, including consideration of their professional competency, language skills, and the potential for triggering fear and mistrust in the detainee (e.g., because of the interpreter's ethnicity, political background, gender, age). Attend to any signals of poor or problematic communication or mistrust from the detainee during the assessment, acknowledge this and stop the interview if necessary, clarify expectations with interpreter, and where necessary, change the interpreter. Explaining the interpreter's professional and ethical duties, including the duty of confidentiality and their role, at the outset is important.

heavily criticized for individualizing, medicalizing, or psychologizing torture as a human rights violation (Bracken et al. 1995; Summerfield 2001; Patel 2003, 2011) and for their cultural specificity and Eurocentric biases (Patel 2003). They are also rigorously critiqued and demonstrated to be both scientifically inadequate and ethically compromised (e.g., Bentall et al. 1988; Caplan and Gans 1991; Young 1995; Boyle 2003; Pilgrim 2007, 2009).

Sources and Availability of Background Information

The range of sources of information is important to note in gathering and comparing information for a psychological assessment. These include the following:

- Observation of the detainee's behavior, mood, and psychological presentation
- Clinical interview
- Self-reports from the detainee
- Reports by significant others (e.g., family members who have contact or visits with the detainee)
- Any available medical or psychological records
- Description of the detainee's general state of health and reports from the detainee regarding their health and torture or ill-treatment from their legal representative where they have had contact with the detainee

The use of formal psychological assessment tools and checklists is inadvisable, particularly in coercive conditions where the detainee may feel watched by guards or under pressure by the interviewer or setting. Formal psychological assessment tools are also inadvisable unless they are professionally and appropriately translated into necessary languages, culturally validated, and reliable. Using formal tools may be seen as a quick way to assess psychological state, but apart from being severely compromised and unethical when used in detention settings, they risk alienating the detainee and deterring them from establishing trust and disclosing other information, including disclosing torture or other ill-treatment.

Again, time constraints and the limit to access to existing medical records, family members, or significant others may limit what information is available. This may mean that the content of a psychological assessment has to be carefully prioritized as noted in Table 5.5.

Psychological Assessment of Torture: Process

Assessing psychological health can be a very complex and sensitive endeavor, requiring time, empathy, and skill. The conditions and constraints of detention settings can make such assessments extremely time pressured and feel unsafe (for the detainee and interviewer), particularly in countries where torture is still practiced. It is crucial to not conduct a psychological assessment where follow-up visits cannot be guaranteed and where there may be a threat of further harm to the detainee (IP, para. 132 [UN 2004]). Further, assessments should not be treated as a checklist of questions, without attending to psychological process and establishing trust and rapport, however restricted the time. This requires skill, patience, and the capacity to discern what the detainee is feeling and what they feel able to talk about at that particular time. Core principles in facilitating trust and the process of a psychological assessment are presented in Table 5.8.

Many factors affect the process of an assessment and conspire to hinder a quality psychological assessment and the disclosure of torture, even where there are indications of psychological vulnerability. These factors are outlined in Table 5.7.

Psychological Documentation of Torture and Other Ill-Treatment

A psychological assessment should be carefully, accurately, and promptly documented. The documentation of a psychological assessment with a detainee should address the overall aim, which is to provide a clinical opinion based on an assessment of the psychological health needs, vulnerability, risks, and coping; on priorities; and on the evidence torture and other ill-treatment, including the testimony given by the detainee. According to the IP, the overall aim of a psychological health assessment is to "assess the degree of consistency between an individual account of torture and the psychological findings during the course of the evaluation" (IP, para. 261 [UN 2004]).

The documentation of psychological assessments should not be confused with psychiatric assessments and a simplistic listing of psychiatric diagnoses. Documentation by medical professionals should provide in the opinion a summary of the psychological state of the detainee. Documentation by psychological health professionals should provide a detailed psychological case formulation of the psychological presentation, psychological difficulties, context, and the relationship with the reports of experiences of torture, other ill-treatment, or significant life experiences.

Documentation involves three steps: first, accurate recording of all assessment information; second, an evaluation of the assessment findings to form a psychological opinion; and third, the preparation of a written report. The content of a psychological report should

TABLE 5.8

Core Principles in Facilitating Trust and the Process of Psychological Assessment

Prepare	• Prepare yourself mentally and be calm, open, and empathic.
	• Give consideration to the gender of the interviewer (female interviewer for female detainees, wherever possible) and the gender, ethnicity, and background of the interpreter, where one is needed.
Introduction	• Introduce yourself and interpreter where one is present.
	• Explain the context and nature of the assessment.
	• Provide clear information to seek informed consent.
	• Even where time is limited, do not rush the introduction and informed consent.
Attend to nonverbal communication	• Notice the detainee's nonverbal communication. Stay alert to the detainee's responses to the detention and interview setting.
	• Adopt an open and relaxed posture and maintain appropriate eye contact.
	• Ensure that your nonverbal behavior is culturally and gender appropriate (e.g., eye contact, posture, gestures).
Questions	• Start with open-ended questions and encourage free narrative with limited interruptions.
	• Use a mixture of open and closed questions and prompts, to ensure flow and the building of trust and sufficient detail in the interview.
	• Avoid a series of questions fired in close succession, as this can feel overwhelming, intrusive and like an interrogation.
	• Closed and direct questions can be used to clarify or seek details and explore the context of the narrative given, but they should not be asked in a harsh and cold manner.
	• Ask questions in reverse order, to facilitate recall but not in a way which is experienced by the detainee as the interviewer trying to "catch them out."
	• Closed questions rigidly and overused can hinder trust and neglect the range of responses which may otherwise follow, including information on psychological difficulties not asked about, nature, frequency, severity, and duration of torture, the meaning this holds for the detainee in relation to their gender, culture, religious and political belief systems, and other factors.
	• Questions should be age-appropriate and take into consideration cultural, gendered, and other norms to ensure sensitivity and clarity.
	• Questions should be appropriate to the detainee's capacity to listen to and retain information (e.g., if there are cognitive difficulties) and to understand complex questions (e.g., if there are learning difficulties or mental health problems).
Flexibility	• Avoid conducting the interview like an interrogation or structured survey or as if you are using a checklist.
	• Use careful clinical judgment to decide which topics need addressing, in what order, in what depth, and how directly, and adapt to the detainee.
Pace	• Do not rush.
	• Allow the detainee to show the pace at which they feel able to talk.
	• Wherever possible, take the lead from the client, allowing more time to topics which are anxiety provoking, distressing, and a priority for the person.
Listen	• An interview should provide an opportunity for the detainee to respond to questions *and* to be heard.
	• Nonverbal and verbal responses to questions are both important to note.
	• Note what is also not said.
"Listen with knowledge"	• Use questions which may indicate relevant background knowledge or experience, for example, about the detention conditions, thereby building trust and enabling the detainee to share more details or disclose relevant information.
	• Avoid only listening to what you expect to hear.
	• Stay attentive to the unique details of each detainee's experiences.

TABLE 5.9

Documenting Outcome of Psychological Assessment

Circumstances of the interview	• Name of detainee, assessing health professional • Name and affiliation of those present at the assessment • Exact date, time, location of the assessment (specific room, address) • Circumstances of the assessment conditions (e.g., interview setting, restraints under which detainee was brought to the assessment, presence of others, threats or warnings to the interviewer)
Source of information and methods used	• All documents read, including clinical records and other medicolegal reports • Observation, interview with detainee, interview with family member(s) • Use of psychological assessment tools, their validity and reliability, including cultural validity, and their limitations • Others
Current, presenting psychological difficulties and coping	• Observations, self-reports, and detainee's responses given during assessment to questions • Details of the nature of psychological difficulties, duration, severity, frequency, onset, triggers, etc. • Meaning given to these difficulties, by the detainee • How the detainee is coping and managing the psychological difficulties; internal, personal, and other social resources and support; social functioning
Risk	• Nature of any identified risks (e.g., risk of self-harm, suicide, harm to others), priority, and mitigating factors • Any health risks impacting the psychological health (e.g., pregnancy by rape, HIV+, epilepsy)
Pre-arrest and pre-detention history	• Relevant aspects of the detainee's history • Developmental, personal, family, psychological, psychiatric, medical, educational, and employment histories
History of detention, torture, or other ill-treatment	• Experiences of previous detentions (circumstances of detention, dates, location, type of detention facility, conditions of detention, duration) • Experiences of past torture and ill-treatment (nature, frequency, duration) • Detailed account of detainee's account of experiences of torture and other ill-treatment in current detention • Detainee's beliefs about why they were detained and subjected to torture or other ill-treatment
Psychological opinion	• Evaluation of assessment findings with an interpretation of the relationship between current psychological difficulties and the report of torture or other ill-treatment • Explanation of psychological health difficulties and any relationship to each other (e.g., cognitive problems and disturbed sleep) • Interpretation of risk concerns, their urgency, and recommended action • Interpretation of the likely reasons for psychological health difficulties, where no report of torture or ill-treatment is given by the detainee • Possible coexisting stressors and likely contribution to the current psychological presentation • Possible physical conditions, injury, or illness and likely contribution to the current psychological presentation • Explanation of the limitations of the psychological opinion, where the assessment was not completed, or compromised, by the circumstances of the interview, setting, time available or other factors

(Continued)

TABLE 5.9 (CONTINUED)

Documenting Outcome of Psychological Assessment

	• Explanation of the limitations of the opinion on the psychological state of the detainee, where the assessment is conducted by a physician, nurse, or other nonpsychological health professional • Possibility of false allegation of torture • Recommendations for follow-up medical or other health investigations and healthcare
Author of report	• Name, qualifications, professional background, affiliation • Brief biography or curriculum vitae • Signature and date of signature

contain, at minimum, key information as outlined in Table 5.9 (see also IP, annex 1, para. 6 [UN 2004]).

Documentation serves several purposes (IP, para. 121 [UN 2004]), including (1) providing a professional record of a psychological assessment; (2) enabling early identification of those detainees who are vulnerable, including those who have been subjected to torture or other ill-treatment; (3) enabling decision-making about the next steps in order to safeguard the detainee's safety and health, including the recommendation of further medical investigation or specialist health assessment and its priority; (4) ensuring legal protection to prevent further harm (in the form of medicolegal reports to support efforts to remove a detainee from detention where there is torture or efforts to contribute to asylum determination processes relevant to the detainee); and (5) contributing to legal proceedings in pursuit of justice and reparation for the detainee.

Even where an assessment is incomplete, documentation must note which areas were not covered in the psychological assessment and reasons for this and that the psychological opinion offered is provisional and interim. The limitations of the opinion on the psychological state of the detainee must be noted.

Conclusions

The psychological assessment and documentation of torture and other ill-treatment of detainees should be considered essential to any investigation to ensure justice and reparation and, essentially, legal protection from further harm and health protection to ensure access to timely, appropriate rehabilitation for the detainee. The breadth, depth, and level of analysis of a psychological assessment will depend on the qualifications and competency of the assessor, although this should not preclude an opinion, however provisional. At the heart of any psychological assessment, and a basic prerequisite, is the capacity to see, to treat, and to listen to each detainee as a human being worthy of dignity and of empathic, respectful communication. This requires not just knowledge and skill, but humility and humanity.

References

Alayarian, A. 2009, Children, torture and psychological consequences, *Torture*, vol. 19, pp. 145–156.

Basoglu, M., Jaranson, J. M., Mollica, R., and Kastrup, M. 2001, Torture and mental health: A research overview, in E. Gerrity, T. M. Keane, and F. Tuma (eds), *The mental health consequences of torture*, Kluwer Academic/Plenum Publishers, New York.

Bentall, R., Jackson, H., and Pilgrim, D. 1988, Abandoning the concept of schizophrenia: Some implications for validity arguments about psychotic phenomena, *British Journal of Clinical Psychology*, vol. 27, pp. 303–324.

Bloche, M. G., and Marks, J. H. 2005, When doctors go to war, *New England Journal of Medicine*, vol. 352, pp. 3–6.

Boyle, M. 2003, *Schizophrenia: A Scientific Delusion?* 2nd edn, Routledge, London.

Bracken, P., Giller, J., and Summerfield, D. 1995, Psychological responses of war and atrocity: Limitations of current concepts, *Social Science and Medicine*, vol. 40, pp. 1073–1082.

Burnett, A., and Peel, M. 2001, Asylum seekers and refugees in Britain. The health of survivors of torture and organised violence, *British Medical Journal*, vol. 322, pp. 606–609.

Caplan, P., and Gans, M. 1991, Is there empirical justification for the category of self-defeating personality disorder? *Feminism and Psychology*, vol. 1, pp. 263–278.

Fazel, M., and Silove, D. 2006, Detention of refugees, *British Medical Journal*, vol. 332, pp. 251–252.

Gaes, G. 1985, The effects of overcrowding in prisons, *Crime and Justice*, vol. 6, pp. 95–146.

Gurr, R., and Quiroga, J. 2001, Approaches to torture rehabilitation, *Torture*, vol. 11, pp. 1–35.

Haney, C. 2003, Mental health issues in long-term solitary confinement and "supermax" confinement, *Crime and Delinquency*, vol. 49, pp. 124–156.

Jacobs, U. 2000, Psycho-political challenges in the forensic documentation of torture: The role of psychological evidence, *Torture*, vol. 10, pp. 68–71.

Patel, N. 2003, Clinical psychology: Reinforcing inequalities or facilitating empowerment? *The International Journal of Human Rights*, vol. 7, pp. 16–39.

Patel, N. 2007, Torture, psychology and the "war on terror," in *Just War, Iraq and Psychology*, Roberts, R. (ed.), PCCS, Ross-on-Wye.

Patel, N. 2011, The psychologisation of torture, in M. Rapley, J. Moncrieff, and J. Dillon, (eds), *De-medicalising misery: Psychiatry, psychology and the human condition*, Palgrave Macmillan, London.

Patel, N., and Cohen, J. 2015, *Identification, health assessment and documentation of rape or other sexual torture of women: Handbook for clinicians*. ICHHR, London.

Peel, M., Hinshelwood, G., and Forrest, D. 2000, The physical and psychological findings following the late examination of victims of torture, *Torture*, vol. 10, pp. 12–15.

Peel, M., Lubell, N., and Beynon, J. 2005, *Medical investigation and documentation of torture: A handbook for health professionals*. Human Rights Center, University Essex, Colchester.

Pilgrim, D. 2007, The survival of psychiatric diagnosis, *Social Science and Medicine*, vol. 65, pp. 536–544.

Pilgrim, D. 2009, Abnormal psychology: Unresolved ontological and epistemological contestation, *History and Philosophy of Psychology*, vol. 10, pp. 11–21.

Quiroga, J., and Jaranson, J. M. 2005, Politically-motivated torture and its survivors: A desk study review of the literature, *Torture*, vol. 15, pp. 1–112.

Steel, Z., Silove, D., Brooks, R., Momartin, S., Alzuhairi, B., and Susljik, I. 2006, Impact of immigration detention and temporary protection on the mental health of refugees, *British Journal of Psychiatry*, vol. 188, pp. 58–64.

Sultan, A., and O'Sullivan, K. 2001, Psychological disturbance in asylum seekers held in long-term detention: A participant-observer account, *Medical Journal of Australia*, vol. 175, pp. 593–596.

Summerfield, D. 2001, The invention of post-traumatic stress disorder and the social usefulness of a psychiatric category, *British Medical Journal*, vol. 322, pp. 95–98.

United Nations (UN). 1982, Principles of medical ethics relevant to the role of health personnel, particularly physicians, in the protection of prisoners and detainees against torture and other cruel, inhuman or degrading treatment or punishment, adopted by General Assembly resolution 37/194 of December 18, 1982, UN, Geneva.

UN. 2004, United Nations manual on effective investigation and documentation of torture and other cruel, inhuman and degrading treatment or punishment (the Istanbul protocol), revised edn, UN Office for the High Commissioner of Human Rights, Geneva and New York.

UN. 2012, General comment 3 of the United Nations' convention against torture (CAT/C/GC/3), adopted by the UN General Assembly, December 2012, UN, Geneva.

Williams A. C. de C., and Amris, K. 2007, Topical review: Pain from torture, *Pain*, vol. 133, pp. 5–8.

Young, A. 1995, The harmony of illusions: Inventing post traumatic stress disorder, Princeton University Press, Princeton, NJ.

6

Assessment of Physical Evidence of Torture or Cruel, Inhuman, and Degrading Treatment during Visits to Places of Detention

Jason Payne-James, Jonathan Beynon, and Duarte Nuno Vieira

CONTENTS

Introduction

The physical or clinical assessment and documentation of injury during visits to places of detention is an important feature of identifying forms of abuse or ill-treatment or torture that may have occurred prior to, or during detention in adults and children (Den Otter et al. 2013). Such ill-treatment is rife throughout the world but varies substantially in nature (Sanders et al. 2009). This chapter focuses predominantly on the assessment of the nature and sequelae of physical assault. Other chapters will address psychological (Chapter 5) and sexual issues (Chapter 10).

The Istanbul Protocol (IP—the *Manual on the Effective Investigation and Documentation of Torture and Other Cruel, Inhuman or Degrading Treatment or Punishment*) provides standardized international guidelines for the documentation of torture and its consequences. It became an official UN document in 1999 (for further details, see Chapter 14). Table 6.1 identifies the chapter and annex contents of the IP. Anyone undertaking an assessment for the purposes of identifying abuse, ill-treatment, or torture should have read this document and understand its contents and implications and preferably undergone specific training in its application.

In relation to this chapter, the IP provides information on, and an appropriate structure and means of interpretation of, injuries, marks, or scars. The assessment of the equally important psychological sequelae is covered in Chapter V. The most relevant parts of the IP with reference to this chapter on physical sequelae are Chapter V and Annex IV. Annex IV provides guidelines for the contents of any report on the medical evaluation of torture and ill-treatment, and the headings are listed in Table 6.2. The term *guidelines* is important to understand—they are there to assist, not provide rigid rules, and the examiner will need to adapt these guidelines to the nature, circumstances, and purpose of individual assessments and with regard to the context and facilities available at the time of assessment (Keten et al. 2013).

During visits to places of detention, whether it is in places with small numbers of detainees such as in police stations or interrogation centers, or with large numbers such as in prisons, the examiner may be faced by allegations of torture, or may have strong grounds to suspect that detainees have been ill-treated. The examiner may not be able to assess all

TABLE 6.1

Chapter and Annex Contents of the IP

Chapters
  I Relevant International Legal Standards
  II Relevant Ethical Codes
  III Legal Investigation of Torture
  IV General Consideration for Interviews
  V Physical Evidence of Torture
  VI Psychological Evidence of Torture
Annexes
  I Principles on the Effective Investigation and Documentation of Torture and Other Cruel, Inhuman or Degrading Treatment or Punishment
  II Diagnostic Tests
  III Anatomical Drawings for the Documentation of Torture and Ill-Treatment
  IV Guidelines for the Medical Evaluation of Torture and Ill-Treatment

TABLE 6.2

IP—Guidelines for the Medical Evaluation of Torture and Ill-Treatment

Possible Considerations for Evaluations
I Case information
II Clinician's qualifications
III Statement regarding veracity of testimony
IV Background information
V Allegations of torture and ill-treatment
VI Physical symptoms and disabilities
VII Physical examination
VIII Psychological history/examination
IX Photographs
X Diagnostic test results
XI Consultations
XII Interpretation of findings
XIII Conclusions and recommendations
XIV Statement of truthfulness
XV Statement of restrictions on the medical evaluation/investigation (for subjects in custody)
XVI Clinician's signature, date, place
XVII Relevant annexes (e.g., clinician's curriculum vitae, images, body diagrams, test results)

detainees and will have to undertake some form of informal triage to determine which detainees they meet and, secondly, will have to conduct rapid assessments of alleged victims of ill-treatment. It will clearly not be possible to conduct a full IP assessment (which may take several hours) in places of detention, but, often with the strong constraints on time and physical space, the examiner must still follow the essential principles of the IP.

For those tasked with the assessment of alleged victims of torture, the IP also highlights principles common to all codes of healthcare ethics, including the need for informed consent, the need for confidentiality, and the duty to provide compassionate care. It also recognizes how these duties and principles are sometimes in apparent conflict with the demands or need of the healthcare professionals' employer, which may include public bodies or state departments (Perera and Verghese 2011).

Chapter III of the IP, "Legal Investigation of Torture," makes specific reference to the need for securing and obtaining physical evidence and medical evidence, and Chapter V, "Physical Evidence of Torture," outlines the key elements of establishing and identifying this evidence. The key elements for consideration are listed in Table 6.3 and will be discussed further in this chapter.

When visiting places of detention, it is usually not practical to enter into all the details covered by Chapter V of the IP, because of constraints of time which may only allow 20 minutes or less to conduct an assessment, but the examiner should apply the essential principles of IP assessment which are summarized in Table 6.4.

The interpretation of findings must be balanced and unbiased and requires appropriate knowledge of published information which should be critically interpreted in the light of documented findings. There are numerous peer-reviewed publications which look at the nature and patterns of ill-treatment and torture allowing regional and geographical differences to be reviewed (Forrest 1995, 1999). Examples include Chaudhry et al. (2008), who explored patterns of alleged police torture in the Punjab, Pakistan; Perera (2007), who looked at physical methods of torture and their sequelae from Sri Lanka; and Morentin et al. (1995),

TABLE 6.3

IP—Chapter V: Physical Evidence of Torture

1. Interview structure
2. Medical history
   - Acute symptoms
   - Chronic symptoms
   - Summary of interview
3. Physical examination
   - Skin
   - Face
   - Chest and abdomen
   - Musculoskeletal system
   - Genitourinary system
   - Central and peripheral nervous systems
4. Examination and evaluation following specific forms of torture
   - Beatings and other forms of blunt trauma
     - Skin damage
     - Fractures
     - Head trauma
     - Chest and abdominal trauma
   - Beatings of the feet
     - Closed compartment syndrome
     - Crushed heel and anterior footpads
     - Rigid and irregular scars
     - Rupture of the plantar aponeurosis and tendons
     - Plantar fasciitis
   - Suspension
     - Cross-suspension
     - Butchery suspension
     - Reverse butchery suspension
     - Palestinian suspension
     - Parrot perch suspension
   - Other positional torture
   - Electric shock torture
   - Dental torture
   - Asphyxiation
   - Sexual torture including rape
     - Review of symptoms
     - Examination following a recent assault
     - Examination after the immediate phase
     - Follow-up
     - Genital examination of women
     - Genital examination of men
     - Examination of the anal region
5. Specialized diagnostic tests

TABLE 6.4

Key Principles When Assessing in Restricted Circumstances or Limited Time

- What are the specific allegations or suspicions of ill-treatment—e.g., methods used, parts of the body targeted, frequency, and duration?
- What were the acute signs and symptoms, injuries, or marks that the victim noticed? And was any medical treatment received at any point? (This may affect wound healing and thus what is found on clinical examination.)
- If seen later after the alleged events, what are the chronic signs and symptoms?
- Upon clinical examination focusing on the targeted parts of the body, the anatomical site, size, shape, and characteristics of any injuries, marks, or scars should be documented using a body diagram (see Annex III of the IP for body diagrams). If possible in the place of detention, photographs should also be taken.
- It may not be possible to arrange any additional diagnostic tests, but any medical records held in the place of detention should be consulted to verify if any assessment and treatment has been provided by the detention or hospital healthcare staff.
- The examiner undertaking the assessment should then make a determination of the correlation between the alleged assault and injuries, with the clinical signs and symptoms found on examination. Are the findings for each sign found either not consistent, consistent, highly consistent, typical, or diagnostic (see Table 6.5)?

TABLE 6.5

Interpretation and Classification of Lesion(s)

This interpretation should be applied to every mark, injury, or scar identified.

Not consistent

- The lesion could not have been caused by the trauma described.

Consistent with

- The lesion could have been caused by the trauma described, but it is nonspecific, and there are many other possible causes.

Highly consistent

- The lesion could have been caused by the trauma described, and there are few other possible causes.

Typical of

- This is an appearance that is usually found with this type of trauma.

Diagnostic of

- This appearance could not have been caused in any way other than that described.

who reviewed alleged methods of torture in the Basque Country. Moisander and Edston (2003) compared torture between six countries and found a wide range of torture methods (including sensory deprivation—isolation/blindfolding; beating—fists, sticks, truncheons; whipping—electric cords; rape; suspension; falaka; electrical, sharp force, burning). More recently, Ghaleb et al. (2014) have explored findings in Cairo. The objective interpretation of findings is crucial, to best assist the complainant of ill-treatment, so that the information is accepted as objective by whichever body (e.g., prison, court, tribunal, judge) is going to use it in their deliberations. This is important because, although the accounts for marks or scars given by victims may be true, they can sometimes be false. If false, this may be as a result of an intention to mislead the medical examiner and courts, poor recall, or misinterpretation due to a variety of causes (e.g., mental health issues). The body adjudicating on the medical assessment will find it easier to accept findings and conclusions if the examiner is clearly seen to be independent and unbiased. It is important when examining individuals to recognize that cruel, inhuman and degrading treatment (CIDT) and torture may leave no visible injuries, marks, or scars. The methods used may leave minimal or no evidence, and any injuries that are produced may heal without visible evidence. This has particular relevance to sexual assault, where penetrative sexual contact only has visible evidence in a minority of cases and that acute injury (whether to the anus or vagina) often heals within 72 hours or so. It is also essential to distinguish between acute (recent) injury and old injury which may manifest as marks or scars. It is also important to distinguish between injury, marks, and scars that are due to ill-treatment and those that are caused by other factors (e.g., employment, sports, and accident).

The nature of injuries and their manifestations must be considered by the examiner at every stage of the assessment. Despite the fact that ill-treatment is often designed such that there may be no, or minimal, visible evidence, short and long-term symptomatology and alteration in function can be extensive, as has been shown in many studies. Examples include Williams et al. (2010), who reviewed persistent pain in survivors of torture, Edston (2009), who reviewed the sequelae of falanga; and Taylor et al. (2013), who studied the interaction of pain and post-traumatic re-experiencing in torture survivors. The gender of the person may also alter the nature and type of ill-treatment. Edston and Olsson (2007) showed female torture victims differed from their male counterparts previously studied in that rape, often both anal and vaginal, several times, and by different persons, was reported by 76% of the women, and physical abuse by use of blunt force was alleged by 95%, but other types of force and specific torture methods was reported infrequently. Eighty-seven percent had a diagnosis of post-traumatic stress disorder (PTSD). Research may also address specific regions of anatomy or areas of science, and as such, such work may be published in specialist journals not generally accessed by those working with complainants of torture. One example is in the specialist journal *Laryngoscope*, which reviews the effects of local torture involving the head and neck (Crosby et al. 2010). Another is Gola et al. (2012) which explored cortisol levels in patients with war- and torture-related PTSD when subject to trauma reminders, published in the journal *Psychoneuroendocrinology*.

Each injury, scar, or mark documented should be interpreted according to the IP Interpretation and Classification of Lesions, as shown in Table 6.5. It is equally important to document the absence of injuries, marks, or scars detected as such absence may also be consistent with or corroborate the allegations. In many cases, as with sexual assault, there may be a complete absence of visible marks or injury (e.g., in hooding [International Forensic Expert Group 2011]). The phrase "absence of evidence is not evidence of absence" (Altman and Bland 1995) is particularly apposite in maltreatment cases—perhaps rephrased and made more clear in this setting as "absence of visible evidence of maltreatment is not evidence of absence of maltreatment," which is why the assessment must be as thorough and complete as the circumstances allow.

Interview Structure

Assessments of alleged victims of torture in detention settings are complicated by several constraints, such as trust (the examinee's relationship with the examiner), not enough time, small space, and lack of privacy. Practitioners must adapt their techniques to optimize the information that can be obtained, while recognizing that poor conditions make the process more difficult for the examiner, but more importantly for the complainant. It is important to find as private a space as possible, at least out of the earshot of guards and of codetainees and to allay the examinees fears, thus reducing their level of anxiety and encouraging them to give information freely and in full. In an ideal setting, the examination should take place in pleasant, purpose-built surroundings with desks, chairs, and examination couch with appropriate high-quality lighting. This is rarely, if ever, going to be the circumstance in which an examination will take place. The visiting team should arrange for interpreters that are acceptable to the detainees, taking into account factors such as language and dialects, gender, ethnicity, and culture.

Once alone with the detainee, the nature and the purpose of the assessment must be clearly explained and described to the detainee. Informed consent should be obtained. The form of that consent (written or verbal) will be dependent on the setting. The examinee must be informed at the beginning of the entire process that they may stop the assessment or examination at any time.

The history taking should begin with a brief narrative account from the individual of what has happened to him or her so that the examiner obtains a broad understanding of the nature and character of ill-treatment alleged. Although this chapter focuses on physical ill-treatment, the examiner must simultaneously record, document, and assess all psychological ill-treatment and its sequelae. As far as possible, the chronology of events should be established, with a particular focus on which law enforcement, security, military, or other forces were responsible and at which places of detention. Having established the pattern and chronology of abuse, a clinical examination must be conducted which may need to be focused on specific anatomical sites due to time constraints. Any healthcare records available from the place of detention should be consulted to, for example, confirm the absence of a condition or to confirm they have attended a doctor or attended a hospital for treatment of an inflicted injury or the complications of that injury (Pounder 2011). The International Forensic Expert Group (2012) recognized the importance of the sight of these records if possible and issued a detailed statement about this. Other examples of documents that can sometimes have evidential value include old photographs and even identification documents with photos. These may confirm the absence of a scar or mark at a particular time. Other considerations during assessment include the nature of any limitation of function caused by musculoskeletal injury and scarring. The need for therapeutic intervention may also become evident during an assessment, and it may be appropriate for the examiner to attempt to arrange appropriate follow-up through the detention healthcare services, but here the consent of the victim is paramount since this would clearly mean that some details of the case (but not necessarily all) might be revealed to the healthcare staff.

Classification of Injuries

When recording and assessing physical evidence, it is important to use a consistent terminology and classification of injury and injury causation. There are many different classifications. The simpler the classification, the more reproducible it is, and the more understood it is by others who are reviewing reports. Table 6.6 is one form of classification and embraces the majority of injuries that will be assessed.

Blunt force injury in particular may give rise to a variety of symptoms and signs dependent on the nature and location of injury. There may be no injury or a spectrum including some or all of tenderness, pain, reddening (erythema) (Figure 6.1), swelling (edema) (Figure 6.2), bruising (ecchymosis, contusion) (Figure 6.3), abrasions (scratches, grazes) (Figures 6.4 and 6.5), lacerations (splits or tears in the skin) (Figure 6.6), and fractures (Figure 6.7). Lacerations

TABLE 6.6

Classification of Injury

Types and Nature of Injury and Examples of Implements or Mode of Causation

Blunt Force

    Not caused by instruments or objects with cutting edges

- Blows
- Traction
- Poking
- Squeezing
- Gripping
- Pinching
- Torsion
- Suspension
- Restraint

Sharp Implement

- Knives
- Bayonets
- Machetes
- Razors
- Glass
- Metal

Burns

- Cigarettes
- Hot liquids
- Flame

Chemical

Suspension

Electrical

- Power sources
- Conducted energy devices
  - Cattle prods
  - Stun devices
  - Taser®

Miscellaneous

---

are particularly seen where bony structures closely underlie the skin (e.g., the orbital margins, the skull, and over the tibia). The color of bruises, once thought to be able to determine bruise age, is now considered to be unreliable and should not be used to age injury (Langlois and Gresham 1991; Stephenson and Bialas 1996; Munang et al. 2002; Maguire et al. 2005). Bruises change and evolve, change shape and migrate (often along tissue plains), and do not necessarily reflect the point of original contact. Abrasions, however, do reflect the initial point of contact. Bruises or abrasions that have distinct patterns may provide evidence or corroboration as to the nature of the weapon used, and any apparent patterned injuries or scars should be accurately recorded with photographic scales (see Figure 6.8). Petechial bruises (pinpoint bruises, generally a couple of millimeters in diameter) (Figure 6.9) may be caused by compression of the neck or chest (e.g., in manual strangulation or

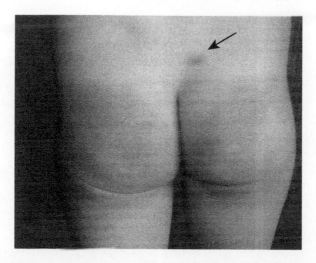

FIGURE 6.1 Reddening (erythema) of the buttocks following repeated smacking with a hand. This should be distinguished from bruising which will not blanch on pressure. This contrasts with non-blanching bruise (see arrow).

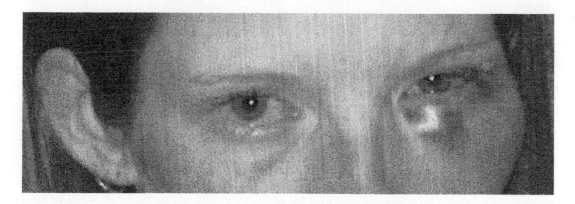

FIGURE 6.2 Swelling (edema) to the left cheek and eye region from direct impact.

crushing injury). Generally, they are present above the level of compression and may be found in skin and mucosa. Examination of all skin surfaces, the nasal cavities, the mouth, and the eyes and ears are important when there is any recent history of compression. They can disappear within hours, but can also coalesce to form apparent larger bruises.

Blunt force injury can result in damage to muscles causing muscle breakdown—rhabdomyolysis—observed as myoglobinuria and which itself can result in subsequent renal failure. Two patients who were systematically tortured and deprived of any oral intake presented with acute renal failure several days later. The authors considered this to

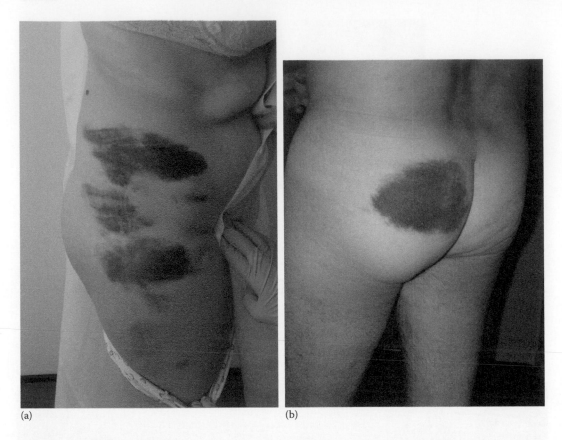

(a)   (b)

FIGURE 6.3 (a) Non-specific bruising to right side of leg and hip (sometimes referred to as ecchymosis or contusion) caused by multiple impacts with blunt object. (b) Non-specific bruising caused by single blunt impact to left buttock.

be a clinical entity wherein repeated direct muscle injury from blunt trauma, in addition to forced dehydration, led to the myoglobinuria and renal failure (Bloom et al. 1995). Naqvi et al. (1996) identified a number of cases of acute renal failure due to prolonged muscular exercise (e.g., squat jumping, sit-ups) and blunt trauma inflicted by law enforcement personnel using sticks or leather belts. None of the patients had a prior history of myopathy, neuropathy, or renal disease. All were critically ill and required renal support in the form of dialysis. Although the morbidity was high, 13 out of 14 of the patients recovered normal renal function. One patient died from sepsis.

Sharp force injury can be broadly classified into slash-type wounds (which are longer than they are deep) (Figure 6.10), stab wounds (deeper than they are long and may damage underlying structures or organs) (Figure 6.11), and chop wounds (from implements such as machetes) (Figure 6.12). Chop wounds may exhibit features of stab or slash wounds, dependent on the nature and sharpness of the implement, and may, particularly with less sharp implements, have features also of blunt contact.

Wounds caused by sharp objects are termed *incised*. They may be differentiated from lacerations (Figure 6.13), described earlier and caused by blunt force, in that incised wounds are clean edged with no evidence of blunt force injury (e.g., maceration, bruising, abrasions at the wound edges) and absence of tissue bridges between the two edges of the wound.

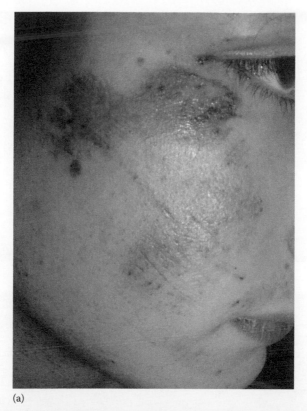

(a)

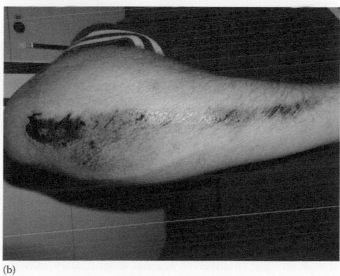

(b)

FIGURE 6.4 (a) Abrasions (sometimes referred to as grazes or scratches) to right cheek region following kick with shod foot. Direction of linearity sometimes assists with direction of impact. (b) Abrasion to right forearm having been dragged across abrasive surface (concrete).

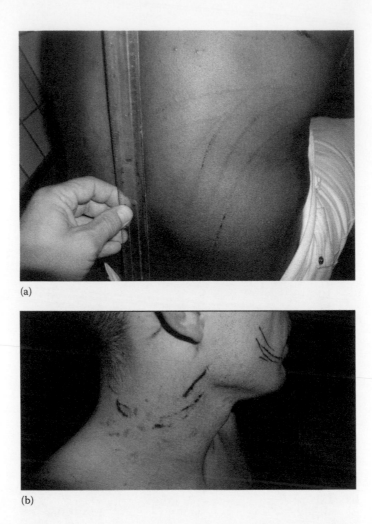

(a)

(b)

FIGURE 6.5   (a) Linear abrasions (scratches) to right side of back. Linear parallel scratches ~0.5 cm across are consistent with fingernail scratches. (b) Irregular abrasions to neck, typical of fingernail scratches in attempted strangulation. Right facial, linear, fine, similar scratches self-inflicted with metal nail by subject.

Some injuries may have elements of both (e.g., a glass bottle breaking on impact may create blunt force injury along with incised wounds). Lacerations and incised wounds may be impossible to distinguish after healing or after suturing or gluing. In the longer term, these physical injuries may cause deformity and loss of function and scars and other cosmetic damage. Certain blunt force and other injuries are still visible in the form of hypo- or hyperpigmentation months and years after the original injury (Peel et al. 2003) (Figure 6.14).

If an individual is defending themselves against assault, they may exhibit patterns of defense injuries, that is to say incisions on the palms and fingers where the victim has tried to grasp the knife (Figure 6.15), or bruises, lacerations, or incisions on the ulna aspect of the forearms and backs of the hands, when the victim holds up their arms to protect the head from assault (Figure 6.16) (Payne-James and Hinchliffe 2011). Injuries may be predominantly on the dominant arm, but can be on both, and there may be multiple, noncontiguous cuts, bruises, or lacerations as the victim struggles. If knocked to the floor, individuals may sustain injuries on the back and torso, as the natural reaction is to curl

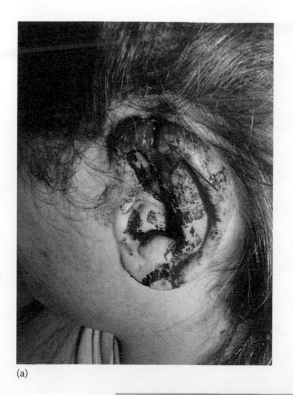

(a)

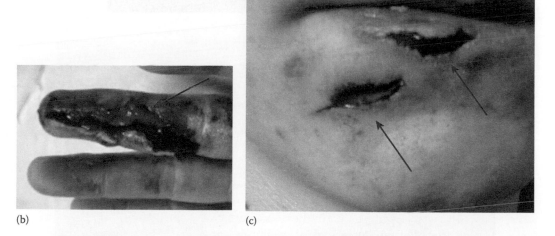

(b)   (c)

FIGURE 6.6 Lacerations (splits or tears in the skin). (a) Laceration to left upper ear caused by direct impact with baseball bat type object, (b) severe laceration to right middle finger caused by crush injury (tendons and nerves damaged), and (c) lacerations to right lower lip and chin caused by single punch.

up into a ball. The examiner should keep in mind that the alleged torture victim may well have been restrained in some fashion during the assault (e.g., wrists bound or handcuffed behind or in front of the torso, suspended by the wrists or ankles, or restrained on a chair or bed) and that this will affect the pattern of injury as certain areas of the body will be shielded and may prevent any attempt at defense against assault. This is true not just for

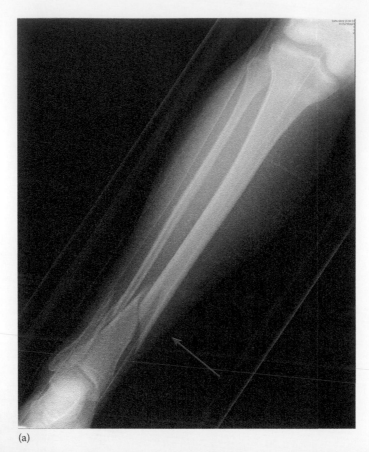

(a)

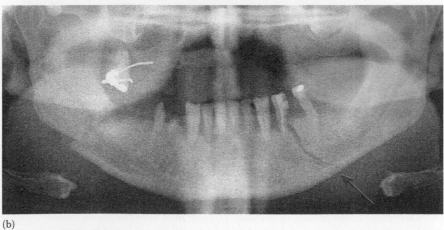

(b)

FIGURE 6.7   (a) Fractured right lower tibia and fibula–caused by a stamping injury on a restrained leg. (b) Fractured mandible (in two places) caused by single punch to jaw.

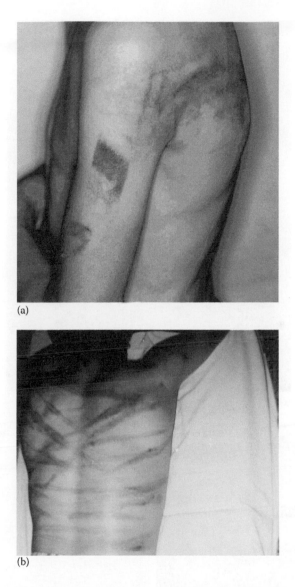

(a)

(b)

FIGURE 6.8 (a) Patterned bruising is seen. Such patterns represent the shape of the impacting object (in this case a 2 × 2″ piece of wood). (b) Patterned "tramline" bruises caused by repeated whipping with a linear object to the back. (*Continued*)

sharp force trauma, but for most forms of assault, such as kicks, punches, or being struck with implements (Figure 6.17).

Other Types of Injury, Torture, and Ill-Treatment

The general nature of injury in the classifications described earlier will often help predict the possible nature of marks, scar, or sequelae of the torture described. There are

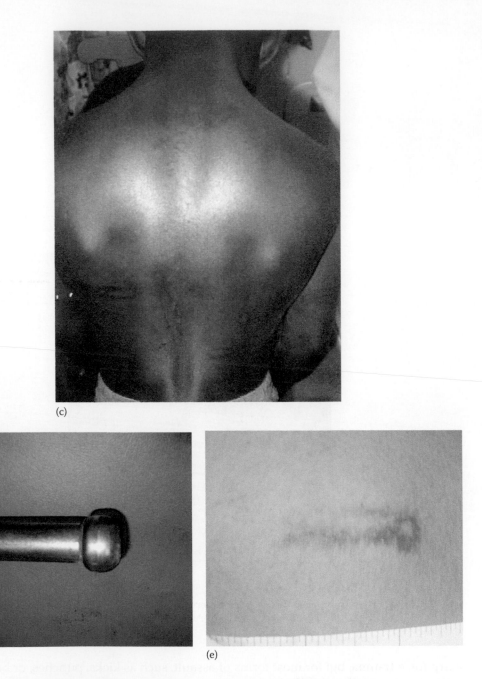

FIGURE 6.8 (CONTINUED)   (c) Persistent patterned tramline hyperpigmentation present some years after initial assault. (d) Rounded end of metal police baton. (e) Patterned imprint of end of baton described in (d).

other types of trauma; some not specific to torture or ill-treatment and others which are more specific or typical of such events, which should also be looked for and described, such as elbow damage when arms are forced up behind the back. Others include beatings to the feet, suspension, other forms of positional trauma, asphyxia, electric shock, and dental torture.

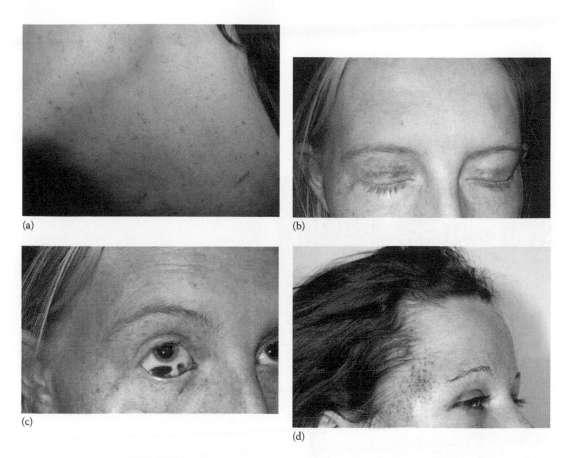

(a)   (b)   (c)   (d)

FIGURE 6.9 (a) Scattered petechial bruises to the neck caused by manual compression of the neck. (b) Multiple fine petechiae to the upper eyelids and around the eyes, caused by neck compression. (c) Same subject with scleral haemorrhage—often associated with coalescence of petechiae. (d) Petechial haemorrhage around the eye and right temple caused by single direct punch.

Beatings to the Feet

Repeated, direct impact to the soles of the feet (falanga or falaka) with some form of rigid implement (e.g., stick, baton, truncheon) can result in substantial and permanent deformity of the foot architecture and disability (Savnik et al. 2000; Prip and Persson 2008). There may be recent evidence of visible bruising or swelling (Figure 6.18). Depending on the intensity of assault, tendons, bones, the heel and footpad, the plantar aponeurosis, neurovascular tissues, and muscles may all be damaged. Edema and hematoma can cause compartment syndrome which can exacerbate neurovascular damage. Acute injury will be self-evident, but evidence of assault of a milder nature in the longer term may be more difficult to determine (Leth and Banner 2005; Torp-Pedersen et al. 2008). Edston (2009) compared different findings between torture survivors subjected to falaka and those who had not. Table 6.7 illustrates those comparative findings.

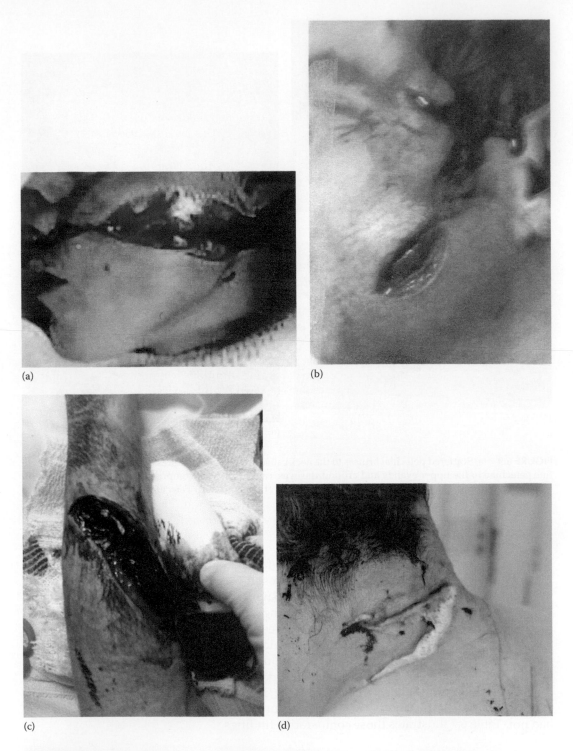

(a)   (b)

(c)   (d)

FIGURE 6.10 (a) Untreated incised slash wound across left face (caused by craft knife). (b) Untreated gaping incised slash wound penetrating oral cavity (caused by kitchen knife). (c) Untreated incised slash wound to left forearm (caused by sharp machete). (d) Irregular incised wound to posterior neck caused by irregular glass fragment.

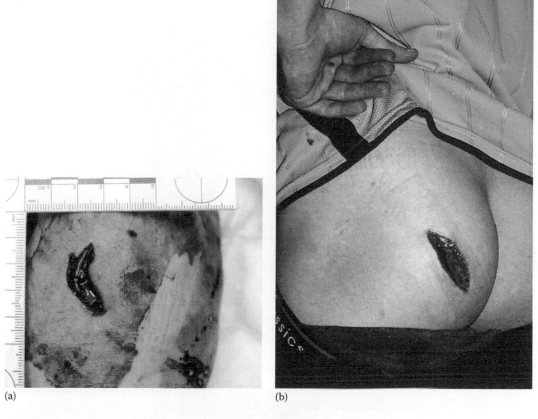

(a)   (b)

FIGURE 6.11   (a) Typical appearance of stab wound with fishtail appearance (underlying organs may need surgical exploration and treatment). (b) Stab wound entrance to left buttock (exploration revealed rectal penetration).

Suspension and Other Positional Torture

Many different types of suspension are described. Most frequent types include cross or crucifix suspension where the arms are abducted and tied to a horizontal bar. Palestinian hanging or suspension is created when the individual is suspended with the hands and forearms tied together in extension behind the back and attached to a horizontal bar, or where the wrists are bound and attached to a ligature, again with the arms in extension behind the back. This type of suspension has great potential for major damage to the shoulder joint complex (Figure 6.19) and creation of brachial plexus damage and may well leave ligature marks. Parrot perch suspension describes suspension with the knees flexed over a pole and the hands or wrists tied to the ankles such that the pole passes anteriorly to the forearms. Neurovascular damage, with motor and sensory neuropathies, are well recognized. Examination needs to determine the extent of structural disruption and the degree of neuropathy with an assessment of functional loss. Forced positions may not involve any form of restraint, but the victim may be made to stand or crouch for prolonged periods (many hours) or even be forced into extremely confined spaces requiring contortion of the body and limbs. Careful history taking and examination will ensure corroboration of accounts if evidence is there to be found since even if there are no

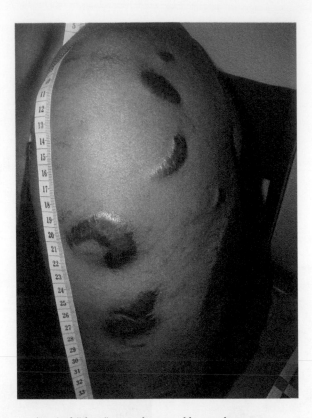

FIGURE 6.12   Healed scars of typical "chop" wounds caused by machete.

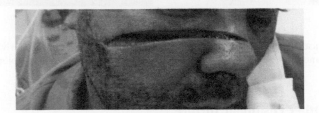

FIGURE 6.13   Typical incised wound caused by razor blade drawn across face (differentiated from lacerations by clean edges, no tissue bridging and runs across skin surface contours).

visible signs at a later date, the victim may provide a clear description of dependent edema, pain, and restricted mobility in the back or limbs.

Electric Shock

There are many ways in which electricity can be applied to the body, and a variety of electrical sources may be used to deliver electric current to the body. Current is delivered via electrodes placed on the body. Substances such as gels or water may be used to ensure good contact and spread the delivery of electricity to avoid any physical traces. Certain devices (e.g., stun guns and other conducted energy devices) have fixed and nonvariable effects. Others may have means of varying the electrical current delivered. Electrodes, crocodile clips, or wires may be attached around the fingers, toes, or tongue; attached to the breast or nipples; attached to the genitals; or inserted in the vagina or anus to provide a return circuit.

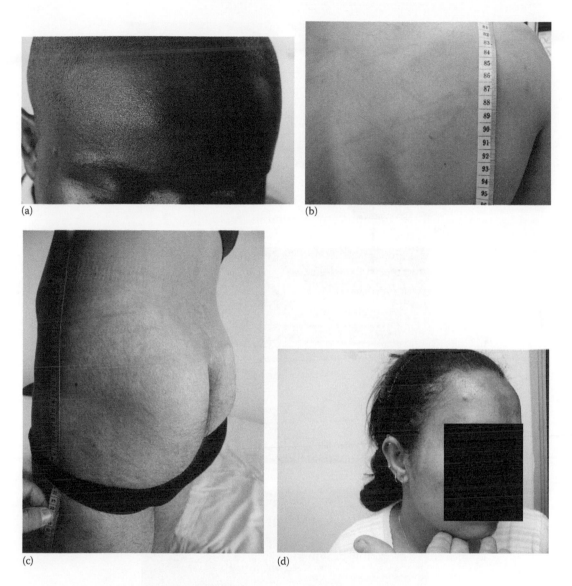

FIGURE 6.14 (a) Hyperpigmentation on forehead from direct impact with gun butt several years previously. (b) Linear hyperpigmentation on back from whipping ~7 years previously. (c) Hypopigmentation to buttocks from previous burn injury (hot fluid). (d) Hyperpigmentation to face and forehead from previous burn injury (forced sun hyper-exposure).

Pain and muscle contraction are the two main effects. Dependent on the type, duration, site of application, current, and voltage, short- and long-term visible effects may include burns and burn scarring. Such changes may be nonspecific and very subtle (Figure 6.20). Those inflicting such treatment try to avoid physical evidence of the use of electrical torture. It is also needed to mention cardiac arrhythmias (and possible death) and compression and avulsion fractures due to violent convulsions. There may be a risk of rhabdomyolysis, myoglobinuria, and renal failure if there has been substantial use of electric shock to stimulate repeated and prolonged muscle contraction. That risk may be increased if the electric shocks have also been accompanied by beating and blunt force trauma to the limb musculature.

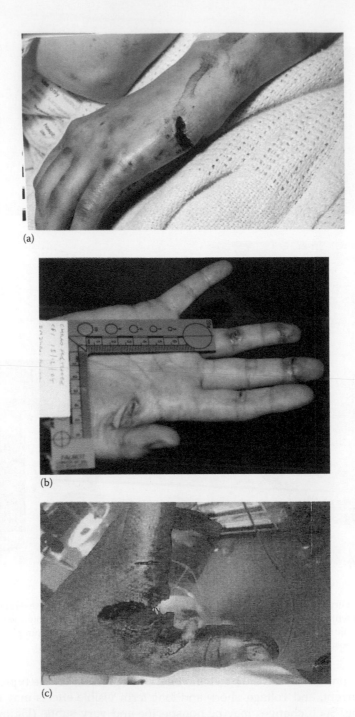

(a)

(b)

(c)

FIGURE 6.15 (a) Defense chop injury to left hand extensor side, caused by hand raised to protect against meat cleaver. (b) Defense incised injuries to right hand where hand raised against knife assault. (c) Defense incised injury to right hand where hand has attempted to grasp assailant's knife.

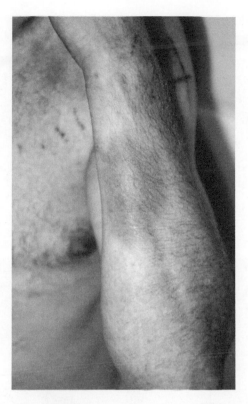

FIGURE 6.16 Defense bruise injury to the forearm, where left arm has been raised to protect against blunt object.

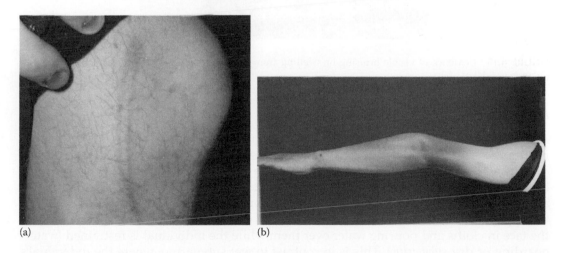

(a)   (b)

FIGURE 6.17 (a) Tramline bruise injury to right outer knee. Bruise caused by impact with police baton. (b) Deformed right elbow caused by joint disruption after arm extension and inward rotation behind back during restraint.

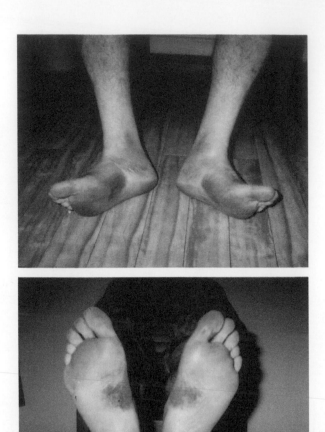

FIGURE 6.18 Evidence of visible bruising or swelling from repeated, direct impact to the soles of the feet (falanga or falaka).

Asphyxiation

Asphyxiation or suffocation can cause a variety of injuries, symptoms, and outcomes ranging from no visible injury to death (Payne-James 2016a). A victim may be asphyxiated directly, by occluding the airways in the sense of a compression force or an occlusive force being exerted on or around the neck (e.g., by hands or ligature), thereby closing off the airways or putting pressure on blood vessels or pressure sensors. Other means of potential asphyxiation include placing plastic bags or gas masks over the heads or covering the face in cloths and pouring water over them while the individual is restrained (waterboarding or dry *submarino*). This is in contrast to wet submarino, where the individual's head is submersed in water. These techniques may leave no visible evidence but inhalation of liquids may provoke drowning phenomena, including electrolyte disturbances and arrhythmias, reactivity of the airways, and produce pneumonias (Beynon 2012). In asphyxia from plastic bags and hooding, there may also be reaction of the mucosa and airways from contaminants deliberately placed in the bag, such as petrol, chilies, or other noxious chemicals. In those where compression has been applied to the neck, a number

TABLE 6.7

Physical Findings and Reported Persistent Symptoms in 131 Alleged Torture Victims

Physical Findings and Symptoms	Falanga ($n = 58$) n (%)	No Falanga ($n = 73$) n (%)	Fisher's Test p Value
Scar foot	38 (66)	14	<.0001
Scar/pigmentation sole	21 (36)	3	<.0001
Soft tissue injury	15 (28)	4	<.0020
Total (one to three findings)	48 (82)	18 (25)	<.0001
Pain and tenderness in soles	28 (48)	4	<.0001
Pain in lower leg	26 (45)	6	<.0001

Source: Edston, E., *Torture*, 19, 27–32, 2009. With permission.
Note: The control group (no falanga) was significantly different from the falanga group.

of effects can be apparent including (apart from visual evidence of application of force to the neck) sore throat; pain during swallowing; hoarseness; stridor; and neck, back, and head pains. The injuries seen are dependent on a number of issues including the type of object or implement causing the compression or occlusion (e.g., hands, arms, elbows, ligatures), relative sizes of hands to neck, force of compression, length of time of compression, whether compression is consistent or intermittent, whether compression is equal around the neck, whether there is anything (e.g., clothes intervening) between assailant's hands and victim's neck. Potential injuries may include no injury seen, pain or tenderness—at site of application of force with no visible injury—reddening which may pass off after a few hours, skin bruising or abrasions at the point of compression—e.g., at sites of finger/thumb/ligature application—this may appear early or later and persist for days (Figure 6.21), or in the line of the ligature or contact with other material (e.g., clothes), pinpoint bruising (petechiae) above the site of compression in skin, eyes, and mucous membranes (e.g., lining of mouth)—such bruises may become confluent and enlarged, damage to larynx—thyroid cartilage—damage to hyoid bone (bone at base of neck), damage to mucosa of mouth and tongue due to direct pressure on teeth internally; bleeding from mucosa where the intravenous pressure has been raised—e.g., from the nose and ears (Duband et al. 2009). Urinary incontinence may be experienced—but its cause may not be clear, as it may be due to a number of factors including unconsciousness and/or fear (Shields et al. 2010). Petechiae may be seen in the skin, the sclera, and conjunctivae and on mucosal surfaces in the mouth, ears, nose, and eyes. It is essential in possible cases of neck compression or strangulation that all areas of the eyes, skin, and mucosa (including inside the mouth, the eyelids, the palate and the uvula, the skin of the scalp) above the level of compression are examined with a good light to identify any localized areas of petechiae. It is important to identify petechiae at an early stage as they fade and disappear within 24 hours or so. It has been shown (Mitchell et al. 2012) that two-thirds of victims subjected to neck compression lost consciousness in a mean of 9.2 seconds, so lack of recall of events may be quite understandable.

Taking the History

As with any clinical examination, it is important to undertake a structured history to elicit any relevant medical findings and to place these in the context of the allegations made. The key elements to determine are the circumstances of the arrest and subsequent detention(s) (e.g., when, where, who by, for what reason), the conditions of detention (e.g.,

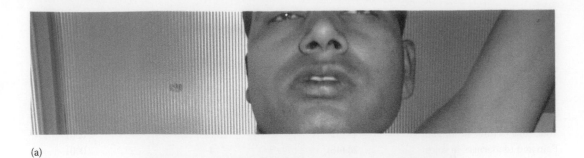

(a)

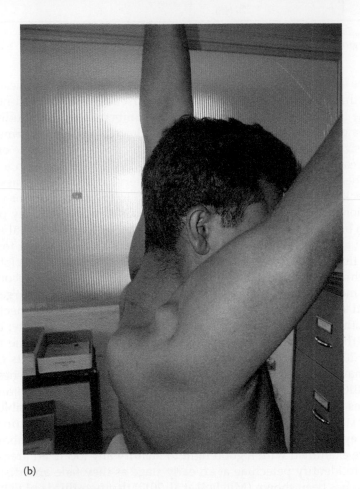

(b)

FIGURE 6.19   Major damage to the shoulder joint complex from Palestinian hanging or suspension. (a) Anterior view. (b) Lateral view.

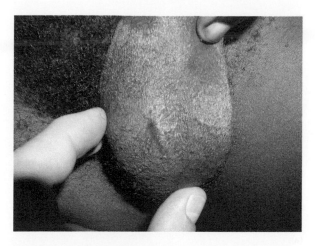

FIGURE 6.20 Visible effects of electric shock may be nonspecific and very subtle. This image shows slight irregular scarring caused by burn at electrode site on scrotum.

type of facility, type of cells, access to the open air, availability of clean water, availability of food, toilet facilities, access to healthcare, access to family visits), and the specific methods of torture or ill-treatment used.

It is important to ask about the general medical and surgical history since these may themselves produce particular physical findings that must be distinguished from those that may result from the alleged ill-treatment. Structured medical examination will inquire about past medical history (e.g., asthma, diabetes, epilepsy, deep vein thrombosis) and whether these conditions are appropriately attended to (or were); past surgical history—to identify operative scars, drain sites, or other iatrogenic marks; past gynecological history (may have relevance in sexual assault allegations); and past psychiatric history (including a history of self-harm and the nature of that harm). A drug, medication, and allergy history must be taken as certain drugs or medications may alter the appearance of the results of trauma (e.g., enhanced bruising due to anticoagulant medication). Skin diseases should specifically be inquired about or previous infectious conditions that may affect the skin (e.g., chicken pox, psoriasis, eczema). A social history should inquire about work and sports to determine whether these have left any specific scars or marks. This is not done to reduce the impact of any report, but to enhance it to show that the examiner has a full understanding of the nature of physical effects of maltreatment. This process elicits a full history of injuries, marks, and scars and medical conditions and surgery before the period of detention and any possible aftereffects related to these.

It is important to avoid leading questions and to structure inquiries to achieve an open-ended, chronological account of events and to find out what the current (acute) and longer-term (chronic) symptoms are that are experienced by the individual and how they relate to events that happened to them. The term *free recall* is relevant as it emphasizes the need for the individual to describe in their own words using their own terms and expressions, which can then be related to physical, as well as psychological findings (if any).

Acute Symptoms

Acute symptoms refer to those active problems that the individual relates to the alleged ill-treatment (e.g., painful arm, burn to leg, cut to head) or to the conditions of their detention

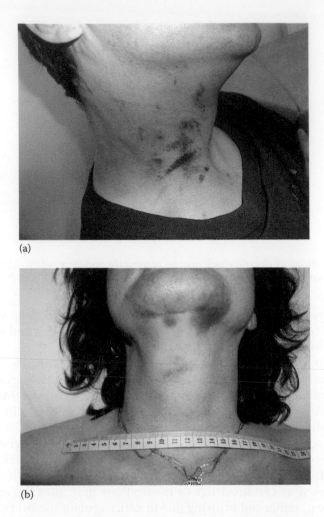

(a)

(b)

FIGURE 6.21 Typical appearances following manual strangulation. Reddening, skin bruising, or abrasions at the point of compression. (a) Scratch marks to neck (may be mixture of victim's and assailant's, as victim tries to remove assailant's hands). (b) Bruises over larynx and chin, caused by direct hand and finger pressure by assailant.

(e.g., skin rash, weight loss). The intensity, frequency, and duration of each symptom should be noted. Often newer, acute lesions are characteristic as they may show a pattern of inflicted injury that differs in character from accidental injuries. Further specific inquiries about ear, eye, skin, respiratory, and musculoskeletal problems may elicit more information that the examiner finds to be relevant to the allegations. Acute symptoms can be broadly taken as those arising from events happening up to 4–6 weeks previously (or in the case of long-bone fractures, up to 3 months). Within this time period, most initial symptoms of torture may have worn off. Beyond 3 months or so, then the symptoms can be considered to be chronic.

Chronic Symptoms

Chronic symptoms relate to those effects that (1) last beyond the time after the initial injury or trauma that it would have been expected to heal or (2) have been caused by the initial injury or trauma but have resulted in prolonged or permanent effects. With the exception of obvious physical deformity, chronic symptoms are often the most difficult to elicit as there may be no physical evidence, and the individual may have difficulty precisely describing the nature of what is experienced. The psychological trauma of ill-treatment can result in symptoms either being minimized or exaggerated. The nature of pain, its duration and how re-experiencing the trauma affects pain perception is a complex area (Taylor et al. 2013). The need for compassionate and patient assessment will enable the most appropriate information to be obtained. Nonspecific symptoms include, but are not limited to, some or all of headache, back pain, gastrointestinal symptoms, sexual dysfunction, and muscle pain, and frequent psychological symptoms include depressive affect, anxiety, insomnia, nightmares, flashbacks, and memory difficulties (Thomsen et al. 2000; Moreno and Grodin 2002).

If there are few, if any, physical signs remaining following ill-treatment, the detail and accounts elicited in the interview and history may be the only evidence of ill-treatment. The better the quality of the interview and its documentation, then the better the opportunity for corroborating such information independently, even in the absence of physical evidence of assault.

Physical Examination

The physical examination is generally undertaken after the interview and medical history has been undertaken as the interview and history will give specific pointers to key elements that will need to be addressed. However, in some cases during visits to places of detention, time and other constraints may mean that there may only be time for a rapid examination, at which time the examiner also asks about the history of the alleged assault, and other nontorture related traumas, such as motor vehicle, work, and sport accidents. It is, however, good practice to conduct as complete a physical examination as possible since there may be marks or sequelae of ill-treatment of which the victim is unaware. Often in detention settings, the psychological assessment may also have to be compressed, and the examiner may only have time to make subjective observations and some focused questions of the victim's mental state throughout the encounter. Chapter 5 reviews the nature of full mental health assessments (which may often be absent or curtailed because of limited time access to the detainee). Any constraints on the interview should be noted so as to make clear the limitations of any assessment in a place of detention.

Standard medical examination (cardiovascular system, abdominal system, neurological system, musculoskeletal, genitourinary system, skin) is carried out in the same way, but in a slightly different format, to reflect the most typical and common findings. General observation of the state of nutrition should be documented, and in the systemic examination, observations should be made about dental state, skin state, and general appearance, all of which may reflect on the conditions of detention in which the individual has been held. Unhygienic conditions may result in poorly healing wounds, insect/tick bites, and outbreaks of scabies among other things. If possible, the weight and height of the individual should be measured, so that a body mass index can be derived as a broad indicator of disease or malnutrition. The nature of the medical complications may be very dependent on the location and conditions of detention, and poor nutritional states are common. This has been explored in a number of studies. Gould et al. (2013) studied the dietary adequacy of prisoners of Beon Prison, Madang, Papua New Guinea, in response to a report of possible nutritional deficiency. They found that from assessment of the prisoners' dietary data, median intakes of calcium (137 mg), potassium (677 mg), magnesium (182 mg), riboflavin (0.308 mg), vitamin A (54.1 µg), vitamin E (1.68 mg), vitamin C (5.7 mg), and folate (76.4 µg) were found to be below estimated average requirements. They concluded that the prisoners' diets are likely lacking in several micronutrients and recommendations for dietary change have been made to the prison authorities. Mathenge et al. (2007) found a high incidence of vitamin A deficiency in a Kenyan prison population. This was manifested as xerophthalmia mostly as night blindness (98.8% of cases), and this was associated with age, length of imprisonment, and previous imprisonment. Men with xerophthalmia were significantly more likely to be in poor health characterized by significant illness, recent hospital admission, persistent cough, diarrhea, fever, or chronic illness. Beriberi has been described (Ahoua et al. 2007) in a setting where a probable case patient was defined as a person detained with at least two of the following symptoms: bilateral leg edema, dyspnea, positive squat test, motor deficiencies, and paresthesia. A definite case patient was defined as a probable case patient who showed clinical improvement under thiamine treatment. Of 712 cases reported, 115 (16%) were probable and 597 (84%) were definite. The overall attack rate was 14.1%, and the case fatality rate was 1.0% (7/712). During the period studied, the prison food ration provided a fifth of the quantity of thiamin recommended by international standards. The authors concluded that systematic food supplementation with vitamins and micronutrients should be discussed when the penal ration does not provide the necessary nutrient intake recommended according to international standards.

See Table 6.8 for the IP systematic approach to examination.

The ideal equipment that the examiner should take to or have available at a place of detention should include a stethoscope, sphygmomanometer, thermometer, otoscope, torch, reflex hammer, urine testing kits, glucose monitoring device, and a forensic scale incorporating rules and color comparisons (Figure 6.22). Ideally, a camera and even a video recorder should be used, but in many places of detention, these devices may be prohibited by national laws and regulations. Even if a camera is permitted, pro forma body diagrams as shown in Annex III of the IP should be used to record the anatomical site, shape, form, and size of all injuries, scars, and marks, including those that are not related to the ill-treatment. Additional means of recording all information on tablets and smartphones and uploading data to a secure server (including digital images, video and audio) for later inclusion in a report are now available (e.g., ForensiDoc®) and will continue to develop to allow best documentation of such data.

Skin

Physical evidence of torture is often revealed in a comprehensive examination of the skin. Detailed external examination may identify marks that may embrace accident, play, sport, work, culture, self-harm, disease, previous surgery, and all forms of ill-treatment. Every site of abnormality should be looked at and palpated. This may elicit features such as bony abnormality or crepitus (if an internal air containing organ has been penetrated— e.g., in rib fracture). Particular attention should be paid to fingernails and toenails which, depending on the nature of injury (e.g., crushing, removal, insertion of objects under the nail), can result in a variety of appearances and remnants of objects still present. Long nails or nails with fungal infections may represent lack of care, or opportunity for appropriate medical treatment. Each abnormality seen on the skin should be described and the

TABLE 6.8

IP—Examination Sequence
_____

Skin

Face

Eyes

Ears

Nose

Jaw, oropharynx, and neck

Oral cavity and teeth

Chest and abdomen

Musculoskeletal system

Genitourinary system

Central and peripheral nervous systems

Examination and evaluation following specific forms of torture

- Beatings and other forms of blunt trauma
  - Skin damage
  - Fractures
  - Head trauma
  - Chest and abdominal trauma
- Beatings to the feet
- Suspension
- Other positional trauma
- Electric shock torture
- Dental torture
- Asphyxiation
- Sexual torture including rape
  - Examination following a recent assault
  - Genital examination of women
  - Genital examination of men
  - Examination of the anal region
_____

Note: Not all may be required—the physical examination will be based on the history obtained.

features as noted in Table 6.9 recorded in written and diagrammatic form for each. It is important to use rules or scales to document injury size accurately as guessing the size leads to inaccuracy in many cases (McLean et al. 2003). Any photographic imaging should provide wider images that identify location on the body, and then in close-up view, with appropriate forensic scales, to capture the detail of the lesion (Marsh 2011; Payne-James 2012; Payne-James et al. 2012; Evans et al. 2014).

Further Investigations

For many, if not most individuals seen in detention, the findings will solely be based on a history and clinical examination. For a small proportion of detainees, there will be access to test and diagnostic tools that may further elicit the nature of injury. The phrase "inspect, palpate, move" is appropriate to all aspects of the clinical examination. The ability to use

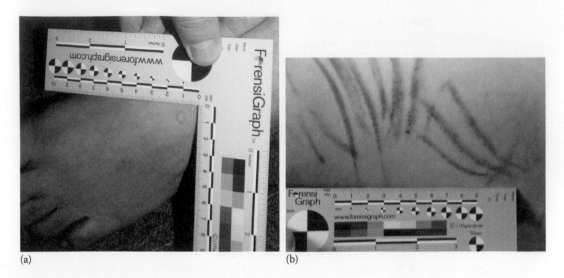

(a)   (b)

FIGURE 6.22 Forensic scales incorporating rules and color comparisons should be used to measure and record any cutaneous injuries, marks or scars. (a) Identifies a cigarette burn scar to the left foot dorsum. (b) Shows multiple fingernail scratches to the torso.

TABLE 6.9

Features to Be Recorded Where Relevant for Each
Mark or Abnormality Seen on the Body

Location (anatomical—measure distance from landmarks)
Pain
Tenderness
Reduced mobility
Range of movement
Type (e.g., bruise, laceration, abrasion)
Size (use metric values)
Shape
Surface (e.g., ulcer, raised, macular, hypertrophied, keloid)
Color
Orientation
Age estimation
Account of causation
Time and date of alleged causation

additional diagnostic techniques (e.g., urine testing, blood sampling, X-ray, ultrasound, magnetic resonance imaging, computerized tomography, bone scintigraphy) will be entirely dependent on the location and are often unavailable luxuries. If available, each technique should be utilized in the same way it would (in terms of indications and timing) in routine medical practice. In many cases, further specialist examination, assessment, and treatment may be recommended (e.g., audiology, orthopedic, ophthalmologist, neurologist) if the facilities are available.

Features that may be identified in specific anatomical regions or organs of the body are discussed in the following.

Face

The face, neck, and scalp need to be examined under optimal light to identify any abnormalities. If the individual is bearded or has a full head of hair, then it is important to closely examine the underlying skin to avoid missing significant lesions. The presence of petechiae in the skin of the face or the scalp, or within the mucosa of eyes, ears, nose, and mouth, may be the only physical sign of neck or chest compression. Bony promontories and anatomical landmarks should be palpated and compared and any deformity noted.

Eyes

Eyes should be examined closely, both around the eyes itself, and inside the eyelids, and the full extent of the sclera. Petechial hemorrhages may be seen. Ophthalmoscopy should be undertaken to detect abnormalities such as retinal hemorrhage (e.g., due to shaking), retinal tears, or detachment (due to blunt trauma). Pupillary responses should be documented; and the eye, movements tested. Visual acuity should be assessed. Direct or indirect trauma to the eyes can result in globe disruption or abrasions to the cornea and conjunctivae (Figure 6.23). Lens dislocation may occur.

Ears

Ears are damaged by direct or indirect trauma. The external ear may be subject to blunt force impact—with a full range of blunt force injury, sometimes damaging the ear cartilages, and may be subject to amputation. Pinching of the ears may result in localized bruising on either side of the pinna. Biting injury may occur (Figure 6.24). Insertion of objects into the ear or slapping one or both ears simultaneously (*telefono*) can disrupt the tympanic membrane. Otoscopic examination is essential, as is the need to test hearing and to observe for injury due to object insertion and the presence of petechiae. Clear fluid leakage may represent cerebrospinal fluid (CSF) indicate an underlying skull fracture.

Nose

The nose is frequently subject to blunt trauma, which can damage bone, cartilage, or septum. Inspection and palpation may give an indication as to whether the injury is new and its extent. The nostrils should be inspected for sources of bleeding, the presence of clear fluid (possible CSF) and petechiae.

FIGURE 6.23 Direct or indirect trauma to the eyes can result in globe disruption, retinal detachments or abrasions to cornea and conjunctivae and it is crucial to properly examine the eye (including using ophthalmoscopy).

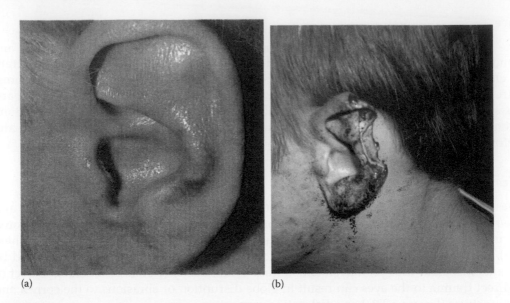

(a)   (b)

FIGURE 6.24   Ear injury is common. (a) Bruising to the pinna after direct impact. (b) Loss of ear structure from human bite.

Jaw, Oropharynx, Mouth, Teeth, and Neck

The face, jaw, and mouth are common sites for injury. Kicking, punching, and hitting with instruments may create a substantial number of injuries including mandibular and maxillary fractures, dental loosening or fracture, soft tissue injuries (internally and externally), and these may be enhanced if the individual is malnourished and has conditions such as gingivitis caused by vitamin C deficiency or dental caries because of lack of access to tooth brushing or dental care. Untreated injuries may leave obvious deformity (e.g., malocclusion, or broken teeth fragments) which may impair eating and feeding. Specific torture (e.g., electric shock) may result (due to teeth clenching) in tooth fracture or self-bites to inner cheek, gums, lips, and the tongue. The teeth may be broken or extracted without anesthetic. Associated injury to the tongue, mandible, and inner mouth is not uncommon (Figure 6.25). The neck may be subject to a variety of insults including direct blows, application of ligatures, and manual strangulation. Examination may reveal damage to the larynx or the hyoid bone and visible evidence of manual strangulation or ligature application in the form of bruises or scratches to the neck, with petechiae above the level of compression.

Chest and Abdomen

The chest and abdomen may be subject to many types of trauma. There may be operative and drain scars from previous unrelated surgical intervention. Unrelated assaults may have left evidence of injury. The main concern in the acute injury is identifying intrathoracic and intra-abdominal trauma related either to blunt force or penetrating injury. It is important for the examiner to identify any potential damage to internal organs. This may include splenic, kidney, liver, and bowel lacerations or perforations. Delayed ruptures of organs such as the spleen is well recognized (Wasvary et al. 1997; Sowers and Aubrey-Bassler 2011). Thus, particular attention should be paid to abdominal examination within

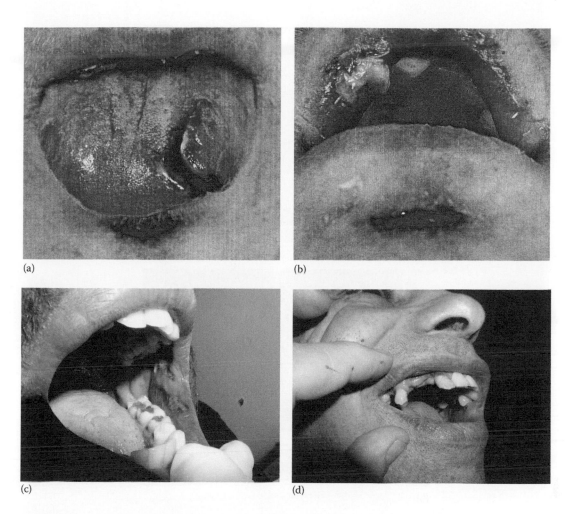

(a)   (b)

(c)   (d)

FIGURE 6.25   (a, b) Laceration to tongue and loss of teeth due to direct impact (and not immediately treated). (c) Abrasion on inner aspect of cheek from external blunt impact. (d) Loss of teeth from direct impact. Poor dental care may be available and teeth and oral hygiene may already be compromised in detention settings.

a week of blunt trauma to the abdomen. It is not uncommon, in the presence of severe internal organ damage, to have no visible external signs of trauma. Examination of the chest and abdomen should include auscultation to identify thoracic complications (e.g., pneumothorax, hemothorax) and absence of bowel sounds (e.g., in ileus caused by retroperitoneal hematoma). Palpable callus or deformity as a result of rib fracture may be identified. Trauma to the kidney, bladder, or ureter may be identified by urine testing for blood. The presence of blood should act an indicator for further investigation of the urinary tract.

Musculoskeletal System and Skin

In some cases, cultural scars may be present (Figure 6.26). Blunt force and positional abuse may result in few if any visible marks in the long term but may substantially affect function and cause chronic pain (Prip and Persson 2008). All parts of the bony skeleton should be palpated for evidence of previous or current fracture or periosteal hematoma.

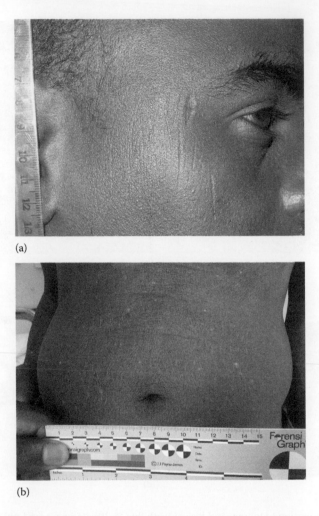

(a)

(b)

FIGURE 6.26 Cultural scars take many forms. (a) Fine vertical linear scars to the cheek and temporal region (for headache). (b) Fine vertical scars to abdomen (said to alleviate abdominal pain).

If penetrating injuries or compound fractures are present, complications such as osteo-myelitis may be identified. All joints should be examined for a range of movement and mobility. If individuals have been subject to substantial soft tissue injury, or severe burns (Figure 6.27), mobility or function may be limited due to contractures. Amputation of dig-its or limbs may have been undertaken (Figure 6.28). The nature of the amputations may reflect on whether medical expertise was used in such procedures. Forced positions, (such as hyperextension of the vertebral column in the hog tie/banana tie) can produce compres-sion fractures of the vertebrae, and electric shocks may produce compression or avulsion fractures due to violent, uncontrolled, muscle contractions. Muscle group function should be tested for power. It is useful to measure muscle power using a 0–5 scale where 0 = no contraction; 1 = slight contraction, no movement; 2 = full range of motion without gravity; 3 = full range of motion with gravity; 4 = full range of motion, some resistance; and 5 = full range of motion, full resistance. In the acute case, compartment syndromes should be sought; and the presence of hematomas (fluctuant collections of blood), identified.

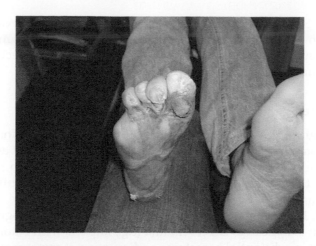

FIGURE 6.27   Resultant burn scars after foot immersed in boiling fluid (nature unknown). No treatment given.

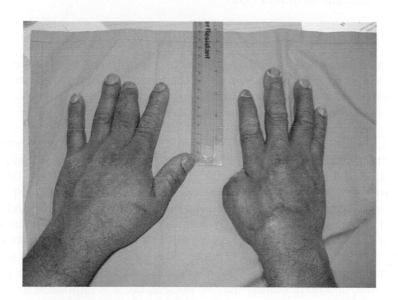

FIGURE 6.28   Judicial amputation of right thumb.

Central and Peripheral Nervous Systems

For both acute and chronic injuries, a full clinical neurological examination is appropriate. A full cranial nerve examination should be undertaken as all cranial nerves can be affected by different types of blunt, direct, or other local trauma. In detention settings, a focused neurological examination may have to be performed. The findings may not only reflect both acute and chronic injuries, but also reflect on standards of care. Neurological examination may identify motor and sensory neuropathies—these may reflect direct trauma (e.g., median nerve or common peroneal palsies), compression neuropathies from ligatures or handcuffs, or conditions such as vitamin deficiencies due to poor nutrition (e.g., dry beriberi). Suspension by the arms can result in brachial plexus damage, which may be manifest in a variety of different ways. Balance and hearing may be affected by head trauma, and such symptoms and signs may require further specialist evaluation at the earliest opportunity.

Genitourinary System

In part, the genitourinary system is addressed in the chest and abdomen examination. Genitoanal examination in the context of penetrative anal or vaginal assault is often not required in historic cases due to the elapsed time. It is important to recognize that the majority of penetrative assaults to the vagina or anus in adults and children do not leave residual evidence and do not cause permanent injury (Royal College of Paediatrics and Child Health 2015; Payne-James 2016b). Thus, it is important to recognize when a genitoanal examination is indicated. Direct trauma (e.g., impacts with batons) to the penis or scrotum may result in substantial hematoma or disruption of structures such as the testes or urethra. These may require further specialist investigation (e.g., cystoscopy, ultrasound) (Norredam et al. 2005). It has long been recognized that sexual difficulties may be present after torture (Lunde and Ortmann 1990).

Self-Injury

Self-injury (sometimes known as deliberate self-harm or intentional self-injury) may be seen in many individuals at times of stress, or for cultural and other reasons. Individuals injure themselves for a number of reasons including psychiatric illness or response to ill-treatment and torture, and other reasons such as attempting to imply events that took place but did not, or for motives of gain, malice, or for other unspecified or unrecognized reasons (Payne-James 2005; Gall and Payne-James 2011a,b). Self-inflicted injuries may have a number of characteristics, which are not diagnostic, but which together may give an indication of self-infliction. In many cases, the individual will admit to having self-harmed. The examiner must try to determine whether an injury is self-inflicted or not—particularly if the injured person denies it or gives an account that conflicts with the wound appearance or the account of witnesses. If there is a belief that self-infliction is a possibility, the type and pattern of wounding should be compared with the various characteristics referred to in Table 6.10. Table 6.10 identifies characteristics of injury which may suggest self-infliction. Some or all of these characteristics—commonly inflicted by some form of implement— e.g., a knife, a nail, or a razor blade—may be present, but it is important to reinforce that only some and rarely all may be present. The absence of a particular feature does not preclude self-infliction nor does the presence necessarily imply self-infliction.

Conclusions

When assessing an individual who may have been subjected to torture or other forms of ill-treatment, it is essential to follow the IP principles when assessing, documenting, and interpreting physical injury, as well as for psychological trauma. This means ensuring that an appropriate history is obtained, differentiating between all injuries, scars, or marks that may be unrelated to ill-treatment (e.g., surgical scars, work-related accidents, sports

TABLE 6.10

Features That Can Be Associated with Self-Infliction

Characteristic	Additional Comments
1. On an area of the body that the individual can access themselves	Sites less accessible, e.g., the middle of the back are less likely
2. Superficial or minor injury	Although more severe injury may be caused—particularly in those with psychiatric disorder
3. If there is more than one cut and they are of similar appearance, style, and orientation	Typically self-inflicted cutting injuries are more superficial, numerous, and similar than those sustained in an assault from another—where the natural reaction of the injured person is to avoid repeated injury
4. If other types of injury (e.g., scratches, cigarette burns) are of similar appearance, style, and orientation	As above—more than one similar injury should raise an index of suspicion as to the possibility of self-infliction
5. Multiple similar injuries	Raise a high index of suspicion as to the possibility of self-infliction
6. Parallel injuries	As above
7. Injuries grouped in a single anatomical region	As above
8. Injuries are grouped on the contralateral side to the patient's handedness	A right handed person will tend to harm themselves on the left-hand side of the body
9. Tentative injuries	Smaller or lesser injuries grouped with the main injuries suggest the initial tentative attempts at self-harm
10. Old healed injuries or scars of a similar age in similar sites	May indicate previous attempts at self-harm
11. Scars of different ages in similar sites	May indicate repeated previous attempts at self-harm
12. Apparently slow-healing injuries	Persistence of wounds that would otherwise have been expected to heal—in the absence of any other factors. The individual may pick at, or reopen wounds
13. Psychiatric and related issues—such as eating disorders, drug and alcohol misuse	
14. Wounds or injuries can be created to imply that someone else has caused such injuries, in which case, none of the features above are necessarily present	

injuries). The physical examination must be thorough addressing all marks and injuries, differentiating between acute and chronic injury and providing an explanation for each, even those that are stated as not being due to torture. The findings must be recorded in writing, on body diagrams and, ideally, photographically. Consistent terminology should be used when describing both the classification, nature, and the features of the injuries. The interpretation must be given, according to the IP classification of the attributability of causation to all clinical findings.

When monitoring places of detention, the examiner may be faced with heavy constraints in making assessments of alleged victims of torture. In particular, having sufficient time to explain the role of the monitoring body and the purpose of the assessment and to gain the trust of the detainees and obtain consent. Furthermore, there may be limitations on the available space and privacy for the examination, and assessments may have to be conducted rapidly, especially in prisons where there may be large numbers of individuals who could be seen. Whatever the setting, applying the principles of the IP will ensure the best available evidence is obtained.

References

Ahoua, L., Etienne, W., Fermon, F., Godain, G., Brown, V., Kadjo, K., Bouaffou, K., Legros, D., and Guerin, P. J. 2007, Outbreak of beriberi in a prison in Côte d'Ivoire, *Food Nutrition Bulletin*, vol. 28, pp. 283–290.

Altman, D. G., and Bland, J. M. 1995, Absence of evidence is not evidence of absence, *British Medical Journal*, vol. 311, p. 485.

Beynon, J. 2012, "Not waving, drowning": Asphyxia and torture: The myth of simulated drowning and other forms of torture, *Torture*, vol. 22, pp. 25–29.

Bloom, A. I., Zamir, G., Muggia, M., Friedlaender, M., Gimmon, Z., and Rivkind, A. 1995, Torture rhabdomyorhexis—A pseudo-crush syndrome, *Journal of Trauma*, vol. 38, pp. 252–254.

Chaudhry, M. A., Haider, W., Nagi, A. H., Ud-Din, Z., and Parveen, Z. 2008, Pattern of police torture in Punjab, Pakistan, *American Journal of Forensic Medicine and Pathology*, vol. 29, pp. 309–311.

Crosby, S. S., Mohan, S., Di Loreto, C., and Spiegel, J. H. 2010, Head and neck sequelae of torture—Regional effects of torture, *Laryngoscope*, vol. 120, pp. 414–419.

Den Otter, J. J., Smit, Y., dela Cruz, L. B., Ozkalipci, O., and Oral, R. 2013, Documentation of torture and cruel, inhuman or degrading treatment of children: A review of existing guidelines and tools, *Forensic Science International*, vol. 224, no. 1–3, pp. 27–32.

Duband, S., Timoshenko, A. P., Morrison, A. L., Prades, J. M., Debout, M., and Peoch, M. 2009, Ear bleeding: A sign not to be underestimated in cases of strangulation, *American Journal of Forensic Medicine and Pathology*, vol. 30, pp. 175–176.

Edston, E. 2009, The epidemiology of falanga—Incidence among Swedish asylum seekers, *Torture*, vol. 19, pp. 27–32.

Edston, E., and Olsson, C. 2007, Female victims of torture, *Journal of Forensic and Legal Medicine*, vol. 14, pp. 368–373.

Evans, S., Baylis, S., Carabott, R., Jones, M., Kelson, Z., Marsh, N., Payne-James, J., Ramadani, J, Vanezis, P., and Kemp, A. 2014, Guidelines for photography of cutaneous marks and injuries: A multi-professional perspective. *Journal of Visual Communication Medicine*, vol. 37, no. 1–2, pp. 3–12.

Forrest, D. 1995, The physical after-effects of torture, *Forensic Science International*, vol. 76, pp. 77–84.

Forrest, D. M. 1999, Examination for the late physical after effects of torture. *Journal of Clinical Forensic Medicine*, vol. 6, no. 1, pp. 4–13.

Gall, J. A. M., and Payne-James, J. J. 2011a, Injury interpretation—Possible errors and fallacies, in J. A. M. Gall and J. J. Payne-James (eds), *Current practice in forensic medicine*, Wiley, Hoboken, NJ.

Gall, J., Payne-James, J., and Goldney, R. 2011b, Self-inflicted injuries and associated psychological profiles, in J. Gall and J. J. Payne-James, *Current forensic medicine*, Wiley, Hoboken, NJ.

Ghaleb, S. S., Elshabrawy, E. M., Elkaradawy, M. H., and Nemr Welson, N. 2014, Retrospective study of positive physical torture cases in Cairo (2009 & 2010), *Journal of Forensic and Legal Medicine*, vol. 24, pp. 37–45.

Gola, H., Engler, H., Schauer, M., Adenauer, H., Riether, C., Kolassa, S., Elbert, T., and Kolassa, I. T. 2012, Victims of rape show increased cortisol responses to trauma reminders: A study in individuals with war- and torture-related PTSD, *Psychoneurolendocrinology*, vol. 37, pp. 213–220.

Gould, C., Tousignant, B., Brian, G., McKay, R., Gibson, R., Bailey, K., and Venn, B. J. 2013, Cross-sectional dietary deficiencies among a prison population in Papua New Guinea, *BMC International Health and Human Rights*, vol. 13, p. 21.

International Forensic Expert Group. 2011, Statement on hooding, *Torture*, vol. 21, no. 3, pp. 186–189.

International Forensic Expert Group. 2012, Statement on access to relevant medical and other health records and relevant legal records for forensic medical evaluations of alleged torture and other cruel, inhuman or degrading treatment or punishment, *Torture*, vol. 22, Suppl 1, pp. 39–38.

Keten, A., Akçan, R., Karacaoglu, E., Odabasi, A. B., and Tümer, A. R. 2013, Medical forensic examination of detained immigrants: Is the Istanbul Protocol followed? *Medicine, Science and the Law*, vol. 53, no. 1, pp. 40–44.

Langlois, N. E. I., and Gresham, G. A. 1991, The ageing of bruises: A review and study of the colour changes with time, *Forensic Science International*, vol. 50, pp. 227–238.

Leth, P., and Banner, J. 2005, Forensic medical examination of refugees who claim to have been tortured, *American Journal of Forensic Medicine and Pathology*, vol. 26, pp. 125–130.

Lunde, I., and Ortmann, J. 1990, Prevalence and sequelae of sexual torture, *The Lancet*, vol. 336, no. 8710, pp. 289–291.

Maguire, S., Mann, M. K., Sibert, J., and Kemp, A. 2005, Can you age bruises accurately in children? A systematic review, *Archives of Disease in Childhood*, vol. 90, p. 187.

Marsh, N. 2011, The photography of injuries, in J. Gall and J. J. Payne-James, *Current practice in forensic medicine*, Wiley, Hoboken, NJ.

Mathenge, W., Kuper, H., Myatt, M., Foster, A., and Gilbert, C. 2007, Vitamin A deficiency in a Kenyan prison. *Tropical Medicine & International Health*, vol. 12, pp. 269–273.

McLean, I., Anderson, C. M., and White, C. 2003, The accuracy of guestimates, *Journal of the Royal Society of Medicine*, vol. 96, pp. 497–498.

Mitchell, J. R., Roach, D. E., Tyberg, J. V., Belenkie, I., and Sheldon, R. S. 2012, Mechanism of loss of consciousness during vascular neck restraint, *Journal of Applied Physiology*, vol. 112, pp. 396–402.

Moisander, P. A., and Edston, E. 2003, Torture and its sequel—A comparison between victims from 6 countries, *Forensic Science International*, vol. 137, pp. 133–140.

Moreno, A., and Grodin, M. A. 2002, Torture and its neurological sequelae, *Spinal Cord*, vol. 40, pp. 213–223.

Morentin, B., Idoyaga, M. I., Callado, L. F., and Meana, J. J. 1995, Prevalence and methods of torture claimed in the Basque Country (Spain) during 1992-3, *Forensic Science International*, vol. 76, pp. 151–158.

Munang, L. A., Leonard, P. A., and Mok, J. Y. Q. 2002, Lack of agreement on colour description between clinicians examining childhood bruising, *Journal of Clinical Forensic Medicine*, vol. 9, pp. 171–174.

Naqvi, R., Ahmed, E., Akhtar, F., Yazdani, I., Bhatti, S., Aziz, T., Naqvi, A., and Rizvi, A. 1996, Acute renal failure due to traumatic rhabdomyolysis, *Renal Failure*, vol. 18, pp. 677–669.

Norredam, M., Crosby, A., Munarriz, R., Piwowarczyk, L., and Grodin, M. 2005, Urologic complications of sexual trauma among male survivors of torture, *Urology*, vol. 65, no. 1, pp. 28–32.

Payne-James, J. J. 2005, Deliberate self-harm, patterns, in J. J. Payne-James, R. Byard, T. Corey, and C. Henderson, (eds), *Encyclopedia of Forensic & Legal Medicine*, vol. 2, Elsevier, Amsterdam.

Payne-James, J. J. 2012, Rules & scales used in measurement in the forensic setting: Measured—And found wanting!, *Forensic Science, Medicine, and Pathology*, vol. 8, no. 4, pp. 482–483.

Payne-James, J. J. 2016a, Asphyxia: Clinical Findings, in J. J. Payne-James and R. Byard (eds), *Encyclopedia of Forensic & Legal Medicine*, 2nd edn, Elsevier, Amsterdam, pp. 280–285.

Payne-James, J. J., 2016b, Sexual offenses, adult: Injuries and findings after sexual contact, in J. J. Payne-James and R. Byard (eds), *Encyclopedia of Forensic & Legal Medicine*, 2nd edn, Elsevier, Amsterdam, pp. 280–285.

Payne-James, J. J., and Hinchliffe, J. 2011, Injury assessment, documentation and interpretation, in M. M. Stark (ed), *Clinical Forensic Medicine: A Physician's Guide*, 3rd edn, Humana Press, New York.

Payne-James, J. J., Hawkins, C., Bayliss, S., and Marsh, N. 2012, Quality of photographic images for injury interpretation: Room for improvement? *Forensic Science, Medicine, and Pathology*, vol. 8, no. 4, pp. 447–450.

Peel, M., Hughes, J., and Payne-James, J. J. 2003, Postinflammatory hyperpigmentation following torture, *Journal of Clinical Forensic Medicine*, vol. 10, pp. 193–196.

Perera, P. 2007, Physical methods of torture and their sequelae: A Sri Lankan perspective, *Journal of Forensic and Legal Medicine*, vol. 14, pp. 46–50.

Perera, C., and Verghese, A. 2011, Implementation of Istanbul protocol for effective documentation of torture—Review of Sri Lankan perspectives, *Journal of Forensic and Legal Medicine*, vol. 18, pp. 1–5.

Pounder, D. J. 2011, The medical contribution to assessing allegations of torture in international fact-finding missions, *Forensic Science International*, vol. 208, pp. 143–148.

Prip, K., and Persson, A. L. 2008, Clinical findings in men with chronic pain after falanga torture, *Clinical Journal of Pain*, vol. 24, pp. 135–141.

Royal College of Paediatrics & Child Health. 2015, *The Physical Signs of Child Sexual Abuse*, 2nd edn, Royal College of Paediatrics & Child Health, London.

Sanders, J., Schuman, M. W., and Marbella, A. M. 2009, The epidemiology of torture: A case series of 58 survivors of torture, *Forensic Science International*, vol. 189, pp. e1–e7.

Savnik, A., Amris, K., Røgind, H., Prip, K., Danneskiold-Samsøe, B., Bojsen-Møller, F., Bartels, E. M., Bliddal, H., Boesen, J., and Egund, N. 2000, MRI of the plantar structures of the foot after falanga torture, *European Radiology*, vol. 10, no. 10, pp. 1655–1659.

Shields, L. B., Corey, T. S., Weakley-Jones, B., and Stewart, D. 2010, Living victims of strangulation: A 10-year review of cases in a metropolitan community. *American Journal of Forensic Medicine and Pathology*, vol. 31, no. 4, pp. 320–325.

Sowers, N., and Aubrey-Bassler, F. K. 2011, Trivial trauma and delayed rupture of a normal spleen: A case report, *Journal of Medical Case Reports*, vol. 5, p. 591.

Stephenson, T., and Bialas, Y. 1996, Estimation of the age of bruising, *Archives of Disease in Childhood*, vol. 74, pp. 53–55.

Taylor, B., Carswell, K., and de C Williams, A. C. 2013, The interaction of persistent pain and post-traumatic re-experiencing: A qualitative study in torture survivors, *Journal of Pain and Symptom Management*, vol. 46, no. 4, pp. 546–555.

Thomsen, A. B., Eriksen, J., and Smidt-Nielsen, K. 2000, Chronic pain in torture survivors, *Forensic Science International*, vol. 108, pp. 155–163.

Torp-Pedersen, S., Matteoli, S., Wilhjelm, J., Amris, K., Bech, J. I., Christensen, R., and Danneskiold-Samsøe, B. 2008, Diagnostic accuracy of heel pad palpation—A phantom study, *Journal of Forensic and Legal Medicine*, vol. 15, pp. 437–442.

Wasvary, H., Howells, G., Villalba, M., Madrazo, B., Bendick, P., DeAngelis, M., Bair, H., and Lucas, R., 1997, Nonoperative management of adult blunt splenic trauma: A 15-year experience, *American Journal of Surgery*, vol. 63, pp. 694–699.

Williams, A. C., Pena, C. R., and Rice, A. S. 2010, Persistent pain in survivors of torture: A cohort study, *Journal of Pain and Symptom Management*, vol. 40, pp. 715–722.

7

Radiology in the Documentation of Torture and Ill-Treatment

H. Vogel

CONTENTS

Introduction

Radiology has an important and specific role to play in the documentation of physical injuries that may be caused by torture, ill-treatment, and other violence during arrest and while in detention. These include injuries caused by the actions of a variety of individuals including the following:

- The police
- Intelligence services
- The military and other official security forces
- Paramilitary forces (including death squads) and other state-controlled contra-guerrilla forces
- Prison officers/detention staff
- Co-detainees acting with the approval or acquiescence or on the orders of public officials

The assessment and treatment of injuries sustained in such settings is commonly under the control of government-run health services and, as such, may be of inadequate standard, not conducted in the acute phase of injury or assault, subject to the healthcare professionals' conflicting duties, or absent altogether. The availability and quality of the health services will also be dependent on the location, country, and jurisdiction.

Torture and ill-treatment are usually committed in a clandestine fashion and using increasingly sophisticated methods with a deliberate attempt to reduce any physical evidence of its practice. It is often carried out in the early stages of confinement, and, if not initially fatal, the physical signs (if any) may be healed by the time the victim is released and can be examined. Therefore, obtaining medical evidence of torture remains difficult, but in certain cases, diagnostic imaging may assist in identifying previous abuse or injury. It must, however, be recalled that diagnostic imaging also has its limits. The uses and the limitations of diagnostic imaging will be highlighted in this chapter.

Background

The data referred to in this chapter have been collected in a project entitled "X-ray Diagnosis of Violence" that commenced some 30 years ago. Violence due to torture was a major part of the project, and during visits to rehabilitation centers for torture victims in Europe, including Turkey, notes and photographs were taken, cases were analyzed, and radiographs of torture victims were copied. The collection was enlarged during travels to other countries (including Chad, Chile, and others) sometimes on official mission, sometimes on self-initiative, and sometimes on invitation. In addition, cases that were documented or reviewed by other professional colleagues were also included in the project. Respecting the wish of the victim or the first observer for anonymity, the location and date of the original event are only rarely mentioned.

The *material is selective*; the *findings*, described being sourced from those who have emigrated or remained in their native country. It is important to state that the role of diagnostic imaging is to provide evidence that may contribute to the determination of whether certain mistreatment amounted to torture or to other cruel, inhumane or degrading treatment (CIDT) or punishment. This overarching determination is made, not by the radiologist, but by the official body tasked with investigating the allegations and compiling all the evidence and testimonies and could thus be, for example, a domestic court, an National Preventative Mechanisms [NPM]*), other UN bodies such as the Special Rapporteur on Torture (SRT) or the Subcommittee for the Prevention of Torture, an international court, and nongovernmental organizations.

Nature of Abuse and Injuries

Diagnostic imaging may be helpful in the documentation of the following types of ill-treatment which will be explored in this chapter.

- Forced positions
- Stabbing and cutting

---

* NPM of the Additional Protocol to the United Nations Convention against Torture.

- Trauma of the fingers, hands, and arms
- Trauma of the toes, feet, and legs
- Compression injuries
- Amputation, e.g., of digits (*petite guillotine*)
- The submersion in, deprivation of, or forced ingestion of water
- Electricity
- Psychological methods
- Malnutrition (e.g., protein deficiency and hypovitaminosis)

Differential diagnosis concerns:

- Other forms of abuse/maltreatment (inflicted injury)
- Accidents, self-inflicted injuries
- Initiation rites and cultural injuries
- Disease or health conditions
- Iatrogenic injuries

Physical ill-treatment may include any part or parts of the body, including hand and arm, foot and leg, torso, genitalia, and head and neck.

Fingers

Fingers are often involved. The resulting injuries may be reversible or permanent. The extraction of fingernails is reversible and seen on inspection. Radiology can visualize the sequelae of some procedures not evident on inspection; furthermore, radiology allows determining the extent of destruction and impairment.

Foreign bodies may remain, when needles, wires, wooden splinters, or other sharp instruments penetrate the fingers or have been inserted beneath the fingernails. These foreign bodies are often directed to the distal interphalangeal joint or even farther. After apparent extraction, the remaining splinters or fragments can show up on a radiograph (Figure 7.1).

There are different causes for *loss of digits and hands*:

- *Compression* of digits by finger, thumb, and toe-screws has been applied since medieval times. Bony damage may be minor (Figure 7.2) or lead to complete loss of a phalanx or digit. Less mechanical compression injuries are accomplished by a variety of means, including stamping with feet or striking with rifle butts or other objects (Moreno and Grodin 2000).
- *Squeezing*: Fingers can also be lost (Figure 7.3) or damaged by direct violence or by neurovascular deficit as a result of squeezing. The squeezing is performed by putting a stick between the fingers and then compressing them against each other in order to damage nerves and vessels without leaving visible traces.
- The petite guillotine was developed in Iran during the times of the Shah but persists. The fingers, or parts of fingers, are cut off in succession (Figure 7.4).
- *Suspension* by fingers is an old method. It had been used in medieval times and in modern times among others as punishment on sailing ships. If extended,

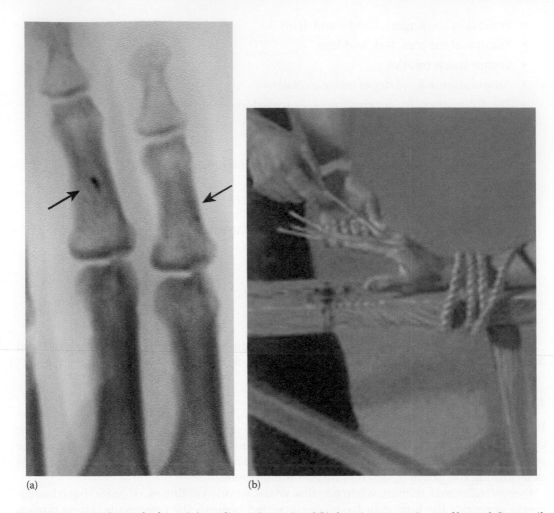

(a)   (b)

FIGURE 7.1   (a) Radiograph of remaining splinters (arrows) and (b) sharp instrument inserted beneath fingernail.

it induces necrosis and loss of the finger (Figure 7.5). The thumb seems to be the
preferred finger, perhaps for anatomical reasons.

- *Cutting or slicing parts of the body* can be used to intimidate or punish. In Sierra
  Leone, it was reported that the hands of possible voters were cut off to prevent
  them from voting. This was a crude but effective method since the national vote
  was controlled by painting the fingers of individuals after they had voted. Cutting
  off the hands and feet of perpetrators of certain crimes is prescribed by Sharia,
  the law of the Koran (Quran 5:38). This punishment is applied in several Islamic
  countries where the Sharia is the official law of the land.

- Fracture of the forearm is a typical *defensive injury*. The detainee (but may also be
  a demonstrator) tries by reflex or intention to protect his/her head against blows
  from a stick or a baton, for example, sometimes resulting in the fracture of the ulna
  alone or the ulna together with the radius (Figure 7.6).

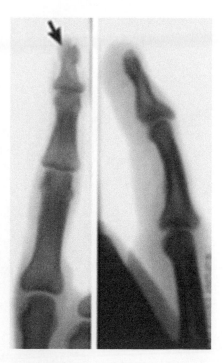

FIGURE 7.2 Contour irregularities (arrow) indicating minor bone damages due to compression of the end phalanx.

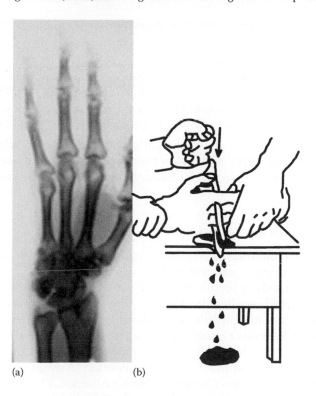

(a)   (b)

FIGURE 7.3 (a) Radiograph: loss of the fifth finger due to squeezing of fingers and (b) the rotation of an instrument, for example a toothbrush, injures the fixed fingers.

FIGURE 7.4 Sharp amputation of the distal part of the end phalanx of the third and fourth fingers (arrows) with the petite guillotine.

- *Injuries meant to hamper and to mutilate*: In Zaire, fractures of the hands and wrists are particularly seen in journalists, writers, and artists (Figure 7.7). The aim is not only to hamper the victim's work, but also to cause psychological injury by mutilating the appendage that is their main instrument of livelihood and personality.
- *Deformation*: Fire and other thermal injuries can create scars, which induce contractures causing deformity and loss of function. In Africa, the use of fire has been reported. Burning with cigarettes is quite common. Scars may be very characteristic.

Postural or Suspension Torture (Arm/Shoulder)

Requiring the victim to maintain a certain normal or awkward posture for long periods, binding the victim in various awkward and painful positions, or suspension of the victim are all widespread methods of torture that take many forms. Victims are sometimes suspended by the arms, which are bent backward and with sudden upward traction applied. Ruptures of the ligaments and capsule of the shoulder joint may result in soft tissue calcification. Fractures can be seen (Figure 7.8) and subluxations may occur (Figure 7.9). Other forms use the hands and feet bound together at the back (Figure 7.10).

Often, forced positions are applied with the intention to avoid evidence of the abuse. Figure 7.10 demonstrates common forms from South America. The forced position induces muscle and ligament damage, when the abnormal position is maintained for a protracted period. An experienced clinician or healthcare professional such as a physiotherapist can

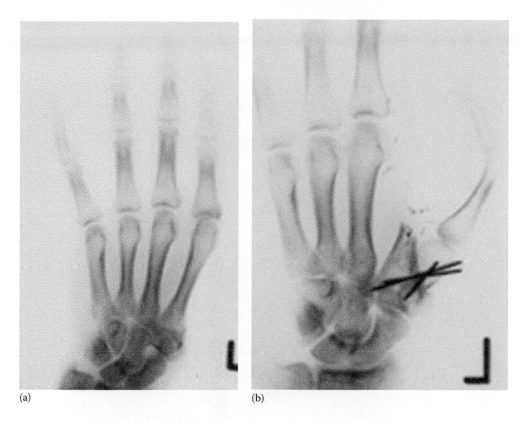

(a) (b)

FIGURE 7.5 (a) Radiograph: loss of the thumb following infection and necrosis due to suspension and (b) Radiograph after reconstructive surgery. The fifth finger replaces the thumb.

identify and characterize such damage. Ultrasonography and magnetic resonance imaging (MRI) can potentially visualize them and confirm clinical findings.

Being confined to cages too small for standing is reported from Kurds and Chinese. Uncomfortable positions can be easily enforced (Figure 7.11).

In Abu Ghraib, Iraq, the prisoners were placed in similar or identical positions as those shown in Figures 7.10 and 7.11, as images that are available on the Internet demonstrate.

Foot and Leg

Feet and legs are common targets of ill-treatment; some procedures are typical or even specific for some regions. Imaging may show typical or even characteristic findings; examples are falaka and palmatoria.

Falaka is a widespread form of torture, sometimes known as *falanga* and, in Spanish-speaking areas, as *bastinado*. Falaka means beating the foot, primarily (but not exclusively) on the plantar aspect of the foot. Falaka is perpetrated in the Near East, especially in Turkey and Iraq, in the Far East, and in some Spanish-speaking areas. Falaka can produce edema, bruising, fractures, and injuries to the ligaments, tendons, fascia, and aponeurosis of the feet and ankle (Figures 7.12 and 7.13). Tissue injury can be confirmed by MRI (e.g., thickening of the aponeurosis after falaka). In the acute phase, ultrasound and computed tomography (CT) may be useful in identifying hematoma and edema. Scintigraphy can be of assistance up to 2 years after the assault. Radiography can confirm or exclude fractures

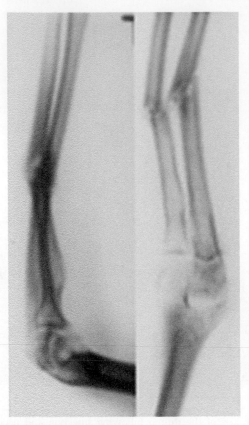

FIGURE 7.6   Defensive fracture of the radius and the ulna due to beating with a truncheon. The victim protected his head with his forearm when being beaten.

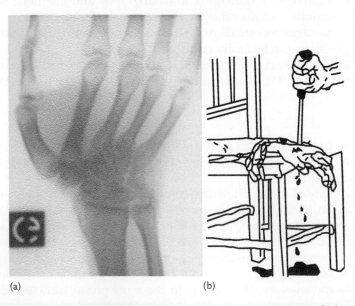

(a)   (b)

FIGURE 7.7   Mutilation of the hand, typical for writers and journalists. (a) Radiograph: fractured carpal bones and (b) screw drive is forced through the carpus.

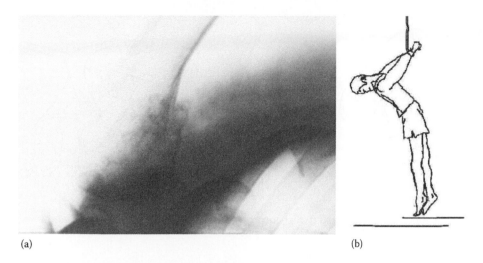

(a) (b)

FIGURE 7.8 (a) Fracture of the proximal humerus due to suspension. (a) Radiograph, rotated 90° anticlockwise to show the shoulder joint in the position during suspension and (b) the victim is suspended by the tied wrist joints. (Available at http://www.pureinsight.org/pi/pi_images/2004-6-20-hang_sill.jpg, retrieved May 06, 2017.)

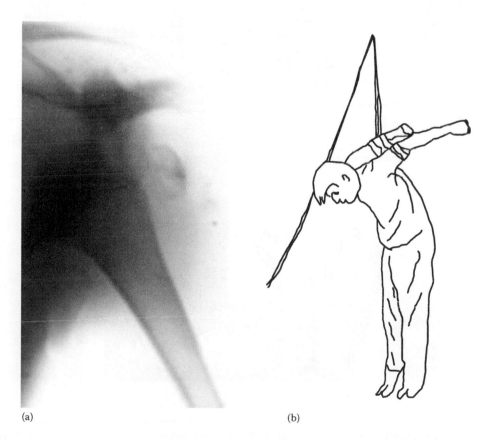

(a) (b)

FIGURE 7.9 Dislocation and fracture of the shoulder joint due to suspension. (a) Radiograph and (b) victim is suspended by the tied elbows.

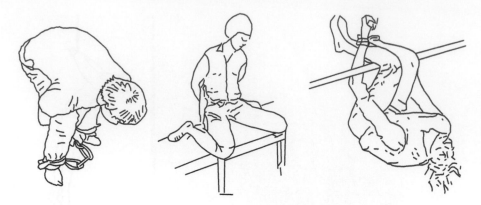

FIGURE 7.10   Different forced positions with bound hands and/or feet.

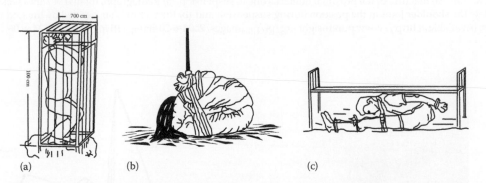

FIGURE 7.11   Different forced positions: (a) penning in a cage shorter than the victim's body height, (b) fixing the victim's trunk in maximum flexion, and (c) bending under a bed.

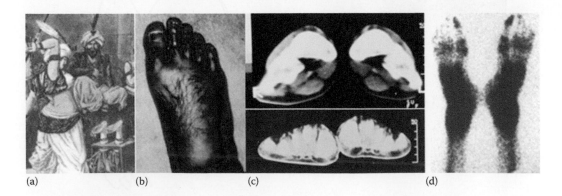

FIGURE 7.12   Falaca: (a) beating on the fixed feet; (b) hematoma and edema of the beaten foot hours after Falaca; (c) computed tomography of the middle foot after Falaca. Above: hematoma and edema hours after Falaca. Below: splayfoot formation weeks after Falaca; (d) Scintigraphy: increased Tc99m uptake indicating increased bone metabolism after Falaca.

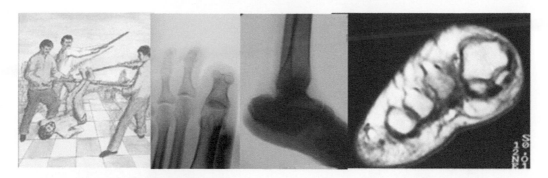

FIGURE 7.13 Further damage from falaka.

and allow estimation of the time interval for years after falaka was used (Bro-Rasmussen et al. 1982; Jensen et al. 1982; Lök et al. 1991; Skylv 1993; Genefke 1986; Lök 1994; Sidel 1996; Brogdon 1998).

In the author's experience, fracture can involve the toes, the metatarsals, the tarsals (especially the calcaneus), and occasionally, the ankle. This pattern is found especially if the feet have been immobilized during the beating. Fractures of the lateral malleolus seem to be an exception; nevertheless, the lower leg near the ankle may be involved. Scintigraphy initially shows increased soft tissue activity after the beating (Figure 7.12). Later, generalized increased bony uptake with degenerative changes that are more often seen in older age groups may be present. When available, MRI is better than computed tomography (CT) in visualizing alterations of soft tissues including capsular thickening, atrophy, edema, and reparative changes. Delayed study may prove falaka by demonstrating thickened aponeurosis of the foot. MRI can also show periosteal hematoma for up to 12 months or persistent edema (Figure 7.13) (Hayes 1997).

Palmatoria is an example of torture that is virtually unique to a specific region—the small West African country of Guinea-Bissau. Palmatoria involves repetitive blows to the shin where the tibia lies closest to the skin. Radiographic examination may show periosteal reaction from subperiosteal hemorrhage and hematoma. A laminar or onion skin periostitis can persist for weeks or even years (Figure 7.14). Somewhat peculiar endosteal and medullary changes may be seen as well. Two case reports have shown that blows by a rod to this area of the tibia can produce a hidden endosteal fracture which is likely to be undetected on plain films but obvious on computed tomography examination (Brogdon and Crotty 1999; Petrow et al. 2001). It is possible, perhaps likely, that some of the cases from Guinea-Bissau would show similar findings with more sophisticated imaging modalities such as CT and MRI.

Compression of digits by toe-screws has been applied in Iran (Figure 7.15). Bony damage can have various degrees; a complete loss of a phalanx or a digit may occur; permanent deformity of the phalanx is one possible consequence.

Other forms: Foreign bodies are introduced into the toes, under the toenails, and into the foot. Sometimes, persistent splinters or fragments may be seen on radiographs. Extraction of toenails is a common technique. The methods are similar to those applied to the fingers and the hand. When the victim is deliberately exposed to low temperatures, the toes may suffer frostbite and dry gangrene, leading to deformity, loss of some digits, or requiring surgical amputation (Gaessner et al. 2001).

Kneecapping is a term originally applied to a gunshot wound in the knee, aimed at the popliteal fossa, usually applied by a hand gun, in order to permanently maim or cripple the victim. In America, it has been attributed to mostly gang warfare. In more recent years,

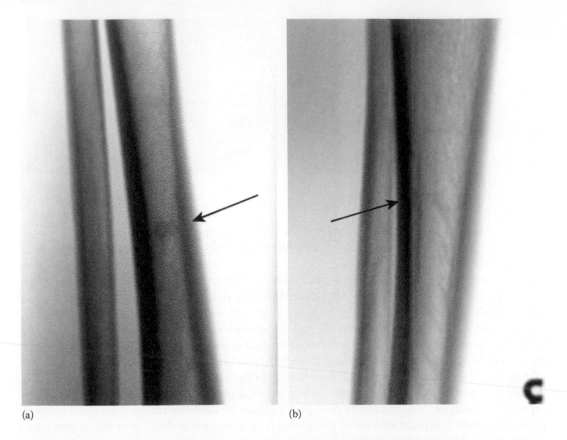

FIGURE 7.14   (a) Bone reaction (arrow), damage from Palmatoria (arrow) and (b) bone reaction (arrow), damage from Palmatoria.

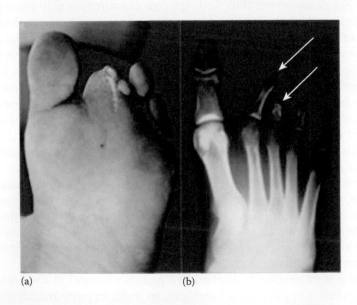

FIGURE 7.15   Loss of the distal phalanx of digits 2 and 3 due to compression: (a) photo and (b) radiograph.

it was commonly seen in Northern Ireland in connection with terrorist and criminal activity. It is not certain which country is the importer and which is the exporter. Kneecapping is no longer limited to the knee; other joints, particularly the ankle and elbow, are also targeted. In one known extreme case both knees, both ankles, and both elbows were shot. Occasionally, other parts of the leg are involved. Radiographs can easily document the extent of injury and may disclose the bullet path, trajectory of fire, and location of the bullet if it has not exited. Bullets are frequently found in situ, since low-velocity weapons are ordinarily employed. Arterial damage is not uncommon, and angiography is frequently employed to assess the damage (Figures 7.16 and 7.17).

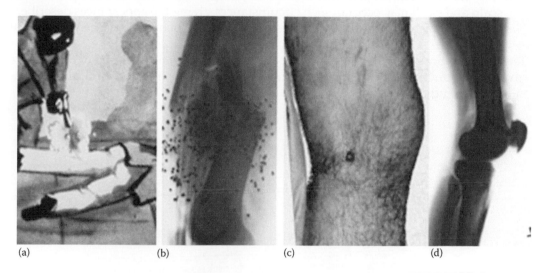

(a)   (b)   (c)   (d)

FIGURE 7.16 Kneecapping, variations: (a) shot into the knee from behind with a handgun from victim fixed in prone position; (b) shotgun injury of the thigh; (c) handgun injury of the knee, photo; and (d) handgun injury of the knee, bullet behind the patella, same victim, radiograph.

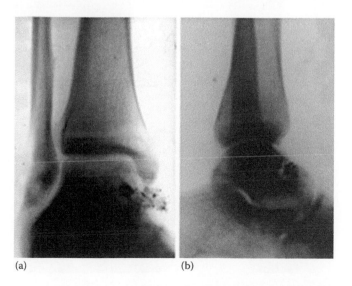

(a)   (b)

FIGURE 7.17 Kneecapping: shot into the ankle joint. (a) Fragments medial of the talus, radiograph, a-p projection and (b) radiograph, lateral projection.

Head and Neck

Ill-treatment involving the head can produce a spectrum of injuries from contusions, to lacerations, to hemorrages, to skull fractures and, in some cases, may be fatal injuries.

Stabbing into the head: An example from the Philippines is shown in Figure 7.18 when a nail was driven into the victim's head. In this case, this was to prevent the spirit of the victim from pursuing the murderers after death (Figure 7.18).

The images in Figure 7.19 are similar; however, the story is quite different in that it referred to a young person not responding to the treatment of a local healer, and thus a nail was introduced into the skull. Although neither of these cases represent torture or CIDT penetration of the scalp and skull may occur in such circumstances giving the appearances described.

Blunt impact to the head: Impacts to the head may fracture bones and cause intracranial bleeding.

Teeth may be broken or dislocated during beating. They may be extracted or drilled as a form of pain induction. These injuries, of course, can be demonstrated by clinical examination as well as radiography.

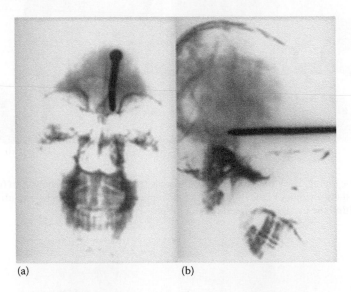

(a)   (b)

FIGURE 7.18   Nail driven into the victim's skull from the forehead (a), parallel to the anterior basis of the skull, up to the pituitary gland (b). Radiographs in two projections.

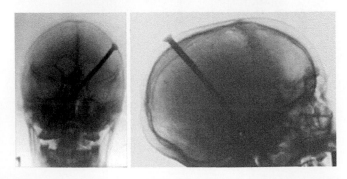

FIGURE 7.19   Nail driven into the victim's skull from left parietal, oblique, up to the basis of the skull. Radiographs in two projections.

In Chad, a rare form of beating on the head involves a detainee being beaten in the face producing fractures of the facial bones that can be radiologically demonstrated. Opacification of the maxillary sinuses is regularly seen due to bleeding, and subsequently, sinusitis will develop (Figure 7.20).

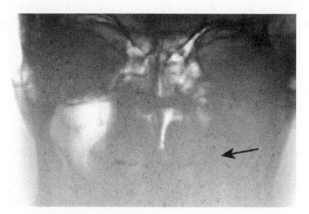

FIGURE 7.20 Sinusitis as a result of bleeding from facial bone fractures: Total opacification of the left maxillary sinus, thickening of the medial wall of the right maxillary sinus (arrow).

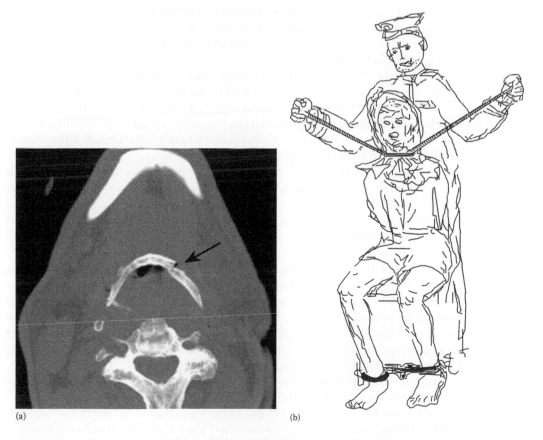

(a)   (b)

FIGURE 7.21 Suffocation and fracture of the larynx. (a) fracture of the hyoid bone (arrow), Computed Tomography and (b) Strangulation, the victim's head and neck in a plastic bag.

Shaking: It has been reported that the Israeli Security Service have used the technique of violently shaking the suspect's upper torso (Alston and Goodman 2013). On occasion, this produced intracranial lesions much like those found in the shaken baby syndrome. The practice has since been outlawed by the Israeli Supreme Court (Sontag 1991).

Neck: *Asphyxiation* in the form of manual or ligature neck compression is a widespread form of suffocation. The larynx may fracture, which is visible on CT (Figure 7.21).

Torso

The torso can be subject to many forms of injury including being beaten and stabbed. Fractures may be caused and foreign bodies introduced. Penetration of genitalia, anus, and mouth are frequent targets of sexual violence; many victims are too ashamed to report sexual abuse.

Beating: Beatings are universal, although implements may vary (M. Peel and V. Iacopino, personal communication). Beating can be as simple as punching, slapping, or kicking a victim. It may happen spontaneously or in conjunction with assaults from other blunt implements. Abusers may attempt to conceal injury. In Chile, those maltreated may be detained until visible bruises have resolved. Few specific findings will be radiologically detected from generalized beating since soft tissue and minor bony injury may have healed by the time the victim comes to medical attention. Such minor bony injury may not always be obvious during X-ray (Figure 7.22). Residual deformities of rib and spinal fractures may be present, as may deformities due to ligamentous tears or ruptures. Scintigraphy (Figure 7.22) shows increased bone metabolism up to 2 years after the beating; sometimes a pattern of the beating may be recognized.

Stabbing: Stabbing of the chest or abdomen incurs a high risk of injuring vital organs or penetrating the hollow viscera, with a chance of immediate fatal hemorrhage or later infection. Therefore, this method is less seen and reported. Certain forms of stabbing can be chosen to frighten or intimidate. In South Africa, the authors examined a young female who was in shock for no apparent reason. An experienced surgeon suggested the inspection of the umbilicus, which showed a tiny bit of blood. It transpired that this was a typical injury inflicted by gangs hunting young women to torment them by introducing bicycle spokes into the umbilicus. A variant of this was stabbing a bicycle spoke into the spine with intent to produce paraplegia.

Foreign bodies: Sometimes, fragments of a projectile or foreign bodies remain and can be documented by a radiological method (Figure 7.23). The identification of such foreign bodies may assist in corroborating accounts of abuse.

Fractures: Rib fractures following beating, stamping by booted feet, or other methods are common (Figure 7.24). Together with scintigraphy, they may show the beating's pattern. Less known is the fracture due to compressing the chest or the pelvis (Figure 7.25), similar to those seen in resuscitation injuries. While radiographs show the fracture, soft tissue injuries become visible with sonography, MRI, and CT. This would cause death more through asphyxiation such as traumatic asphyxia, in which the movement of the rib cage are impeded by the weights, thus impairing respiratory exchange.

Genitals and anus: It is well recognized that rape and sexual assault of females are common violations in war and among detainees who are subject to torture. This also takes place in a significant minority of males. In Abu Ghraib, prisoners were forced to commit sexual acts among each other (https://www.google.de/search?q=Falun+Gong+torture&source=lnms&tbm=isch&sa=X&ved=0ahUKEwjZ6qfDoNTTAhVEbhQKHVi7B6cQ_AUIBigB&biw=1382&bih=1205#tbm=isch&q=abu+ghraib+folter-fotos).

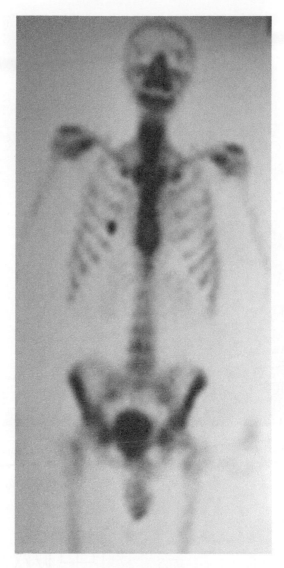

FIGURE 7.22 Whole body scintigraphy showing increased bone metabolism in the anterior part of a rib on the right due to beating. Scintigraphy may be positive up to two years.

Violence is often directed against genitalia (Figures 7.26 and 7.27). Hours after the abuse, scintigraphy can show an increased activity at the site of the injury.

Diagnostic imaging only occasionally provides additional information. In most cases, detailed assessment and clinical examination will be superior to any imaging. However, where there is more substantial injury (e.g., perforation or hemorrhage), plain film and CT may identify free air in the peritoneum or retroperitoneal space. Ultrasound, CT, and MRI may all have a place in identifying other lesions, e.g., collections of blood.

Rape, including penetration of the vagina or anus by foreign objects, may be accompanied by injuries. Foreign bodies may remain. If perforation of the vagina or intestinal walls occurs, there may be the risk of fatality from infection or hemorrhage before diagnostic imaging is done.

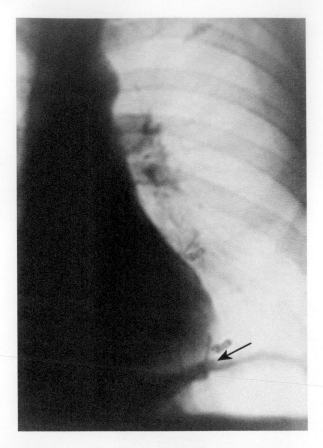

FIGURE 7.23 Needle in the back, reaching the left kidney. Rare observation: punctures of the chest and the abdomen often induce infections of the pleura and the peritoneum; untreated, these punctures are often lethal.

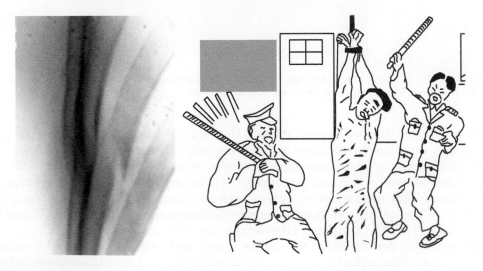

FIGURE 7.24 Rib fracture due to beating.

FIGURE 7.25 Compression of pelvis. Falun Gong. (Available at https://www.google.de/search?q=Falun+Gong+torture&source-lnms&tbm=isch&sa=X&ved=0ahUKEwjZ6qfDoNTTAhVEbhQKHVi7B6cQ_AUIBigB&biw=1382&bih=1205#imgrc=jkPGd89VCFaONM.)

Stabbing into the anus is sometimes performed to make the victim suffer until his/her death and/or to hide the killing: Edward II (1327), King of England, was killed in custody by stabbing him into the anus; this procedure was chosen in order to hide the wound and, thereby, the murder from the public, who were entitled to view the corpse. Killing by impalement has been reported in wars from our time; the death struggle may last from hours to days.

Electricity

Electricity as an instrument of ill-treatment can be used in multiple ways. In the Near East, it is common to place the electrode between the toes, on the tongue, at the teeth, or on the penis or scrotum, in the anus, and in the vagina. The location between the toes and on the tongue is chosen in order to hide the place of entrance of the electric current. The placement on the penis is selected not only to inflict pain but also humiliation. In Africa, the electrodes may also be placed on the teeth. In the Near East, large electrodes are used on wet skin and collar-like electrodes are placed on the neck. Electric current induces muscle contractions. The consequences may be bone fractures and soft tissue injuries, with secondary degencrative change in bony structures (Figure 7.28). Electroshock can produce compression fractures of the vertebrae

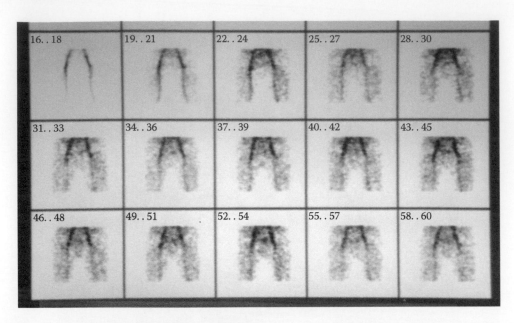

FIGURE 7.26   Compression of the penis and the scrotum. Increased uptake hours after the ill-treatment (image 43–54) due to the injury. Dynamic scintigraphy.

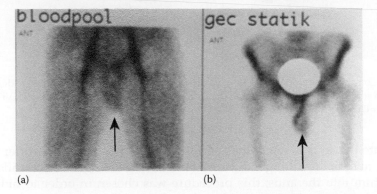

FIGURE 7.27   Increased uptake hours after compression of the genitals (arrow). (a) Scintigraphy without cover of the bladder and (b) with cover of the bladder for improving the visualization of the neighboring anatomy.

(Figure 7.29) and, along with grand mal seizures, is one of the few causes of high thoracic vertebral fractures. Teeth can be lost and jaws can be broken (Figure 7.30) (Vogel 2003).

If the victim was immediately available, it is likely that torture by electricity could be confirmed by MRI due to possible signal alteration, although the likelihood of an immediate MRI appears to be unlikely. At the point of contact or entry, whatever is conducting the current (e.g., a wire or needle) may produce an area of local necrosis which should be documented. Skin biopsy at the entry point may also have diagnostic changes.

Water

In *submersion*, often called *submarino*, the victim's head is forced underwater until near-drowning (Figure 7.31). The water is often polluted with excrement or other matter.

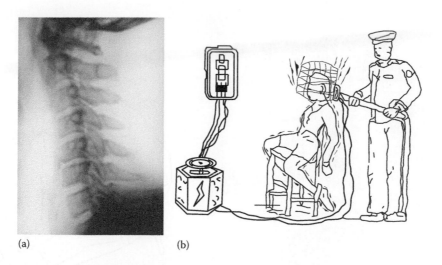

(a)   (b)

FIGURE 7.28 Malposition of the cervical spine after exposure to electricity via a collar made of an iron wire. (a) Partial kyphosis replaces the physiologic lordosis, radiograph. (b) Possible application of electricity for ill-treatment.

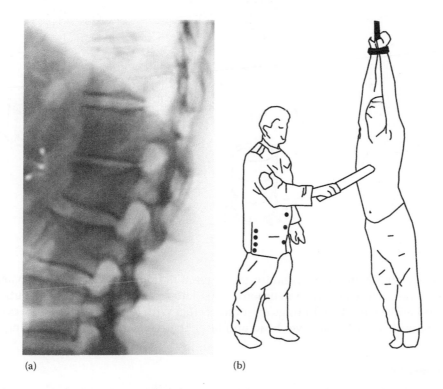

(a)   (b)

FIGURE 7.29 Wedge-shaped thoracic vertebra corresponding to a compression fracture induced by electricity. (a) Radiograph and (b) application of electricity with a stick (modified truncheon).

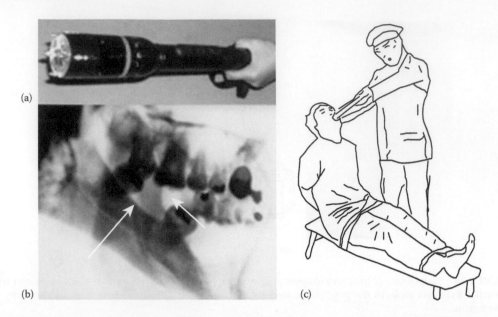

FIGURE 7.30 Loss of teeth due to contractions induced by electricity (combined with beating). (a) Stick for application of electric current, (b) lost molars in the lower jaw (arrows) on the right and the upper jaw on the left (arrows, superimposition of the right and the left upper jaw) and (c) example for intraoral application of electricity.

FIGURE 7.31 Examples of submersion.

Aspiration is virtually inevitable, and the subsequent radiography changes may vary from pulmonary edema to extensive pneumonia. The latter may lead to residual pulmonary scarring and adhesions. The findings are nonspecific. With dry submarino (e.g., occlusion of breathing with a plastic bag over head and face), there may be no visible findings.

Forced Ingestion

Prisoners in Chad, Africa, have reported that they were bound with their arms behind them, then forced to ingest several liters of water in a very short time. Thereafter, they were

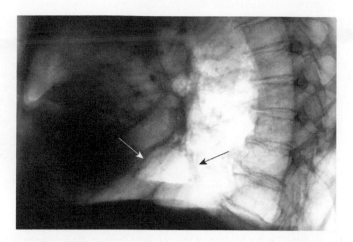

FIGURE 7.32   Diaphragmatic hernia, gastric cavity filled with air behind the heart (arrows). With hands bound on the back, the victim had to swallow several liters of water and was thrown on his stomach out of several meters height. Lateral chest radiograph.

thrown, or caused to fall, from a height of several meters to land on their anterior chest and abdomen, with the possibility of visceral rupture. One survivor was found to have a diaphragmatic hernia (Figure 7.32) which might have been caused by this forced trauma, although its causation cannot be confirmed in the absence of other concurrent injuries.

Waterboarding

Waterboarding was characterized in 2005 by former Central Intelligence Agency (CIA) director Porter J. Goss as a "professional interrogation technique." A cloth or plastic wrap is placed over or in the person's mouth, and water is poured onto the person's head (Figure 7.33). CIA officers who have subjected themselves to the technique have lasted an average of 14 s before capitulating (Bennett and Shambaugh 2009). There is a real risk of death from actually drowning or suffering a heart attack or damage to the lungs from inhalation of water, which would be visible in radiographs. Long-term effects include

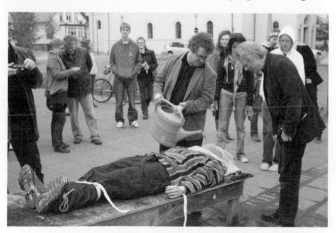

FIGURE 7.33   Protest against Waterboarding in Iceland 2008. (Available at https://upload.wikimedia.org /wikipedia/commons/2/26/Waterboarding.jpg, retrieved May 06, 2017.)

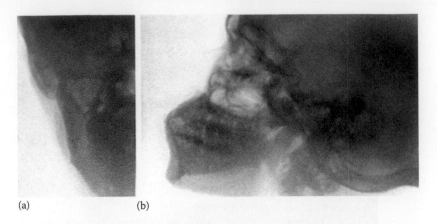

(a)   (b)

FIGURE 7.34   Russian roulette. Defect healing of the jaw joint (arrow). Radiographs. (a) a-p projection and (b) lateral projection.

panic attacks, depression, and post-traumatic stress disorder. Up until now, there are no signs of these long-term effects, which have been visualized in diagnostic imaging.

Execution, Russian Roulette, Simulated Execution

By the state, executing a death penalty is often celebrated as a demonstration. Of what? Mistreatment and torture of others are instruments to torment prisoners. This is valid too for execution and killing: Prisoners are forced to assist; they see what they have to expect; being forced to assist the execution of a companion, a friend, or a relative aims to obtain intelligence or cooperation or to torment. Simulated killing has the same goals. A special form is Russian roulette, in which the victim's life is at risk (Figure 7.34). In Russian roulette, a player places a single bullet in a revolver chamber, spins the chamber, places the muzzle against his head, and pulls the trigger. There is normally a six-bullet capacity in a chamber, so there is a one in six chance of fatally injuring oneself. In isolated cases, injuries of Russian roulette can be visualized with later radiographs.

Infectious and Deficiency Diseases

Detainees generally have an increased risk of infection. This risk increases with the time of imprisonment. Tuberculosis, hepatitis C, and HIV are common in many countries. A chest X-ray may show pulmonary tuberculosis. Sonography, CT, and MRI furnish only limited information on hepatitis; they can contribute to show accompanying diseases in a detainee with HIV/AIDS. Advanced infectious diseases often have findings which diagnostic imaging methods can visualize. The same is valid for deficiency diseases. Protein deficiency, and the lack of sufficient food, and vitamin deficiency induce pathologies, which diagnostic imaging methods are able to show. Such imaging is supportive but not diagnostic of torture.

Selection and Constraint

The availability of imaging techniques varies widely. Imaging studies are usually scarce in countries where ill-treatment of detainees is common. Consequently, the literature on imaging of detainees involves selective material. Multiple forms of ill-treatment are designed and applied in a manner to avoid telltale evidence by subsequent clinical or radiologic inspection. However, some methods produce changes that can be demonstrated by imaging. There are regional differences in dealing with detainees and in the design and infliction of ill-treatment throughout the world. Analysis by imaging is rare in the acute phase. Often, the victim is held in custody until visible traces have disappeared. Even after being freed, the victim is usually frightened or shamed and is hesitant to seek diagnosis, treatment, or documentation of the trauma. This is especially true when the ill-treatment is tolerated or performed by the state and when physicians and medical facilities are felt to be an active part of the system.

The interests of the victim, the courts, and the state influence the assessment, documentation, and interpretation of cases, where torture and ill-treatment has occurred. In Syria, forensic physicians must examine a prisoner before he/she is brought before a judge for the first time and must differentiate between abuse and self-inflicted trauma, both in the acute stage (Iacopino 1996). Unquestionably, in regimes that countenance torture and other infringements of human rights, the medical community is under great pressures and coercion to look the other way, or to go along with the policy (Amnesty International 2002). In a retrospective case study of 200 alleged survivors of torture from 18 different countries, the Danish Medical Group of Amnesty International documented that 20% of those victims reported that medical personnel were involved in their torture (Bro-Rasmussen et al. 1982).

Radiologic studies can be particularly useful in the evaluation of victims who have eventually come to rehabilitation centers where newer imaging modalities can be employed to assess the late findings of ill-treatment and torture. However, the cost of such procedures prevents widespread utilization (Genefke 1986; Brogdon 1998; Lök 1994; Sidel 1996).

CT is used by centers for the rehabilitation of torture victims only in exceptional cases because of its cost and limited availability. Nevertheless, there are some strong indications for its use, and when employed, the findings can be quite impressive. CT of the central nervous system is rarely employed early after torture has occurred. However, late studies can show sequelae such as subdural hematomas, hygromas, old intracerebral bleeding, and hydrocephalus (Hayes 1997). Cerebral atrophy has been associated with previous beatings. Scintigraphy can verify that beating has indeed taken place, when clinical examinations and plain film diagnosis fail to document anything. In soft tissue, an increased activity can be demonstrated for days and even weeks; in bones, it is demonstrated over months and even years, long after edema and hematoma have disappeared (Jensen et al. 1982; Meier and Andersen 1985; Lök 1994).

The differential diagnosis for torture and ill-treatment includes common trauma and other pathologies. Injuries such as scars due to cuts in African initiation rites have to be carefully distinguished. Cultural scars are frequent in many countries. Once obtained, diagnostic images must be carefully evaluated as to whether specific findings of forms of abuse can be documented. Such evidence must be discussed and presented compellingly to physicians, lawyers, and officials usually not involved in the actual case (Rasmussen 1990; Kintzel 1992; Vogel 1997, 1999; Brogdon 1998).

Only sometimes do diagnostic imaging demonstrate lesions so characteristic that they can be considered legal proof of previous ill-treatment and verify a presumed victim's claims. In general, a validity check is indicated. Criteria that support claims of ill-treatment are as follows:

- Correlation between the type of torture and the findings derived from imaging procedures

- Correlation between the date of torture and the imaging appearance of the lesion
- Specific alterations, such as the periosteal reactions from palmatoria
- Correlating findings in a particular situation, such as imprisonment and nutritional deficiencies or sequelae from denial of treatment or surgery
- Patterns of beatings (proven by imaging) typical for a particular geographic location and corresponding with the victim's story

Summary

Before referring to diagnostic imaging, a person claiming to have been maltreated or tortured must have a detailed history taken. The interviewer must try to assess whether diagnostic imaging can add additional information that may either confirm or exclude torture and other abuses. If the information obtained from interview suggests that there may be a role for diagnostic imaging methods, then it should be (if the equipment and the radiographer or radiologist or a practitioner skilled in interpreting images is) a routine practice to use one or more of ultrasound, scintigraphy, plain film, CT, or MRI. Diagnostic imaging is a potentially very important part of the complex jigsaw of investigation of those who are claiming torture or other abuses.

References

Alston Ph., and Goodman, R. 2013, *International Human Rights*, Oxford University Press, Oxford. p. 246.

Amnesty International 2002, Doctors and torture: Amnesty International annual report, Amnesty International, London.

Bennett, A., and Shambaugh, G. 2009, *Taking Sides: Clashing Views in American Foreign Policy*, 5th edition. McGraw-Hill, New York. p 317.

Brogdon, B. G. 1998, Human rights abuse, torture, terrorism. Chapter 17, in *Forensic Radiology*, CRC Press, Boca Raton, FL.

Brogdon, B. G., and Crotty, J. M. 1999, The hidden divot: A new type of incomplete fracture? *American Journal of Roentgenology*, vol. 172, p. 789.

Bro-Rasmussen, F., Henriksen, O. B., and Rasmussen, O. et al. 1982, Aseptic necrosis of bone following falanga torture, *Ugeskrift for Laeger*, vol. 144, pp. 1165.

Gaessner, S., Gurris, N., and Pross, C., (eds) 2001, *At the Side of Torture Survivors*, Johns Hopkins University Press, Baltimore, MD.

Genefke, I. K. 1986, *Torturen I Verden: Den Angar os Alle*, Hans Reizels forlag, Copenhagen, pp. 1–27.

Hayes, E. 1997, MRI illustrates history of torture, *Diagnostic Imaging Europe*, vol. 13, p. 17.

Iacopino, V. 1996, Turkish physicians coerced to conceal systematic torture, *The Lancet*, vol. 348, p. 1500.

Jensen, T. S., Genefke, I. K., Hyldebrandt, N., Pedersen, H., Petersen, D., and Weile, B. 1982, Cerebral atrophy in young torture victims, *New England Journal of Medicine*, vol. 307, p. 1334.

Kintzel, R. 1992, Röntgenbefunde von Folteropfern, Dissertation, Hamburg, Germany.

Lök, V. 1994, *Oral Communication*, International Torture Meeting, Istanbul.

Lök, V., Tunca, M., Kumanlioglu, K., Kapkin, E., and Dirik, G. 1991, Bone scintigraphy as clue to previous torture, *Lancet*, vol. 337, p. 846.

Meier, J., and Andersen, J. G. 1985, Sclerosing of the calcaneus following phalanga torture, *Ugeskrift for Laeger*, vol. 147, p. 4206.

Moreno, A., and Grodin, M. A. 2000, The not-so-silent marks of torture, *Journal of the American Medical Association*, vol. 284, p. 538.

Petrow, P., Page, P., and Vanel, D. 2001, The hidden divot fracture: Brogdon's fracture, a new type of incomplete fracture, *American Journal of Roentgenology*, vol. 177, p. 946.

Rasmussen, O. V. 1990, Medical aspects of torture. Laegerforenigens Forelag, Kopenhagen, pp. 1–85.

Sidel, V. W. 1996, Commentary: The social responsibilities of health professionals: Lessons from their role in Nazi Germany, *Journal of the American Medical Association*, vol. 276, p. 1679.

Skylv, G. 1993, Falanga: Diagnosis and treatment of late sequellae, *Torture*, vol 2, pp. 11–15.

Sontag, D. 1991, A strike against brutality, *Mobile Register*, September 9, vol. 1. Cited in Thali, M., Viner, M., and Brogdon, B. G. (eds), *Brogdon's Forensic Radiology*, 2nd edition, CRC Press, 2011, Chapter 17, Child abuse, 255–278.

Vogel, H. 1997, *Gewalt in Röntgenbild*, Wcomed verlagsgesellschaft mbH, Landsberg/Lech.

Vogel, H. 1999, Imaging helps unveil torture's dark secrets, *Diagnostic Imaging Europe*, vol. 37, p. 22.

Vogel, H. 2003, Electric torture, in B. G. Brogdon, H. Vogel, and J. D. McDowell, *A Radiologic Atlas of Abuse, Torture, Terrorism, and Inflicted Trauma*, CRC Press, Boca Raton, FL.

8

Management of Hunger Strikes in Detention

Hernán Reyes

CONTENTS

Introduction

The issue of hunger strikes is a complex one. This chapter reviews all aspects of this complex subject, gives pointers for adequate management, and scrutinizes the ethical issues that arise when dealing with prisoners who—rightly or wrongly—state they are, or they are said to be, on hunger strike, refusing food, or fasting.

The medical role of physicians monitoring detention and torture and cruel, inhumane, and degrading conditions is different to that of a prison physician who is responsible on a daily basis for the healthcare of prisoners. Prison physicians must be aware of the issues of relevance to hunger strikes even if only encountered infrequently.

Doctors monitoring detention conditions may be faced with a range of different scenarios. They may find that the prison doctors are unfamiliar with the principles of management of hunger strikes, including the monitoring and assessment required for such patients. In some cases, the prison doctors may be acting more as agents of the prison administration, rather than in the best interests of the hunger-striking detainees. This can be of detriment to the detainee's health and well-being. This is a frequent example of the nature of conflicting roles between duties to the patient based on medical ethical principles and the duties to, and requirements of, the employer. The monitoring doctor's intervention in such cases will be to evaluate the situation and then to consult with the prison doctors to consider what management should be in place. Monitoring doctors may find that their main role is to support their prison medical colleagues, who may be being pressured by the prison administration to act unethically by, for example, force-feeding fasting prisoners.

As discussed in previous chapters, the complexities arise when a doctor-patient relationship has to be balanced with all the external factors that are specific to custodial settings. Both the prison doctor and the monitoring doctor must attempt to avoid being used or manipulated by either the prison authorities or by the detainees themselves.

Background

Terminology is crucial in this setting. The term *hunger strike* is often misused, including by the detainees who are not eating.

The term *hunger strike* refers to a means of protesting by fasting, generally associated with a demand of some kind. The World Medical Association (WMA) clearly states in the Preamble to the 1991 Malta Declaration on Hunger Strikes (revised in 2006):

> ... (hunger strikes) are often a form of protest by people who lack other ways of making their demands known. In refusing nutrition for a significant period, they usually hope to obtain certain goals by inflicting negative publicity on the authorities.

A prisoner, or group of prisoners, decides at some point to stop taking nourishment and declares that they are on a hunger strike, with the intention either of demonstrating against some action or circumstance or demanding something that would otherwise not be obtained. The term *hunger strike* thus covers many different forms of protest fasting. The term *hunger strike* is very emotive and has a connotation of intransigence and of demands made that, if refused by the authorities, could in extreme cases even lead to the death of the protestors. To members of the general public, examples such as Mahatma Gandhi, who used fasting as a political weapon, or Bobby Sands, who along with 10 others in the Irish Republican Army movement died from self-imposed lack of nourishment, taking only water, in 1981, are representative of hunger strikes. The vast majority of hunger strikes, however, are straightforward protests calling for negotiations, wanting to draw outside attention to a specific cause and attempting to seek some support, often as a last resort, when other means of protest have failed. Generally, a fatal outcome is certainly not the intention and does not occur.

The monitoring physician can be confronted with hunger strikes in shorter-term custodial settings (e.g., police custody or remand prisons) or in prisons, with sentenced prisoners, with long-term inmates. The difference between the two settings is important, as the former group usually needs a noisy protest to try to make things move with a certain urgency, but may be less coordinated and planned, whereas those inmates in longer-term custody may have spent considerable time on the organization and nature of any protest.

If an external monitoring physician attends a detention setting for an emergency visit to a detainee on hunger strike, due to media attention or other outside factors, such as family pressure, it is essential to have a clear understanding of the situation not only of the fasting detainee individually but also of the environment in which the detainee is incarcerated. In some cases, it may even be the prison physician who calls the external monitoring physician for assistance, so as to be able to resist complying with unethical orders from the facility administration, such as having to force-feed the hunger strikers.

The essential information to establish initially, from reliable sources, is as follows:

- How many detainees are involved in this protest fasting?
- How long has the fasting been going on?
- What is the nature of the fasting (e.g., all food and drink [dry fast]; all food but not water; all prison food, but not family food)?

The information provided earlier may be gathered before any interviews with the fasting detainees—for example, from the authorities, or prison physicians and nurses, or family members. The answers to these questions will help determine the nature of the hunger strike or whether it is merely what has been called *food refusal*. The latter term was defined following discussions by the author of this chapter with the Chief Medical Officer of the prisons of Northern Ireland in the mid-1980s, who had been present during the major hunger strike in 1981. It was only in 1998 that it was possible to openly define these categories. See Figure 8.1 (Reyes 1998).

It is important to determine the detaining authorities' attitude toward the protest and whether it is indeed a hunger strike. Are the authorities calm and allowing their prison physician to deal with the issue appropriately or are the authorities concerned and intent on avoiding any damaging outcomes? Such scenarios can lead to preemptive action by the authorities (e.g., punishment of the protesting prisoners by sending them to solitary

FIGURE 8.1 The clinical framework for time and diet is defined by the 72/72 rule of thumb. This is 72 hours defining the beginning of a hunger strike; 72 days, the probable longest survivable time of anyone on total fasting. Diet is defined by total fasting or nontotal fasting.

confinement) or insisting the physician intervene (Reyes et al. 2013a). This is usually a counterproductive attitude and has to be reversed by patient and professional explanations by the monitoring physician, so as not to worsen the situation. The authorities sometimes take hasty and untoward actions, wanting to break the protest movement.

Another important factor is to determine which type of detainee is protesting by refusing to eat. Are they categorized, for example, as security risks or political prisoners or convicted criminals? In each case, the motivation and attitude may differ. For example, political prisoner hunger strikes may be more structured and planned.

Food Refusers and Hunger Strikers

There is an essential difference between food refusers and hunger strikers.

Prisoners who refuse to eat, may be just that—food refusers—a prisoner or a group of prisoners quite distinct from that of real hunger strikers. While both categories will have a stated motive for not taking nourishment, the mind-set is very different in each case.

The food refuser wants to have influence on higher authorities, usually for some petty or minor reason, by having outside pressure exerted on those with the power to ask for concessions. However, food refusers have no intention of fasting in such a way as to cause themselves any serious harm.

A hunger striker, as has been mentioned, has a specific motivation for protesting by refusing nourishment and sees fasting as a last resort. At least initially, the hunger striker is willing to put his health on the line. Whether or not fasting is prolonged in case of a deadlock in discussions with the authorities will depend mainly not only on motivation, but also on external factors.

Food refusers never get themselves to a point where their health is in danger and create an ethical dilemma for medical staff. Hunger strikers, on the other hand, may sometimes (although rarely) find themselves fasting to a point where their health and even life can be put in jeopardy.

It is important for the medical personnel involved to differentiate these two categories from the outset, as the way the fasting is approached and managed will be very different.

The generic term *hunger striker* is often misused when describing both situations. Any monitoring physician must be aware of the difference between these two categories. Prison physicians may not have a clear understanding of these two categories and may react inappropriately to the sense of emergency which may be created by the facility administration around hunger strikes.

Food refusers do protest and do stop taking food indeed—for a while at least. They may certainly have complaints or demands—but, generally speaking, their situation is anything but a last resort for protest. They do protest by making as much noise as possible around their claims. Their motives may often be, or be perceived to be petty or minor, but despite whatever claims they make, they rarely have the intention of going all the way, and in fact, they may even count on the prison doctor to make sure they do not risk their health, let alone their lives. Thus, they often appeal to the prison doctor for help and support. Whatever intransigent message they communicate toward the outside may be totally opposite to what they tell the doctor. Recent research from French remand prisons showed that almost 100% of physicians had encountered what they called *hunger strikes*, but that the vast majority (85%) of these hunger strikes were in fact food refusals—lasting a week or less—and needing no medical intervention (Fayeulle et al. 2010) (Figure 8.2).

In contrast, true hunger strikers (according to the definition in the WMA Declaration of Malta [2006]) are prisoners who have somewhat more solid motivations for their protest (political, social, local related to prison conditions) and who refuse food and often proclaim they intend to do so until they obtain what they want. These hunger strikers protest by refusing food most often as a last resort, as they feel, rightly or wrongly, that this is the only way to make their plight known. Hunger strikers may be individuals or be part of a group. They may be determined at the start, and motivated, through deep

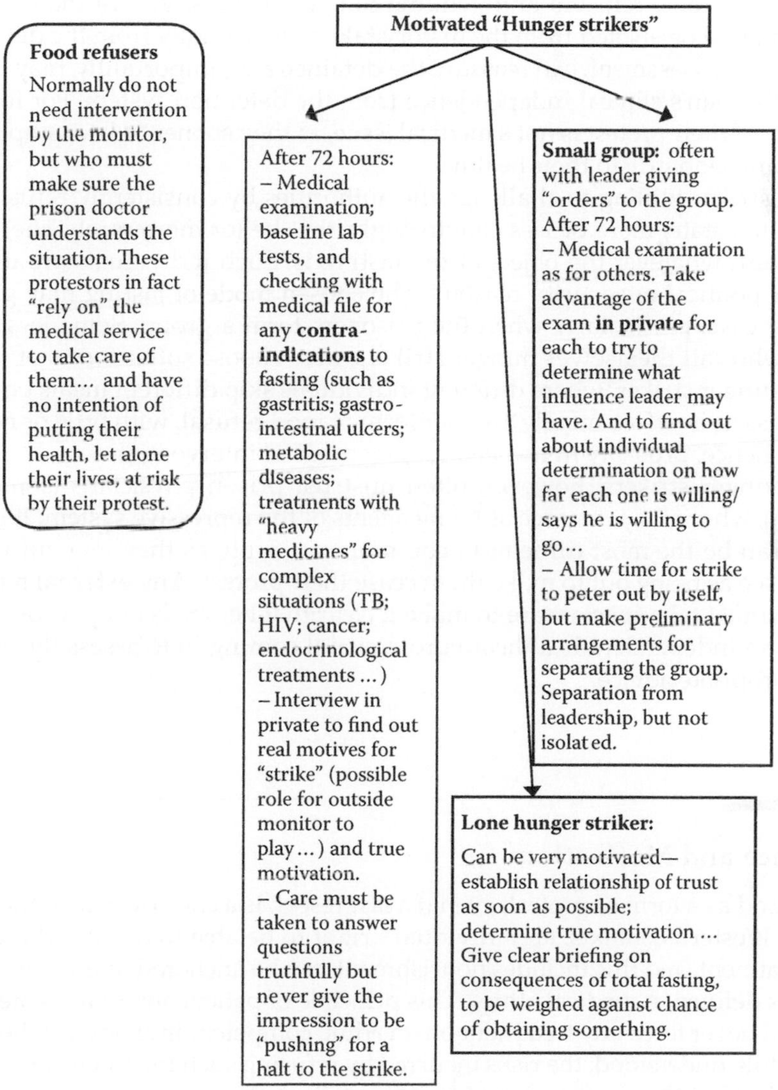

Motivated "Hunger strikers"

Food refusers

Normally do not need intervention by the monitor, but who must make sure the prison doctor understands the situation. These protestors in fact "rely on" the medical service to take care of them… and have no intention of putting their health, let alone their lives, at risk by their protest.

After 72 hours:
– Medical examination; baseline lab tests, and checking with medical file for any **contra-indications** to fasting (such as gastritis; gastro-intestinal ulcers; metabolic diseases; treatments with "heavy medicines" for complex situations (TB; HIV; cancer; endocrinological treatments …)
– Interview in private to find out real motives for "strike" (possible role for outside monitor to play…) and true motivation.
– Care must be taken to answer questions truthfully but never give the impression to be "pushing" for a halt to the strike.

Small group: often with leader giving "orders" to the group. After 72 hours:
– Medical examination as for others. Take advantage of the exam **in private** for each to try to determine what influence leader may have. And to find out about individual determination on how far each one is willing/says he is willing to go…
– Allow time for strike to peter out by itself, but make preliminary arrangements for separating the group. Separation from leadership, but not isolated.

Lone hunger striker:

Can be very motivated—establish relationship of trust as soon as possible; determine true motivation … Give clear briefing on consequences of total fasting, to be weighed against chance of obtaining something.

FIGURE 8.2   Food refusers and hunger strikers.

personal convictions—or sometimes by peer pressure, which can seriously complicate the issue.

It is important to note that all categories of prisoners who protest by refusing to take nourishment call themselves—and are called so by the authorities, and the press, and their families—*hunger strikers*. It is not relevant for a physician, whether from prison or an external monitor, to insist on using the correct label (hunger striker or food refuser) for each case. Food refusers will invariably insist they are genuine hunger strikers—which, in the vast majority of cases, they are not. The physician needs to be able to make the distinction so as to determine the best medical approach—but should not get involved in the political determination of the label ascribed, either by the protestor, their family, or the administration.

Those physicians with experience in these settings may be better able to detect the difference between food refusers and genuine hunger strikers. Where there is doubt, the distinction should be elicited from the history taken individually from the detainees. This, and the physical assessment, can reassure the detainee and, importantly, may help demonstrate the physician's clinical independence from the detention system. For food refusers, management of their protest is not a medical issue, as they sooner or later stop their fasting well before any jeopardy to their health.

A hunger striker willing to challenge the authorities by consistently refusing nourishment will often state, more or less convincingly, that he (or more rarely, she) is prepared to die to obtain whatever the object of the fasting is. Such individuals are usually those detained for political or security reasons. The chosen mode of fasting may greatly differ from case to case, particularly when the prisoners form a group. Some less determined protestors, who call themselves hunger strikers, may choose softer forms of fasting, such as rotating hunger strikes, where different individuals skip different meals on a rota basis. Such a process is, in effect, merely another form of food refusal, with little or no danger for health, and, hence, probably in no need for any medical intervention.

Political hunger strikers, however, often mistrust prison physicians (sometimes with good reason), whom they may see as being agents of the repressive system. It is these prisoners who can be the most difficult to communicate with, as they may mistrust anyone whom they see as being out to make them cease their protest. Any external medical monitor called in must take special care to make it clear that he/she is not part of the custodial system, but an independent healthcare professional coming in to assess the situation and provide appropriate advice.

Competence and Motivation

Refusal of food as a form of protest, even if a last resort, is a controversial notion at the best of times. In Western contexts, an individual's right to be able to decide whether or not to take any treatment, and this includes nourishment, can be anchored in this basic principle of autonomy as defined in medical ethics. This principle of patient autonomy states that a physician should never force any treatment on an adult, competent individual, who is informed of, and has duly understood, the risks incurred by refusing such treatment (or food). In 2006, the WMA decided that in the case of hunger strikes, the principle of patient autonomy overrides another basic principle of medical ethics, that of beneficence, which determines the duty to assist or look after a patient, and to prevent death. Authorities, both medical and nonmedical, often evoke this principle of beneficence for recommending or imposing forcible treatment or feeding. Not to do so, not to respect beneficence, is thus said to be equivalent to nonassistance of a person in danger of death. Before deciding that autonomy is to prevail, the prison physician, or the external or other monitoring physician, has, first of all, to ascertain that the protesting prisoner is a fully competent adult, has full mental capacity, and understands what the situation is and what the outcome of a continuation of a total hunger strike entails.

The principle of autonomy is, however, not always accepted or may be interpreted differently according to the country and jurisdiction. This is often the case in some non-Western contexts where an individual's rights are considered subservient to the rights of the community or of the state. In the former Soviet Union, for example, a physician's loyalties were first and foremost to the state, duties to patients coming only afterwards, and the principle of autonomy was seen as a foreign, Western concept (author's field experience as physician working in Transcaucasia for the International Committee of the Red Cross in the 1990s). In many countries in Asia, both a prisoner's right to protest by fasting and a physician's right to decide whether or not to intervene are not recognized—the state defining what is good for the community as a whole and any individualistic approach being also considered as contrary to tradition. Religious considerations can further complicate the issue, as some physicians will, for such personal reasons, refuse to accept what they see as condoned suicide by fasting.

Together with determining a fasting prisoner's mental capacity, the prison physician and any external monitor will have to determine the state of physical health of the potential hunger striker, as there are many health contraindications to total fasting. The presence of a preexisting health problem that could be readily exacerbated by a hunger strike (such as insulin-dependent diabetes or a stomach ulcer) would be reason enough to try to persuade an individual from not participating in any prolonged fasting.

Baseline parameters for total fasting need to be known by prison doctors and monitors alike, so that appropriate management can be undertaken when a prisoner decides to fast totally (World Medical Journal 2006). These parameters must be considered for the beginning and the end of a total hunger strike, i.e., taking water only. Until 72 hours of total fasting have passed, there is no reason for a physician to intervene (unless there are preexisting physical or mental health issues). If the mental health condition is one which also affects capacity, then this may negate the detainee's status as a hunger striker. Any physical condition which would deteriorate for mere physiological reasons when fasting should be considered a contraindication to go on hunger strike, and the protestor should be advised of this. Upper gastrointestinal disorders can fall into this category. Prisoners should be informed of possible risks—such as gastric bleeding or peptic ulcer perforation—and many may decide against pursuing a hunger strike. Diabetes (particularly Type 1) can rapidly destabilize with risk of both hypo- and hyperglycemia. Although not all mental health conditions will affect the capacity to decide to fast, an evaluation by a psychiatrist should be done if there is any doubt in this respect. An initial screening mental state examination should in this case be undertaken by the prison physician. If there is preexisting known mental health diagnosis (e.g., schizophrenia, bipolar disorder) or if the screening mental state examination suggests undiagnosed conditions, then an external psychiatric opinion must be sought to assist with management of the case.

A fast of 72 hours is considered to define the true beginning of a hunger strike. It was demonstrated during the 1981 hunger strike in Northern Ireland that it was exceptional to live beyond 72 days when taking only water. Irish hunger striker Maze prisoner Kieran Doherty died on his 73rd day of fasting (Beresford 1987).

As of 72 hours, the prison physician should make an initial assessment of the situation, attending the protesting detainees, taking a medical history (including past history of protest fasting, length of time previous fasting lasted, length of imprisonment, baseline decision-making capacity, possible external pressures from peers or authorities), and undertaking a clinical examination (including body weight, body mass index, blood pressure, pulse, general physical conditions) and order, using clinical judgment, baseline laboratory tests such as urea and electrolytes and magnesium. Many facilities and healthcare staff will have their own local protocols of frequency of testing (e.g., how often electrolytes and which ones should be measured). Only if fully informed on their actual health can protesters make an informed decision on whether to embark on a hunger strike (Smeulers 1995).

Pressures on Hunger Strikers

Problems arising from a hunger strike situation can present in various ways. Harm by prolonged lack of nourishment may take time to develop. While medical monitoring is essential, both the prison physician and external monitor may have other useful roles to play during the initial days and weeks of fasting, such as discussing the situation calmly and in the privacy of the medical consultation, to see whether a compromise solution can be found. Experience has shown, however, that custodial authorities, refusing to accept any such protest fasting, try to impose certain measures to force fasting prisoners to relent. Such measures hamper any effort by the prison doctor to try to find a solution.

Some punitive measures may be relatively lenient such as suppression of visits and mail or access to leisure facilities (e.g., television). Other more severe punishments may be the placement of the/each hunger striker(s) in solitary confinement. In some cases, custodial authorities may order the medical staff to intervene and feed the protesting detainees by force. The authorities often justify this extreme measure as being issued to prevent any fatal outcome. This, however, may often be a mere pretext, particularly when force-feeding is ordered early on in the protest, when there is no medical need to intervene. Jacobs (2012) has undertaken a comprehensive review on legal precedents and judicial decisions to force-feed prisoners which highlights the difficulties for all practitioners in the field. Some recent medical studies are robust about sanctions that are required for healthcare professionals involved in force-feeding, recommending that organized medicine must appeal to civilian state oversight bodies and federal regulators of medical science to revoke the licenses of health professionals participating in such activities at Guantanamo Bay (Dougherty et al. 2013). Such ethical and legal implications have also been reviewed in other settings, for example, in detained asylum seekers in Australia (Kenny et al. 2004). Pressure from prison or other authorities (judicial, political) is not unexpected. Less expected to those unfamiliar with the situation are other sources of pressure (Figure 8.3) such as from prison guards observing the protest, from fellow inmates, and from the families of the fasting prisoners.

Prison physician and external monitor will need to determine what the pressures in their specific situation are and how they influence the commitment of the hunger striker(s). Talking to each hunger striker alone in the privacy of a medical consultation is paramount and physicians should never allow the custodial authority or other detainees to limit such contacts. A physician's duty is primarily to his/her patient, but in custodial settings, there will inevitably be conflicts and demands made, implicitly or explicitly, for the prison physician to do

Pressures on hunger strikers...

> Some determined hunger strikers may declare they will *not* back down unless their goal is attained. Individually or in groups, they may differ in their mode of fasting but share a common determination to put their health (or even lives) at risk for their "cause." Politically motivated hunger strikers often fall into this category. Unlike food refusers, who rely on medical staff to make sure they do not harm themselves, this category of prisoners often mistrust the prison doctor, whom they see as belonging to the "system"...

Pressures on the · *Hunger striker*

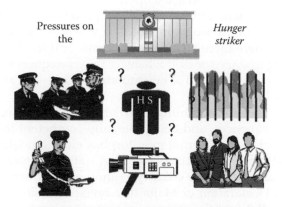

> Pressures may come from all sides, from inside the prison as well as from the outside. The above diagram illustrates pressures from (clockwise from the top) the governmental authorities; from fellow inmates; from families; from the media; from the prison guards; and last but not least from the prison management... prison doctors and nurses can also exert pressure, either in complicity with the prison management or for their own moral or religious reasons...

FIGURE 8.3 Pressures on the hunger striker. (From the author's personal slides from his course on hunger strikes.)

everything possible to support the administration by getting the protest to cease. The extent (if any) of such demands will depend on the country, context, and jurisdiction. While this goes against what should ethically be done, it is a reality that the external monitor has to be aware of and accept, as the prison physician may, for example, have been threatened with loss of job or harm to himself or family. The role of any external monitor, however, should be very clear—it is not to persuade the hunger striker one way or the other, but to see that there is fair play on all sides and appropriate management. The hunger striker's motive and intentions need to be established through frank dialogue, determining what his/her expectations are from the protest and what the outcome will be in the event that it does not work. External monitors must make it clear that they are there to act or advise, as the need may be, in the prisoner's best interests. Allowing the prisoner to make an informed choice, by explaining the situation and the consequences of total fasting, is legitimate and appropriate and, when handled properly, can help achieve an end to the protest in a majority of cases.

Prison authorities may justify interventionism arguing that suicide prevention must be a priority—and that prisoners do not have the right to commit suicide by starving themselves to death. This argument is fallacious. The cliché image of the prisoner starving himself to death is exactly that—a cliché; although in rare cases, a fatal outcome may end up being achieved. Any prisoner who truly wants to commit suicide will choose a less painful way of taking his or her life. Death by slow starvation is certainly not the aim of the hunger striker but only what a very determined prisoner may be able to accept, when all other avenues of protest are seen to be impossibly blocked.

Prisoners around the world go on hunger strikes to protest for many different issues, reasonable and unreasonable alike. The hunger striker wants to have pressure put on the authorities from the outside. This can only occur if the hunger strike becomes public knowledge and gets widespread outside coverage.

The majority of hunger strikers want to live, not die, (Reyes 1998) and to see their particular complaint or demand taken seriously and acted upon. A hunger strike uses a shaming approach, shaming the authorities who refuse to negotiate protest demands and let a prisoner die... However, this approach only works in a context where authorities can feel shame of some kind. In a context where there are no such notions, or if the hunger strike is not at all publicized, threatening to starve oneself whatever the consequences will have no effect whatsoever. Some hunger strikers need to be reminded of this—yet another role for the prison physician or external monitor.

In the very rare case of a truly determined hunger striker being intransigent about totally fasting, whatever the consequences, and being mentally competent to decide to do so, the attending prison physician (or external monitor) has clear guidelines to follow, as set down by the WMA (already in 1991). As has been stated, custodial settings and cultural values vary considerably from one country to another; the doctor will have some leeway, foreseen by WMA Declaration of Malta (the revised version in 2006), to adapt them to the circumstances, all the while acting in respect of basic ethical principles (Reyes et al. 2013b).

It is also necessary for prison physicians to know and understand the different clinical phases of total fasting.

It is essential, when following (prison doctor) or monitoring (external doctor) a hunger strike, to not just focus on weight charts and electrolyte balance, however important that may be in some cases. This is not to minimize the need to understand the physiology of total fasting, so as to follow and counsel hunger strikers adequately and professionally (Kalk et al. 1993; Peel 1997). The doctor knowledgeable about his/her holistic role must not only monitor medical parameters, but also take advantage of the time at hand to discuss with the detainee before any medical deterioration becomes a problem.

Where protesters appear to be fasting under duress, peer pressure for example, a solution may be to separate those individuals into the medical ward or hospital on a medical pretext, thereby extracting them from such negative influence. This may allow some of them to immediately resume nutritional intake on what they are free to call medical grounds, as they can legitimately say that they are "following the doctor's orders." External monitors may be in a better position than the prison physician to suggest such separation—and to counsel individuals on how best to find a way out.

Experience suggests that in the majority of cases of group hunger strikes, the cohesion and determination of the group is affected once the conditions and health deteriorate. These may be manifested by unpleasant symptoms such as the oculomotor phase, which begins at around 35 days of total fasting. The hunger striker needs to be informed in advance of the risks of these symptoms developing and when they might develop. These are nystagmus and ophthalmoplegia, due to vitamin B1 (thiamine) deficiency, this concept is discussed in the paragraphs below.

Well before approaching this phase, the prison physician should have seen each fasting prisoner individually. Any external monitor will obviously also do so, as soon as he/she is called to intervene. In extreme situations, where prisoners mistrust (as aforementioned, sometimes for good reason) the custodial authorities, separation of hunger strikers may be difficult to carry out, the prisoners themselves refusing to be separated. The physician (prison or external) should use negotiating skills to persuade the hunger strikers to accept, as far as possible, being placed in decent, relatively comfortable cells or hospital wards, for better follow-up. They should not be put in punishment cells, or in any other form of isolation or solitary confinement, which would clearly break any relationship of trust and could lead to a breakdown of any possible negotiation, as well as being ethically inappropriate.

If the physician presents a rational argument, many hunger strikers and prison authorities will accept the (alleged) reason of being better able to follow each case medically and examine each individual in private. Most hunger strikers will go along with the proposal, as long as isolation is not the result. Even hunger strikers who really want to show their determination to go all the way will also find a space for confiding in the prison doctor being in an individual setting. Experience shows that a favorable setting allows many hunger strikers to state in confidence that they in fact do not want to die and are willing to accept medical assistance. Voluntary nasogastric feeding is rarely warranted; most prisoners who accept an intravenous infusion very soon begin taking food again for medical reasons. Nasogastric feeding has acquired a very bad reputation since used forcibly at Guantanamo Bay (Crosby et al. 2007; Annas 2011; Chrispin and Nathanson 2013), although it is widely and appropriately used in routine medical practice.

The majority of hunger strikers, if the fasting becomes prolonged, desperately wants to find a way out of the confrontation. They will often stop fasting if they obtain some minor form of concession from the authorities. Both prison and external monitor physicians may be in the best position to negotiate some compromise between the two parties. When the demands of hunger strikers are very obviously out of reach, prison physicians must not fall into the trap of pretending otherwise or insinuating that a solution is achievable through mediation, if this obviously will not be the case. They should make clear that they are outside the actual negotiation (political or other) process. This does not mean that they cannot influence if an occasion to do so presents itself.

An example of this type of influence occurred during a hunger strike in Northern Ireland, some years after the 1981 hunger strike. An impasse had been reached—the hunger strikers told the prison doctor they had to obtain something before desisting; otherwise, they would lose face with their peers back in the general population. They decided to ask for Kentucky Fried Chicken (KFC) dinners for all the protestors. The doctor, knowing the prison administration would never agree to what would be seen as a whim, finally paid for the KFC dinners out of his own pocket, and the strike was thus resolved peacefully (personal communication to author by a prison doctor in Northern Ireland).

The physicians have a duty to respect the hunger strikers' right to medical confidentiality, as any maintenance of trust depends upon the prisoner knowing that he/she can trust the doctor (prison or monitor). This applies not only to medical matters but also to nonmedical information given to physicians by patients, although this duty may be modified by professional regulatory bodies in some countries (e.g., the United Kingdom) if there is risk of harm to others (Reyes 1997). For example, a physician interviewing a hunger striker might learn the names of the ringleaders of the protest, but he/she would lose all credibility with the hunger strikers and the other prisoners as well were he/she to disclose that information to the authorities. As in normal medical practice, unless there is a serious and credible threat to a third party being harmed, physicians should retain discretion on such issues—and resist pressures from the prison authorities to use the medical function to obtain such information. For prison physicians, this may be difficult, because of their issue of dual loyalties and conflicts of interest.

Clinical Stages of a Hunger Strike

Refusal to take nourishment leads to a clinical syndrome that resembles, but is not equivalent to, starvation. In the latter case, body depletion is a prolonged process, with little caloric intake, but still minimum absorption of vital elements such as vitamins, minerals, and (some) proteins. It is this intake that differentiates total fasting in a total hunger strike situation (with the ingestion of water only) from that of starvation, such as in concentration camps.

The 72/72 rule of thumb stated previously (see Figure 8.1) gives the starting and end benchmarks for a total—water-only—hunger strike. This being said, 72 hours may be considered by some as too generous for the attribution of hunger striker to a fasting prisoner. Some authors have extended that period to 14 days, defining hunger strikers as "those going for more than 14 days without food" (Arnold 2008). Objectively, in most cases, anyone initially in good health who stops eating for a week or 19 days (as long as he/she drinks some 2 L of water a day) will not have any grave consequences, so long as there are no contraindications to fasting. What should be understood by the physician is that these days should already be used to establish some rapport of trust with the protestor(s) and not merely to take the necessary baseline measurements and blood tests that have been mentioned.

It is important to identify a midpoint, a clinical stage—relatively easy to identify in total fasting, which is an alarm signal for what follows. This stage has been called the *oculomotor stage*, whereby acute lack of vitamins and thiamine in particular result in specific neurological complications resulting in altered function of the small motor muscles controlling eye movements with severe symptoms related to this paresis. It is best to summarize all the different clinical stages of total fasting (Figure 8.4).

The 72-day limit for a total, water-only hunger strike has been defined thus because it is a medically documented figure, established from the 1981 Northern Ireland hunger strikes. The fatal outcomes of total fasting were first documented during the 1980 and 1981 hunger strikes in Northern Ireland where death generally occurred between 55 and 75 days. Similar experiences have confirmed this wide time bracket. The 3-week interval is due to differences in initial physical constitution and individual adaptation (personal communication by a prison doctor involved in the 1981 hunger strikes in Northern Ireland). Hunger strikers, who do take some form of nourishment, with or without vitamin supplements, may live longer, in some cases up to 80–90 or even 100 days, but will still be in a very serious condition of malnutrition.

It is not possible to predict any time span more precisely as it may be dependent on many factors including prehunger strike body weight and other concurrent medical conditions. Protesters need to be made clearly aware that death can occur some (unpredictable) time after 6 full weeks of fasting. Survival after 10 weeks of total fasting is essentially impossible. The protestors also need to know that in the final clinical stages of fasting, they will no longer be capable of discernment and need to make clear in advance what they expect physicians to do for them then. This is explored by Oguz and Miles (2005) when considering

Clinical stages of a Total Hunger strike: The first weeks

The first week

- Fasting generally well supported, as long as water intake is sufficient
- Hunger pangs and stomach cramps disappear after the 2nd and 3rd days

after 15–18 days

- The hunger striker suffers from dizziness and "feels faint"...
- Ataxia : can be quite severe...
- Orthostatic hypotension
- "Lightheadedness" or inversely "mental sluggishness" can occur
- Sensation of "cold"...
- General sensation of overall weakness
- Fits of hiccoughs can occur
- Loss of sensation of thirst, leading to less water intake than the 2 litres minimum required !

—From Chapter 5, Lesson 3 of the WMA Internet course for prison doctors (www.wma.net)

(a)

Clinical stages of a Total Hunger strike: the benchmark "oculo-motor phase"

Between 35–42 days

- Troubles of ocular mobility due to progressive paralysis of the small motor muscles of the eye:
  - Uncontrollable nystagmus : constant sensation of getting off a carousel
  - Diplopia (prisoners report "seeing double")
  - Extremely unpleasant sensations of vertigo...
  - Incoercible vomiting: cannot keep water intake in...
  - Swallowing is also very difficult, if not impossible...
  - Converging strabismus (prisoners report being "cross-eyed")

This phase has been described by those who have actually survived "total fasting" as the most unpleasant one, and is in fact the phase "most dreaded" by potential hunger strikers...

One week *after* the "ocular" phase...

- Once paralysis of the oculo-motor muscles is quasi total, the nystagmus ceases and with it, all the associated problems (vertigo, vomiting...)

—From Chapter 5, Lesson 3 of the WMA Internet course for prison doctors (www.wma.net)

(b)

FIGURE 8.4 Clinical stages of total fasting: (a) the first weeks; (b) the oculomotor phase. *(Continued)*

Clinical stages of a Total Hunger strike: the final stages of Total fasting

From ≈ 42 days onward

- Progressive asthenia...
- Turpitude...
- Increasingly confused state of mind...
- Concentration becomes difficult or impossible...
- Somnolence...
- Anosognosia...
- Indifference to surroundings...
- Progressively incoherent...

At this stage, it becomes impossible to evaluate intellectual functions and to thereby determine what the hunger striker's state of mind is. Any decision made to ascertain what action is to be taken by the medical staff after this stage will have had to be made beforehand!

Further, even more serious complications follow soon after:
- Loss of hearing
- Partial or total blindness
- Diverse forms of haemorrhage: gingival, oesophageal, gastro-intestinal...
- The body "shuts down" progressively: extreme bradycardia; Cheyne-Stokes respiration; all metabolic activity diminishes...

Between 45~72 days...

- Death occurs from cardio-vascular collapses and/or severe arythmias...

—From Chapter 5, Lesson 3 of the WMA Internet course for prison doctors (www.wma.net)

(c)

FIGURE 8.4 (CONTINUED)   Clinical stages of total fasting: (c) the final stages of total fasting. (From Norwegian Medical Association, https://nettkurs.legeforeningen.no/enrol/index.php?id=39, accessed May 10, 2017.)

the Turkish hunger strikers of the 1990s, dozens of whom died from nontotal fasting, after months of what became in fact a situation of chronic starvation (Basoglu et al. 2006).

Physicians should use this available time to discuss with patients any flaws or lack of logic in their expressed wishes without exercising undue pressure. Experience shows that particularly in highly political hunger strikes, decision-making is far from simple. There may be situations where physicians need to challenge the patient rather than accept that person's views at face value (WMJ 2006; case example 1). It is here that trust and confidentiality become of paramount importance. There are cases in which physicians, confronted with an apparently fanatical hunger striker, can use their position of trust and medical authority to gain the protestor's confidence and bring the protestor to reason.

Sometimes, nontotal fasting (meaning taking nourishment on the sly) is considered by the authorities as cheating and an unacceptable form of hunger strike. This can lead to controversy about the seriousness of the protest. The prison doctor can explain when useful that prolongation of the period for potential negotiation can often be beneficial to the final outcome and helps avoid deaths. Thus the so-called cheating may actually work in favor of a positive outcome.

Prison physicians and external monitors must be very wary about not assigning fasting prisoners into such categories of serious and not-so-serious (i.e., cheating) categories. The differences that have been spelled out here between the types of fasting should clarify the reality of different situations, separating those that will imply ethical dilemmas from those that do not. As far as the prisoners themselves are concerned, all of them, even food refusers, may consider themselves as true hunger strikers. It is not for the physician to get embroiled in this kind of debate, as to do so will do nothing toward building up a relationship of trust between them and the prisoners (Reyes et al. 2013c). Prison physicians will generally have a good idea which fasting prisoners may really pose a medical problem; outside monitors need to assess the situation and not let themselves be manipulated.

This defining of categories, serious and not-serious, is, however, time and again demanded from the prison physician by the authorities, or by the media—as, for example, when one or the other of these entities wants to discredit or raise the profile of the hunger strikers for whatever reason. Any external monitors should not allow themselves to be made to challenge the motives of the nontotal hunger strikers on the quality of their protest fasting, whatever the position of the local prison physician is on this issue. Nontotal or partial fasting for a lengthy period can be a different form of protest and, by providing more time to find a face-saving solution for all, can be instrumental in reducing the risk of fatal outcomes.

There have been reports of prison physicians giving inaccurate or inappropriate clinical advice, for example, by threatening hunger strikers that medical sequelae of hunger strikes can include effects such as impotence, in order to make them stop their protest (personal communication with head of Prison Medical Service in the Middle East). Whether this was done to please, or to comply with, the prison hierarchy, or whether it was done out of genuine desire to have them stop the fast, is irrelevant. Physicians should never provide inappropriate or wrong or fabricated medical information. Professional credibility must be maintained at all times; otherwise, the credibility and influence will be lost with the hunger strikers.

In cases where the prison physician does not have, and cannot obtain, the trust of the hunger strikers, alternative solutions must be sought. This can be the role for an external monitor, perceived by all parties to be impartial, but only if he/she can stay on long enough to gain trust and to assess the ongoing situation. Access to a doctor who can offer such impartial, independent, and expert counseling is absolutely essential (Lancet 2008).

Medicalization of the Hunger Strike

Medicalization in this context refers to the transformation of a management issue into a medical problem by a nonmedical authority. This authority may be the custodial one, the prison governor, or the prison service. It may in some cases be a political one, by the governmental authorities of the country.

Medicalization could be considered a noncoercive way of providing a solution to a controversial situation by imposing a medical solution implemented by or carried out by prison medical staff. A prisoner in good physical condition when he/she began (total) fasting can survive without significant long-term danger to his/her health for some 3 or 4 weeks, if he/she has adequate water intake (2 L per day).

To summarize what has been said on this point, this can provide a window of opportunity in which a solution can be peacefully sought, if there is goodwill and trust prevailing between the hunger strikers and the physician. After the 72 initial hours of total fasting, it is not particularly useful to systematically launch a battery of controls and tests unless there is a specific indication for them. This can be done when commencing the second week, if the fasting persists and unless there are medical indications to undertake tests earlier. Dialogue and careful, individual clinical observation are much more important to determine the likely outcome of the hunger strike and the potential for future medical and ethical dilemmas.

Frequently, however, nonmedical authorities try to impose some sort of medical intervention—often force-feeding—to stop the protest at a very early stage, often the second or third week (Rubenstein and Annas 2009), and the question is raised as to why this is done, when there is no immediate danger of any fatal outcome. The explanation is often that lives have to be saved. In cases where an external monitor advises that nobody is going to die after 2 weeks of fasting, the explanation by the authorities is often that force-feeding is performed to prevent health problems, or "preserve health." Generally speaking, any normal adult initially in good health will not die from fasting before a month, or even the sixth week of fasting (Beresford 1997). The imposing of a medical solution (force-feeding) to end the protest might be interpreted as an outward means of the authorities merely attempting to appear beneficent (Wolff and Gétaz 2012a,b).

Protest fasting also creates a situation which is intolerable to many custodial or judicial authorities, who consider a hunger striker as blackmailing the system, which is the real reason they may attempt to impose the force-feeding of the prisoners onto the medical staff. Such orders would oblige the prison doctor to flout recognized guidelines of medical ethics issued by the WMA, which forbid it in any situation (WMA Declaration of Malta, article 13 [2006]).

When such medicalization occurs, two outcomes are possible. In the first case, the authority orders the prison physician to force-feed the hunger strikers. If this happens, any external monitor should remind the prison physician of his or her medical and ethical duties and inform the prison authorities to this effect. In the second case, the prison doctor abides by the ethical and clinical approaches discussed in this chapter and refuses to intervene, with then the support of any external monitor (Figure 8.5).

In some cases, the prison physician could protest against unethical orders from above—but chooses not to. This may be for a variety of reasons. Some, as already referred to, will have religious beliefs that make them feel they have to intervene. For whatever reason, physicians who comply with orders to force-feed hunger strikers are breaching Article 5 of the WMA Declaration of Malta (2006). Religious reasons do not constitute a legitimate reason for acting unethically, as personal objections by physicians are taken into the account by the 2006 declaration, who then should find another physician to take over care of the hunger strikers.

More often, prison doctors may be unwilling to comply with unethical orders, but need support from outside. In such a situation, the role and support of an external monitor can be paramount, as it may ensure that the authorities revise their decision or at least rescind the order.

In a recent high tribunal at an international court, the judge had decided to impose force-feeding on a hunger striker in their charge. The prison physician refused to do so, for ethical reasons and because there was no medical reason to intervene. The hunger striker had lost more than 12 kg—from an initial weight of over 100 kg. If the case had not been highly politicized, there would have been no cause for any intervention at this stage. The judge, however, apparently upset by the stance of the prisoner, wanted to impose medical action—in this case, force-feeding.

Medicalization of the controversy: Physicians complying with orders vs. physicians refusing unethical orders…

First case: Second case:

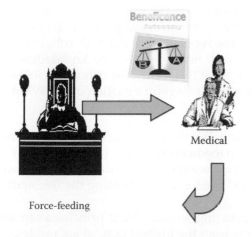

The authorities may issue a decree, or otherwise "oblige," prison doctors to force-feed a hunger striking prisoner. In most cases, this will not be motivated by "medical necessity" but to make the prisoner comply with prison rules. The reason given will often be an interpretation of the principle of "beneficence"—assistance to a person in danger. Some doctors, for personal or religious reasons, or if military doctors, following orders, will comply with this ruling, going against the guidelines given by the World Medical Association as stated in the 2006 WMA Declaration of Malta on Hunger strikes.

(a)

The authority may issue a decree or otherwise "oblige" prison doctors to force-feed a hunger striking prisoner, and have this order *refused* by the prison doctors, who evoke the principles of medical ethics as stated in WMA Malta 2006. The principle overruling the principle of "beneficence" is that of "autonomy" of the patient. Any competent adult has the right to refuse any treatment as long as s/he has been duly informed of, and has understood, the consequences of such a refusal. This applies to any form of feeding as well.

(b)

FIGURE 8.5 Medicalization: (a) Physicians accepting orders to force-feed and (b) physicians refusing orders to force-feed. (From the author's personal slides from his course on hunger strikes.)

The author of this chapter provided the following opinion in this case:

1. The high tribunal (this was in Europe) was a high profile court—How would it look if such a tribunal gave an order to force-feed and this was reported by the media? What example would that give to the hundreds of smaller tribunals worldwide, in countries where human rights may be less respected, or absent? For this high tribunal to order force-feeding, an act which the WMA Declaration of Malta clearly states is "never justified" and which constitutes a form of "inhuman and degrading treatment," would be a definitely bad example to give to countries where medical ethics are less known or, worse, already ignored.

2. The prison physician in this specific context was aware of his ethical responsibilities and would refuse to force-feed if so ordered—and if necessary, he could appeal to his national medical association for support—which he would get. If necessary, he could then appeal to the WMA, and would receive support from that instance as this concerned implementation of the WMA Declaration of Malta (2006). The question was put as "how would the high tribunal look quarrelling

over an indefensible point of view of medical ethics, with the highest of medical authorities?"

3. The judge in this instance at one point had suggested he could get doctors from [an Eastern European country] to comply with the orders to force-feed, implying that these doctors would be less "intransigent." Such an order, given by the judge, would certainly have an adverse effect on the reputation of the high tribunal. It could not be justified to call upon doctors with no respect—or no knowledge— of medical ethical principles, to implement what the WMA has defined as inhuman and degrading treatment by force-feeding, a flagrant violation of the WMA Declaration of Malta.

The judge did not respond directly to these points, but the following day, issued a directive that "the prison doctor would act according to medical necessity" (of which there was none in this case) and "the prison medical service would henceforth refer to acknowledged medical guidelines as issued by the WMA" (hence acknowledging the Declaration of Malta indirectly).

This example is given here to show that supporting sound ethical principles can and should always be done—and can produce results from the highest judicial authorities.

Resolving Hunger Strikes and the Refeeding Phase

The resolution of hunger strikes is mainly a question of competent negotiation, patience, ability to listen, and ability to communicate. The prison doctor is the one best placed to play this role. In some cultures, the chaplain or other religious representative may also possibly play a role—but without the essential component of medical counselor.

It is important that risks of refeeding syndrome in those who are malnourished after many weeks of total fasting taking only water is recognized. These risks may be present in some cases after only 7–10 days of fasting (Crook et al. 2001; Miller 2008). While the main principle of nutrients being given slowly and progressively is certainly true, if the hunger striker was in good health and not nutritionally deficient to begin with, such complications are rare. Severe electrolyte and fluid shifts associated with metabolic abnormalities mainly occur in chronically malnourished individuals. The major electrolyte problem in the refeeding syndrome is hypophosphatemia. Increasing levels of insulin during refeeding stimulate cellular uptake of minerals such as phosphorus, magnesium, and potassium, leading to low plasma levels. This may have negative consequences on metabolism and on the well-functioning of leukocytes and platelets (Mehanna et al. 2008, 2009). Of all the vitamins the human organism deprives itself by total fasting, it is by far lack of thiamine which is most dangerous. A total fast pursued to the final demise of the hunger striker leads to death by acute thiamine depletion and its effects on cardiac (mal)function (Gétaz et al. 2012).

Thiamine depletion can be considerably worsened by the administration of carbohydrate without administering vitamin B1 at the same time—and preferably even before giving any sugars. Lack of thiamine through total fasting has been found to cause a form of Wernicke encephalopathy (Kopelman et al. 2009), and glucose metabolism certainly plays a role, although the precise mechanism is as yet unclear, hence, the need to administer thiamine before carbohydrate infusions are started.

The few studies carried out on long-term hunger strikers retaking nourishment have shown that if the premise of "good initial health" is respected, even a prolonged strike of 2 months would seem to be insufficient for severe tissue damage or metabolic consequences (Faintuch et al. 2001). The refeeding syndrome was found to be in most cases associated to chronically nutritionally depleted individuals. This should of course be fully taken into account when confronted with hunger strikers who have been on repeated fasting for long periods.

The most serious and most frequent intolerance to enteral refeeding has been found to be diarrhea, due to bowel atrophy associated with the prolonged fasting.

An external monitoring physician should always ensure that whatever prison or outside hospital is in charge of the hunger strikers has personnel with experience and knowledge in refeeding those who have been fasting. Many countries have multiprofessional nutrition support teams in their hospitals—and wherever possible, it is recommended to seek advice from such teams where available.

The Hunger Striker Intent on a Fatal Outcome

Since the 1981 hunger strike in Northern Ireland, during which 10 Irish prisoners died on what was to be an open-ended total fasting-type strike, there have been very few fatal hunger strike cases. The Turkish hunger strikes in the 1990s were not total—which did not make them any less fatal, as many more prisoners died than in Ulster—but were in a different scenario. During the hunger strikes in Turkey, there was the additional complication of family members of prisoners fasting as well outside the prison (Oguz and Miles 2005; Kirbas et al. 2008).

In the case of Northern Ireland (Beresford 1997; Walker 2006), medicalization was never an issue. The U.K. government fully respected the principle of autonomy, and force-feeding was never considered. One of the senior physicians informed the author that any such action would have been "considered as an assault on their person." This stance was in 1981, a full 10 years before the WMA 1991 Declaration of Malta on hunger strikes, which makes the attitude of the British physicians all the more commendable in their recognition of their duties and respect for medical ethics.

In more recent times, other countries have implemented force-feeding. Guantanamo Bay is a case in point, as the actions there triggered the full revision of the WMA Declaration of Malta into the current 2006 version (Okie 2005). The current declaration states within its principles (WMA 2006; Reyes 2007)

> Article 2: Respect for autonomy. Physicians should respect individuals' autonomy. This can involve difficult assessments, as hunger strikers' true wishes may not be as clear as they appear. Any decisions lack moral force if made involuntarily by use of threats, peer pressure or coercion. Hunger strikers should not be forcibly given treatment they refuse. Forced feeding contrary to an informed and voluntary refusal is unjustifiable. Artificial feeding with the hunger striker's explicit or implied consent is ethically acceptable.
>
> Article 3: "Benefit" and "harm". Physicians must exercise their skills and knowledge to benefit those they treat. This is the concept of "beneficence", which is complemented by that of "non-maleficence" or primum non nocere ("first do no evil"). These two concepts need to be in balance. "Benefit" includes respecting individuals' wishes as well as promoting their welfare. Avoiding "harm" means not only minimising damage to

health but also not forcing treatment upon competent people nor coercing them to stop fasting. Beneficence does not necessarily involve prolonging life at all costs, irrespective of other values.

Article 5: Clinical independence. Physicians must remain objective in their assessments and not allow third parties to influence their medical judgement. They must not allow themselves to be pressured to breach ethical principles, such as intervening medically for non-clinical reasons.

And guidelines from the same Declaration state

Article 6: Physicians need to satisfy themselves that food or treatment refusal is the individual's voluntary choice. Hunger strikers should be protected from coercion. Physicians can often help to achieve this and should be aware that coercion may come from the peer group, the authorities or others, such as family members. Physicians or other health care personnel may not apply undue pressure of any sort on the hunger striker to suspend the strike. Treatment or care of the hunger striker must not be conditional upon suspension of the hunger strike.

Article 11: Physicians may consider it justifiable to go against advance instructions refusing treatment because, for example, the refusal is thought to have been made under duress. If, after resuscitation and having regained their mental faculties, hunger strikers continue to reiterate their intention to fast, that decision should be respected. It is ethical to allow a determined hunger striker to die in dignity rather than submit that person to repeated interventions against his or her will.

Article 12: Artificial feeding can be ethically appropriate if competent hunger strikers agree to it. It can also be acceptable if incompetent individuals have left no unpressured advance instructions refusing it.

Article 13: Forcible feeding is never ethically acceptable. Even if intended to benefit, feeding accompanied by threats, coercion, force or use of physical restraints is a form of inhuman and degrading treatment. Equally unacceptable is the forced feeding of some detainees in order to intimidate or coerce other hunger strikers to stop fasting.

It should thus be clear that force-feeding is never acceptable and that the reasons given by authorities for doing so is often an excuse for breaking the strike and intimidating other prisoners into not starting a new one. Physicians who comply with orders to force-feed are committing a serious breach of medical ethics, thus participating in what the WMA has deemed "inhuman and degrading treatment."

Conclusions

The management of hunger strikes is a difficult issue. It is important that those responsible for the healthcare of prisoners understand that motivations for hunger strikes or food refusal may vary and require different approaches. Prison physicians most often find themselves caught in dilemmas, often in conflict between detainees and prison authorities who have widely varying agendas. Sometimes, a range of external authorities or bodies may attempt to influence medical management. Physicians must be aware that nonmedical bodies should not be giving medical orders in the first place and may need to be made aware of the medical ethical position.

The prison physician and the external monitoring physicians have clear roles in establishing the aims of the hunger striker or food refusers. Medical management needs to take into account the individuals' clinical condition, the need for regular monitoring to establish the effects of absence or reduction of nutrients, and the need for expertise when refeeding patients who have been on prolonged hunger strike. Those who continue their hunger strike until a fatal outcome ensues are particularly complex, and those responsible for their care need to be aware of their professional and ethical duties with regard to issues such as force-feeding.

References

Annas, G. J. 2011, American vertigo: "Dual use," prison physicians, research and Guantanamo, *Case Western Reserve Journal of International Law*, vol. 43, pp. 631–650.

Arnold, F. 2008, Practical notes on hunger strikes. *The Lancet*, vol. 372, p. 1544.

Başoğlu, M., Yetimalar, Y. B., Gürgör, N. et al. 2006, Neurological complications of prolonged hunger strike, *European Journal of Neurology*, vol. 13, pp. 1089–1097.

Beresford, D. 1987, *Ten men dead: Story of the 1981 Irish hunger strike*, Harper Collins, New York City.

Beresford, D. 1997, *Ten men dead*, Grove Atlantic, New York City.

Chrispin, E., and Nathanson, V. 2013, Force feeding of mentally competent detainees at Guantánamo Bay, *British Medical Journal*, vol. 347, p. 4454.

Crook, M. A., Hally, V., and Pantelli, J. V. 2001, The importance of the refeeding syndrome, *Nutrition*, vol. 17, pp. 632–637.

Crosby, S. S., Apovian, C. M., Grodin, M. A. et al. 2007, Hunger strikes, force-feeding and physicians' responsibilities, *Journal of the American Medical Association*, vol. 298, pp. 563–566.

Dougherty, S. M., Leaning, J., Greenough, P. G., and Burkle, F. M. Jr. 2013, Hunger strikers: Ethical and legal dimensions of medical complicity in torture at Guantanamo Bay, *Prehospital and Disaster Medicine*, vol. 28, pp. 616–624.

Faintuch, J., Soriano, F. G., Ladeira, J. P. et al. 2001, Refeeding procedures after 43 days of total fasting, *Nutrition*, vol. 17, pp. 100–104.

Fayeulle, S., Renou, F., Protais, E. et al. 2010, Prise en charge médicale de la grève de la faim en milieu carcéral [Management of a hunger strike in custody], *La Presse Médicale*, vol. 39, pp. 217–222.

Gétaz, L., Rieder, J. P., Nyffenegger, L. et al. 2012, Hunger strike among detainees: Guidance for good medical practice. *Swiss Medical Weekly*, vol. 142, p. w13675.

Jacobs, P. 2012, *Force-Feeding of Prisoners and Detainees on Hunger Strike: Right to Self-Determination Versus Right to Intervention*, Intersentia, Cambridge.

Kalk, W. J. , Felix, N., Snoey, E. R. et al. 1993, Voluntary total fasting in political prisoners—Clinical and biochemical observations, *South African Medical Journal*, vol. 83.

Kenny, M. A., Silove, D. M., and Steel, Z. 2004, Legal and ethical implications of medically enforced feeding of detained asylum seekers on hunger strike, *Medical Journal of Australia*, vol. 180, pp. 237–240.

Kirbas, D., Sutlas, N., Kuscu, D. Y. et al. 2008, The impact of prolonged hunger strike: Clinical and laboratory aspects of twenty-five hunger strikers, *Ideggyogy Sz*, vol. 61, pp. 317–324.

Kopelman, M., Thomson, A. D., Guerrini, I. et al. 2009, The Korsakoff syndrome: Clinical aspects, psychology and treatment, *Alcohol and Alcoholism*, vol. 44. pp. 148–154.

Lancet Editorial 2008, Clinical care of hunger strikers, *The Lancet*, vol. 372, p. 777.

Mehanna, H. M., Moledina, J., Travis, J. et al. 2008, Re-feeding syndrome: What it is, and how to prevent and treat it, *British Medical Journal*, vol. 28, pp. 1495–1498.

Mehanna, H. M., Nankivell, P. C., Moledina, J. et al. 2009, Re-feeding syndrome—Awareness, prevention and management, *Head and Neck Oncology*, vol. 1, p. 4.

Miller, S. J. 2008, Death resulting from overzealous total parenteral nutrition: The refeeding syndrome revisited, *Nutrition in Clinical Practice*, vol. 23, pp. 166–171.

Oguz, N. Y., and Miles, S. H. 2005, The physician and prison hunger strikes: Reflecting on the experience in Turkey, *Journal of Medical Ethics*, vol. 31, pp. 169–172.

Okie, S. 2005, Glimpses of Guantánamo—Medical ethics and the war on terror. *New England Journal of Medicine*, vol. 353, pp. 2529–2534.

Peel, M. 1997, Hunger strikes: Understanding the underlying physiology will help doctors provide proper advice, *British Medical Journal*, vol. 315, pp. 829–830.

Reyes, H. 1997, Medical neutrality: Confidentiality subject to national law: Should doctors always comply? *Medische Neutraliteit*, vol. 45, pp. 1456–1459.

Reyes, H. 1998, Medical and ethical aspects of hunger strikes in custody and the issue of torture, in M. Oehmichen, (ed.), *Maltreatment and torture*, Research in Legal Medicine/Rechtsmedizinische Forschungsergebnisse, vol .19, Verlag Schmidt-Römhild, Lübeck.

Reyes, H. 2007, Force-feeding and coercion: No physician complicity, *American Medical Association Journal of Ethics*, vol. 9, pp. 703–708.

Reyes, H., Allen, S., and Annas G. 2013a. Physicians and hunger strikes in prison: Manipulation, medicalization and medical ethics. *World Medical Journal*, vol. 59(1), February, pp. 27–36.

Reyes, H., Allen, S., and Annas, G. 2013b. Physicians and hunger strikes in prison: Manipulation, medicalization and medical ethics. *World Medical Journal*, vol. 59(2), April, pp. 60–67.

Reyes, H., Allen, S., and Annas, G. 2013c. Physicians and hunger strikes in prison: Manipulation, medicalization and medical ethics. *World Medical Journal*, vol. 59(3), June, pp. 97–101.

Rubenstein, L. S., and Annas, G. J. 2009, Medical ethics at Guantánamo Bay detention center and in the US military: A time for reform, *The Lancet*, vol. 374, pp. 353–355.

Smeulers, J. 1995, Medical background of hunger strikers, in *Assistance in hunger strikes: A manual for physicians and other health personnel dealing with hunger strikers*, Johannes Wier Foundation for Health and Human Rights, Amersfoort.

Walker, R. K. 2006, *The hunger strikes*, Lagan Books, Belfast.

WMA (World Medical Association) Declaration of Malta 2006. Available from: http://www.wma.net/en/30publications/10policies/h31/index.html.

WMA (World Medical Association) Declaration of Malta on Hunger Strikers 1991; revised 2006. Available from: https://www.wma.net/policy/current-policies/.

WMA Internet course *op cit*, at www.wma.net, Chapter 5, lessons 1–4 and https://nettkurs.legeforeningen.no/enrol/index.php?id=39.

WMJ (World Medical Journal), Reyes, H, and Sommerville, A, (unattributed) 2006, World Medical Association Declaration of Malta: A background paper on the ethical management of hunger strikes, *World Medical Journal*, vol. 52, pp. 36–43.

Wolff, H., and Gétaz, L. 2012a, Grève de la faim en détention: Prise en charge et enjeux éthiques, *Forum Médical Suisse*, vol. 12, pp. 477–479.

Wolff, H., and Gétaz., L. 2012b, Grève de la faim et alimentation forcée: Enjeux thérapeutiques et éthiques, *Revue Médicale Suisse*, vol. 8, pp. 182–183.

9

Legal Aspects of Detention in Military Detention*

Peter Glenser and Kirsty Sutherland

CONTENTS

Introduction

General Principles of the Law of Armed Conflict

This chapter will explore the legal instruments and military procedure regarding detention of combatants and civilians in a conflict zone, using examples from the United Kingdom (UK).

Captured persons is the generic term given to all individuals captured and held by the UK Armed Forces on overseas operations, whether prisoners of war, internees, or detainees (MOD [Ministry of Defence] 2015, para. 103). The UK MOD states that an individual

---

* Review of legal instruments and military procedure regarding the detention of combatants and civilians in a conflict zone.

becomes a captured person "at the point of capture or when a member of the UK Armed Forces deprives the individual of his liberty on transfer to UK Armed Forces by another State or non-State actor" (MOD 2015, para. 103). The MOD draws a distinction between deprivation of liberty, deprivation of movement, and restriction of liberty. Deprivation of liberty involves the exercise of physical control over an individual (MOD 2015, para. 103).

The capture of combatants is practically beneficial in that it reduces the enemy party's numerical strength and capacity and may constrain enemy tactics. The MOD also notes that captured persons may be an important source of intelligence and states that "the exploitation [of captured persons] is a legitimate military activity" (MOD 2015, para. 104).

The UK Armed Forces are bound by customary international law, treaties to which the UK is party, and UK domestic law.

International humanitarian law is defined by the MOD as "those treaties, conventions, rules, regulations and customary international law that govern the conduct of hostilities during an armed conflict and/or during a military occupation" (MOD 2015, para. 113). It aims to limit the adverse humanitarian effects of armed conflict by protecting persons who are not, or no longer, participating in hostilities and restricting the means and methods of warfare. It is binding on all parties to a conflict, whether states, nonstate armed groups, organizations, or individuals.

In addition, and in circumstances where international humanitarian law does not apply, captured persons also have rights under international human rights treaties such as the International Covenant on Civil and Political Rights, the United Nations Convention against Torture and Other Cruel, Inhuman or Degrading Treatment or Punishment (CAT), and the European Convention on Human Rights (ECHR).

International humanitarian law is applicable only during armed conflicts that cross a threshold of intensity. Human rights law, on the other hand, is generally applicable at all times. Derogations from certain provisions of international human rights law are permissible under certain conditions, such as under a de jure and de facto state of emergency, or where derogable human rights are in conflict with each other. Nonderogable human rights include the right against torture and the right to a fair trial; these cannot be violated at any time.

The normative frameworks of international humanitarian law and human rights are diametrically opposed in how they confer rights as well as obligations. International humanitarian law seeks to regulate the conduct of individuals as well as states, while human rights law imposes obligations on states.

International human rights law is applicable during all armed conflicts, whether international or non-international (ICJ [International Court of Justice] 2004a, para. 11). The ICJ has further affirmed that "international human rights instruments are applicable 'in respect of acts done by a State in the exercise of its jurisdiction outside its own territory', particularly in occupied territories" (ICJ 2005, para. 216).

The extraterritorial application of human rights obligations hinges on "effective control" (UNHRC [United Nations Human Rights Council] 2004, para. 10; ECHR 1996, para. 62; ECtHR [European Court of Human Rights] 2011a,b). Effective control can be exercised over persons, even if this control is merely temporary. Clearly, this covers situations where UK Armed Forces are performing arrests and/or detaining people (ECtHR 2011a,b).

In *Legal Consequences of the Construction of a Wall in the Occupied Palestinian Territory* (ICJ 2004b, para. 106), the ICJ has described the relationship between international humanitarian law and human rights law thus

> As regards the relationship between international humanitarian law and human rights law, there are thus three possible solutions: some rights may be exclusively matters of

international humanitarian law; others may be exclusively matters of human rights law; yet others may be matters of both these branches of international law, namely human rights law and, as *lex specialis*, international humanitarian law.

Under this *lex specialis* approach, in the event of any conflict between the two legal frameworks, international humanitarian law should prevail in situations of armed conflict. In *General Comment 31*, on the other hand, the UNHRC (2004) states

> While in respect of certain [ICCPR] rights, more specific rules of international humanitarian law may be specially relevant for the purposes of the interpretation of [ICCPR] rights, both spheres of law are complementary, not mutually exclusive.

Under this complementary approach, whichever legal framework is more advanced and detailed should be considered authoritative.

In order to properly avoid breaching its legal obligations, the UK Armed Forces must adhere to the very highest standards available to them at all times. Aside from the ethical responsibilities concomitant with international military intervention, the practical benefits of maintaining the highest attainable conduct include the potential reduction of inciting retributive action.

Some of the standards of detention articulated in the following are contained in treaties to which the UK is party. These legally bind the UK Armed Forces. Other standards are contained in "soft law" instruments such as declarations, resolutions, or principles. While not strictly binding, such standards are, having been negotiated by states and/or adopted by international political bodies, persuasive.

International humanitarian law must be adhered to at all times during armed conflicts. Unlike international human rights law, international humanitarian law confers individual criminal responsibility upon those who violate its provisions. Thus, individuals who intentionally or recklessly commit or attempt to commit serious violations of international humanitarian law are responsible for war crimes. Military commanders and civilian leaders may also bear personal responsibility under command responsibility if they knew or should have known about the commission of war crimes, but failed to prevent or punish them. Where war crimes are committed as part of a widespread or systematic attack against a civilian population, these may constitute crimes against humanity (see, for example, Rome Statute, Article 7).

Applicable Law

The legal basis for a military operation could be individual or collective state self-defense, UN Security Council Resolution, or humanitarian intervention or at the invitation or consent of the host state. Due attention should be paid to any specific legal provisions pertaining to a particular situation.

The Geneva Conventions (GC) of 1949 and their Additional Protocols (AP) of 1977 constitute the core of international humanitarian law. They seek to protect persons who are not, or no longer, taking part in hostilities. The GC are considered to have attained the status of customary international law and are therefore universally binding. The UK is party to all three additional protocols and is thus bound by these.

All Armed Conflicts

Common Article 3 to the Geneva Conventions of 1949

Common Article 3 to the GC of 1949 sets out the very minimum standards of treatment to be afforded to all persons not, or no longer, taking part in hostilities. Such persons must be treated humanely in all circumstances. The Article absolutely prohibits the following:

- Violence to life and person, in particular murder of all kinds, mutilation, cruel treatment, and torture
- Taking of hostages
- Outrages upon personal dignity, in particular humiliating and degrading treatment
- The passing of sentences and the carrying out of executions without previous judgment pronounced by a regularly constituted court, affording all the judicial guarantees which are recognized as indispensible by civilized peoples (GC Common Article 3(1)).

Convention against Torture

The prohibition of torture or CIDT is absolute (see, for example, GC Common Article 3, AP I, AP II, UN CAT, Rome Statute, ICCPR, ECHR). There are no circumstances whatsoever that can justify the use of such treatment (UN CAT, Article 2(2)). The prohibition of torture is considered jus cogens, meaning that it cannot be contradicted by treaty law or by any other rule of international law. It holds nonderogable status in international human rights law (see, for example, ECHR, Article 3).

Article 1(1) of the UN CAT articulates an internationally agreed definition of *torture*:

> [T]orture means any act by which severe pain or suffering, whether physical or mental, is inflicted on a person for such purposes as obtaining from him or a third person information or a confession, punishing him for an act he or a third person has committed or is suspected of having committed, or intimidating or coercing him or a third person, or for any reason based on discrimination of any kind, when such pain or suffering is inflicted by or at the instigation of or with the consent or acquiescence of a public official or other person acting in an official capacity. It does not include pain or suffering arising only from, inherent in or incidental to lawful sanctions.

Although the distinction between torture and other forms of CIDT may be blurred, ill-treatment must additionally be for a specific purpose to constitute torture.

An order from a superior officer or a state authority cannot be invoked as a justification for torture (UN CAT, Article 2(3)). Any order to inflict torture or CIDT is null and void. Interrogation rules, instructions, methods and practices, and arrangement for the custody and treatment of detainees must be kept under systematic review (UN CAT, Article 11).

The right of an individual to be protected against torture and other forms of ill-treatment extends to the right not to be returned or transferred to a country where there are substantial grounds to believe that he or she might be subjected to such treatment (UN CAT, Article 3).

States party to the CAT are obliged either to prosecute or extradite for prosecution elsewhere any person suspected of torture found in their territory (UN CAT, Article 5). The

UK is therefore obliged to try those suspected of administering, or being complicit in the administration of, torture, or CIDT (UN CAT, Article 4). Since the prohibition on torture is considered to be jus cogens, even those states not party to the CAT may similarly exercise universal jurisdiction over torture.

In addition to the clear moral and legal obligation to refrain from mistreating captured persons, such treatment may well be counterproductive. The MOD states that

> Cruel, inhuman or degrading treatment, as well as being unlawful, will further con-
> vince the [captured persons] of the justice of their cause and reinforce their view that
> the UK Armed Forces fail to comply with [International Humanitarian Law]. Humane
> treatment, however, will assist in challenging any misconceptions. It may undermine
> their negative beliefs, and may cause them to re-assess their view of the overall situa-
> tion, and thus the UK's legitimacy. It will ensure the greatest possibility of successful
> intelligence exploitation and in some cases the complete rejection of the [captured per-
> sons'] previous beliefs and convictions. (MOD 2015, para. 210)

European Convention on Human Rights

The European Convention on Human Rights applies in situations in which UK officials exercise "control and authority" over foreign nationals (ECtHR 2011a). Articles 3 (the right not to be subjected to torture or inhumane or degrading treatment), 5 (the right to liberty), and 6 (the right to a fair trial) are of particular importance (ECtHR 2011b).

International Armed Conflicts

Geneva Conventions

Geneva Convention III applies to prisoners of war.

Geneva Convention IV affords protection to civilians, including those in occupied territory. It contains a specific regime for the treatment of civilian internees.

Additional Protocol I bolsters the protection to be afforded to victims of international armed conflicts.

Non-International Armed Conflicts

Additional Protocol II

Additional Protocol II governs the protection to be afforded to victims of noninternational conflicts.

Copenhagen Principles

The Copenhagen Process Principles and Guidelines were born of recent concern regarding insufficiencies of international humanitarian law in protecting detainees in international military operations in the context of non-international armed conflicts and peacekeeping operations. As UK guidelines demand a higher standard of treatment than that articulated in the Copenhagen Guidelines, the existence of these is perhaps useful merely as an indication of the need for international humanitarian law to be updated to meet the require-
ments of modern conflict.

The transfer of persons between states has emerged as one of the defining features of recent armed conflicts particularly in situations where multinational forces transfer persons to a host state, their country of origin, or a third state. Captured persons are extremely vulnerable to abuse during transfer between countries. The European Court of Human Rights has held European states responsible for torture and inhumane and degrading treatment contrary to Article 3 of the European Convention on Human Rights for their involvement in the United States' extraordinary rendition program (see, for example, *El-Masri v. The former Yugoslav Republic of Macedonia* 2012). The UK is prohibited from transferring persons in its charge to situations in which there is a real danger that they may be subject to serious ill-treatment (UN CAT, Article 3).

Categories of Conflict

The governing law applicable during any conflict is determined by the status of the conflict. The simplest distinction is between international and noninternational, which the ICRC articulates as follows:

> International armed conflicts exists whenever there is resort to armed force between two or more States.
>
> Non-international armed conflicts are *protracted armed confrontations* occurring between governmental armed forces and the forces of one or more armed groups, or between such groups arising on the territory of a State. The armed confrontation must reach *a minimum level of intensity* and the parties involved in the conflict must show *a minimum of organisation*. (ICRC 2008, para. 5)

This is not always a straightforward determination: during the Vietnam conflict, for example, the Republic of South Vietnam and the United States characterized the conflict as international, while North Vietnam viewed the conflict as internal; the Soviet Union held that it was assisting the Government of Afghanistan in quelling a rebellion, but much of the international community, including the ICRC, considered it to be an international armed conflict between Afghanistan and the USSR (Provost 2005, paras. 252–253). Recent conflicts such as in Iraq and Afghanistan have involved coalitions of states fighting one or more nongovernmental armed groups in a host country. Such conflicts would arguably be categorized as noninternational, despite prima facie appearances. Categorization as an international armed conflict brings with it a more rigorous standard of conduct.

International Armed Conflicts

In an international armed conflict, all captured persons are protected by the GC and Additional Protocol I.

Armed conflicts in which peoples are fighting against colonial domination, alien occupation, or racist regimes are to be considered international conflicts (AP I, Article 1(4)).

Non-International Armed Conflicts under Common Article 3

Common Article 3 applies as a minimum. Hostilities must meet a threshold of confrontation. It is generally accepted that the lower threshold found in Additional Protocol II, which excludes internal disturbances and tensions (such as riots or isolated or sporadic acts of violence), also applies to Common Article 3. The first criterion is that hostilities must reach a minimum level of intensity (ICTY [International Criminal Tribunal for the former Yugoslavia] 1997, paras. 561–568; ICTY 2005a, para. 84). This may be the case when a government is obliged to use military force against insurgents, instead of merely relying on police forces (ICTY 2005b, paras. 135–170). Secondly, those involved in the conflict must amount to parties, meaning that they possess organized armed forces, under a command structure and with the capacity to sustain military operations (ICTY 2005c, paras. 94–134).

Non-International Armed Conflicts under Additional Protocol II

Additional Protocol II applies to armed conflicts which take place between the armed forces of a state and "dissident armed forces or other organised armed groups which, under responsible command, exercise such control over a part of its territory as to enable them to carry out sustained and concerted military operations and to implement [Additional Protocol II]" (AP II, Article 1(1)). This definition is narrower than that under Common Article 3 in that it introduces a requirement of territorial control and applies only to armed conflicts between State armed forces and organized nonstate armed groups.

Categories of Detainee

It is necessary to distinguish the legal status of a conflict, as this will determine to which categories captured persons are to be assigned. The MOD states that "commanders are entitled to expect clear direction on this matter" (MOD 2015, para. 127).

For a detailed list of the categories of captured persons, see Table 9.1. Regardless of which category they belong to, all captured persons must be treated humanely and in accordance with Common Article 3 at all times. Beyond these basic standards, certain categories of captured persons will be entitled to additional rights and protections. The status of an individual immediately prior to capture will normally dictate the category to which he/she belongs, although it may be necessary to formally decide this through an Article 5 Tribunal or similar institution.

Broadly speaking, captured persons could be enemy forces or insurgents who are no longer willing or able to continue fighting, persons who merit internment for imperative reasons of security, or persons suspected of criminal offences.

Categories of Captured Persons—International Armed Conflict

The key distinction to be drawn between captured persons during an international armed conflict is between combatants and civilians.

Combatants

The MOD defines a *combatant* as "a member of the armed forces of a party to the armed conflict (other than medical personnel and chaplains) who has the right to participate directly in hostilities" (MOD 2015, para. 134). Under Additional Protocol I, this includes irregular forces who are under responsible command, are subject to internal military discipline,

TABLE 9.1

Table of Applicable Law

Operation	Captured Persons	Examples	Applicable Law
International armed conflict	Prisoners of war	• Combatants • Others entitled to prisoner of war status: Those authorized to accompany armed forces (e.g., war correspondents, supply contractors); levée en masse	• Geneva Convention III • Additional Protocol I
	Retained persons	• Medical staff • Chaplains	
	Internees	• Civilians belonging to opposing state interned for imperative reasons of security • Criminal detainees sentenced to internment	• Geneva Convention IV
	Detainees	• Civilian criminals • Civilians taking direct part in hostilities • Criminal detainees prior to sentence • Insurgents/Agitators • Spies • Mercenaries	• Additional Protocol I, Article 75
Non-international armed conflict	Internees	• Organised armed groups interned for imperative reasons of security	• Common Article 3
	Detainees	• Civilians detained for committing a criminal offense under host nation law • Civilians taking a direct part in hostilities	• Additional Protocol II
Other (e.g., noncombatant evacuation, peace support operation)	Internees	• Individuals threatening mission accomplishment	• UK Law • Host state law
	Detainees	• Individuals threatening mission accomplishment • Individuals committing criminal acts	

carry their arms openly, and otherwise distinguish themselves from the civilian population (AP I, Articles 43 and 44).

A combatant is immune from prosecution for legitimate acts of war committed before his/her capture. Generally, combatants are entitled to prisoner of war status. Medical and religious personnel, however, become "retained persons."

The MOD defines a *prisoner of war* as "a combatant or a person who accompanies the armed forces without being a member thereof (provided that he is authorized by the armed force which he accompanies) who is captured by the armed forces of the enemy" (MOD 2015, para. 135). Prisoners of war are not convicted criminals. They are not detained for punishment or rehabilitation; they are members of the armed forces who were, until capture, performing their professional duty.

Those entitled to prisoner of war status under Geneva Convention III are:

• Members of the armed forces of a party to the conflict, as well as members of militias or volunteer corps forming part of such armed forces

• Members of other militias and members of other volunteer corps, including those of organized resistance movements, belonging to a party to the conflict and operating in or outside their own territory, even if this territory is occupied, provided that such militias or volunteer corps, including such organized resistance movements, fulfill the following conditions:

- That of being commanded by a person responsible for his/her subordinates
- That of having a fixed distinctive sign recognizable at a distance
- That of carrying arms openly
- That of conducting their operations in accordance with the laws and customs of war

- Members of regular armed forces who profess allegiance to a government or an authority not recognized by the detaining power
- Persons who accompany the armed forces without actually being members thereof, such as civilian members of military aircraft crews, war correspondents, supply contractors, members of labor units or of services responsible for the welfare of the armed forces, provided that they have received authorization from the armed forces which they accompany, who shall provide them for that purpose with an identity card
- Members of crews, including masters, pilots, and apprentices, of the merchant marine, and of civil aircraft of the parties to the conflict, who do not benefit by more favorable treatment under any other provisions of international law
- Inhabitants of a nonoccupied territory, who on the approach of the enemy spontaneously take up arms to resist the invading forces, without having had time to form themselves into regular armed units, provided they carry arms openly and respect the laws and customs of war (GC III, Article 4A).

Although not prisoners of war, the following categories of persons are to be treated in the same way as prisoners of war:

> Persons belonging, or having belonged, to the armed forces of the occupied [territory], if the occupying Power considers it necessary by reason of such allegiance to intern them, even though it has originally liberated them while hostilities were going on outside the territory it occupies. . .
>
> The persons belonging to any of the categories enumerated [in Article 4A] who have been received by neutral or non-belligerent Powers on their territory and whom those powers are required to intern under international law. . . (GC III, Article 4B)

Uniforms or other clear demarcations of combatant status are important; in order to qualify for prisoner of war status, guerillas and militias must distinguish themselves as combatants.

Mercenaries are not combatants and do not qualify for prisoner of war status (AP I, Article 47); they are entitled to the fundamental guarantees articulated in Additional Protocol I, Article 75. Mercenaries "will generally be treated as civilian criminals," and "any suspicion that [a captured person] may be a mercenary must be reported to higher headquarters immediately" (MOD 2015, para. 139).

Members of the armed forces engaged in espionage lose their right to prisoner of war status (AP I, Article 46). They remain entitled to the protection of Additional Protocol I, Article 75. Suspicion that a captured person is a spy or engaged in espionage must be reported to higher headquarters immediately.

Determining whether a captured person is entitled to prisoner of war status can be complex. Geneva Convention III, Article 5, states

> Should any doubt arise as to whether persons, having committed a belligerent act and having fallen into the hands of the enemy, [be entitled to prisoner of war status], such persons shall enjoy the protection of the present Convention until such time as their status has been determined by a competent tribunal.

Civilians

Additional Protocol I defines *civilians* as "persons not members of an armed force" (AP I, Article 50(1)). In cases of doubt, people are to be assumed to be civilians (AP I, Article 50(1)). An internee is a civilian "interned for imperative reasons of security" (GC IV, Article 78). Internees are protected by Geneva Convention IV. A detainee is a civilian "detained because he has committed, or is suspected of committing, a criminal offence against the laws of the territory in which he has been captured, or against UK Armed Forces, or an offence against the law applied in an occupied territory" (MOD 2015, para. 143). Such persons are entitled to the protections afforded by Additional Protocol I, Article 75.

Categories of Captured Persons—Non-International Armed Conflict

The MOD defines internees in non-international armed conflicts as "normally . . . persons who are involved in actively and violently resisting the mission or presence of UK Armed Forces or seeking to undermine the host nation government" (MOD 2015, para. 148). UK Armed Forces may have powers to detain criminal suspects. Civilians found to have taken a direct part in hostilities may also be detained as detainees.

Standards of Detention

It must always be remembered that persons detained, no matter why or for how long, are rendered extremely vulnerable by their absolute dependence on the detaining authority. This vulnerability will be exacerbated by animosities generated by the conflict and the general deterioration of social and other structures.

International humanitarian law contains detailed rules on conditions of detention for international conflicts (see GC III and IV). It does not, however, contain adequate provisions for noninternational conflicts, especially those governed only by Common Article 3.

The MOD Joint Doctrine Publication 1–10: Captured Persons (CPERS) provides a detailed overview of the standards and practices to be applied in handling captured persons.

The MOD prohibits in all circumstances the following acts (MOD 2015, para. 214):

- Violence to the life, health, and physical or mental well-being of captured persons, in particular murder as well as cruel treatment and torture, mutilation, or any form of corporal punishment (GC Common Article 3; GC III, Article 13; GC IV, Article 27; AP I, Articles 11 and 75; AP II, Article 4; ICC Act, Schedule 8, Articles 7(1) and 8(2); UN CAT; ECHR, Articles 2 and 3)
- Collective punishments (AP I, Article 75; AP II, Article 4)

- Taking of hostages (GC Common Article 3; AP I, Article 75; AP II, Article 4; ICC Act, Schedule 8, Article 8(2))
- Acts of terrorism (*terrorism* remains undefined in international law, although the jurisprudence of the Special Tribunal for Lebanon may eventually address this)
- Slavery and the slave trade in all their forms (ICC Act, Schedule 8, Article 7(1))
- Outrages upon personal dignity, in particular humiliating and degrading treatment, rape, sexual slavery, enforced prostitution, forced pregnancy, forced sterilization, and any other form of sexual violence (GC Common Article 3; AP I, Articles 75 and 76; AP II, Article 4; ICC Act, Schedule 8, Articles 7(1) and 8(2))
- Pillage
- Physical mutilation or medical or scientific experiments of a kind which are neither justified by medical, dental, or hospital treatment of the person concerned nor carried out in his/her interest (AP I, Article 11; AP II, Article 4)
- The passing of sentences and the carrying out of executions without previous judgment pronounced by a properly constituted court, affording all the judicial guarantees, which are recognized as indispensible by civilized peoples (GC Common Article 3; GC III, Articles 82–88 and 99–108; GC IV, Article 117; AP I, Article 75; AP II, Article 4)
- Reprisals
- Threats to commit any of the foregoing acts
- The taking or possession of photographs of live captured persons or dead bodies for any reason other than official purposes of identification, evidence, or intelligence (GC III, Article 13; GC IV, Article 27)
- Identification by tattooing or imprinting permanent signs or markings on captured persons (GC IV, Article 100)

The UK government, in the wake of allegations of inhumane treatment from former internees in Northern Ireland, prohibited the use of the five techniques as an aid to interrogation: hooding; wall-standing; subjection to noise; deprivation of sleep; and deprivation of food and drink (ECtHR 1978, para. 102).

The interrogation practices of the UK Armed Forces again came under intense scrutiny following the death of Iraqi detainee Baha Mousa. Among other acts of ill-treatment, the prohibited five techniques were inflicted on the individual leading to his/her death, although the names given to the methods were redefined, e.g., by replacing wall-standing with stress positions. The MOD states that these techniques "must never be used as an aid to tactical questioning or interrogation, as a form of punishment, discriminatory conduct, intimidation, coercion or as deliberate mistreatment" (MOD 2015, para. 218).

At the time of writing, the MOD faced calls for a public inquiry in the face of allegations of systemic violations of international humanitarian law.

The circumstances under which a person is captured are likely to be fraught and chaotic. The MOD notes that treating a captured person humanely from the point of capture is "not only a legal necessity," but "also sets the conditions for subsequent exploitation through tactical questioning and interrogation" (MOD 2015, para. 702).

All reasonable steps are to be taken to control situations without resorting to the use of force. The circumstances under which force may be used, and to what degree, are governed by the legal status of the conflict and the operational rules of engagement.

The guidelines for conducting searches of persons at the point of, or prior to, capture are contained in Chapter 7 of the Joint Doctrine Publication 1–10: CPERS. Put simply, all searches at this stage are to be conducted with due regard for the individual's personal dignity, taking into account religious sensibilities (MOD 2015, para. 708.d). Intimate searches are not permitted at the point of capture or during an initial search (MOD 2015, para. 708.e). An intimate search involves the searching of body cavities and orifices; a captured person may be asked to open his/her mouths to be assessed by sight, but nothing may be inserted into his/her mouth (MOD 2015, para. 912). Females, juveniles (defined as those aged between 15 and 17 by AP I, Article 77), and children (defined as those aged under 15 by AP I, Article 77) should, unless absolutely impossible, be searched by female service personnel. Male service personnel should search male captured persons. In the event that a captured person cannot be searched by a person of the same gender, the search must be supervised and details recorded by another member of the UK Armed Forces.

To accord with the requirements under the GC and the AP, each captured person must be properly documented. Efficient documentation procedures also facilitate efficient intelligence gathering. To this end, any equipment or documents evacuated with a captured person should be treated as potential evidence. Chains of custody must be recorded. Each captured person is to be allocated a unique serial number to enable his/her identification and handling. The Joint Doctrine Publication advocates the use of an automated data process for the documentation and tracking of captured persons.

GC III and IV require the UK to inform the Prisoner of War Information Bureau or the National Information Bureau, respectively, of the capture and every subsequent significant event affecting prisoners of war or internees. The MOD demands the operation of a similar system even during conflicts not governed by these provisions (MOD 2015, para. 719).

Captured persons will be interned only as an exceptional measure and where it has been found to be necessary for imperative reasons of security. The Article 5 tribunal, or equivalent, should consider the case for internment within 48 hours of a potential internee's capture (MOD 2015, para. 132 and Annex 1B5). The internment of captured persons should be reviewed every 28 days (MOD 2015, para. 132 and Annex 1B5). An internee must be released as soon as it is determined that it is no longer necessary to intern him/her for imperative reasons of security.

An internee against whom there is sufficient evidence to support a criminal charge should be reclassified as a criminal detainee and transferred to the host nation for prosecution. If so requested, the UK may continue to detain such individuals, but as a criminal detainee.

Captured persons are to be removed from the theatre of combat as soon as practicable. They are to be afforded protection from the dangers of the conflict as much as possible.

Living conditions are to be, where possible, as favorable as those for the UK Armed Forces (GC III, Article 25; GC IV, Article 85). It is desirable that these standards be applied even when a conflict is not governed by these instruments. Living conditions must under no circumstances be prejudicial to the health of the captured persons. To accord with the GC, food must be sufficient to support good health and maintain weight. Access to water must be provided, at the very minimum, "to the same extent as the local civilian population" (AP II, Article 5(1)(b)), although it is of course preferable that water is accessible "at all times either by request or default" (MOD 2015, para. 211c).

Captured persons shall be afforded at least 8 hours of rest in every 24-hour period, including an interrupted 4-hour period (MOD 2015, para. 211g).

Captured persons are entitled to complete freedom to exercise their religious practices (GC III, Articles 34, 35, and 37; GC IV, Article 93; AP II, Article 5).

Tactical questioning is that which is routinely conducted at the point of capture. Interrogation is conducted by specialist members of the UK Armed Forces at approved and appropriately equipped facilities provided for the purpose.

Oppressive questioning is that which is "by its nature, duration or other circumstances (including the fact of custody) excites hopes (such as hope of release) or fears, or so affects the mind of the subject that his will crumbles and he speaks when otherwise he would have stayed silent" (UK House of Lords 2005, *per* Lord Carswell at para. 64, citing the Court of Appeal in *R v Prager* [1972] 1 WLR 260, at 266). Shouting is held to be a lawful interrogation technique (*Ali Hussein v. Secretary of State for Defence* 2013).

Conclusion

UK Armed forces are bound by customary international law, treaties to which the UK is Party, and UK domestic law. International humanitarian aims to limit the adverse humanitarian effects of armed conflict by protecting persons who are not, or no longer, participating in hostilities and restricting the means and methods of warfare. It is binding on all parties to a conflict, whether states, nonstate armed groups, organizations, or individuals. In circumstances where international humanitarian does not apply, captured persons also have rights under international human rights treaties such as the International Covenant on Civil and Political Rights, the UN CAT, and the European Convention on Human Rights. Such international humanitarian law is applicable only during armed conflicts that cross a threshold of intensity. Human rights law, on the other hand, is generally applicable at all times. Derogations from certain provisions of international human rights law are permissible under certain conditions and nonderogable human rights include the right against torture and the right to a fair trial which cannot be violated at any time. International humanitarian law seeks to regulate the conduct of individuals as well as states, which while human rights law imposes obligations on states. It is important for all those who may encounter those in detention at times of conflict are aware of national and international principles and statutes which apply in the given setting.

References

Ali Hussein v. Secretary of State for Defence (2013) EWHC 95 (Admin).

Council of Europe, European Convention for the Protection of Human Rights and Fundamental Freedoms, as amended by Protocols Nos. 11 and 14, 4 November 1950.

ECHR (European Convention on Human Rights) 1996, *Loizidou v. Turkey* (15318/89), para. 62.

ECtHR (European Court of Human Rights) 1978, *Ireland v UK* (5310/71), para. 102.

ECtHR 2011a, *Al-Skeini and Others v. UK* (55721/07).

ECtHR 2011b, *Al-Jedda v. UK* (27021/08).

El-Masri v. The former Yugoslav Republic of Macedonia (2012) 39630/09.

Geneva Conventions: International Committee of the Red Cross, Common Article 3 to the Geneva Conventions, 12 August 1949.

ICJ (International Court of Justice) 2004a, *Legality of the Threat or Use of Nuclear Weapons*, Advisory Opinion of 8 July 1996, General List 95.

ICJ 2004b, Legal Consequences of the Construction of a Wall in the Occupied Palestinian Territory, para. 106.

ICJ 2005, Armed activities on the territory of the Congo (*Democratic Republic of the Congo v. Uganda*), *ICJ Reports*, para. 216.

ICRC Opinion Paper, March 2008, available at https://www.icrc.org/eng/assets/files/other/opinion-paper-armed-conflict.pdf

ICTY [International Criminal Tribunal for the former Yugoslavia] 1997, *The Prosecutor v. Dusko Tadic*, Judgment, IT-94-1-T, paras 561–568.

ICTY 2005a, *The Prosecutor v. Fatmir Limaj,* Judgment, IT-03-66-T, para. 84.

ICTY 2005b, *The Prosecutor v. Fatmir Limaj,* Judgment, IT-03- 66-T, paras 135–170.

ICTY 2005c, *The Prosecutor v. Fatmir Limaj,* Judgment, IT-03-66-T, paras 94–134.

International Committee of the Red Cross (ICRC), Protocol Additional to the Geneva Conventions of 12 August 1949, and relating to the Protection of Victims of International Armed Conflicts (Protocol I), 8 June 1977, 1125 UNTS 609.

International Committee of the Red Cross (ICRC), Geneva Convention Relative to the Treatment of Prisoners of War (Third Geneva Convention), 12 August 1949, 75 UNTS 135.

International Committee of the Red Cross (ICRC), Geneva Convention Relative to the Protection of Civilian Persons in Time of War (Fourth Geneva Convention), 12 August 1949, 75 UNTS 287.

MOD (Ministry of Defence) 2015, Joint Doctrine 1–10: Captured Persons (CPERS), Development, Concepts and Doctrine Centre, 3rd edn, Ministry of Defence, London. Available from: https://www.gov.uk/government/uploads/system/uploads/attachment_data/file/455589/20150820-JDP_1_10_Ed_3_Ch_1_Secured.pdf.

Provost, R., *International Human Rights and Humanitarian Law,* Cambridge University Press, 2005.

UK, International Criminal Court Act 2001 (c. 17).

UK House of Lords 2005, *R v. Mushtaq*, 1 WLR 1513, 21 April 2005, *per* Lord Carswell at para. 64, citing the Court of Appeal in *R v Prager* [1972] 1 WLR 260, at 266.

UN General Assembly, Convention Against Torture and Other Cruel, Inhuman or Degrading Treatment or Punishment, 10 December 1984, United Nations, Treaty Series, vol. 1465, p. 85.

UN General Assembly, Rome Statute of the International Criminal Court (last amended 2010), 17 July 1998.

UNHRC (United Nations Human Rights Council) 2004, *General Comment 31*, para. 11.

UNHRC 2004, *General Comment 31*, CCPR/C/21/Rev.1/Add.13, para. 10.

10

Sexual Assault in Detention

Jason Payne-James

CONTENTS

Introduction

Sexual assault within established detention facilities such as police stations, civil prisons, military prisons or other secure custodial settings, or in other closed settings where an individual is not completely free to come and go (e.g., refugee camps, secure psychiatric facilities, homes for the elderly or for juveniles), and whether run by State or non-state actors or by private entities, is often unreported and unidentified. The term 'detention' in this chapter will thus broadly utilize the Optional Protocol to the Convention against Torture (OPCAT) definition—"deprivation of liberty means any form of detention or imprisonment or the placement of a person in a public or private custodial setting which that person is not permitted to leave at will by order of any judicial, administrative or other authority" (UN Human Rights Office of the High Commissioner, 2002).

In detention, it should also be recognized that consensual sexual contact may be experienced, and it is important to ensure that the nature of consensuality versus nonconsensuality is understood within this setting in which coercion as well as violence may coexist. Data on sexual activities within detention settings are lacking, and it is clear that much more research should be undertaken on this subject. Often sexual contacts are associated with other types of physical, violent, interpersonal assault. This chapter seeks to provide an overview of the themes and issues relevant to sexual assault (of any kind) in detention. There may be substantial overlap with rape and other forms of sexual assault being used as weapons or means of control in conflict settings.

The Problem

Where allegations of sexual assault in detention facilities, such as prisons, are received, the majority of complainants are male (by virtue of the demographics of most detention facilities). However, other settings (such as refugee camps) may have a female predominance. Sexual contact may be between those in detention or between those in detention and those personnel detaining them. Recording and documenting and investigating such assaults is difficult, even in structured detention facilities within political or legal frameworks with established reporting mechanisms. But in some countries and in conflict zones where the nature of detention may hugely vary, and where reporting mechanisms may be absent or nonfunctioning, then the task becomes almost impossible. The physical effects of unwanted and unconsented sexual contact can result in a wide range of physical and psychological problems. Physical problems include the complete range of sexually transmitted infection including HIV and hepatitis. Genital injuries from penetrative assault may be present and nongenital injuries as a result of restraint and resistance to the assault may be present. If documented at an early stage, these may provide strong corroborative evidence. Psychological effects can be widespread including depression, anxiety, self-harm (in all its forms), and suicide. Post traumatic stress disorder (PTSD) may develop. Loncar et al. (2010) studied 60 cases of sexual abuse of men during the war in Croatia and Bosnia and Herzegovina. They found that the men were exposed to physical torture of their genitals, psychosexual torture, and physical abuse. The most common symptoms of traumatic reactions were sleep disturbances, concentration difficulties, nightmares and flashbacks, feelings of hopelessness, and different physical stress symptoms such as constant headaches, profused sweating, and tachycardia. In addition to rape and different methods of sexual abuse, most of the victims were heavily beaten. The authors also concluded that the number of sexually abused men during the war must have been much higher than reported.

Such issues are global and their nature and location depend on the geopolitical setting. Reporting and interpretation may be subjective, and data are lacking. Lack of accurate prospective data is a problem for many of the settings in which sexual assault in detention is an issue. It is likely that the problem is widely underreported, and the real incidence and prevalence, as of now, is unknown.

Examples originate worldwide. Olujic (1995, 1998) has reviewed and explored elements of coercion, rape, and torture—and in particular sexual assault—related to the war in the former Yugoslavia and determines that the number of rapes was in many thousands and often occurring in "rape camps" where women were forcibly held by Serb soldiers. Among the rape victims, there were a number who died, and these were recorded as being from a variety of causes including gunshot wounds, hemorrhage as a consequence of injuries from sexual assault, and suicide motivated by shame. Zawati (2007) and Oosterhoff et al. (2004) make reference to the end of the war in the former Yugoslavia, when the medical records of healthcare centers provided evidence of male rape and sexual torture of Croatian and Bosnian Muslim men including castration, genital beatings, and electroshock. Testimonies collected at the Medical Center for Human Rights in Zagreb from 55 men, who were captured by Serb militants, showed they had been exposed to five categories of systematic and organized sexual torture. These assaults included rape, deviant sexual acts, total and partial castrations, injuries to the testes with blunt objects, and a combination of other traumatic insults.

Recent reviews (Brown 2012; Guy 2014) touch on some of these issues when exploring violence against women in the Democratic Republic of Congo (DRC) where it is estimated that 5.5 million people have died since the beginning of the war in 1994 and where rape is used as a weapon. Data for the most recent year (2013) suggest that more than 15,000 rapes were reported. What is not clear is what proportion of those assaults took place in any form of detention.

Similarly O'Connor (2014) further addresses these issues and makes the point that there is a huge variation in the levels of sexual violence in armed conflicts. O'Connor points out that the Israeli–Palestinian conflict have extremely low levels, whereas in Bosnia and many African states, the prevalence of sexual violence is at epidemic levels. There are several factors which may account for these differences. Elements, which reduce such events, may include strong military discipline, improved gender balance in armed forces, better political awareness by combatants of the aims of a campaign, and predeployment training in the humanitarian law (the laws of war).

Black (1998) expanded on the potential sexual assault of females as isolated atrocities and, with reference to the civil war in Uganda, pointed out that guerrilla forces in the late 1990s had kidnapped 6,000–10,000 children and had forced the "most desirable" girls to become "wives" of warlords. At that time, families in refugee camps in Burundi and Somalia began to submit their young daughters to early marriage, ostensibly to protect female honor. A resurgence in forced marriages and sexual enslavement by armed groups is currently being seen across war-torn parts of the Middle East.

Incidence, Nature, and Predictors for Assaults

It is important to understand the nature of sexual contact within the broad range of detention settings. In some cases, it may be purely consensual between consenting adult detainees. In some cases, there may be clear nonconsensual sexual assault, either by detainees or by staff. However, there are other instances where consent may not be completely freely given and where coercion is used, due to the nature of the detention setting—and this is particularly the case in staff–detainee sexual contact. For those reviewing or investigating complaints of sexual assault, the setting and context must be clearly understood. Often, governments or authorities may be unclear or ambiguous in their approach.

Over two decades ago, when it was already recognized that sexual contact within prisons of the UK was widespread, Linehan (1993) identified the failure of the UK government to ensure the provision of condoms for fear of being construed as encouraging illegal behavior. Similarly, although many jurisdictions acknowledged that HIV and other bloodborne infections are spread by illicit intravenous drug use within detention settings, there was a reluctance to introduce measures to make injecting practices safer, since this would appear to condone the illegal activity. While numerous states have introduced harm reduction strategies aimed at reducing the spread of HIV and other infections within places of detention, through measures such as needle exchange programs, condom distribution, drug dependence treatment (UNODC 2006), in many countries and jurisdictions, no such measures exist, despite the size of the problem. This is illustrated, for example, in a recent study from Papua New Guinea (PNG) (Kelly-Hanku et al. 2015) where semistructured interviews were undertaken with 56 prisoners and detainees and 60 key stakeholders. The authors found that women in detention are vulnerable to sexual violence and exploitation and are at greatest risk of HIV while detained in police holding cells, where they are typically supervised by male officers, in contrast to prisons, where they have little contact with male staff. HIV risk for men in prison is associated with consensual and nonconsensual sex; this risk is perpetuated by a pervasive culture of denial and institutionalized homophobia. The unlawful nature (in PNG) of anal penetrative sex and of men having sex with men provides prisons with the legal grounds by which to refuse access to condoms for prisoners. Addressing HIV risk among detained men and women in PNG requires the reform of legislation, police, and prison practices and an understanding of broader structural problems of gender-based violence and stigma and discrimination.

Studies concerning inmate-on-inmate sexual assaults within male correctional facilities remain sparse in the sociological and correctional literatures (Hensley et al. 2005). The largest studies have originated from the United States where Beck and Harrison (2007) showed that an estimated 60,500 inmates (4.5% of all state and federal inmates) experienced one or more incidents of sexual victimization involving other inmates or staff and that nationwide, about 2.1% of inmates reported an incident involving another inmate and 2.9% reported an incident involving staff. Of the 146 prison facilities in the 2007 study, 6 had no reports of sexual victimization from the sampled inmates; 10 had an overall victimization rate of at least 9.3%. Among the 10 facilities with the highest overall prevalence rates, three had prevalence rates of staff sexual misconduct that exceeded 10%.

Only a few studies have specifically examined the characteristics of male inmate sexual assault victims. Hensley et al. (2005) sought to address this gap by providing an examination of factors related to victimization likelihood. Using data gathered in March 2000 from 142 inmates in one Southern maximum-security prison, the authors examined demographic and behavioral characteristics of male inmate sexual victims. Based on inmates' self-reports of sexual victimization—threatened and/or forced sexual assault encounters—the correlates of victimization were identified. Approximately 18% of the inmates reported inmate-on-inmate sexual threats, and 8.5% reported that they had been sexually assaulted by another inmate while incarcerated.

Sexual orientation may have impact on risk. One research studied self-reported transexual male prisoners HIV risk behaviors in a state penal system (Stephens et al. 1999). The specific research question was whether or not sexual orientation of inmates influences the level to which they evidence HIV risk behaviors. A total of 153 participants volunteered to participate in the study, of which 31 described themselves as being transsexual. Based on risk ratios and using transsexual inmates (TIs) as the reference group, they were 13.7 times more likely to have a regular sex partner while in prison (95% CI = 5.28, 35.58). Additionally, TIs were 5.8 times more likely than non-TIs to report having more than one sex partner while in prison (95% CI = 2.18, 15.54). These findings indicate that TIs require more preventive support than nontransexual codetainees.

Wolff and Jing Shi (2009) showed that physical and sexual assaults are a common accompaniment of incarceration in US prisons. They showed that approximately 21% of male inmates were physically assaulted during a 6-month period. Sexual assault is estimated to be between 2% and 5%. The authors assessed approximately 2200 physical and 200 sexual victimizations reported by a random sample of 6964 male inmates. On average, the victims, independent of the type of assault, were in their early 30s, African American, had spent 2 years at the prison they were currently in, had 4–5 years left on their current sentences, and had spent roughly 8 years in prison since turning 18. Mental health problems were more frequently reported by victims of sexual assault than victims of physical assault. Physical injury occurred in 40% of physical assaults and 70% of sexual assaults between inmates and in 50% of assaults perpetrated by staff. When sexual assault involved a staff perpetrator, nearly 30% of the victims reported being coerced into sexual acts in an effort to protect themselves from future harm. Emotional reactions to assaults were experienced by virtually all victims. The authors emphasize that context is vital in the development and implementation of prevention and therapeutic interventions.

Richters et al. (2012) conducted a computer-assisted telephone survey of a random sample of 2018 male prisoners in New South Wales (NSW) and Queensland, Australia. Of 2626 eligible and available inmates, 76.8% consented and provided full responses. Most men (95.1%) identified as heterosexual. Of the total sample, 13.5% reported sexual contact with males in their lifetime: 7.8% only outside prison, 2.8% both inside and outside, and 2.7% only inside prison. Later in the interview, 144 men (7.1% of total sample) reported sexual contact with inmates in prison; the majority had few partners and no anal intercourse. Most did so for pleasure, but some for protection, i.e., to avoid assault by someone else. Before incarceration, 32.9% feared sexual assault in prison; 6.9% had been sexually threatened in prison; and 2.6% had been sexually coerced ("forced or frightened into doing something sexually that [they] did not want"). Some of those coerced reported no same-sex contact. The majority of prisoners were intolerant of male-to-male sexual activity. This study, in this setting, suggested that both consensual sex and sexual assault were less common than had been anticipated.

Rowell-Cunsolo et al. (2014) explored the extent to which incarcerated African American males were exposed to sexual assault and identified possible predictors of such exposure in a study conducted from April to August 2008 within one of the largest maximum-security male correctional institutions in the United States which houses 2800 inmates. Sixty-eight percent of the inmates were African American, and 20% were Caucasian. One hundred and thirty-four incarcerated African American males participated in this study. African American male prisoners were eligible if they had been incarcerated within the facility for at least 1 year and had achieved at least a sixth grade reading level. Prisoners segregated from the general prison population during recruitment were excluded from participating in this study, including those experiencing behavioral and serious medical problems. Fifty percent ($n = 67$) of all participants reported being previously incarcerated. Almost 18% ($n = 24$) were on probation and 30% ($n = 40$) were on parole when they were arrested for committing their current offense(s). The vast majority of the participants were currently incarcerated for committing at least one violent offense (69%, $n = 93$); 22% ($n = 30$) had committed property and drug offenses, and 7% ($n = 10$) were sex offenders. Participants had spent an average of 13 years in prison and were sentenced to 37 years (excluding life sentences). Forty-three percent ($n = 57$) of the sample reported hearing one or more of their fellow inmates being sexually assaulted, and 16% ($n = 21$) reported they had witnessed a sexual assault while incarcerated. There were slight differences between those who were exposed to sexual assault and those who were not, with a few exceptions. Generally, participants who were exposed to sexual assault were older, received sentences that were 6 years longer, and had been incarcerated more than 2 years longer than participants who were not exposed to sexual assault. There were no significant relationships between exposure to sexual assault and demographic characteristics such as age, education, marital status and number of children, previous imprisonment, and nature of the offense committed.

One particular category of such assaults involves hostage-taking. A Canadian study (Mailloux and Serin 2003) reviewed 33 hostage-takings/forcible confinements spanning 11 years. The incidents were classified as 20 hostage-takings (3 with sexual assault) and 13 forcible confinements (7 with sexual assault). Sexual assaults were always perpetrated against women, and 36.6% of the women were sexually assaulted. A quarter of the perpetrators had a forcible confinement or hostage-taking in their current conviction; half had a prior history of such incidents. Those serving sentences for rape were overwhelmingly implicated in incidents that resulted in a sexual assault. Most perpetrators were below the age of 30 and serving sentences of less than 10 years in medium- or maximum-security institutions.

Sexual assaults in conflict zones will have their own particular characteristics and nuances. Bartels et al. (2013) studied sexual violence survivors presenting to Panzi Hospital (South Kivu, DRC) between 2004 and 2008 to describe the patterns of sexual violence described by survivors and to analyze perpetrator profiles. The authors analyzed 4311 records. Perpetrators were identified as follows: (1) 6% were civilians; (2) 52% were armed combatants; and (3) 42% were simply identified as assailant(s) with no further identifying information. Those identified simply as assailants perpetrated patterns of sexual violence that were similar to those of armed combatants, suggesting that this group included a large number of armed combatants.

Tsai et al. (2012) examined medical evidence of human rights violations against non-Arabic-speaking civilians in Darfur, Sudan. They undertook a retrospective review and analysis of medical records of 325 patients seen from 2004 to 2006 at the Nyala-based Amel Centre for Treatment and Rehabilitation of Victims of Torture. Two hundred and ninety-two (89.8%) patients from 12 different non-Arabic-speaking tribes disclosed in the medical notes that they had been attacked by the Government of Sudan (GoS) and/or Janjaweed forces. Nearly all attacks (321 [98.8%]) were described as having occurred in the absence of active armed conflict between Janjaweed/GoS forces and rebel groups. The most common alleged abuses were beatings (161 [49.5%]), gunshot wounds (140 [43.1%]), destruction or theft of property (121 [37.2%]), involuntary detainment (97 [29.9%]), and being bound (64 [19.7%]). Approximately one-half (36 [49.3%]) of all women disclosed that they had been sexually assaulted, and one-half of sexual assaults were described as having occurred in close proximity to a camp for internally displaced persons. The authors point out that the quality of documentation was similar to that available in other conflict/postconflict, resource-limited settings (i.e., not ideal).

One of the problems with sexual (and physical) assault of any kind is that there may be a perception by both victim and perpetrator that such abuses are to be expected. This perception implies a lack of training, education, and discipline, and awareness of what is acceptable, appropriate, and legal behavior. Holmes et al. (2007) explored these views and assessed detainee abuse acceptance and variables associated with it. Outpatients from a veterans' hospital were administered questionnaires with three increasingly severe scenarios of a US soldier abusing a detainee. Three questionnaire versions differed in the final line of each version's scenarios, describing abuse either as soldier initiated, superior ordered, or wrong by a whistleblower soldier. Three hundred fifty-one veterans participated, 80% with service during the Vietnam War. Zero tolerance for abuse—"completely unacceptable" regardless of who the detainee was—increased with abuse severity (16% for exposure, 31% for humiliation, and 48% for rape of detainee) and with soldier initiation. The strongest, most consistently significant odds were of depressed veterans, veterans with comorbid depression/PTSD, and men being approximately 2, 3, and 4–20 times more tolerant of abuse than those without depression/PTSD and women, respectively. The authors conclude that there may be potential value to using similar scenario-based questionnaires to study active duty military perceptions of detainee abuse and that results may inform prevention policies. Certainly, such scenarios could be used in training in ethics. Clearly, however, this can only apply where the detaining authority is structured and accountable.

Reporting Assaults

Garland and Wilson (2013) have identified the fact that although the prevalence of sexual assault in US prisons is debated, it is known that the consequences for victims can be quite severe. The Prison Rape Elimination Act (PREA) requires prison officials to keep track of incidents of sexual assault, but these data will be generated only to the extent that inmates regularly report these acts. Male rape itself is a highly underreported phenomenon and even less reported in prisons due to inmate cultural norms that frown upon disclosing inmate information to correctional authorities (often referred to as snitching or grassing which in itself may stigmatize the detainee). They identified that inmates are less likely to view the reporting of prison rape as snitching (or grassing) in the early part of their detention, and Caucasian inmates are more likely than African American inmates to view disclosing rape as snitching. The authors recommend the need to study this matter in order to increase the appropriate reporting and proper identification of the true incidence of such assaults.

Sequelae of Assault

The sequelae of detention-based sexual assault have been poorly studied, and data are lacking. Physical consequences may include injury, infection (e.g., HIV, hepatitis B and C, and other sexually transmitted infections), and pregnancy. The incidence and prevalence of long-term physical effects (e.g., hepatitis, HIV, and other sexually transmitted diseases) and psychological effects (e.g., PTSD, depression, suicidal and self-harm behaviors) for victims of sexual assault in detention populations is unknown. It is unknown whether being a victim of such assaults predisposes the victim to becoming a perpetrator of such assault in the future.

A small number of studies have explored some of these themes.

Schneider et al. (2011) undertook a study aimed to determine associations between current psychological distress and history of having experienced sexual coercion and/or physical assault. Their subjects were drawn from prisoners in two Australian states (Queensland and NSW). Prisoners were asked about forced sexual encounters in or outside prison and physical assault in prison. Psychological distress was estimated using a dichotomized score obtained from the Kessler 6-Item Psychological Distress Scale (K6), and a logistic regression analysis was employed to investigate associations. Schneider et al. interviewed 2426 prisoners. They categorized 236 men (12%) and 63 women (19%) as "severely" psychologically distressed, and 13% of the men and 60% of the women reported that they had been sexually coerced prior to imprisonment. Physical assault in prison was common, reported by 34% of the men and 24% of the women. On a multivariate analysis, prisoners were more likely to be psychologically distressed if they had ever been threatened with sexual assault in prison or physically assaulted in prison. Sexual coercion outside prison was an important associate of psychological distress among men but not among women. The authors concluded that because psychological distress and experiences of assault are closely statistically linked among male prisoners and both are very common among female prisoners, screening for psychological distress in these settings should include routine inquiry about sexual and violent assaults against them both before and during imprisonment. The authors also suggested that further research is required in order to understand causal relationships.

Disease Prevention

Prisoners are at increased risk for infection with HIV, hepatitis B and C, and other sexually transmitted infections, due to overcrowded prisons, unprotected sex and sexual assault, unsafe injecting practices, and inadequate HIV prevention, treatment, and care. Saliu and Akintunde (2014) undertook a study to describe the knowledge, attitude, and preventive practices toward HIV/AIDS by male inmates in Ogbomoso Prison at Oyo State, South West Nigeria. Fifty (29.9%) were in the age group of 20–24 years with mean age of 30.99 ± 11.41. About half (50.3%) had been married before incarceration. Family and friends (30%), healthcare workers (25%), prison staff (20%), and mass media (25%) were the most common sources of information on HIV/AIDS. Knowledge about HIV was found to be high (94.6%). About 68.9% believed that people with the disease should be avoided. The knowledge about HIV/AIDS among inmates was high, but misconceptions about HIV/AIDS are still rife among the prisoners, and the authors advised that educational programs would be appropriate to correct this.

Such problems are recognized at international level, and organizations such as the UN have outlined, in a number of publications, frameworks, and strategies to address these issues (UNODC 2006, 2013). Emphasis on the need for appropriate healthcare is now made in Rules 24–27 of the UN Standard Minimum Rules for the Treatment of Prisoners (UN 2015).

Reducing Incidence and Improving Outcomes

Yap et al. (2011) reviewed evidence from population-based surveys of a steady decrease in male prisoner sexual assaults in NSW between 1996 and 2009. The authors conducted in-depth interviews with former and current inmates, and using a "systems" approach, they discussed the complexity of sexual assaults in prison, incorporating a multiplicity of perspectives. Of these, changes in power structures and control in a modern prison, the attitudes of older and younger prisoners, the concept of "duty of care," introduction of prison drug programs, and prisoner attitudes toward gender and sexuality may all have influenced this reduction.

The United States has taken a proactive but somewhat slow approach to sexual assault of those in correctional facilities. The PREA (2003) was the first US federal law passed dealing with the sexual assault of prisoners. The bill was signed into law on September 4, 2003 (Mair et al. 2003). However, it was not until 2012 that the US Department of Justice released a final rule to prevent, detect, and respond to sexual abuse in confinement facilities, in accordance with the PREA (Department of Homeland Security 2014). The rule set national standards in the United States for four categories of facilities: adult prisons and jails, lockups, community confinement facilities, and juvenile facilities. It was announced as the first ever federal effort to set standards aimed at protecting inmates in all such facilities at the federal, state, and local levels. The attorney general stated at that time that "the standards we establish today reflect the fact that sexual assault crimes committed within our correctional facilities can have devastating consequences—for individual victims and for communities far beyond our jails and prisons… These standards are the result of a thoughtful and deliberative process—and represent a critical step forward in protecting the rights and safety of all Americans." These standards are shown in Table 10.1 and have three clear goals: to prevent, detect, and respond to sexual abuse in detention facilities.

There is a need for structures to be in place to adequately record allegations, investigate them, undertake appropriate clinical examinations to document relevant findings, and to take forensic evidential samples with an appropriate chain of custody for those samples. Such processes are clearly not going to be in place or manageable.

Assessment of Sexual Assault

If the facilities and personnel are available, any sexual assault complaint should be dealt with in the same ways as any criminal investigation for such assault (Payne-James et al. 2016).

TABLE 10.1

Standards to Combat Sexual Abuse in Confinement Facilities

Prevent: To prevent sexual abuse, the standards require, among other things, that facilities

- Develop and maintain a zero-tolerance policy regarding sexual abuse;
- Designate a PREA point person to coordinate compliance efforts;
- Screen inmates for risk of being sexually abused or sexually abusive and use screening information to inform housing, bed, work, education, and program assignments;
- Develop and document a staffing plan that provides for adequate levels of staffing and where applicable, video monitoring;
- Train employees on their responsibilities in preventing, recognizing, and responding to sexual abuse;
- Perform background checks on prospective employees and not hire abusers;
- Prevent juveniles from being housed with adult inmates or having unsupervised contact with adult inmates in common spaces;
- Ban cross-gender pat-down searches of female inmates in prisons and jails and of both male and female residents of juvenile facilities;
- Incorporate unique vulnerabilities of lesbian, gay, bisexual, transgender, intersex, and gender nonconforming inmates into training and screening protocols;
- Enable inmates to shower, perform bodily functions, and change clothing without improper viewing by staff of the opposite gender;
- Restrict the use of solitary confinement as a means of protecting vulnerable inmates; and
- Enter into or renew contracts only with outside entities that agree to comply with the standards.

Detect: To detect sexual abuse, the standards require, among other things, that facilities

- Make inmates aware of facility policies and inform them of how to report sexual abuse;
- Provide multiple channels for inmates to report sexual abuse, including by contacting an outside entity, and allow inmates to report abuse anonymously upon request;
- Provide a method for staff and other third parties to report abuse on behalf of an inmate;
- Develop policies to prevent and detect any retaliation against those who report sexual abuse or cooperate with investigations; and
- Ensure effective communication about facility policies and how to report sexual abuse with inmates with disabilities and inmates who have limited English proficiency.

Respond: To respond to sexual abuse, the standards require, among other things, that facilities

- Provide timely and appropriate medical and mental healthcare to victims of sexual abuse;
- Where available, provide access to victim advocates from rape crisis centers for emotional support services related to sexual abuse;
- Establish an evidence protocol to preserve evidence following an incident and offer victims no-cost access to forensic medical examinations;
- Investigate all allegations of sexual abuse promptly and thoroughly and deem allegations substantiated if supported by a preponderance of the evidence;
- Discipline staff and inmate assailants appropriately, with termination as the presumptive disciplinary sanction for staff who commit sexual abuse;
- Allow inmates a full and fair opportunity to file grievances regarding sexual abuse so as to preserve their ability to seek judicial redress after exhausting administrative remedies; and
- Maintain records of incidents of abuse and use those records to inform future prevention planning.

Source: Department of Homeland Security, *Federal Register*, 79, 13099–13183.

It is acknowledged that for many of the settings described, there may be no means of undertaking such assessments, and the skills and competences of those conducting forensic medical examinations of complainants and suspects of alleged sexual assault may be limited or absent. It is important that any individual asked to assess a potential sexual assault understands the basic principles of such an examination and, if necessary recognizes when to seek additional or corroborative assistance. A forensic medical and forensic scientific examination potentially assists the investigation of sexual crime in a variety of ways including identifying perpetrators, corroborating accounts, excluding accounts, and confirming detail. The forensic medical assessment comprises a comprehensive examination, identifying injury, and obtaining appropriate samples for forensic scientific assessment and contemporaneous documentation (which may include photodocumentation) (Payne-James 2016). The interpretation of the significance of genital and nongenital injuries will be crucial in the assessment of findings and is dependent on accurate documentation and nonambiguous use of terms to described findings (Crane 2013; White 2013). The forensic scientific input is directed at analyzing scenes, recovering relevant evidence, and using a wide variety of analytic and technical methods (including fiber analysis, deoxyribonucleic acid analysis, and toxicology) to assist the investigation. Such techniques are reviewed elsewhere and where possible, applied. Medical care must be arranged appropriately to address (1) treatment of injuries, (2) risk of pregnancy, and (3) sexually transmitted infection (including hepatitis and HIV). Forensic science can help determine the nature of sexual acts, the gender and possible identity of the assailant, and the potential links with other offenses. From the medical examination, the majority of samples taken are biological (e.g., samples from the mouth, vulva, vagina, anus, penis) as swabs and/or blood and urine for toxicology.

Support to the Complainant

In the nondetention setting, standards are set for the immediate needs of complainants after sexual assault, and these should apply in detention. Such needs include safety and privacy, followed by treatment of injuries and prevention of unwanted pregnancy and sexually transmitted infections, including HIV. The management should also include risk identification of self-harm and suicide, as well as safeguarding children and vulnerable adults. For nonacute or and past sexual assault, consideration must be given to risks of conditions such as PTSD (Mason and Lodrick 2013). Pregnancy prevention may be required using oral or mechanical methods of emergency contraception, and the availability may vary between districts and countries, depending on local laws and cultural or religious beliefs. Sexually transmitted infections, including gonorrhea, chlamydia, hepatitis B, and HIV, are an important part of the management of victims of sexual assault and is best prevented immediately by offering bacterial and viral prophylaxis followed by sexual health screening 2 weeks later. Ideally, awareness of local prevalence of infections and resistance to antibiotics should decide treatment. Prophylaxis against HIV infection after sexual exposure should be discussed and offered in high-risk cases for up to 72 hours after exposure. In high-prevalence areas, prophylaxis HIV infection after sexual exposure should be offered as a routine.

Summary

Sexual assault in detention embraces a huge range of possible abuses and contacts, all of which should be investigated as criminal acts. Adults and children, males and females, may all be affected, and the abuses may be between those detained or between those detained and the personnel detaining them. Many (perhaps the majority) will be unreported and uninvestigated. Many that are investigated will be investigated inadequately. There are a number of initiatives that are assisting (in those settings with the capability) in highlighting the issues and which provide guidelines and strategies to prevent, detect, and respond to such abuses. The US PREA is perhaps a model with which local practice can be compared and contrasted. Often, the abuses will be associated with poor care; cruel, inhumane, and degrading treatment; and torture. As with all such allegations, the key issues are to ensure that all those involved in detaining individuals are made aware of the appropriate standards of behavior and how those standards are defined in national and international laws and instruments. If such allegations of abuses are raised, then they must be properly investigated and, if appropriate, brought to trial. Clearly, this will not be practical in many of the settings described. It is, however, crucial that governments and states, those in authority, and individuals ensure that where such matters can be pursued, that they are and with vigor.

References

Bartels, S., Kelly, J., Scott, J., Leaning, J., Mukwege, D., Joyce, N., and VanRooyen, M. 2013, Militarized sexual violence in South Kivu, Democratic Republic of Congo, *Journal of Interpersonal Violence*, vol. 28, pp. 340–358.

Beck, A. J., and Harrison, P. M. 2007, Sexual victimization in state and federal prisons reported by inmates, in *Bureau of Justice Statistics Special Report*, Bureau of Justice Statistics, Washington, DC. Available from: https://www.bjs.gov/content/pub/press/svsfpri07pr.cfm.

Black, M. 1998, Girls and war: An extra vulnerability, *People Planet*, vol. 7, pp. 24–25.

Brown, C. 2012, Rape as a weapon of war in the Democratic Republic of the Congo, *Torture*, vol. 22, pp. 24–37.

Crane, J. 2013, Interpretation of non-genital injuries in sexual assault, *Best Practice & Research Clinical Obstetrics & Gynaecology*, vol. 27, pp. 103–111.

Department of Homeland Security 2014, Standards to prevent, detect, and respond to sexual abuse and assault in confinement facilities: Final rule, *Federal Register*, vol. 79, pp. 13099–13183.

Garland, B., and Wilson, G. 2013, Prison inmates' views of whether reporting rape is the same as snitching: An exploratory study and research agenda, *Journal of Interpersonal Violence*, vol. 28, pp. 1201–1222.

Guy, K. M. 2014, Mai-Mai militia and sexual violence in Democratic Republic of the Congo, *International Journal of Emergency Mental Health and Human*, vol. 16, pp. 366–372.

Hensley, C., Koscheski, M., and Tewksbury R. 2005, Examining the characteristics of male sexual assault targets in a Southern maximum-security prison, *Journal of Interpersonal Violence*, vol. 20, pp. 667–679.

Holmes, W. C., Gariti, K. O., Sadeghi, L., and Joisa, S. D. 2007, Abuse of war zone detainees: Veterans' perceptions of acceptability, *Military Medicine*, vol. 172, pp. 175–181.

Kelly-Hanku, A., Kawage, T., Vallely, A., Mek, A., and Mathers, B. 2015, Sex, violence and HIV on the inside: Cultures of violence, denial, gender inequality and homophobia negatively influence the health outcomes of those in closed settings, *Culture Health & Sexuality*, vol. 17, pp. 990–1003.

Linehan, T. 1993, Barred from safe sex, *Nursing Times*, vol. 89, pp. 16–17.

Loncar, M., Henigsberg, N., and Hrabac, P. 2010, Mental health consequences in men exposed to sexual abuse during the war in Croatia and Bosnia, *International Journal of Emergency Mental Health and Human*, vol. 25, pp. 191–203.

Mailloux, D. L., and Serin, R. C. 2003, Sexual assaults during hostage takings and forcible confinements: Implications for practice, *Sexual Abuse*, vol. 15, pp. 161–170.

Mair, J. S., Frattaroli, S., and Teret, S. P. 2003, New hope for victims of prison sexual assault, *Journal of Law, Medicine & Ethics*, vol. 31, pp. 602–606.

Mason, F., and Lodrick, Z. 2013, Psychological consequences of sexual assault, *Best Practice & Research Clinical Obstetrics & Gynaecology*, vol. 27, pp. 27–37.

O'Connor, M. 2014, Sexual violence in armed conflict: The least condemned of war crimes, *Journal of Law, Medicine & Ethics*, vol. 21, pp. 528–542.

Olujic, M. B. 1995, Coercion and torture in former Yugoslavia. *Cultural Survival Quarterly*, vol. Spring, pp. 43–45.

Olujic, M. B. 1998, Embodiment of terror: Gendered violence in peacetime and wartime in Croatia and Bosnia-Herzegovina, *Medical Anthropology Quarterly*, vol. 12, pp. 31–50.

Oosterhoff, P., Zwanikken, P., and Ketting, E. 2004, Sexual torture of men in Croatia and other conflict situations: An open secret, *Reproductive Health Matters,* vol. 12, pp. 68–77.

Payne-James, J. J. 2016, Sexual offenses, adult: Injuries and findings after sexual contact, in *Encyclopedia of forensic and legal medicine*, 2nd edn, pp. 280–285.

Payne-James, J. J., Newton, M., and Bassindale, C. 2016, Forensic science, forensic medicine and sexual crime, in *Witness Testimony in Sexual Cases*, Oxford University Press, Oxford.

Richters, J., Butler, T., Schneider, K., Yap, L., Kirkwood, K., Grant, L., Richards, A., Smith, A. M., and Donovan, B. 2012, Consensual sex between men and sexual violence in Australian prisons, *Archives of Sexual Behavior*, vol. 41, pp. 517–524.

Rowell-Cunsolo, T. L., Harrison, R. J., and Haile, R. 2014, Exposure to prison sexual assault among incarcerated Black men, *Journal of African American Studies (New Brunswick)*, vol. 18, pp. 54–62.

Saliu, A., and Akintunde, B. 2014, Knowledge, attitude, and preventive practices among prison inmates in Ogbomoso Prison at Oyo State, South West Nigeria, *International Journal of Reproductive Medicine*, vol. 2014, 364375. doi: 10.1155/2014/364375.

Schneider, K., Richters, J., Butler, T., Yap, L., Richards, A., Grant, L., Smith, A. M., and Donovan, B. 2011, Psychological distress and experience of sexual and physical assault among Australian prisoners, *Criminal Behaviour and Mental Health*, vol. 21, pp. 333–349.

Stephens, T., Cozza, S., and Braithwaite, R. L. 1999, Transsexual orientation in HIV risk behaviours in an adult male prison, *International Journal of STD & AIDS*, vol. 10, pp. 28–31.

Tsai, A. C., Eisa, M. A., Crosby, S. S., Sirkin, S., Heisler, M., Leaning, J., and Iacopino, V. 2012, Medical evidence of human rights violations against non-Arabic-speaking civilians in Darfur: A cross-sectional study, *PLOS Medicine*, vol. 9, p. e1001198.

UN Human Rights Office of the High Commissioner. 2002, Optional Protocol to the Convention against Torture and other Cruel, Inhuman or Degrading Treatment or Punishment, Article 4 para 2. Available from: http://www.ohchr.org/EN/ProfessionalInterest/Pages/OPCAT.aspx.

UN Nations Third Committee of the UN General Assembly, 2015, United Nations Standard minimum rules for the treatment of prisoners (the Nelson Mandela Rules), UN, Geneva.

UNODC (United Nations Office on Drugs and Crime) 2006, *HIV/AIDS prevention, care, treatment and support in prison settings, a framework for an effective national response*, UNODC, Vienna.

UNODC 2013, *HIV prevention, treatment and care in prisons and other closed settings: A comprehensive package of interventions*, UNODC, Vienna.

US Department of Justice 2012, *Justice Department releases final rule to prevent, detect and respond to prison rape*, US Department of Justice, Washington, DC. Available from: http://www.justice .gov/opa/pr/justice-department-releases-final-rule-prevent-detect-and-respond-prison -rape. [November 25, 2015].

White, C. 2013, Genital injuries in adults, *Best Practice & Research Clinical Obstetrics & Gynaecology*, vol. 27, pp. 113–130.

Wolff, N., and Jing Shi, J. 2009, Contextualization of physical and sexual assault in male prisons: Incidents and their aftermath, *Correct Health Care*, vol. 15, pp. 58–77.

Yap, L., Richters, J., Butler, T., Schneider, K., Grant, L., and Donovan, B. 2011, The decline in sexual assaults in men's prisons in New South Wales: A "systems" approach, *Journal of Interpersonal Violence*, vol. 26, pp. 3157–3181.

Zawati, H. M. 2007, Impunity or immunity: Wartime male rape and sexual torture as a crime against humanity, *Torture*, vol. 17, pp. 27–47.

11

Children in Detention

Peter Green

CONTENTS

Introduction

In this chapter, the terms child and young person are meant to apply to any individual under the age of 18 years, the internationally agreed age of the majority as expressed on the United Nations Convention on the Rights of the Child (UNCRC 1989).

"Independent and qualified inspectors should be empowered to conduct inspections on a regular basis and to undertake unannounced inspections on their own initiative; they should place special emphasis on holding conversations with children in the facilities in a confidential setting" (UN Committee on the Rights of the Child, General Comment 10).

This chapter is written using predominantly the jurisdiction of England and Wales as an example, but the principles that will be discussed will be applicable to other jurisdictions. It is important for any practitioner to be aware of the local laws, statutes, and protocols that apply in the relevant jurisdiction.

The significance of putting children in detention is very real; the effects of detention on children are rarely positive and can be very damaging (The Australian Human Rights Commission 2014; Lorek 2009; Ashton et al. 2009). A consideration of the needs and management of children and young people should always be undertaken by all agencies who have dealings with detainees, and this particularly applies to healthcare practitioners whose ethos is governed by the principal of the well-being of humanity.

Children and young people (i.e., those under the age of 18 years) are by definition vulnerable (Brown 2015). Particular and additional vulnerabilities will be described, and practical strategies for effectively dealing with their needs and development will be outlined.

Incidence

Criminal Age of Responsibility

There is a wide range of ages across countries and international systems within which it is presumed that the capacity to commit crime has been achieved. The relevance of this benchmark is that it recognizes that a child has attained a sufficient degree of emotional, mental, and intellectual maturity to be held accountable for his or her actions (PRI [Penal Reform International] 2013). In England and Wales, the criminal age of responsibility (CAR) is 10 years old. In Scotland, it is 8 years old for some cases, but the government is currently consulting on changing this to 12 years (Scottish Government 2016). The majority of the rest of the world chooses ages above this up to the International Criminal Court and Brazil where the age of majority (18) is used. Below the CAR, children cannot be formally charged and are therefore immune from criminal prosecution. The median age is 12 years old (Cipriani 2009).

Specific Issues, Risks, and Vulnerabilities Related to Children

Under the terms of the UNCRC (1989), children and young people are entitled to a full range of rights that cover all aspects of their lives. These include the principles of the right to be heard, their views to be taken seriously in all matters which affect them, and the right of access to the best possible health and restorative therapy if they have been harmed. The health needs of children and young people should therefore be the highest priority when they are held in detention.

In England and Wales, national legislation and statutory guidance make the needs of children and young people the paramount concern of those that deal with them and make their well-being the responsibility of all. Local legislation puts local authorities at the heart of coordinating multiagency working which is seen as the key to ensuring a holistic approach to child safeguarding and the promotion of child well-being (Children Act 1989, 2004). Multiagency safeguarding children boards include representatives from detention authorities such as the police, and youth offending teams, as well as having access to prison representatives. Mental health authorities, among other things, are responsible for the compulsory detention of those individuals who have mental illness and who have been criminally active.

Throughout history, there has been an almost universal inclination to see children as small adults when it comes to processes to deal with their detention rather than individuals in their own right. Their innate vulnerabilities were not fully and internationally recognized until the UNCRC of 1989. Nearly three decades later and the situation has barely changed despite the almost complete global acceptance of the convention.

As a consequence, children and young people in detention quickly lose the following:

- The right to be heard
- Respect as an individual (seen as a nuisance)
- Respect for their views
- A normal supportive structure of family or care

Without being able to exercise their right to be heard, children and young people are unable to establish or maintain any control over their lives or their future. This is in itself dehumanizing and creates or exacerbates further vulnerabilities. At the same time, a lack of respect for their individual needs, because they are not adults, very often entrenches the notion that they are a nuisance because attending to their needs requires additional time, effort, and expense, all of which commodities are universally in short supply in places of detention. There is therefore an inevitable lack of respect for their views and opinions. The absence of a normal supportive family structure (which would normally include adult advocates who could speak up for them) only exacerbates the isolation and vulnerabilities that they experience.

Detaining children and young people isolates them from family protection, which further compounds an almost inevitable lack of understanding of the processes of detention. This lack of understanding of detention processes denies them opportunities to speak up for themselves when processes or treatments are unfair or abusive. In these situations, children and young people are at risk of coercion to make compromising statements that may disadvantage them and/or codefendants (Physicians for Human Rights—Israel 2011).

It always helps to have detention facilities that allow easy and regular access by a juvenile's family and parts of the community to provide support to the detainee. Such community access helps detention facilities to remain accountable in recognizing, in an appropriately transparent manner, the rights of the children in their care. It also further helps with the rehabilitation and reintegration process both during detention and on release into society for the juvenile in question. The ultimate ambition of maintaining contact between the child and the family/community is to build child and adolescent resilience that in turn will minimize the likelihood of reoffending.

Further, removal from linguistic and ethnic origins without appropriate transitional arrangements are likely to have a significant and damaging impact on the development and well-being of individual children (Robjant et al. 2009). Educational opportunities being in short supply in places of detention only compounds the vulnerability to illiteracy that many children in detention are exposed to. This lack of educational and cultural stimulation further adds to the losses experienced by children and young people in detention. These, in turn, add to the immediate and long-term financial impoverishment that child detainees almost inevitably end up suffering from.

All these losses greatly enhance the risks of drugs and alcohol misuse which themselves lead to an increased risk of ongoing criminality and consequent developmental failures (Hawkins et al. 2000). There are also clear and concomitant risks to health and psychological problems, which include an abnormally high level of hyperactivity disorders and special learning needs. Specialist care and understanding is required to effectively support such children and young people: without it, detention will only exacerbate their problems.

Further, there are risks of bullying to children and young people in detention. In mixed adult and children detention institutions, this will usually be carried out by fellow adult detainees; and in child institutions, by fellow child detainees. Detention staff also bully children and young people, commonly under the pretext of a punishment regime (CPT [European Committee for the Prevention of Torture and Inhuman or Degrading Treatment or Punishment] 2015a, para. 126). Such justification cannot take away from the fact that such treatment is not in the best interest, either in the short or long term, of the child or young person, but is instead inclined to ingrain a violent attitude in a developing mind. Detention of children also exposes them to the risks of witnessing violence, which is itself a damaging and regressive influence on minors.

Children and young people in detention can also experience malnutrition, which has a disproportionate impact on a growing and developing individual. It must therefore be a particular concern for monitoring and inspection organizations to ensure that food and nourishment are of a good standard at all times (CPT 2015b, para. 118).

Similarly, the lack of appropriate education, leisure facilities, and opportunities to both rest and normal play can have a lifelong impact on young people leading to lifelong difficulties with relationships and with authority if these deficiencies are not recognized and ameliorated.

Female children and young people have singular vulnerabilities. Places of detention exposed them to the risks of sexual harassment and/or maltreatment from fellow inmates (of both genders) and staff alike. This puts female detainees at a greater risk of psychological illness, which is itself a greater risk for female detainees. This, in turn, leads to greater risk of deliberate self-harm and suicide attempts (The Australian Human Rights Commission 2014). A further challenge for young females is the common lack of support for menstrual needs and appropriate standards of care for those who are pregnant. There is also an associated common failure of concern for the children of young mothers in detention and the harm this can do to both parties in such a critical relationship.

Young people with disabilities may have particularly complex needs while in places of detention, such as specialist feeding or therapy regimes, and are commonly found in social care homes where various degrees of restriction on liberty may be necessary to keep the individual safe. Here, a balance has to be struck with the consequent loss of liberty. Relatively recent English and Welsh legislation has sought to address this problem which requires careful consideration of each individual case (Mental Capacity ACT 2005). Oversight and review processes are a necessary part of the structures to allow the full implementation of the rights of young people held in these circumstances.

A significant principle, while not being the whole answer, for dealing with many of these vulnerabilities is that of the custodial separation of children from adults. It is recognized that in many countries, this is observed only in part, for example, in the United States, Dubai, Indonesia, Cambodia, the Philippines, and Zambia. One of the practical risks is that the provision of separate child cells in an otherwise adult-dominated detention area only increases adult overcrowding. Nonetheless, the benefits of separation from adults significantly reduces the risks of bullying, sexual maltreatment, and other forms of neglect.

Specific Conventional Protections

There are a significant number of international standards that are in place to protect children and young people and foster their rights while in detention. In date order, these include the Body of Principles for the Protection of All Persons under any form of detention or imprisonment (UN 1988), the UNCRC (1989), the UN Rules for the Protection of Juveniles Deprived of their Liberty (UN 1990; also known as the Havana rules), The European Prison Rules (Council of Europe 2006), The Principles and Best Practices on the Protection of Persons Deprived of Liberty in the Americas (Inter-American Commission on Human Rights 2008), *The European Rules for Juvenile Offenders subject to Sanctions or*

Measures (2009), Standard Minimum Rules for the Treatment of Prisoners (UN 2015; also known as the Nelson Mandela Rules), and the Standards Document of the Council of Europe Committee for the Prevention of Torture and Inhuman or Degrading Treatment or Punishment (CPT 2015c).

An overarching and universally agreed principle is that the detention of children should always be a sanction of last resort and always for the least possible time (UNCRC 1989). It cannot be ignored, however, that significant numbers of children and young people are still detained by state institutions, commonly in breach of this principle and with little or no recognition of the very significant additional vulnerabilities outlined earlier.

Inspection Mechanisms: Ambitions, Standards, and Processes

There are a significant number of different organizations and institutions that may be involved in the monitoring and detention facilities for children. These can include governmentally established organizations such as children's commissioners or ombudspersons; NPMs; lawyers and bar institutions; judicial bodies; UN subcommittee to the Convention against torture; the CPT; the Special Rapporteur on Prisons and Conditions of Detention in Africa; independent custody and prison visiting institutions; nongovernmental investigative organizations, and the UN SRT.

It is to be hoped that with increasing recognition of the special vulnerabilities of children in detention, monitoring groups will develop within existing bodies with sufficient specialist knowledge and understanding to have an impact on breaches of children's rights in detention. This requires inspectors who are knowledgeable, experienced in children's rights, and have appropriate and necessary authority and duties. This positive state of affairs is by no means universal and much remains to be done to enhance the respect due to all children and young people in detention.

Ambitions

The actions whereby monitoring bodies can help safeguard the rights of children in detention are shown in Table 11.1.

It is generally agreed that monitoring organizations that have the best chances of fulfilling these ambitions have the need to have the following appropriate characteristics. Table 11.2 identifies these characteristics.

Monitoring organizations must also be free to write reports that are published and are systematically followed up. Without the opportunity to work freely and independently, monitoring arrangements will not be effective in finding and reporting inappropriate, abusive, or neglectful behavior. With regard to monitoring the detention of children and their particular vulnerabilities, it is proportionate for specialist teams to be developed, although they do not need to be completely outside adult monitoring arrangements. It is the specialist expertise and understanding that should be provided.

TABLE 11.1

Actions whereby Monitoring Bodies Can Help Safeguard the Rights of Children in Detention

- Ensuring children in detention are given a voice
- Preventing violence and maltreatment of children
- Holding child-detaining authorities accountable
- Encouraging, supporting, and protecting detention staff who whistle-blow
- Encouraging the replication of good practice
- Identifying and challenging poor practice
- Raising challenges and identifying changes required in strategic policy and legislation

TABLE 11.2

Ideal Characteristics of Monitoring Bodies

- Independent, i.e., not part of the detention facility management team
- Appropriately qualified and include medically trained inspectors
- Required to include women when monitoring detention facilities that hold girls and young women
- Required to make regular visits
- Free to make unannounced visits
- Authorized to visit all places were children are detained
- Authorized to speak to all employees where children are detained
- Authorized to inspect all records regarding conditions and treatment of children
- Free to choose which places of child detention they visit and which children they interview
- Able to process specific allegations of maltreatment

Standards

The fundamental standards that are to be applied must all ensure that the children and young people are in receipt of all their rights as outlined in the UNCRC. All children in detention have the same rights as those outside except the loss of their liberty. It is the primary function of monitoring organizations to do all it can to ensure that there are no other deficiencies in the child's life. Not least, children should only be detained as a matter of last resort and for the shortest period of time. The principal objective of detention for children is rehabilitation and reintegration into society once they are ready to be released. In all other respects, their childhoods should not suffer during detention. To undertake the monitoring process effectively an inspection must refer to the following issues (PRI 2011) (see also Table 11.3):

Protection from torture and ill-treatment: It is a fundamental tenet of child safeguarding that children should be kept safe and free from maltreatment. Detention considerably increases the risks because codetainees and detention officials commonly use violence or the threat of it to achieve control over their lives or organization.

Separate detention from adults: Places of adult detention contain individuals whose behaviors are not societally acceptable and commonly violent or abusive and represent poor role modeling for children. It has long been a fundamental principle of child detention that they should not be kept in such company as it is damaging and corrupting.

TABLE 11.3

Issues That Should Be Referred to in Each Inspection by the Monitoring Body

- Protection from torture and ill-treatment
- Separate detention from adults
- Good recordkeeping
- Complaints
- Material conditions
- Community and family contact
- Education and recreation
- Right to healthcare
- Professional competence
- Girls and young women
- Staff training and management
- Rehabilitation

Good record keeping: When the state detains an individual, it is important that good records are kept. These should demonstrate attention to due process from the moment of arrival to the moment of release. A full record of all incidents, both positive and adverse, is to be expected as well as compliance with regime routines such as food provision, education, exercise, free association, and family contact. It is particularly important that all medical records, the creation of which is an obligation on all healthcare professionals, are maintained but kept separately from the main detention record. They must also only be accessible to healthcare professionals. This principal applies whether they are on a separate computer system or on paper.

Complaints: When children are mistreated or have concerns or complaints about any aspect of their detention, there must be an effective system to hear them and to record and investigate their concerns. If these concerns contain a medical or healthcare element, they must be passed to the healthcare staff in a completely unfettered manner. Detention officials, who do not act in the best interests of the children and control and do not heed their complaints or concerns, represent a serious risk to the well-being of the child involved.

Material conditions: The environment in which children and young people are detained must be equipped and furnished in a child- or young person-centered manner with adequate bedding and toilet facilities, washing facilities that are hygienic and usable, access to good and regular nutrition, facilities for recreation or sports, preferred pastime activities, space that allows for privacy, and the maintenance of dignity. While a place of detention can never be a true replacement for home, the environment must be as homelike as possible to ensure that the untrammeled development of the child and young person continues much as it would have done in the community.

Community and family contact: All children and young people need to maintain contact with family and friends just as they would do when living in their community. This is why it is vital that places of detention of children must provide as unmoderated access as possible for family and friends to maintain the ties with home and to encourage rehabilitation. Without this kind of contact, children will become inappropriately isolated—in itself a damaging influence on psychological development and resilience.

Education and recreation: Education and recreation are two very important planks of childhood development and must be provided in a manner equivalent to outside life, i.e., regular, organized, and progressive education with associated facilities for hobbies, sports, and vocational activity. Clear educational objectives must be developed as part of the educational plan and evidence must be sought to show if and when targets are being achieved.

Right to healthcare: Provision of healthcare is a fundamental right for those children held in detention. This includes access to specialist treatment for those that need it and where necessary must be provided by institutions outside the detention area. Monitoring organizations should check for each of the seven following fundamental principles (CPT 2015d, para. 32):

1. *Access to a doctor*: Access to a doctor must be unfettered by interference from detention staff and should not be used as a bargaining chip to coerce detainees for the benefit of the officials or management.

2. *Equivalence of care*: Tthe standard of healthcare offered to children and young people held in detention must be no less than that available to those children and young people in the community. Institutions of detention should have healthcare practitioners available at all times, who are qualified to give appropriate and specific advice and have access to further specialist care should the need arise.

3. *Consent and confidentiality*: It is a fundamental and universal ethic that all healthcare practitioners are required to work only with the consent of their patients. This is as true in the place of detention as in the community. Monitoring bodies should ensure that the standard is not breached. Similarly, the same degree of confidentiality that is applied in the community should be found in places of detention. Consequently, healthcare records must be secured and managed by the healthcare professionals alone. While it is recognized that on occasions, detaining authorities needs to know something about the well-being of the detainees to safely care for them, such information sharing can only be on a strictly proportionate need-to-know basis and, with rare exceptions, only with the patient's consent. (For example, a medical emergency such as meningitis in which the detainee has lost mental functioning with a consequent loss of mental capacity to consent).

4. *Preventive healthcare*: In as much as healthcare professionals are required to provide treatment and advice and healthcare support, they are also mandated to provide advice and information to prevent illness, e.g., the spread of infectious diseases such as tuberculosis and hepatitis.

5. *Humanitarian assistance*: There is a requirement on all practitioners to provide good healthcare. There is also a further expectation that healthcare professionals will provide humanitarian support for all detainees. This particularly applies to children and young people where responsible adults such as healthcare professionals are expected to respond to the broader needs of their patients, taking time to build relationships and fulfilling the function of a role model, while also drawing the attention of the authorities to the needs of their charges as and when they are made aware of them. This approach is consistent with the UK model of child safeguarding in which it is the responsibility of all professionals who deal with children to respond in a supportive way to the children's needs.

6. *Professional independence*: The need for independence in healthcare is never more important than in the area of child detention. Practitioners must be robust in defending the rights of the young patients when they see the risk of transgression or maltreatment, e.g., unauthorized force being applied to a child. A similarly robust attitude is also required to maintain the messy professional standards with regard particularly to confidentiality and consent.

7. *Professional competence*: Working in the area of custodial healthcare requires particular competencies. In child detention, healthcare practitioners should have a primary care understanding of pediatrics, juvenile psychiatry, and infectious diseases and ready access to specialists in these and all other conditions that affect children and young people. When in detention, this population requires specialist carers and support as outlined earlier. A female presence in the monitoring organization is therefore required as is specialist female healthcare support in the place of detention to respectfully deal with the gender-specific needs of the girls and young women.

Staff training and management: The organization and management of a place of child detention requires the staff to have specialist training and the institute to be well aware of their special responsibilities with regard to the rights of the child. Monitoring organizations should appraise the understanding demonstrated by the staff and management of these responsibilities. They should assess training and assessment records to find assurances that appropriate safeguarding standards are in place.

Rehabilitation: All child detention institutions must provide programs of rehabilitation for the children and young people in their charge with a view to facilitating the reintegration of the child or young person back into the community in a better position to resist attempts to reoffend and to make a positive contribution to society. This therefore involves not only providing education and training but also programs of personal development, which will lead to continuing education or employment once the detainee is released.

Processes

In fulfilling their functions, monitoring institutions need to gather and process evidence in an organized manner. The following apply particularly to institutions of detention for children but have a significant overlap with the monitoring of places of adult detention. It should always be remembered that children and young people are most vulnerable when they first enter a new institution, whether a police station, a prison, a detaining hospital, or a care home.

The sources of information for monitors are the observation of conditions and interviews. It is important that they listen to the experiences of children and young people of all ethnicities and linguistic backgrounds. It is also important to gather statistics on the number and kind of children in detention with a specific focus, for example, on numbers imprisoned in adult prisons, whether detention is actually a measure of last resort, and whether there are excess delays in case processing in the pretrial period. Monitors can also provide fresh ears for complaints and allegations from the young people (which should be immediately referred to the authorities), as well as a source of contact with the outside world that is supportive. Wider information about the general experience of the systems they are held in, such as the courts and police processes, can also be usefully gathered and fed back to the relevant authorities even if they are not responsible for the institution which they are being seen.

Any monitoring organization should have its own child safeguarding policy in place to ensure that monitors are appropriately recruited, screened, and supervised during the monitoring process. They should be given appropriate training in interviewing children and recording, maintenance, and safe storing of the personal data that they will be provided with. An example of such a policy is that of Her Majesty's Inspectorate of Prisons (2008).

Interviews with children and young people should be undertaken with care, bearing in mind the fact that children in detention often have substantial difficulties trusting unfamiliar adults. Conversations with children should follow specialty interview techniques that build trust, and adequate time should be allowed to ensure that the truth of the child experience will be relayed to the monitor. Without attention to such details, conversations with children will be of little real purpose. There is no place for a tick box approach to this subject. Children should therefore be encouraged to give their own accounts of their experiences. Particular awareness should be demonstrated concerning the risks of reprisals for a child who discloses concerns or makes allegations about maltreatment. This calls for particular care in planning interviews, making sure they are held out of the hearing and preferably out of sight of detaining officers or codetainees, and, above all, ensuring that the best interests of the child prevail throughout the process.

No inspection can meaningfully evaluate a detaining institution without interviewing representatives of the management. Assessments must be made of the awareness of the needs of the children they are in charge of, their professionalism putting those principles into practice, their capacity for good team working, leadership and appropriate recordkeeping, and support and encouragement they provide to the front line staff.

Institutional records are a vital source of information with regard to the health and safety of the children detained, the education and recreational opportunities that they are given, and the rehabilitative and integration processes that are in place. Healthcare monitors should scrutinize healthcare records to ensure that appropriate therapeutic actions have being taken, that health preventative programs are in place, that medicine management is appropriate and not exclusively dependent on nonhealthcare staff, and that healthcare access in practice complies with the standards laid out earlier.

Interviews with, and observations at work of, frontline staff should also be structured to evidence their true understanding of the needs of children and the culture of the staff toward their charges. Quotations from child interviews must not be made because this breaches the confidentiality principle under which all such interviews are conducted. As well as their views about their charges, their opinions and observations about the management should also be sought in an effort to triangulate managerial assertions about example training frequency, policy document availability, workload, and capacity.

Monitoring reports should be written as soon as possible following the visit and sent to the detention authorities straightaway. The report should be structured, make mention of all the identified concerns or issues, and provide a list of actions to improve deficiencies. The report should describe any changes found since the last visit and commend good practice whenever it is found. If recommendations relate to issues of, for example, national policy, then a separate report should be sent to the appropriate authorities (see also Table 11.4).

TABLE 11.4

Example of Monitoring Report Structure

Visit reports should contain a chapter with general information, including (at a minimum) the following:
* Details about the composition of the visiting team
* Date and time of the visit
* Specific objectives of the visit
* A discussion of how information was gathered and checked before, during, and after the visit.

The substantive part of the report should be thematically divided, rather than chronologically. It should clearly present, at a minimum, the principal concerns about the following:
* The treatment of children and young people
* The protective measures employed
* The material conditions encountered
* Issues concerning detention personnel

For each theme, the report should
* Describe the objective situation observed
* Offer an analysis of the risks
* Provide recommendations

Source: Association for the Prevention of Torture, *Monitoring Police Custody, A Practical Guide*, Association for the Prevention of Torture, Geneva, 2013.

Conclusion

Monitoring institutions that hold children and young people in detention calls for not only a thorough understanding of basic monitoring practice, but also a real understanding of the specific vulnerabilities of children and young people, their rights to be treated as individuals in their own right, the skills and personnel to find out the truth of their experiences, and a recognition of the very positive role they can play in the lives of some of the most vulnerable in society. It is to be hoped that this chapter will help to develop some of these characteristics.

References

Ashton, L., Collins, P., Katona, C. et al. 2009, *Significant harm—The effects of administrative detention on the health of children, young people and their families*, London: Royal College of Paediatrics and Child Health. Available from: http://www.rcpch.ac.uk/pdf/significant%20harm%20inter collegiate%20statement%20Dec09.pdf.

Association for the Prevention of Torture 2013, *Monitoring police custody, a practical guide*, Association for the Prevention of Torture, Geneva.

Brown, K. 2015, *Vulnerability and Young People: Care and Social Control in Policy and Practice*, Bristol, UK: Policy Press.

Children Act 1989.

Children Act 2004, Section 10.

Cipriani, D. 2009, *Children's rights and the minimum age of criminal responsibility: A global perspective*, Routledge.

Council of Europe 2006, *The European prison rules: rec(2006)2*, Council of Europe, Strasbourg.

Council of Europe 2009, *The European Rules for Juvenile Offenders subject to Sanctions or Measures*, Council of Europe, Starsbourg.

CPT 2015a, *CPT Standards: Extract from the 24th General Report [CPT/Inf (2015) 1]*, CPT, Strasbourg, para. 126.

CPT (European Committee for the Prevention of Torture and Inhuman or Degrading Treatment or Punishment) 2015b, *CPT Standards: Extract from the 24th general report [CPT/Inf (2015) 1]*, CPT, Strasbourg, para. 118.

CPT 2015c, *Standards document CPT/Inf/E (2002) 1—rev. 2015*, CPT, Strasbourg.

CPT 2015d, *CPT standards: Extract from the 3rd general report [CPT/Inf (93) 12]*, CPT, Strasbourg, para. 32.

Hawkins, J. D., Todd, I., Herrenkohl, D. P. et al. 2000, Predictors of youth violence, *US Department of Justice Juvenile Justice Bulletin*, p. 7.

Her Majesty's Inspectorate of Prisons 2008, *Child safeguarding policy*, Her Majesty's Inspectorate of Prisons, London. Available from: https://www.justiceinspectorates.gov.uk/hmiprisons/wp-content/uploads/sites/4/2014/02/HMIP-Child-Protection-Policy-2015.pdf.

Inter-American Commission on Human Rights 2008, *The principles and best practices on the protection of persons deprived of liberty in the Americas*, Inter-American Commission on Human Rights, Washington, DC.

Lorek, A., Ehntholt, K., Nesbitt, A. et al. 2009, The mental and physical health difficulties of children held within a British immigration detention center: A pilot study, *Child Abuse & Neglect*, vol. 33, pp. 573–585.

Mental Capacity Act 2005, Sections 4A and 4B.

Physicians for Human Rights—Israel 2011, *Graciela Carmon coerced confessions: The case of Palestinian children*, Physicians for Human Rights—Israel, Jaffa.

PRI (Penal Reform International) 2011, *Safeguarding children in detention: Independent monitoring mechanisms for children in detention in MENA*, PRI, London.

PRI 2013, *Justice for child briefing no. 4*, PRI, London.

Robjant, K., Hassan, R., and Katona, C. 2009, Mental health implications of detaining asylum seekers: Systematic review, *British Journal of Psychiatry*, vol. 194, pp. 306–312.

Scottish Government 2016, *Consultation on the minimum age of criminal responsibility*, Scottish Government, Edinburgh. Available from: https://consult.scotland.gov.uk/youth-justice/minimum-age-of-criminal-responsibility.

The Australian Human Rights Commission 2014, *The forgotten children: National inquiry into children in immigration*, The Australian Human Rights Commission, Sydney.

UN 1988, *United Nations body of principles for the protection of all persons under any form of detention or imprisonment: Resolution 43/173*, UN, Geneva.

UN 1990, *United Nations rules for the protection of juveniles deprived of their liberty (the Havana rules): Resolution 45/113*, UN, Geneva.

UN 2015, *United Nations standard minimum rules for the treatment of prisoners (the Nelson Mandela rules): E/CN.15/2015/L.6/Rev.1*, UN, Geneva.

UNCRC (UN Convention on the Rights of the Child) 1989, *Resolution 44/25 1989*, UN, Geneva.

UNCRC 2007, *General Comment 10*, UN, Geneva.

12

Investigation of Ill-Treatment during Detention

Hernán Reyes

CONTENTS

Introduction

This chapter will focus on the way to tackle the issue of detainees who may have been submitted to some form of torture or cruel, inhuman, and degrading treatment (CIDT). While legally speaking, there is a difference between these two entities, they are both illegal under international human rights law. This chapter shall deal with a range of mistreatments, some that qualify as forms of torture according to international legal definitions, and others that are considered less intense in nature or in their effects, including "cruel, inhuman and degrading treatment"—but also even lesser forms. The term *ill-treatment*, a term often used so as to not distract from the real issue by launching a futile discussion on definitions, is also meant to encompass all categories of mistreatment that are not a form of torture.

The documentation of ill-treatment and torture has different important aspects that the outside monitor has to consider. Chapter 6 covers the physical aspects based on the Istanbul Protocol (IP) (IP 2004). The documentation of the psychological effects of torture is discussed in Chapter 5. This chapter addresses additional aspects of visits to places of detention by outside monitors, the actual interview with the interviewees, and will attempt to identify pitfalls to avoid. It is useful to remember at this point that it is the people (the detainees, inmates, prisoners, etc.) who are being visited, not buildings, and an empathic approach is the key to ensure that such visits are of maximum value to all.

Visits by outside monitors not only seek to document what has happened in the way of torture, both physical and psychological, but should also have a preventive role. The visits should assist in the preparation, carrying out, and following up of visits to victims of torture who are still in custody, as opposed to interviews with torture survivors in safe, therapeutic environments outside a custodial setting. Monitors who have worked in torture rehabilitation centers are aware that time for interviews is not a limiting factor in such settings. Furthermore, torture survivors can feel objectively safe from any reprisals. When interviews are carried out in custodial settings, with limited time and the fear of reprisals for talking to outsiders, monitors should be aware that these very real factors must be taken into consideration (British Medical Association 1991; Cassese 1996).

Background to Visits

Monitoring and prevention of ill-treatment in custodial situations covers a wide range of situations that will require different strategies. Even if one is able to visit a specific place of detention in the most favorable way (having access to all persons and not being restrained by an uncooperative detaining authority), such visits can vary considerably. A prison for sentenced prisoners who normally do not move anywhere may be visited, for example, twice a year. A police lockup, where detainees are held for only a week or two before being transferred elsewhere, may be visited more often. Many factors intervene, depending on the visiting modalities agreed upon, the size of the visiting teams, the composition of these, with interpreters, one or several doctors, and the actual objective of the visits in a given country and context.

The following guidelines will need to be adapted according to context, timing, and strategy adopted in each case. The prison doctor is often a key source of information (Reyes 2008; Staiff 2000). This can be in a positive way, if indeed that the doctor is doing his/her level best to provide care for the prisoners and has not been involved in any wrongdoing, or in a negative way, if the doctor has participated in interrogations and other coercive actions—in which case, the violation of medical ethics will be an additional issue to consider and document.

The premise here is that such visits have as their main objective to document whatever torture may have been inflicted on the people visited, so as to have a solid case to make, for it ceasing to happen, with the higher authorities. Such documentation will undoubtedly hopefully have a preventive action by putting an outside spotlight on the place and on the more general context where torture is condoned and implemented. This may set in motion mechanisms that will help put a stop to torture, or at least start to do so.

Another objective of any visit to is to have a humane approach toward the persons interviewed. Showing true empathy for them is essential for the detainee—perhaps more even so than getting the actual testimonies and any factual evidence. To document torture without, at the same time, providing as much solace and empathy to those persons who have been submitted to harsh and rigorous conditions, and ill-treatment or outright torture, would be inappropriate, however worthy the primary objective in itself could be.

Monitors from the outside are sometimes the only ones able to provide some solace and comfort to the prisoners, who are often deprived of outside contacts, even with their families. The personal contact and rapport established can be a most important contribution to the morale of a prisoner who has often been treated as subhuman by the torturers (Iacopino 1996;

Stover and Nightingale 1985). Thus, any privileged encounter with outsiders will often, in itself, implicitly give such a prisoner acknowledgment that he/she is not forgotten.

One initial question monitors often ask is how many prisoners should be seen and interviewed in a large prison, so as to get a significant sample that can be used for the documentation. This question leads to knowing then "which ones to choose," when there are a great number of them. The answers to these questions will depend on the actual situations. There are no foolproof sampling techniques or methods in a torture situation.

Prisoner populations in any situation are anything but homogeneous. Identifying whom to interview is a major problem. Choosing to document "the prisoners in the eastern half" of the courtyard is *not* a correct way for defining a random sample! Prisoners tend to cluster in groups of similar ethnic, political, same-village affiliation. Thus, to just choose one side instead of determining first what the distribution is may result to completely missing out on the theme to be documented. In a situation where torture is the main issue, just such crude sampling may miss the problem altogether.

All prisoners who have been alleged to have been ill treated should be at least offered a chance to come forward and speak in the privacy of the interview, if they so desire and according to their needs. Prisoners having been kept in isolation for months and years will have a greater need of contacting visitors from the outside than prisoners who live together and are allowed visits (Daudin and Reyes 1996). Likewise, prisoners held in extremely harsh disciplinary conditions are also more likely to be in need of some contact with an outsider than those in less stringent conditions.

Initial safeguards must be established with the authorities so that the visit itself does not put anyone in danger from any sort of reprisal. The main principle to adhere to, as a healthcare professional when interviewing prisoners in a coercive situation, is a principle that overarches all medical practice—*primum non nocere*—above all do no harm. Wanting to document torture at all costs will never justify putting prisoners at risk of reprisals for having spoken out. This core question of potential risk to the persons visited should be constantly kept in mind and reevaluated as the need arises during the visit.

To illustrate this from personal experiences, in one prison in Central Asia, a team was doing the first general tour of the premises, a visit of all facilities and cells where prisoners lived, worked, and generally had access to. While explaining to the prisoners that during the following days they would be able to speak in private to members of the team and to the doctor, the team leader asked the prisoners in the cell how many would want to speak to someone on the team. A small number of hands were raised. This procedure was repeated in several cells—until it was noticed that an accompanying member of the prison security staff was discretely taking down the names or numbers of all the prisoners who volunteered to speak to members of the team. It was immediately decided to ask nothing more during the general tour, as it was quite possibly putting prisoners in danger if they had to single themselves out.

Detaining authorities often coach prisoners as to what they can or cannot say to visitors. This may come out during talks with prisoners, if a brave soul reports it. The main point is that if talks are allowed in private and a sufficient number of inmates approach the visiting team, sooner or later, this type of issue will be mentioned, and thus, whatever information comes out will be judged accordingly. It is thus important to call a good number of prisoners, even from those who have nothing to say, so as to blur the list of those who come to talk.

In another example from personal experience, it was found out some time later, after the visit, and during the second repeat visit, that the chief security officer had been doing the same general tour of the premises as the visiting team—only several cells in front of the team. The security officer reminded prisoners in each cell that *"they* (the visitors) leave the prison—remember that *you* (the prisoners) do not!" It is only through the safeguard of having interviews in private that prisoners may decide if it is safe for them to speak freely and divulge information about torture.

A one-shot visit may be useless and even cause more harm than any good. The first visit in fact ends when the second, the repeat visit begins. A repeat visit is absolutely necessary if torture is the issue. First of all, it will show prisoners that one is serious about following them up and that one keeps promises made (to come back). Secondly, and more importantly, it will allow the team to find out whether anyone was harassed, or worse, because he or she talked to the outside visitors. If only one visit is planned, there will be no way of knowing for sure what happened *after* the team left.

Thus, repeat visits to *individuals*, and not just to prisons, are necessary to ensure the safety of all prisoners interviewed who are potentially at risk for retaliation. In order to effectively be able to locate these persons and personally (again, in privacy) interview them about any such reprisals, it is necessary to have some way of localizing each individual. There thus can be an objective need for some kind of system for taking down names and personal data so as to ensure reliable identification of the individuals concerned during a follow-up visit. The ICRC has such a system, based on its experience of its Central Tracing Agency, responsible initially for creating a file system for documenting all prisoners of war, and later extended to civilian victims of war as well. Other visiting mechanisms, the Council of Europe (CPT), for example, do not take down individual identities of interviewees and have to rely on making interviews as anonymously as possible, for example, by seeing a large number of prisoners, so as not to identify any one informer.

One visit alone may provide information about torture, but if it is not repeated, it will provide no safeguard to those prisoners who have put their trust in the monitors by speaking out.

Trust

Visits to prisoners in a context where torture may be or is known to be an issue will require careful planning. An initial interview with the detaining authority will be a necessary first step. This will usually be with the custodial service responsible for the prisoners—more rarely, the actual authorities responsible for their maltreatment. Needless to say, this initial interview must be carefully managed, as any false step could compromise the visit and access to the people to be seen and interviewed. Some information will always be obtained—for example, number of prisoners, how long they have been there, what regimes are applied to possible different categories of prisoners.

The most important information should be obtained from the prisoners. For this to happen, there has to be a relationship of trust between the prisoners and the outside monitor(s). This is not self-evident to the prisoners anymore than it is to the authorities allowing the visit. The authorities may have received orders to allow the outside visitor in and to even speak to prisoners in private—that does not mean they trust the outside visitor. They may try to "listen in on the interviews." This may be through a variety of ways, from insisting on having a guard be present (which should be politely but firmly refused); by installing microphones in whatever area the talks with prisoners are to take place; or, more commonly, simply by debriefing all those prisoners who have spoken to the outside monitor after the visit. Rather than recommend what some teams do—some teams are allowed to bring in sophisticated equipment that can detect electronic eavesdropping—the simplest way to avoid anyone listening in is to have the interview in private in a more or less foolproof place, such as out in the open. By speaking softly out of earshot of anyone, whispering if need be, the confidentiality of the interview should be guaranteed.

Prisoners may not necessarily trust the outside monitor if it is the first time they see someone from that visiting team. Proper identification and explanation of the role of the monitoring group must be shown to the prisoners, and clear explanations should be given as to the purpose and remit of the visit. Group interviews to begin with may be useful so as to break the ice. Such group talks are also useful for obtaining information on general conditions of imprisonment or details about (usually) safe subjects such as the food, sanitary conditions, and access to health care.

It should be kept in mind that even these apparently innocent subjects may sometimes be highly touchy—particularly when there are internal clans or hierarchies among the prisoners themselves, often with internal coercion. Access to food, for example, has sometimes turned out to be strictly decided, not by the detaining authorities, but by clan bosses inside the prisoner population. Hence, prisoners may be reluctant to speak about the food, merely saying all is well—which in fact it is not. The skilled interviewer will be able to recognize such issues and later come back to them in the privacy of the individual talk.

Internal hierarchies and rival clans exist practically worldwide in prisons, with local contexts of course dictating internal practices. Coercion, and sometimes extreme violence, is known to occur, however, between rival clans or exerted from top to bottom by the hierarchy. Coercion and reprisals do not always come from the detaining authorities, although they may know about them and condone them, so as maintain internal order. Interviewers should try to learn as much as they can about the internal situation in each context, so as to not be fooled by appearances. If the visit is the first one in a given context, the assessment may take time and not be completely meaningful until several visits have been conducted.

Great care should be taken to protect those prisoners from any form of reprisal for having spoken to the outside monitor. For this reason, it is not advisable to speak about torture in groups. In a group, there may be an undetected "agent provocateur" who may lead to the subject, hoping to encourage others to speak out. This may put them at risk for reprisals after the visit. Other prisoners, perhaps naively trusting the outside visitor to offer them protection, may broach the subject and do the same—put those who speak out in danger. For the prisoners' safety, if torture is the issue at hand, the principle should be to speak about it only during individual interviews.

Prisoners may understandably not be willing to come forward and may be too frightened to say anything, either about themselves or about torture—even when there are clearly visible signs of torture on their bodies. In this case, the visit will have to proceed slowly, and the interviewers clearly explain about the objectives and the limitations of the visit. If the prisoners are fearful of reprisals, and unless there is a rock-solid guarantee from the detaining authorities as to being allowed to repeat the visit, it may be best in some cases to not broach the subject of torture at all.

Never take for granted that prisoners will "blindly" true a monitor from the outside. Trust has to be gained and deserved. Inversely, one should warn any possibly "naive" prisoner, who, putting blind trust in the presumed protection provided by an outsider, might take risks speaking out in presence of the authorities—and get into trouble. Clearly explain to prisoners the limitations of the visit.

Prisoners may be too afraid to even ask for interviews in private, as they may fear that by doing so they point themselves out to the authorities—and may be called up after the visit to be interrogated as to what was said. Experience has shown this to be common precisely in those contexts where reprisals are likely to occur. The only way to avoid this is to interview as many prisoners as feasible, so as to dilute those who are the ones with most to say. The detaining authorities however usually "know" who are the ones most likely to speak out. In some cases, particularly in prisons with a not too big number of political or security prisoners, it may be necessary to interview each and every prisoner. This is time consuming and may seem discouraging, but must be done if it is the only way to avoid prisoners being singled out.

There may be cases where the vast majority of the prisoners have visible scars of physical torture on their bodies, but all are reluctant to say anything about it out of fear of reprisals. In such cases, it may be useful to conduct what is known as a sanitary inspection of all prisoners, dressed only in shorts or something similar, in the courtyard, thereby making it possible for the outside visitors to see them and observe and document at least the visible physical scars of torture. This should be done in full view of guards and authorities. Thus, they will know that such an inspection has taken place and will not have anyone to pinpoint as having talked about torture. More to the point, the prisoners will feel confident that no one can accuse them of having spoken out.

By thus doing everything possible to avoid prisoners being singled out, the element of trust will hopefully develop, and prisoners will come forward to speak with the interviewer. The "medical consultation" is the best alibi, as well as often being the real reason, for requesting an individual interview. Health issues are always a problem in prisons, and the privacy of the medical interview is usually accepted. In cases where the authorities refuse even medical interviews in private, the bottom line should be to have any guards out of earshot. It may not be possible to have them out of sight altogether, as many prison systems have strict rules to this effect, to protect prison medical staff from aggressions—which do occur. Out of earshot distance at least guarantees that some information may be passed.

The shame and stigma around sexual assault is such that torture victims even once they have been released from custody will often prefer not to go to a treatment center, as this could make "other people [rightly] suppose" that they might have been sexually assaulted or raped (Skylv 1992). The complex issue of sexual assault and torture is discussed in Chapter 10.

Retraumatization

While the objective of a visit to prisoners may be indeed to document torture, with the next step being some sort of outside intervention to stop the practice of torture—the first consideration should be, however, for those actual victims of torture. It is on purpose here that the term *victims* and not the term *survivors* is used. When prisoners having suffered torture are still in custody, they are still working on survival—for the moment, they are still victims. Hopefully, the visit by the outside monitor will contribute to them ultimately becoming survivors.

These victims of torture should never be forced to relive their torture experience by the outside monitors. They should not have to undergo retraumatization during the interview. The interviewer must be extremely cautious in approaching such issues and should stop if there is any evidence of distress, anxiety, or reluctance to discuss events that have happened.

Great care must be taken in any such interview by carefully observing the prisoner as the subject is approached. Body language, voice inflections, and any physical reactions must be observed. A prisoner being interviewed should be given the option of stopping at any time—and, if desired, allowed to continue later or on a different day if possible. Outside physician monitors should also sense if a particular interviewee is unwittingly tormenting him/herself too much and gently offer these options as well.

Benefits to Detainees

The objective of visits to places of detention should be not only to document ill-treatment, but also ideally to offer persons having been tortured some direct benefit.

During the visit, for a brief moment, prisoners will have access to someone from the outside world—and with medical knowledge and expertise. Thus, prisoners should also get something out of the visit for themselves, such as medical counselling, or answers to any specific questions—and not just feel they are providing data for a report! They can, therefore, feel free to ask any questions they have about their bodies and minds and the effects of their traumatic torture experience. Torturers intentionally break bodies and minds, and concerns about body integrity and soundness of mind are prevailing worries in the minds of their victims. To be able to have access to medical assessment of one's condition, by a physician who can be trusted, can be a major benefit. It should be explained to the torture victim that the effects of torture are long lasting. Explanations will have to be given, again and again, that the many different reactions the victims may have are normal reactions to what was an abnormal situation (Suedfeld 1990). Getting answers to questions about possible long-term sequelae, or about the possibility of treatment once they are free, may provide some comfort and reassurance to those who need it. It is important to clearly explain what can be done in the given circumstances relevant to the case. Tell the prisoner if and when you expect to come back; never make promises you are not really confident you can keep. If you suggested bringing up the prisoner's medical case with the local doctor, make sure you do it. Do not promise to come back yourself, unless you are certain to be able to.

The outside monitor should also be very clear about what he/she can offer and what he/she cannot. Basic needs and shortcomings may vary considerably from one context to another—on top of any issue of maltreatment or torture—and prisoners should be told clearly what external monitors can and cannot provide.

In extreme cases, prisoners may show outright aggressiveness toward any visitors from the outside, and no degree of communication will be able to create any useful communication let alone a rapport of trust. While very rare, this may be a case of prisoners merely protecting themselves, using such anger as the only degree of freedom they still have left. To refuse to see and talk to an outside visitor in this case may be their way of asserting themselves or having some semblance of control. Such prisoners' wishes should be respected, and outside monitors should simply come back later and try again.

Nature of the Interviewee

Interviewees alleging ill-treatment hugely vary in nature. For example, an interview with a political activist or a political prisoner will obviously be very different from that with a young girl having been raped by her oppressors.

Empathy is a key quality for anyone working with victims of torture.

This may mean putting down one's pen and paper and merely listening to the victim's story. The visit will be your first contact with that prisoner—hopefully, there will be a follow-up visit. It is more important to provide personal empathy and establish trust, than to absolutely fill out a "torture check list" one may have in mind for documentation. In all cases, direct and full attention is required. The interviewer may try to remember the important points and write them down *only after* the interview is over. When it becomes obvious that the victim feels uncomfortable with what may be taken to resemble as new interrogation, the discussion about torture should stop, and the interview should ever so gently go back to different, hopefully more pleasant topics. Interviewers should never take the risk of enhancing the psychological injuries of torture by uncalled for assertiveness or aggressive interviewing. The persons interviewed should never feel that they are being obliged to talk about their torture experience.

In the same light, interviewers should not forget that each individual has his or her own story to tell. When visiting a large number of prisoners, it is easy for the interviewer to forget this. The last prisoner of the day, who has been waiting for his/her interview all day, and who has, from the interviewer's point of view, "nothing new" to tell, should never be brushed away with the attitude of "I-have-heard-this-story-already." Each individual deserves the same amount of attention and empathy, whether or not the details of the torture experience have already been heard.

Outside monitors often mistakenly think that prisoners who have been tortured talk among themselves about their torture experiences. Whether this is done or not depends a great deal on cultural and social circumstances. In most cultures, talking about torture is simply not done, at least not about the intimate aspects of torture and their consequences.

Interviewers should know the difference between the shame culture experience as opposed to guilt culture as documented by Skylv (1992). In very general terms, Western and many Latin American contexts will correspond to the guilt culture—whereby torture is a horrible experience—but there is a sense of survival guilt, which can be compensated by speaking out about the experience, so those who have succumbed to it will not have done so in vain. In the shame culture, predominant in Asian contexts, torture itself is bad enough, but for the experience to become known to others, particularly its almost sexual component, practically always present to some degree, is even worse. Hence, the victims will be most reluctant to speak to anyone about it.

The Interviewer

Monitors who visit prisoners and want to document torture should expect difficult interviews. Many interviewers may often find it very difficult to cope with the stories they hear and the reactions of the torture victims they interview. The anguish of the victims may be extreme, understandably so, and the interviewer is most often in a situation with little to offer besides some on-the-spot empathy.

Interviewers should be well prepared for their tasks and be knowledgeable about the outside circumstances in the country where they work. Background homework on the political, cultural, and historical facts pertaining to the context of the interviewee is essential. Interviewers should make themselves familiar with the specific objectives of torture within the given country, as well as with the local methods used by the torturers and any coping mechanisms relevant to the culture at hand.

However, being knowledgeable should not lead to a preconceived categorization of torture. Interviewers should approach torture and its consequences as a whole and not reduce the information received to groupings of methods and symptoms.

The question of whether outside monitors should be physicians or lay (nonmedical) persons is always a moot issue and may depend on local skill base and availability. There is undoubtedly a role for monitors from different backgrounds (e.g., medical, legal, psychological). What is most important is for different interviewers to know their limits and to complement each other's talents and know-how. The documentation of torture for preventive purposes must always be carried out with an experienced physician on the team who is familiar with all aspects of the IP. One of the added values for the prisoners will be the provision of medical advice answers to the many questions the victims of torture will have. A physician will have the unquestionable advantage of being able to answer specific questions about the effects and sequelae of torture, both physical and psychological. These two aspects of monitoring go together and should be inseparable. A follow-up visit in a context where new cases of torture are unlikely to be present might appropriately be carried out without a physician.

Visits to prisoners by preventive instruments such as National Preventive Mechanisms (as defined in the Guide to the Establishment and Designation of NPMs [APT 2006]) have attempted to carry out visits without an accompanying medical doctor—this author considers that this is not the optimal way of either documenting torture or providing expert advice and counseling to those persons who have been tortured and are still in custody.

The Interview

The information about torture obtained from the interview with the torture victim will obviously vary between contexts and according to the time elapsed since the torture actually took place.

The use of questionnaires when visiting prisoners, such as the one in *Monitoring Places of Detention—A Practical Guide*, issued by the APT in 2004, is debatable. The humane aspect of the visit, which is the restoration of personal contact with the prisoner, will be diluted if not altogether lost, if the essential part of the interview is to be conducted through a written impersonal checklist.

Investigating torture will often require more than just one interview with the same person. Indeed, it is not rare to learn much more about torture concerning a given individual on a second visit than on the initial interview. A victim of torture will frequently not tell everything during the first interview.

The structure of the interview will depend on the context and on the personal situation of each interviewee. Directed, closed questions should be avoided ("Were you tortured when they arrested you?") in favor of open, very general questions ("When you were arrested, how did it go?").

Cultural norms should be taken into account, which may in some cases imply asking roundabout questions first, about family, for example, before getting to the situation in the prison and the issue of actual torture. Elsewhere, it might be considered impolite to ask about a prisoner's family before a rapport of trust has been established and the objective of the visit and interview fully understood by the interviewee. There are no one-fits-all methods for conducting interviews.

Interviewers should be aware of the effect of potentialization. It is necessary to be aware of and understand the different modes and techniques of torture, if the interviewer is to fully comprehend the victim's story. Several methods of torture applied simultaneously will have greatly enhanced effects—more severe than one would expect from simply applying them one by one to the same person. This is particularly true for the psychological effects. A hooded or blindfolded person submitted to beatings or applications of electricity, for example, if they are blindfolded, is not able to anticipate what direction the blow or electric shock is coming from. Applying electrical current, for example, to someone suspended by the arms tied behind his/her back and blindfolded can provoke spasmodic contractions much more severe and painful than if the victim can see (and prepare himself for) the same torture. The unpredictable and uncontrollable aspects of torture have been described in detail (Başoğlu and Mineka 1992), as well as the effects of hooding as a factor of potentialization (IFEG [International Forensic Expert Group] 2011).

Transcribing Findings of Ill-Treatment and Torture

Once the outside monitor has collected the information about torture—and given back some positive elements to the interviewees, in the form of advice, medical or otherwise, and hopefully being able to reassure them about their health, both physical and mental—the information will have to be recorded and presented as a demarche to the authorities.

A mere listing of methods approach to documenting torture, meaning merely recording the different forms of torture used by the oppressors, may be counterproductive if presented as a sort of catalog in a report. The clinical picture produced by torture will obviously greatly vary between individuals, even more so between cultures and contexts. Such a listing has been called by this author the package deal approach for the documentation of torture, to be avoided at all times (Reyes 2002). Such an approach may reduce any dialogue with the alleged perpetrators to a discussion of the lowest common denominator. Instead of discussing the victims, and how they are affected, list of methods will lead to sterile discussions and arguments about which methods from the list actually qualify as torture—and which do not—and to which of the methods are absolutely unwarranted and should not be on the list to begin with, "as they never happened."

Another pitfall interviewers often fall into is that of focusing on "scars and visible *evidence...*" It is now generally accepted that "the worst scars are in the mind," as has been extensively commented by this author in 2007 in *Psychological Torture*, an international review of the Red Cross. These scars can be the result of both physical and psychological methods of torture—most often a combination of both. Victims of torture themselves have unequivocally stated that the psychological effects of torture can often be far worse than those effects caused by brutal, physical ones. Several seasoned political prisoners have told the author of this chapter that "electric shocks are but *child's play* compared to the effects of months of absolute solitary confinement in an empty, windowless cell, with no human contact whatsoever..." (Reyes 2007a).

Why is it then that again and again, reports by well-meaning and professional nongovernment organizations and other reporting bodies always insist on the physical evidence documented? Physical scars and other physical evidence may be present, but is it necessarily most important when evaluating the effects of torture?

An approach concentrating on "visible evidence" is thus only partially useful and can be counterproductive. Most authorities will deny that their subordinates have been involved in torturing prisoners, sometimes out of ignorance, but most often out of bad faith. To submit to them the lists of cases with documented evidence not only will not necessarily convince them to accept the facts, but will also give them an additional argument to refute any allegations of torture by (the majority of) prisoners who have nothing to show. Psychological torture by definition leaves no such physical signs; and furthermore, physical signs wane and eventually disappear. To concentrate on physical evidence will thus allow the authorities to reject outright any claims "without physical evidence." The author has witnessed such rejection of any claims not "supported" by "something to show" by authorities either acting in bad faith or having no knowledge about psychological sequelae. Before the UN IP affirmatively dealt with the issue of psychological sequelae, such argumentation was often thrown out of any discussion by such authorities.

The IP states that "...the absence of such physical evidence should not be construed to suggest that torture did not occur, since such acts of violence against persons frequently leave no marks or permanent scars."

Outside monitors should thus refrain from concentrating merely on physical scars. A solid and well restructured description of torture, and not only the methods used, but also the effects on the individual, can, of course, include description of scars if there are any. Torturers have known for a long time how to minimize any physical marks left on the body, and psychological torture, while it may indeed have physical effects on the system, leaves nothing at all to show on the body.

Torture methods involving third persons, particularly when family members are concerned, are usually even more traumatic than torture to the person: "I didn't mind the pain so much. It was the cries next door I couldn't bear."

Finally, interviewers should be aware of coping mechanisms used, unconsciously in most cases, by victims of torture. The IP specifically recognizes that memories of torture, for this reason, often are blurred and fuzzy to recollect exactly. In the past, some judges had taken this imprecision of precise recollection as an argument against veracity. It is now recognized, thanks to the IP, that such imprecision is normal and is not to be held against the victim of torture.

Translation and Interpretation

It has already been mentioned how important it is for outside monitors to be knowledgeable about the historical, cultural, and ethnic background of the context their interviewees are in. As in the majority of cases, interviewers shall work through interpreters, this also obviously applies to them. Some monitors try to get around the cultural obstacles by using interpreters from the same local background as the victims, but this use of local staff as interpreters raises other problems.

Local interpreters, no matter how devoted and trustworthy (and determining this may in itself be a problem), may be putting themselves into dangerous situations by working with interviewers when documenting torture. Experience has shown that such interpreters can be put under pressure, themselves or their families, by the authorities, to reveal information about interviews in which they have served as interpreters. Apart from the danger this may mean to interpreters and their families, this could also jeopardize the trust between interviewers and prisoners and might even put the latter in danger as well if the interpreters were forced to divulge delicate information given during the talks.

Even before these issues, the use of local interpreters can lead to mistrust by either the prisoners themselves or the detaining authorities. One example occurred in some instances during the civil war at the demise of former Yugoslavia. There were, to simplify the example here, Croatian prisoners in Serbian hands and Serbian prisoners in Croatian hands. If local interpreters were to be used—and supposing that these persons were irreproachably neutral in the positive sense of the word, meaning able to show empathy for the opposite ethnic group—was it better to have a Croatian interpreter to visit Croatian prisoners in Serbian hands, in order to "please" the prisoners, but not the detaining Serbs? Or to have, inversely, Serbian interpreters to visit Croatian prisoners held in Serbian custody to please the authorities, but not have the trust of the Croatian prisoners?

It became evident that the best and only way to work was with interpreters who were from neither ethnic groups.

The best policy if practical is *not* to use local interpreters but to rely on expatriate ones. This may complicate (and make more expensive) the task at hand, but is a necessary condition if the work is to be done in a professional way, avoiding any possible situations as described earlier.

Experience has shown that the choice of the interpreter goes well beyond just knowing the words of the language and that the sensitivity rightly demanded of all who interview torture victims need to be all the more present in the interpreters. It should be fully realized that it is the interpreters who are on the front line of the torture interview, which is why it is so important that all these sensitivities be fully grasped beforehand. Whether professional interpreters or merely trained dual-language speakers are used for interpretation during visits to prisoners, it is necessary to offer a full, tailored-to-the-context briefing to all those persons who will thus be front-line listeners, having the know-how to manage their emotions when hearing what can be very depressing histories from those who have suffered torture. The ICRC has learned from years of field experience that interpreters need such training. Monitors working with them should also learn to listen to not only the words translated, but also the translated emotions.

Interviewing via interpreters is not necessarily intuitive. The interviewer should always look at the interviewee when presenting her or himself and when asking questions. Likewise, when the prisoner answers or speaks for him or herself, it is the prisoner who should be observed, even if not a word is understood—and even when the prisoner looks at the interpreter and not the interviewer. Observing body language, gestures, and facial expressions, as well as nonverbal communication, is of paramount importance.

Some words concerning known methods of torture in the given context will invariably be used by the prisoner and should hopefully be recognized. Prisoners will often use terms directly used in their recounting of events. Examples such as *teléfono* in Latin America in the 1980s; *darmashakra* torture in Sri Lanka in the 1990s, *cheera* and *roller* in India; *waterboarding* in this century are cases in point. The acknowledgment of such terms, even by just nodding, will show the interviewee that one is familiar with the local situation. The victims of torture themselves will invariably talk to the interpreter, often at great lengths. This is quite normal, and the interviewer should certainly not take offense at this understandable reaction.

If the interpreter is not a trained professional, there is the risk of the actual monitor losing control of the interview. A nonprofessional interpreter might also lead the interview or launder what the torture victim has to say, according to preconceived opinions, modesty, or even personal bias. Some information will inevitably be lost during any translated interview, but this should be kept to a minimum; and outright distortions absolutely avoided. The interviewer and the interpreter have to learn how to work together as a team.

Sometimes a word-for-word translation will be required. More often, the interpreter will have to provide as accurate a linguistic connection as possible between what involves two different cultures, all the while remaining as objective as possible. When preparing a visit to prisoners, it is necessary to compare notes with the interpreter beforehand and exchange any notions of vocabulary that may come up during the interviews. This is particularly true regarding any medical terminology. As most interpreters for such visits will not be knowledgeable about anatomical terms or body system functions, the outside monitor should explain what terms are to be expected, so as to keep any awkward exchanges in front of the interviewee to a minimum. Interviewers should avoid esoteric words or internal jargon, so as to avoid any misunderstandings in front of the interviewee.

Fellow detainees should not be used as interpreters, except for topics that cannot possibly put anyone in a difficult situation. For example, explaining the workings of the septic tank in a prison should not necessarily need a professional expatriate interpreter, and a prisoner can be used for such interpretation. For interviews about torture, however, as for any other touchy or controversial subject, fellow prisoners should be avoided. As has been mentioned, prisons have internal hierarchies and clan systems that are difficult to know about. Using a prisoner from one group to interpret for members of another group can be tricky or downright dangerous.

Finally, the issue of confidentiality about any information received applies to interpreters as much as to interviewers, as they, of necessity, are the only ones to have the full story. Interpreters working for the ICRC are required beforehand, in a written agreement, to fully respect confidentiality in the same terms as what is required of all interviewers.

Medical Consultations

One important consideration is that medical doctors will often be swamped by medical demands. Some will be serious medical issues—many will not. This will greatly affect the number of cases related to torture that can be actually seen. Outside monitors should prepare their visit accordingly, hopefully getting information from preceding visits which will help them organize their time and working methods accordingly. Prisoners must be advised that outside investigating doctors are not there to replace the prison healthcare service—hopefully speaking to their ward leaders or other hierarchy, the real importance of the visit in such contexts will be understood, and doctors will not be overwhelmed by ordinary medical questions from the prisoners.

The role of physicians in general when visiting prisoners has been described in some detail (Reyes 1996; see also "Monitoring Places of Detention" by the APT [APT 2004]). It will, however, be necessary in most cases for the outside monitor to have at least a summary understanding of how the medical system in the prison works (or does not). Some medical cases may therefore be selected to concretely see how the medical system handles consultations and referrals for example—but certainly keeping in mind that the monitors are not going to replace the prison doctor's role.

Gender

Whether the outside monitor should be of the same gender as the interviewee will have greater or lesser importance according to the context. In countries where men and women can exchange conversations without any hesitation, and where female doctors as well as male doctors work interchangeably with either gender, this should be less of a problem. However, many of the countries where the ICRC works, visiting prisoners in detention worldwide, are precisely the countries where gender may be a decisively limiting factor in assessments.

In much of the Middle East, and in Asian countries in general, whether or not Islam is the religion of the country, and in a few other places, it will be impossible for a male doctor to interview a female prisoner, let alone examine her. Mainly, but not only, in Islamic contexts, it is out of the question for a man who is not the husband of a woman to speak to her alone, let alone set a hand upon her, even for a medical examination. A man and a woman not married cannot even be alone without a chaperone, as Rafael Patai has clearly documented in his chapters on sexuality in *The Arab Mind*. The interaction goes both ways—many Islamic men will never even shake the hand of a woman not their wife, for example. In most of these countries, the opposite will also be true—female doctors will not be allowed to touch or examine any male prisoners.

When torture is the issue, by its very nature, as it is meant to humiliate and degrade those submitted to it, sexual torture or torture targeted on the sexual organs will invariably have taken place in many cases. Gender differences can complicate matters, and can seriously aggravate any kind of exchange between outside monitor and the prisoner. For any even perfunctory assessment of a person having been tortured, a clinical examination will be warranted. Such a medical examination may be simply out of the question because of the gender difference between the interviewer and the interviewee. If sexual torture is suspected, and an examination of the genital area is deemed necessary (although in many cases it is not), the (same-sex) interviewer will have to be particularly careful in explaining why this is necessary and only do so with informed consent.

Sexual torture and harassment are opposite extremes of the same phenomenon. As this author has developed elsewhere (Reyes 2007b), any form of sexual assault, verbal or physical or even innuendo, can take on major proportions depending on the person it is directed against. Such sexual ill-treatment, to use a term covering the full spectrum, can take on many forms and be applied to males and females. In females, it by no means restricted to rape. Sexual torture will begin with the threat to rape, as a constant form of mental harassment and coercion—women know only too well what can happen in custody in many countries. Forced undressing, lewd remarks and threats, and "pawing" all can constitute a form of sexual torture. In males, what is much more common than anal penetrative assault is the infliction of any form of torture which targets the genitals. In all these cases, gender sensitivities need to be considered and taken into account before broaching the subject and obviously before suggesting an examination be performed.

Experience has shown that such examinations reveal a great deal more than what may have been insinuated during the interview, but this is not a sufficient reason to push for such exams to be systematic. Examples from fieldwork are numerous. One example, interviewed by the author of this chapter, was that of a Sri Lankan woman who told a horrific story of rape and other sexual assault *only* in the strict privacy of the medical consultation. In India, men who had "nothing particular to say" during the mere interview and history taking, somewhat reluctantly showed severely traumatized scrotums and inner thighs, results of beatings targeted, as has been mentioned, on the genitalia. A physical examination should always be negotiated with the person, whenever possible, and again, with respect for gender when this is an issue.

Sexual assault is perhaps the most traumatic form of torture, and many victims of torture will not even mention it.

In many countries where torture takes place, for religious or cultural reasons—or both—men are not supposed to address unmarried women directly, and it will be out of the question for a male doctor to approach a woman, let alone examine her unclothed in any circumstance. For such reasons, it will be necessary to provide for interviewers of both sexes. This may be a complication and involve additional difficulties and costs, but cannot be avoided.

There are exceptions. Apart from the culturally extreme cases, there may be times when the function of the interviewer is intrinsically more important than his or her gender. For example, in a case where women have been raped and are afraid of being pregnant, or are fearful for their future fertility, it may be most important for them to be able to ask questions to a physician coming from outside, as they may not trust a doctor working in the prison, seen as "part of the repressive system." These women want a doctor who can provide answers they can believe. Thus, they may prefer a male doctor from outside whom they feel they can trust, to a female one from inside. Ideally, however, gender should be respected, and interviewing teams should provide for physicians from both sexes so as to respect cultural sensitivities regarding gender.

Conclusions

Documenting ill-treatment or torture by outside monitors by interviewing prisoners still in custody is a difficult task. It is completely different from encounters with torture survivors in rehabilitation centers.

Care should be taken to ensure that such prisoners are not put in danger by talking to the monitors. Great care must be taken to not unwittingly provoke a retraumatization of the prisoners, making them relive their torture experience more than they may want to.

Establishing a relationship of trust will be paramount if any information is to be obtained. Explaining why getting information from them to the prisoners is essential—all the more so as the outside monitor will most often have little to offer. Genuine empathy transmitted to the prisoners may be, in many cases, the very least any outsider could deliver to prisoners still living their traumatic experience.

Working through interpretation takes practice and skills acquired through experience. The medical interview in private will provide a history of what happened. Closed, directed questions and the use of questionnaires should be avoided if possible.

Once obtained, the information should never be delivered as a list of methods of ill-treatment. Examining the prisoners interviewed should be done with tact and care and with respect for gender—but should not be focused only on getting evidence. It should always be remembered that "absence of evidence is not evidence of absence."

Appropriately trained physicians are essential members to any team documenting ill-treatment or torture, as they can interpret signs and symptoms and demonstrate patterns between methods and clinical findings or explain untoward effects on health. Doctors can also explain symptoms and effects to prisoners themselves, hopefully in clear common language when the need arises. They should, however, never forget the psychological importance of their contact with human beings who have been abused and whose dignity has been trampled on. Just as important as getting documentary information are the empathy and professional counseling that should in all cases also be a prime concern when encountering prisoners still victims of torture in custodial settings.

References

Association for the Prevention of Torture (APT) 2004, *Monitoring Places of Detention: A Practical Guide*, APT, Geneva.

APT 2006, *Guide to the Establishment and Designation of National Preventive Mechanisms*. APT, Geneva.

Başoğlu, M., and Mineka, S. 1992, The role of uncontrollable and unpredictable stress in post-traumatic stress responses in torture survivors, in *Torture and its consequences*, CUP, Cambridge, pp. 182–226.

British Medical Association (ed.) 1992, *Medicine Betrayed*, Zed Books, London.

Cassese, A. (ed.) 1996, *Inhuman States: Imprisonment, Detention and Torture*, Polity Press, Cambridge.

Daudin, P., and Reyes, H. 1996, Armed conflicts and analogous disturbances: How visits by the ICRC can help prisoners cope with the effects of traumatic stress, in Y. Danieli, N. S. Rodley, and L. Weisaeth, (eds), *International Responses to Traumatic Stress*. Baywood, Amityville, NY, pp. 219–255.

Iacopino, V. 1996, *Torture in Turkey and Its Unwilling Accomplices*, Physicians for Human Rights, Boston.

IFEG (International Forensic Expert Group) 2011, Statement on hooding: International forensic expert group, *Torture: Journal on Rehabilitation of Torture Victims and Prevention of Torture*, vol. 21, pp. 186–189.

IP (Istanbul Protocol) 2004, *Manual on the Effective Investigation and Documentation of Torture and Other Cruel, Inhuman or Degrading Treatment or Punishment*, Professional Training Series No 8/Rev. 1, Office of the United Nations High Commissioner for Human Rights, Geneva. Available from: available at www.ohchr.org/english/about/publications/docs/8rev1.pdf.

Patai, R. 2014, *The Arab mind*, Recovery Resources Press, Tucson, AZ. ISBN-10: 0967201551; ISBN-13: 978-0967201559.

Reyes, H. 1996, Doctors at risk, in *Healthy Prisons: A Vision for the Future*, Report of the 1st International Conference on Healthy Prisons, Liverpool, pp. 24–27.

Reyes, H. 2002, Chapter 5: Visits to prisoners and documentation of Torture, in M. Peel and V. Iacopino, (eds), *The Medical Documentation of Torture*, Cambridge University Press, London.

Reyes, H. 2007a, The worst scars are in the mind: Psychological torture, *International Review of the Red Cross*, vol. 89, pp. 591–617.

Reyes, H. 2007b, The worst scars are in the mind: Psychological torture, *International Review of the Red Cross*, vol. 89.

Reyes, H. 2008, Doctors in prison: Documenting torture in detention, *Torture*, vol. 18, pp. 176–182.

Skylv, G. 1992, *The Nature of Human Experience: Some Interfaces Between Anthropology and Psychiatry*, Lecture at the Royal Society of Medicine, London.

Staiff, M. 2000, Visits to detained torture victims, *Torture*, vol. 10, pp. 4–7.

Stover, E., and Nightingale, E. 1985, *The Breaking of Bodies and Minds*, WH Freeman, New York.

Suedfeld, P. 1990, *Psychology and Torture*, Hemisphere Publications, New York.

Further Reading

Reyes, H. 1995, Torture and its consequences, *Torture*, vol. 5, pp. 72–76.

Reyes, H. 1997, Visits to prisoners by the ICRC, *Torture*, supplementum 1, pp. 28–30.

13

Investigation of Deaths in Custody

Marc Bollmann, Morris Tidball-Binz, Bernice Elger, and Patrice Mangin

CONTENTS

Introduction

There is great variability in different jurisdictions as to when and who undertakes investigations of deaths in custody and sometimes whether any investigation is done at all. In many jurisdictions, there is little awareness about the importance and relevance of a proper investigation of those deaths. Because a detainee has little freedom in many aspects of normal life, the detaining authority has to take on full responsibility for every detainee. Any death occurring in the hands of the detaining facility, and in the end, of the acting government or state or authority, should be fully and independently investigated in order to identify failings and learn lessons and to reassure the general public. This chapter identifies the key elements that should form the basis of all investigations following a death in custody. It has to be kept in mind that in many detaining facilities, violent deaths and self-inflicted deaths are much more frequent than in the general population (which may reflect management or personnel issues) and that even a natural death might still involve the responsibility of the detaining authority, which controls access to health professionals, medication, hygiene, and nutrition.

It is appropriate that all deaths in custody should be treated as suspicious until an investigation has been completed. Special attention should be paid to any possible involvement of other parties, which may also relate to clinical negligence, side effects and interactions of prescribed medication, insufficient access to medical care, nutrition, or adequate hygiene. However, in cases of deaths in custody that are expected, such as those that are the consequence of a diagnosed terminal illness, the investigation may be simplified. Certain groups are more at risk of death in custody (e.g., those with circulatory conditions), and this may relate to poor or delayed medical care. The Prison and Probation Ombudsman in the United Kingdom reviews deaths in prisons in the United Kingdom and regularly publishes theme-specific reports (Ryan-Mills 2010; Prison and Probation Ombudsman 2012, 2015). The extent of the investigation is highly variable and often insufficient. It is, for example, unacceptable to rely on a medical death certificate that is not based on objective observations. The scientific literature gives only little oversight into the extent of the death investigation in many countries, and the closed nature of prisons certainly contributes to this state of affairs.

In some jurisdictions (e.g., the United Kingdom), any death in custody (whether police, prison, or mental health facilities) will be supervised by a judicial officer (in England & Wales, a coroner), and they will have access to the relevant expertise required to properly investigate the circumstances of the death. Death investigation should be performed by a team of qualified and independent persons in order to determine the cause and the circumstances of the death. Key competences include crime scene forensics, medicolegal postmortem examination, criminal investigation, and medical management. This chapter also indicates basic evidence-taking acts that can and should be immediately undertaken by any other less-qualified independent investigator if the required competencies mentioned earlier are not completely met. Ideally, all cases of death under custody should be submitted to autopsy, in order to determine the cause of death. In many cases, the cause of death will only be the first step in the determination of the circumstances. Even in cases of a natural death, the responsibility of a third party is not automatically excluded, and where there are possible failings in access to, or standards of care for health conditions such as diabetes, asthma and epilepsy, these will need exploration by relevant professionals.

The death investigation, independently of the place, the circumstances, and the cause of death, consists of several steps including the following:

- Death scene investigation
- Examination of the medical history and the medical documents
- Clothes examination
- External and internal examinations of the body (postmortem examination)
- Additional investigations
- Reporting of the results

Several international standards for the medicolegal investigation are available, most importantly *The Minnesota Protocol on the Investigation of Potentially Unlawful Death* (2016) and the Council of Europe's *Harmonisation of Medico-Legal Autopsy Rules*, Recommendation No. R (99) 3. These provide clear guidance on the expected methods of investigation.

The Death Scene Investigation

The location in which a death occurs as well as the location of the body are to be treated as one crime scene, which means that access is strictly limited and given only to those personnel who have a specific role to reduce the risk of scene disturbance or contamination. Each movement in and out of the scene should be restricted and documented. The access restriction commences immediately for the place of death and as soon as the resuscitation efforts stop for the body and its surroundings. If resuscitation efforts are undertaken prior to the death, a detailed statement should be obtained from all those present and those involved in any resuscitation.

Confirmation of death is crucial and must first be verified by a physician. Once the death has been confirmed, tampering with the scene, if any, needs to be investigated and documented in itself. Where doubt exists about the identity of the deceased (a mutilated body, for example), it is necessary to scientifically identify the body.

The scene investigators need to take certain steps very rapidly after the death (such as preserving the scene, securing evidence, and estimating the time since death). Any delay could compromise the investigation.

The body and associated evidence should be left in place and examined by a qualified team—whose members should be independent from the detaining authority. A physician with forensic expertise, preferably a forensic pathologist, must be part of the team. An independent death investigation partly depends on the nation-specific system put into place for investigating deaths. If the death investigation is too closely interconnected with the detaining authority, it might be advisable to outsource the investigation to other departments, ministries or nongovernmental organizations, international organizations, or other countries. Lack of, or perceived lack of independence of the investigators, may jeopardize the credibility of the conclusions, even if the investigation has been properly led.

It is recommended that all central detention authorities (whether prisons, police, military, or mental health facilities otherwise) draw up policies and procedures to be followed in the event of any death in custody. These policies should form the basis for an emergency action plan (or standard operating procedures [SOPs]) in every place of detention under the control of the central authority. SOPs will ensure the rapid reporting of the death to the competent authority, facilitate the preservation of the scene, and prepare the ground for a professional scene investigation. The procedures should be short, understandable, and contain up-to-date contacts, so should be reviewed regularly. The SOP should address the following:

- Who to inform (e.g., the detaining authority, the investigating authority, and the next of kin of the deceased person)
- Timing of the different steps of the investigation (e.g., immediate information of the detaining and the investigating authorities, protection of the scene, secure relevant data)
- Content of the information (e.g., identity of the deceased, the circumstances of the death, the medical history, history of drug abuse, and all other information that may help to provide an appropriate response by the investigators)

Scene Management

The scene is the location in which the death occurred as well as the location of the body and its immediate surroundings. The scene is considered a crime scene until the scene investigation is concluded and the investigating authority has released the area to normal usage again. This will be dependent on the specific investigating authority (e.g., in the United Kingdom for prisons, the Prison and Probation Ombudsman and for police, the Independent Police Complaints Commission). Both these organizations publish reports of all their investigation which are available online. The release of the scene can be quick if no evidence of a third-party intervention is found. Other places and objects can be part of the scene. Personal property and all documents about the deceased are of crucial importance to the investigating authority and need to be made available to them. The scene should be placed under the jurisdiction of the investigating authority, which will only grant access to the investigators and medicolegal specialists. The body and the areas associated with the death need to be preserved in their original state, until the investigators properly document everything of interest.

The main objectives of the scene management include the following:

- Preservation of the scene and the evidence until it is documented and processed by the investigators
- Collection of information and securing evidence linked to the death
- Controlled removal of the body and proper conservation until the full postmortem examination

The physician should check for the presence of any evidence of violence and record all data for the estimation of the time of the death. The latter can be important for the verification of statements and can give supportive evidence for some causes. This step can, however, be postponed for a short time, to secure the evidence on the access path to the body. Particularly if there was a struggle shortly before death, or if the deceased was prescribed psychotropic medication, and there is a suggestion of stimulant intoxication or excited delirium, a rapid deployment to the death scene is of crucial importance. Early measurement of the body and environmental temperature can assist in determining some specific causes of death. Table 13.1 identifies the procedural steps to be undertaken.

In addition to the procedures outlined in Table 13.1, the staff in charge of the deceased should be interviewed at an early stage (before any internal debriefing procedure). Their statements have to be written down, dated, and signed. The medical personnel of the detaining facility should be interviewed as well and asked about medication and medical conditions of the deceased. It has to be established when the deceased was last seen by a nurse or a physician. All medical documents of the deceased as well as remaining biological (e.g., blood, urine) samples should be secured. All relevant documents that have to remain on-site for a good reason must be documented by copy or photographs. All prison documents concerning the deceased and units where the deceased was detained should be secured (e.g., notes and observations of guards, reporting of rounds, fights). Recordings of security cameras, logs of electronic locks, and similar data should be secured at an early stage, as they are often overwritten after some time. If any phone calls of the deceased have been recorded, they must be made available to the investigators.

TABLE 13.1

Procedures to be Undertaken at Scene and Immediately after Death

- The body, its position and the surroundings are to be documented (by both written description and imaging—which may be photograph and video). If available, digital color photo documentation is the preferred method. Making a sketch is an acceptable alternative. Color photographs should include general views as well as detailed photographs with a scale. Blood trace evidence should be documented and photographed.
- Those entering the scene of a suspicious death should minimize disruption and avoid its contamination. Everybody having accessed the scene should be listed.
- All evidence, documents, and personal objects concerning the deceased are to be gathered and secured.
- Evidence has to be documented, collected, labeled, and secured. All evidence should be accompanied by a chain of custody listing (a signed record of the date, time, and person to whom the evidence is passed at each stage). This prevents undetected tampering with the evidence.
- If the body and associated evidence (e.g., clothing and personal effects) have been moved, this needs to be documented. All medical interventions must be noted, including any drug administration, cardio-pulmonary resuscitation, and defibrillation. This also includes resuscitation measures by wardens or detainees.
- The external forensic medical examination of the body usually is only summary at this stage and should not interfere with the following detailed postmortem examination including autopsy.
- Evidence for electricity-related deaths and intoxication should be actively sought, because of the benefit of context with the scene. Electrical marks can be very discrete and are often located on the hands. Any powder residues and residues of medication might be located on or next to the body, or within biological liquids.
- Consider protecting the hands of the body with paper bags, especially in cases of struggle or the use of firearms.
- Clothing can often be left on the body at this stage. Wounds of any kind should not be explored at the scene.
- The physician should also make all measurements for estimating the time of death. The later he/she is given access, the less precise his/her estimation of the time of death will be. The parameters that need to be recorded in any case are the location, color and degree of fixation of lividity, the presence or absence of rigidity, any signs of decomposition, the measurement of the deep rectal (body core) and ambient temperatures. This must be performed with care, not to interfere with sampling for sexual assault (consider performing a rectal swab before the measurement), and without inflicting postmortem injuries. It must be stressed that the estimation of the time of death always has an inherent tolerance (i.e., error factor) of several hours. Any heat source or any influencing factors concerning the cooling of the body have to be identified and documented for estimating the time of death (e.g., exposure to the sun, floor heating, removed or added bedspread, any change of ambient temperature, opened doors/windows). Estimating the time of death needs specialist knowledge and experience. Even though it can be performed on the basis of thorough scene documentation and complete measurements, it is preferable to have the scene examined by an experienced forensic pathologist in the first place.

An initial written report detailing all observations of the preliminary examination has to be given to the investigating authority. The investigators need to be allowed access to any section of the facility. The staff of the detention facility is responsible for the security of the investigators. After the completion of all medicolegal investigation, the body should be transported to a cooled storage.

Management of the Body

After the preliminary examination of the body, it must also be protected from postmortem change. This is best achieved by storing the body in refrigeration as soon as possible, ideally between 2 and 4°C. The removal of the body and its transfer to the morgue where the full postmortem examination will be carried out has to be closely supervised by the investigating team. The body must at all times be treated with respect for the dignity of the person. Care must be taken in the proper identification and labeling of the body.

Informing the Next of Kin

The next of kin has the right to be immediately informed of the death of their relative (as soon as the body is identified) and that an inquiry is opened. They should be treated in a proper, respectful, and dignified manner and reminded of their right to send a representative to the autopsy. They must be informed of the results of the inquiry. If available, counseling services (i.e., support therapy) should be offered. As soon as possible after the death, a complete death certificate should be issued to the next of kin. Upon completion of the examination, the body must be returned to the next of kin in a manner affording all respect for the human dignity of the deceased, such that the funeral rites/customary procedures can be conducted with the shortest possible delay. The personal effects of the deceased should be returned to the next of kin as soon as possible.

Postmortem Examination

The external and internal examination of a dead body is known as a postmortem examination. The postmortem examination of a body goes from an external examination of the body to a full forensic autopsy (external and internal examination) completed with ancillary analyses.

The aim of the postmortem examination is to determine and record the identity of the deceased; the estimation of the time of death; the documentation of external and internal injuries and pathological changes; the cause of death (e.g., physiological process and reason that a person died, such as injuries, diseases, intoxication); the manner of death (i.e., natural, accidental, suicidal, homicidal, undetermined [although in some jurisdictions, e.g., England & Wales, it is the coroner who will make the final determination]); and the possible sequence of events that led to the death and those that eventually occurred after death.

Answers to other forensic questions according to the nature of the case (e.g., surveillance, ill-treatment, quality of the medical care, hunger strike, sexual assault, drug abuse) may require additional forensic specialists such as clinicians and toxicologists. The extent of the postmortem examination of the body can depend on the local resources and customs. Since a dead body undergoes natural postmortem changes, which can mask or imitate injuries, the postmortem examination has to be performed as soon as possible after death by a trained pathologist.

It is of paramount importance to understand that the autopsy in itself is destructive and cannot be repeated in the same manner. Thus, every postmortem examination should be thoroughly documented to ensure the possibility of a later review by external experts. A thorough photographic documentation of the whole body and all injuries and features is mandatory even in regions with low resources.

Some funeral rites can modify or completely destroy the body, preventing any further forensic examination. For this reason, the body should be released by the competent authority to the next of kin only after the postmortem examination. Contacting the next of kin and, if necessary, a relevant religious authority can be very helpful in order to manage conflictual situations arising from cultural or religious differences concerning the potential interference of autopsy with funeral rites and customs.

Basic Principles

The threshold for conducting a full forensic autopsy in deaths in custody should be particularly low—in other words, there should be very strong, convincing, and properly recorded arguments for *not* conducting an autopsy. The means the capability of carrying out a forensic autopsy and the full range of ancillary investigations must always be available in those cases. Accepted international standards should be followed when conducting a medicolegal autopsy in cases of deaths in custody, and any major deviations from such standards along with the supporting reasons should be fully noted (e.g., *Model Autopsy Protocol of the United Nations*, endorsed by the General Assembly in 1991 [*United Nations Manual on the Effective Prevention and Investigation of Extra-Legal, Arbitrary and Summary Executions* {UN 1991}] and the Council of Europe's *Harmonisation of Medico-Legal Autopsy Rules*, Recommendation No. R 3 (99)).

All deaths in custody should be examined by a forensic pathologist. Countries where a forensic pathologist is not locally available should make provisions in advance how to have access to a forensic pathologist within the shortest possible timeframe using all available means.

If no medicolegal expert is available, SOPs should specify which independent physician takes this role. Whenever possible the medicolegal expert attending the scene of death also carries out the postmortem examination. The body should be entrusted to the pathologist for at least 24 hours in order to assure an adequate examination. He or she must be given full independence concerning the investigation and the presentation of results, which must be impartial and objective. He or she must also be allowed to order ancillary examinations and analyses. All limitations that could affect the quality of the examination should be duly noted.

A detailed written, color photographic, and video record (if available), as well as sketches of the procedure and findings should be made. All evidence must be fully documented; and relevant items and samples collected (ensuring chain of custody). A detailed written report, if possible with photographs of all findings, concludes the postmortem examination. In addition, a summary of the relevant findings, the cause of death, and comments about the cause of any pathological finding and injuries should figure in the report. If, however, the independency and safety of the pathologist are not guaranteed, he or she can refrain from making any conclusions and comments. The same principles apply to any second autopsy that may be conducted in cases of deaths in custody (see the following).

Procedures

The procedures described are based upon the *UN Manual on the Effective Prevention and Investigation of Extra-Legal, Arbitrary and Summary Executions* (UN 1991). With rare exceptions, postmortem examinations (including autopsies) in cases of death in custody should be performed as for a homicide case, with appropriate investigating personnel in attendance and, if available a forensic-trained photographer. The following checklist is derived from the UN model protocol for a legal investigation of extralegal, arbitrary, and summary executions. This checklist is not exhaustive and needs to be adapted for each individual case. The listed investigations should however be carried out whenever possible. Failure to do so should be duly explained in the report. Older injuries might be very important in this context, and evidence of torture has to be actively sought. The last country-specific reports of the UN Special Rapporteur on torture and other CIDT or punishment are a good starting point, in order to direct the search on specific methods of torture or cruel treatment.

A record of resuscitative measures undertaken by first-aid and ambulance personnel, warders, or prisoners should be made available to the pathologist prior to the autopsy. The medical documents of the deceased should be reviewed by the pathologist prior to autopsy. Any weapons or suspect substances from the scene should be shown to the pathologist. Photographic imaging of all pathological autopsy findings and injuries is mandatory in all cases and must be especially extensive if the autopsy is performed by less experienced or not specialized doctors. The imaging is of crucial importance for a later external review of the case. Detail photographs should have a scale on them. Especially if several cases are examined at the same time, the case number should also be on each photograph. One should be able to attribute each detail photograph to the corresponding body part. This is achieved by also taking some more general, distant photographs. Whenever possible the photographs should be taken perpendicularly to the body surface and in neutral zoom to minimize distortion. Rules and color scales should be used. The quality of each photograph should be checked before continuing. Ensure adequate lighting conditions and equipment for the examination. Table 13.2 identifies all the actions that need to be taken during the external examination.

Internal Examination

A very thorough autopsy procedure is crucial for shedding light on controversial deaths such as those occurring in custody. Partial autopsies are insufficient and should not be accepted unless there are compelling reasons which must be documented. In most cases, a full autopsy with subcutaneous dissection including of the back side of the body and layered in situ neck dissection should be performed, and ancillary investigations should be ordered if appropriate.

A systematic internal examination is undertaken. The examination should be performed either by body regions or by systems, including the cardiovascular, respiratory, biliary, gastrointestinal, reticuloendothelial, genitourinary, endocrine, musculoskeletal, and central nervous systems. The weight, shape, color, and consistency of each organ must be recorded, and any neoplasia, inflammation, anomalies, hemorrhage, ischemia, infarcts, surgical procedures, or injuries should be properly noted. Sections of normal and any abnormal areas of each organ must be taken for microscopic examination, as well as samples of any fractured bones for radiographic and microscopic estimation of the age of the fracture. It is essential that proper consents have been obtained for removal and retention of any biological materials. After the internal examination, the organs should be replaced in the body. Consideration should be given to embalming the body. All incisions should be closed, and the body should be released to the next of kin in a state of apparent integrity.

Thorax

Note any abnormalities of the breasts. Record any rib fractures, noting whether cardiopulmonary resuscitation was attempted. Before opening the chest, check for pneumothoraces.

TABLE 13.2

Actions to be Undertaken during External Examination of the Body

- Complete photographs and sketches of the body including close-up (detail) photographs of the face (including teeth), hands, and feet. Taking photographs must be performed before and after undressing and washing.
- Whenever possible, consider a full body radiological investigation (X-ray, CT, MRI) before the internal examination.
- Collect all DNA samples and evidence from the body before washing. Ensure the proper labeling and chain of custody for all evidence.
- Consider taking swabs for semen and DNA from the oral cavity, anus, rectum, low and high vagina (or penis), even if there is no suspicion of sexual assault at the time of the autopsy.
- Describe the clothing and store it as evidence. If wet, the clothes must be dried before storing them separately in paper bags.
- Document and photograph any jewelry and other personal items.
- Note and photograph any bite marks and swab for DNA.
- Record the deceased's apparent age, sex, length, weight, nutritional status, and color of skin, hair, eyes.
- Record the degree, location, and fixation of lividity and the presence of rigor mortis, especially if the pathologist has not recorded these data on the scene. Note any signs of decomposition.
- Document absence/presence of petechial hemorrhages to the conjunctivae, buccal mucosa and periorbital, retro-auricular, and neck skin.
- Consider fingerprinting in order to establish the identity (generally, the fingerprints of prisoners are listed).
- Record the dental condition and any dental work.
- Document and photograph all identifying features (e.g., distinctive birthmarks, prominent moles, scars, tattoos).
- Document (nature of injury type, size, shape, color, pattern, and location) and photograph all injuries on the body. Shaving might be necessary to correctly assess injuries of the scalp. Photography should be taken before and after shaving.
- When injuries cover large areas (such as burns/scalds), it is important to note the regions that are intact. Body hair should also be carefully documented in the presence of burns or scalds, and an estimation of the burnt body surface should be given.
- In gunshot injuries, make sure to document the presence or absence of abrasion, stippling, soot, and residues. The skin defect should be measured. Excision and storage of gunshot injuries are recommended.
- In gunshot injuries, pedestrian injuries, incised wounds, or other injuries that could be important for a later reconstruction, the distance from the middle line and the distance from the heel should be measured.
- Document the absence/presence of injuries to the external genital organs/anus (see Specimens section).
- Be especially aware of injuries in less exposed regions of the body as they could be related to ill-treatment or torture. The locally used methods of torture and ill-treatment need to be known in order to find the sometimes very discrete residues.

Record the thickness of subcutaneous fat. Consider checking for gas embolism. Immediately after opening the chest, evaluate the pleural cavities and the pericardial sac for the presence of blood or other fluid and describe and quantify any fluid present. Save any fluid present until foreign objects (detected at radiology or suspected after the external examination) are accounted for. Trace any injuries before removing the organs. Collect a blood sample directly from the heart and make sure that it is labeled as heart blood. Check the pulmonary arteries for thrombotic material and save it in formalin if it could be an antemortem thrombus. Examine the heart, noting the degree and location of coronary artery disease or other abnormalities. If thrombotic material is present in the coronary arteries, a section of the artery should be collected in the area of interest and saved in formalin. Examine the lungs, noting any abnormalities. Examine the major blood vessels.

Abdomen

Examine the abdomen and record the amount of subcutaneous fat. Consider retaining adipose tissue in a hermetic glass container if intoxication with volatile substances is suspected. Note the interrelationships of the organs. Trace any injuries before removing the organs. Note any fluid or blood present in the peritoneal cavity and save it until foreign objects are accounted for. Remove, examine, and record the quantitative information on the liver, spleen, pancreas, kidneys, and adrenal glands. Remove the gastrointestinal tract and examine the contents. Note any food present and its degree of digestion. All gastric contents should be collected (as these may be required for toxicology and time of death issues). The entire small and large bowels should be opened. Examine the rectum and anus for burns, lacerations, or other injuries. Locate and retain any foreign bodies present. Examine the aorta, inferior vena cava, and iliac vessels.

Pelvis

Consider a formal perineal dissection if appropriate. Examine the organs in the pelvis, including ovaries, fallopian tubes, uterus, vagina, testes, prostate gland, urethra, and urinary bladder. Trace any injuries before removing the organs. Note any evidence of previous delivery. Save any foreign objects within the cervix, uterus, vagina, urethra, or rectum.

Head

Examine the external and internal surfaces of the scalp, noting any trauma or hemorrhage. Note any skull fractures. Remove the calvarium carefully and note epidural and subdural hematomas. Quantify, date, and save any hematomas that are present. Remove the dura to examine the internal surface of the skull for fractures. Remove the brain and note any abnormalities. In cases with suspected pathology of the central nervous system, the brain should be examined after fixation. The unfixed brain is difficult to examine and can only detect gross pathologies, such as important hemorrhage. It may be important to seek the advice of a neuropathologist to determine the optimum means of preserving the brain. Evaluate the cerebral vessels. Dissect the brain and describe any injuries including cortical atrophy (whether focal or generalized).

Neck

After the brain and visceral block have been removed (through excision at the thoracic inlet), in order to obtain a bloodless field, a formal neck dissection should be performed. Examine the subcutaneous layer. Dissect the anterior neck muscles in situ and describe any injuries or hemorrhage. Open and examine the jugular veins and carotid arteries. Remove the neck organs, taking care not to fracture the hyoid bone. Check the mucosa of the larynx, pyriform sinuses, and esophagus and note any petechiae, edema, or burns. Note any articles or substances within the lumina of these structures. Examine the thyroid gland. Examine the tongue. Dissect the hyoid bone and laryngeal cartilages and note any fractures.

Spine

Examine the cervical, thoracic, and lumbar spine and note any hemorrhage in the paravertebral muscles. Examine the vertebrae from their anterior aspects and note any fractures, dislocations, compressions, or hemorrhages. In cases in which spinal injury is suspected, dissect and describe the spinal cord.

Specimens

Remember to consider the need for consent for taking and retaining specimens. All specimens must be collected in separate containers. For most specimens, disposable hard plastic or glass tubes are recommended. Each sample must be labeled with the identification of the deceased, specimen type, collection site, date/time of collection, and initials of the individual collecting the sample. Samples should be stored at a maximum of 4°C when analyzed promptly after autopsy; otherwise, at −20°C. When liquid specimens are to be frozen, it is recommended to leave a small (10%–20%) headspace in the specimen tubes.

Swabs for deoxyribonucleic acid (DNA) may usually be taken directly from the mouth, anus, and vagina. If the sampling area is dry, the cotton swabs should be humidified with sterile water before swabbing the area, followed by a second dry swab. Swabs should be dried in air and protected from any contamination (e.g., in a paper envelope). Other samples that should be taken are blood: 10 mL of peripheral blood (usually from the femoral veins) and 30 mL of central (heart) blood with sodium fluoride/potassium oxalate as preservative; some serum should also be taken (needs centrifugation); samples of urine, bile, vitreous humor, and cerebrospinal fluid should be taken where possible; all gastric contents should be retained; small samples (25 g) of liver, muscle, kidney, lung, and brain should be retained and frozen; fingernail scrapings/cuttings and one strand of hair should be cut at the vertex as closely at the scalp as possible—the proximal part (scalp side) should be indicated (e.g., rubber band); body hair can be taken if no head hair is available—hair samples are stored at room temperature; samples of all vital organs should be fixed in a formalin solution for histology. Consider taking samples of injuries for histology: in cases of suspected systemic infection, microbiological samples should be taken (usually blood) from a noncontaminated site with sterile equipment. Storage and analysis should be coordinated with the local microbiology lab. Consider taking alcohol swabs for presence of oleoresin capsicum (or similar antiriot substances) if the context indicates that such agents have been used. Such agents can often be found on facial skin or clothing. All foreign objects that have been found in the body must be preserved. If the identity is unknown after the autopsy, consider removing the mandible and maxilla (only if an in situ dental examination is not possible), taking a DNA sample and fingerprints of all fingers. Also, take photographs of all identifying features and a presentable photograph of the face.

Table 13.3 summarizes the nature of samples, reasons for sampling, and the nature of the analysis.

Examination of the Medical History and the Medical Documents

All medical information (e.g., hospital notes, prison medical records, medication charts, radiographs) about the case should be available to the medicolegal investigator(s), including interviews with treating doctors, nurses, and next of kin. This information should be studied and relevant findings taken into consideration in the final report. It may be appropriate for independent physicians (e.g., forensic physicians or prison physicians) to review any healthcare that the deceased was subject to, to see whether there were any suggestions of clinical negligence and whether the standards of medical care are comparable or better than for the general population.

TABLE 13.3

Nature of Samples, Reasons Taken, and Storage Requirements

Specimen Type	Specimen Site	Analysis	Storage
DNA (foreign)	Swabs for foreign DNA near injuries and natural orifices	DNA profile of another person than the victim	Dry storage, protection from contamination
DNA (victim)	Blood or tissue from the body	DNA profile of the victim in order to recognize foreign DNA, hereditary diseases	Blood and tissue frozen at −20°C, or blood on filter paper fast technology for analysis of nucleic acid [FTA®] and dried
Peripheral blood	Femoral vessels	Toxicology and clinical chemistry	If analyzed within 2 days, 4°C; otherwise, 20°C, at least one tube with sodium fluoride/potassium oxalate as preservative
Urine, bile, vitreous humor and CSF		Toxicology and clinical chemistry	If analyzed within 3 days, 4°C; otherwise, 20°C
Gastric content (totality)	Stomach	Toxicology (way of administration, quantity not absorbed)	If analyzed within 3 days, 4°C; otherwise, 20°C
Tissue fragments (25 g)	Liver, muscle, kidney, lung, and brain	Toxicology (if no peripheral blood is available, chronic intoxication)	If analyzed within 3 days, 4°C; otherwise, 20°C
Histology samples	Brain, heart, lungs, kidneys, liver, and all abnormal macroscopic findings	Microscopy	Samples in formalin solution, paraffin blocks at room temperature (20°C)
Head hair or, if unavailable, pubic hair		Toxicology, mitochondrial analysis	Dry storage
Fingernails	Cut or scrapings		Dry storage
Swabs for antiriot agents	Site of application with alcohol swabs	Toxicology	Dry storage
Heart blood (sterile)	Right atrium or vena cava	Microbiology	According to the local laboratory protocols

Note: FTA, fast technology for analysis of nucleic acids.

Additional Investigations

Table 13.4 shows the additional investigations that may be required dependent on the nature of the case, the facts of the case, and whether or not the postmortem examination has identified a definite cause of death.

Report

The autopsy report includes the major positive and important negative findings (e.g., absence of conjunctival petechiae, genital injuries), the date, time and place of the

TABLE 13.4

Additional Investigations Which May Be Required

- Full routine toxicology (whenever possible)
- Sexual assault screen
- Radiology
- Histology
- Neuropathology
- Microbiology
- Postmortem chemistry
- Molecular biology
- Technical investigations (e.g., in suspension or restraint cases)
- Forensic odontology

postmortem examination, the name of the medicolegal investigator and the participating assistant(s), and all other persons present during the autopsy, including the medical and/or scientific degrees and professional, political, or administrative affiliations(s) of each. The report summarizes all important findings and usually concludes to a cause of death. In the report the medicolegal investigator should also attribute any injuries to external trauma, therapeutic efforts, postmortem change, or other causes. Results of ancillary investigations and any other forensically important questions according to the specific case should also be commented on. The manner of death may be referred to in the report.

If for any reason, perhaps because of pressure from the authorities, or risks of sanctions against himself/or herself, the medicolegal investigator feels that it would not be appropriate to include his/her interpretation of the cause and mechanism of death, he/she may refrain from doing so, only truthfully and accurately describing his/her findings, without providing an interpretation. This is especially the case when the investigator could be subjected to intimidation or worse. In such cases, an independent expert opinion can be sought later on, based on the objective findings.

Special Considerations

Expected Natural Deaths

Even though every death in custody should be treated as suspicious, in cases of expected deaths in custody, such as those that are the consequence of a previously diagnosed and medically well-documented terminal illness, there must still be an investigation, although it may be simplified. The minimum requirement in those cases is an external examination and the provision of a death certificate established by a medical doctor. Information must be given to the next of kin and the body released to them, as well as a clinical death report, written by the treating physician. The next of kin have the right to ask for further investigation into the death. Some nations have put agencies into place in order to receive complaints and demands from families, to investigate, and to render recommendations. The power of such agencies should be enhanced, so they can overrule decisions of the detaining facilities and their hierarchy. The UK Prison and Probation Ombudsman is a good initiative in this direction, and the annual reports give good insight into many aspects of prison life, conflictual situations, and also deaths (Prison and Probation Ombudsman 2013). Similar issues are annually reviewed in short-term police custody by the Independent Police Complaints Commission (2016).

The Second Autopsy

Sometimes a second autopsy has to be performed, sometimes because of doubts on the results of the first autopsy and sometimes at the request of others, e.g., families. One has to be aware that a first autopsy is always a destructive process and that the initial situation cannot be restored. Another factor to take into account is the postmortem change the body undergoes after death. This is why the result of such an autopsy mainly depends on the condition of the body. A second medicolegal autopsy or counterautopsy can however be performed even years after the death. The questions a second autopsy can answer are as follows: Was the original autopsy performed according to good practice? Can the initial findings be confirmed? Are there additional relevant findings that were not detected at the first autopsy? Are the findings consistent with the initial interpretation of the results?

If the first autopsy has been well documented and the findings photographed, it can sometimes suffice to submit the documentation of the first autopsy to the appointed expert instead of performing a second autopsy. This is especially true in cases where a full-body computed tomography (CT) scan and maybe even magnetic resonance imaging (MRI) have been performed. If a second autopsy is performed, the same principles as for a first postmortem examination apply.

Conclusion

Investigations into deaths in custody are still very incomplete and insufficiently independent in many countries. Each case of death in custody has to be approached very openly without preformed opinions. Ideally, all investigations of deaths in custody in any jurisdiction should be open and transparent. National statistics should be annually published. Violent deaths are much more frequent in places of detention than in the general population. Without a full scene investigation, autopsy, and toxicology, such causes can neither be confirmed nor excluded. The use of illicit substances is widespread in many detention settings. Also, a natural death in a detention setting does not mean that there is no third-party involvement, mainly because of the often-restricted access to health professionals and medical infrastructure. However, overmedication, undermedication, prescribed drug interactions, and side effects are also very problematic in many countries. All sources of information should be taken into consideration, not to forget the next of kin. Many deaths of undetermined cause can have a hereditary origin, and the next of kin may be able to provide decisive information on that regard, as molecular analysis only gives very incomplete answers.

The complete investigation of a death in custody is often a complex and difficult task. An adequate investigation and reliable conclusions depend on the competence of the investigators, the available means, and on a high degree of independence. The investigators who are in charge will usually be familiar with the procedures described in this chapter.

Only at the very end of the investigation is one enabled to conclude if a death is natural without any third-party involvement or responsibility, or not. The investigators must be given all necessary powers and access in order to complete the task. A high level of credibility can only be achieved if all those requirements are met and if the investigation is fully transparent.

Lastly, it has to be kept in mind that even the most complete investigation will not always be able to deliver all answers. In a certain percentage, not even the cause of death can be determined. For this reason, any death investigation has to be measured by the means put into place and not the results.

References

Independent Police Complaints Commission 2016, Police complaints; statistics from England & Wales 2015/2016, Independent Police Complaints Commission London. Available from: https://www.ipcc.gov.uk/sites/default/files/Documents/research_stats/complaints_statistics_2015_16.pdf.

Minnesota Protocol on the Investigation of Potentially Unlawful Death 2016, Advanced version, UNOHCHR, New York. Available from: http://www.ohchr.org/Documents/Issues/Executions/MinnesotaProtocolInvestigationPotentiallyUnlawfulDeath2016.pdf. Accessed on 2 June 2017.

Prison and Probation Ombudsman. 2012, Learning from PPO Investigations: Natural cause deaths in prison custody 2007–2010. London.

Prison and Probation Ombudsman. 2015, Learning from PPO Investigations: Self-inflicted deaths of prisoners—2013/14. London.

Prison and Probation Ombudsman. 2016, *Annual report 2015–2016*, Prison and Probation Ombudsman, London. Available at: http://www.ppo.gov.uk/wp-content/uploads/2016/09/PPO_Annual-Report 201516_WEB_Final.pdf.

Ryan-Mills, D. 2010, *Learning from PPO Investigations: Deaths from Circulatory Diseases*, Prison and Probation Ombsudsman, London.

United Nations Manual on the Effective Prevention and Investigation of Extra-Legal, Arbitrary and Summary Executions 1991, UN Doc. E/ST/CSDHA/.12, New York. Available from: https://www.un.org/ruleoflaw/blog/document/united-nations-manual-on-the-effective-prevention-and-investigation-of-extra-legal-arbitrary-and-summary-executions/.

Further Reading

Allen, S. A., Rich, J. D., Bux, R. C. et al. 2006, Deaths of detainees in the custody of US forces in Iraq and Afghanistan from 2002 to 2005, *Medscape General Medicine*, vol. 8, p. 46.

Amnesty International 2000, *Council for the development of social science research in Africa. Monitoring and investigating death in custody*, Amnesty International, London. Available from: http://www.codesria.org/Links/Publications/amnesty/custody.pdf.

Arnold, R., Giebe, W., Winnefeld, K., and Klein, A. 2002, An initially unexplained death during prison sentence: Diagnostic verification by atomic absorption spectrometry, *Archiv Fur Kriminologie*, vol. 209, pp. 14–19.

Bennewith, O., Gunnell, D., Kapur, N., Turnbull, P., Simkin, S., Sutton, L., and Hawton, K. 2005, Suicide by hanging: Multicentre study based on coroners' records in England, *British Journal of Psychiatry*, vol. 186, pp. 260–261.

Best, D., Havis, S., Strathdee, G., Keaney, F., Manning, V., and Strang, J. 2004, Drug deaths in police custody: Is dual diagnosis a significant factor? *Journal of Clinical Forensic Medicine*, vol. 11, pp. 173–182.

Bhana, B. D. 2003, Custody-related deaths in Durban, South Africa 1998–2000, *American Journal of Forensic Medicine and Pathology*, vol. 24, pp. 202–207.

Biles, D., and McDonald, D. 1992, *Deaths in custody Australia, 1980–1989. The research papers of the Criminology Unit of the Royal Commission into Aboriginal Deaths in Custody*. Australian Institute of Criminology. Available from: http://www.aic.gov.au/media_library/publications/dic/dic1992.pdf.

Bobrik, A., Danishevski, K., Eroshina, K., and McKee, M. 2005, Prison health in Russia: The larger picture, *Journal of Public Health Policy*, vol. 26, pp. 30–59.

Camilleri, P., and McArthur, M. 2008, Suicidal behaviour in prisons: Learning from Australian and international experiences, *International Journal of Law and Psychiatry*, vol. 31, pp. 297–307.

De la Grandmaison, L., Durigon, M., Moutel, G., and Herve, C. 2006, The international criminal tribunal for the former Yugoslavia (ICTY) and the forensic pathologist: Ethical considerations, *Medicine, Science and the Law*, vol. 46, pp. 208–212.

Dogra, T. D., Bhardwaj, D. N., Sharma, G. A., and Lalwani, S. 2008, Postmortem examination in cases of custodial death in India, *Journal of the Indian Medical Association*, vol. 106, pp. 101, 104, 106.

Elger, B. S., Tidball-Binz, M., and Mangin, P. 2009, Mort en detention: Vers un cadre international d'investigation et de prevention, *Revue Médicale Suisse*, vol. 5, pp. S41–S43.

Fazel, S., and Benning, R. 2006, Natural deaths in male prisoners: A 20-year mortality study, *European Journal of Public Health*, vol. 16, pp. 441–444.

Frühwald, S., Frottier, P., Eher, R., Aigner, M., Gutierrez, K., and Ritter, K. 2000a, Assessment of custodial suicide risk—Jail and prison suicides in Austria 1975–1996, *Psychiatrische Praxis*, vol. 27, pp. 195–200.

Frühwald, S., Frottier, P., Eher, R., Gutierrez, K., and Ritter, K. 2000b, Prison suicides in Austria, 1975–1997, *Suicide and Life-Threatening Behavior*, vol. 30, pp. 360–369.

Gaeta, P. 2004, May necessity be available as a defence for torture in the interrogation of suspected terrorists? *Journal of International Criminal Justice*, vol. 3, pp. 785–994.

Gallagher, C. A., and Dobrin, A. 2006, Deaths in juvenile justice residential facilities, *Journal of Adolescent Health*, vol. 38, pp. 662–668.

Grant, J. R., Southall, P. E., Fowler, D. R. et al. 2007, Death in custody: A historical analysis, *Journal of Forensic Sciences*, vol. 52, pp. 1177–1181.

Grant, J. R., Southall, P. E., Mealey, J., Scott, S. R., and Fowler, D. R. 2009, Excited delirium deaths in custody: Past and present, *American Journal of Forensic Medicine & Pathology*, vol. 30, pp. 1–5.

Grellner, W. 2008, Fatal electrocution in prison, *Archiv Fur Kriminologie*, vol. 222, pp. 145–151.

Gunnell, D., Bennewith, O., Hawton, K., Simkin, S., and Kapur, N. 2005, The epidemiology and prevention of suicide by hanging: A systematic review, *International Journal of Epidemiology*, vol. 34, pp. 433–442.

Heide, S., Kleiber, M., and Stiller, D. 2009, Legal consequences in cases of deaths in police custody, *Gesundheitswesen*, vol. 71, pp. 226–231.

ICRC, 2013, *ICRC guidelines for investigating deaths in custody*. Available from: http://www.icrc.org/eng/assets/files/publications/icrc-002-4126.pdf.

Kariminia, A., Law, M. G., Butler, T. G. et al. 2007a, Factors associated with mortality in a cohort of Australian prisoners, *European Journal of Epidemiology*, vol. 22, pp. 417–428.

Kariminia, A., Butler, T. G., Corben, S. P. et al. 2007b, Extreme cause-specific mortality in a cohort of adult prisoners—1988 to 2002: A data-linkage study, *International Journal of Epidemiology*, vol. 36, pp. 310–316.

Koehler, S. A., Weiss, H., Songer, T. J., Rozin, L., Shakir, A., Ladham, S., Omalu, B., Dominick, J., and Wecht, C. H. 2003, Deaths among criminal suspects, law enforcement officers, civilians, and prison inmates: A coroner-based study, *American Journal of Forensic Medicine & Pathology*, vol. 24, pp. 334–338.

Leese, M., Thomas, S., and Snow, L. 2006, An ecological study of factors associated with rates of self-inflicted death in prisons in England and Wales, *International Journal of Law and Psychiatry*, vol. 29, pp. 355–360.

Miyaishi, S., Yoshitome, K., Yamamoto, Y., Naka, T., and Ishizu, H. 2004, Negligent homicide by traumatic asphyxia, *International Journal of Legal Medicine*, vol. 118, pp. 106–110.

O'Driscoll, C., Samuels, A., and Zacka, M. 2007, Suicide in New South Wales prisons, 1995–2005: Towards a better understanding, *Australian & New Zealand Journal of Psychiatry*, vol. 41, pp. 519–524.

Okie, S. 2005, Glimpses of Guantanamo—Medical ethics and the war on terror, *New England Journal of Medicine*, vol. 353, pp. 2529–2534.

Petschel, K., and Gall, J. A. 2000, A profile of deaths in custody in Victoria, 1991–96, *Journal of Clinical Forensic Medicine*, vol. 7, pp. 82–87.

Rainio, J., Lalu, K., and Penttila, A. 2001, Independent forensic autopsies in an armed conflict: Investigation of the victims from Racak, Kosovo, *Forensic Science International*, vol. 116, pp. 171–185.

Roessler, B., Fleischhackl, R., Fleischhackl, S. et al. 2007, Death in correctional facilities: Opportunities for automated external defibrillation, *Resuscitation*, vol. 73, pp. 389–393.

Sailas, E. S., Feodoroff, B., Lindberg, N. C., Virkkunen, M. E., Sund, R., and Wahlbeck, K. 2006, The mortality of young offenders sentenced to prison and its association with psychiatric disorders: A register study, *European Journal of Public Health*, vol. 16, pp. 193–197.

Seijeoung, K., Ting, A., Puisis, M., Rodriguez, S., Benson, R., Mennella, C., and Davis, F. 2007, Deaths in the Cook County Jail: 10-year report, 1995–2004, *Journal of Urban Health*, vol. 84, pp. 70–84.

Southall, P., Grant, J., Fowler, D., and Scott, S. 2008, Police custody deaths in Maryland, USA: An examination of 45 cases, *Journal of Forensic and Legal Medicine*, vol. 15, pp. 227–230.

South Worchestershire Primary Care Trust NHS 2005, *Death in custody guidelines*, South Worchestershire Primary Care Trust, Worcester. Available from: http://www.worcester shirehealth.nhs.uk/Internet_Library/Primary_Care_Trust/policies_and procedures/Clinical /040607Deathincustody.pdf.

Spencer, J. 1989, Aboriginal deaths in custody, *Australian & New Zealand Journal of Psychiatry*, vol. 23, pp. 164–165.

Stover, E., Haglund, W. D., and Samuels, M. 2003, Exhumation of mass graves in Iraq: Considerations for forensic investigations, humanitarian needs, and the demands of justice, *Journal of the American Medical Association*, vol. 290, pp. 663–666.

UN Special Rapporteur on Torture and Other Cruel, Inhuman or Degrading Treatment or Punishment. 2010, *Introduction*, Office of the High Commissioner for Human Rights, Geneva. Available from: http://www.ohchr.org/en/issues/torture/srtorture/pages/srtortureindex.aspx.

Vilke, G. M., Johnson, W. D., III, Castillo, E. M., Sloane, C., and Chan, T. C. 2009, Tactical and subject considerations of in-custody deaths proximal to use of conductive energy devices, *American Journal of Forensic Medical Pathology*, vol. 30, pp. 23–25.

Wobeser, W. L., Datema, J., Bechard, B., and Ford, P. 2002, Causes of death among people in custody in Ontario, 1990–1999. *Canadian Medical Association Journal*, vol. 167, pp. 1109–1113.

14

The Istanbul Protocol: Development, Practical Applications, and Future Directions

Vincent Iacopino

CONTENTS

Introduction

Torture is one of the most serious violations of fundamental human rights. It is prohibited in international human rights and humanitarian law in all circumstances without exception. Despite the absolute prohibition of torture in international law, it continues to be practiced in more than 100 countries around the world (Amnesty International 2008). Torture not only destroys the bodies and minds of individuals and their communities; it also undermines the rule of law and democratic institutions in civil society.

This chapter addresses two of the most critical factors in torture prevention, accountability, and redress—effective investigation and documentation. Ending impunity for torture and ill-treatment requires effective legal investigation and documentation practices. In addition, effective forensic medical investigation and documentation of torture and ill-treatment often provides one of the most powerful forms of material evidence in corroborating a victim's allegations of abusive treatment. This chapter reviews the development of international standards for the effective investigation and documentation of torture and ill-treatment known as the Istanbul Protocol (IP), practical application of IP standards, and examines future directions for IP implementation.

The content of this chapter is based on the author's 24 years of forensic medical documentation of torture with Physicians for Human Rights (PHR) and experience in leading the development of the IP together with colleagues Önder Özkalıpcı, MD, and Caroline Schlar, MS, and implementing the IP standards on behalf of PHR in nearly 30 countries during the past 14 years. PHR is a nongovernmental, nonprofit organization, founded in 1986, that uses medicine and science and the authority of health professionals to prevent gross abuses of human rights and establish justice and accountability. PHR applies critical scientific and medical evidence as the basis for authoritative advocacy, policy reform, capacity building measures, and redress for those who suffer gross violations of human rights. PHR was a corecipient of the 1997 Peace Prize for its role in the International Campaign to Ban Landmines.

Development of the Istanbul Protocol

What Is the Istanbul Protocol?

The *Manual on Effective Investigation and Documentation of Torture and Other Cruel, Inhuman or Degrading Treatment or Punishment*, commonly known as the IP, outlines international and legal standards on protection against torture and sets out specific guidelines on how effective legal and medical investigations into allegations of torture should be conducted (Iacopino et al. 1999, 2001a).

The IP is a key source of information as it both reflects existing obligations of states under international treaty and customary international law and aids states to effectively implement relevant standards. It became a UN official document in 1999 (see Figures 14.1 and 14.2).

The IP is intended to serve as a set of common, international guidelines for the assessment of persons who allege torture and ill-treatment, for investigating cases of alleged torture, and for reporting such findings to the judiciary and any other investigative body. The investigation and documentation guidelines also apply to other contexts, including human rights investigations and monitoring (including monitoring places of detention), assessment of individuals seeking political asylum, the defense of individuals who "confess" to crimes during torture, and the assessment of needs for the care of survivors of torture. In the case of health professionals who are coerced for a variety of reasons to neglect, misrepresent, or falsify evidence of torture, the manual also provides an international point of reference for health professionals and adjudicators alike and gives information on their professional ethical as well as legal obligations.

The documentation guidelines apply to individuals who allege torture and ill-treatment, whether the individuals are in detention, applying for political asylum, refugees or internally

FIGURE 14.1 *Manual on Effective Investigation and Documentation of Torture and Other Cruel, Inhuman or Degrading Treatment or Punishment*, the IP.

displaced persons, or the subject of general human rights investigations. The guidelines cover a range of topics including the following:

- Relevant international legal standards
- Relevant ethical codes
- Legal investigation of torture
- General considerations for interviews
- Physical evidence of torture
- Psychological evidence of torture

Many procedures for a torture investigation are included in the manual, such as how to interview the alleged victim and other witnesses, selection of the investigator, safety of witnesses, how to collect alleged perpetrator's statement, how to secure and obtain physical evidence, and detailed guidelines on how to establish a special independent commission of inquiry to investigate alleged torture and ill-treatment. The manual also includes comprehensive guidelines for clinical examinations to detect physical and psychological evidence of torture and ill-treatment, as well as providing information on additional diagnostic tests that may assist in corroborating the clinical findings.

The IP also outlines minimum standards for state adherence to ensure the effective documentation of torture in its *Principles on the Effective Documentation of Torture and Other Cruel, Inhuman or Degrading Treatment or Punishment*, or Istanbul Principles (Table 14.1). The guidelines contained in the IP are not designed to be fixed; rather, they represent an elaboration of the minimum standards contained in the Istanbul Principles and should be applied in accordance with a reasonable assessment of available resources.

Despite being officially recognized, and often cited by the UN, the IP is a nonbinding document. However, international law obliges governments to investigate and document incidents of torture and other forms of ill-treatment and to punish those responsible in a comprehensive, effective, prompt, and impartial manner. The IP is a tool for doing this and has received worldwide recognition.

According to the IP, medical evaluations must include detailed assessments and documentation of both physical and psychological evidence by one or more qualified experts. Unfortunately, lawyers, judges, and others within judicial or investigative systems and processes often fail to recognize the critical value and legitimacy of psychological

TABLE 14.1

Summary of Istanbul Principles

Legal Principles	Medical Principles
Prompt, effective, independent investigations	Medical evaluations must conform to established IP standards
Empowerment of investigative authority	Medical evaluations must be under the control of medical experts, not security personnel
Safety of alleged victims and witnesses	Medical evaluations must be conducted promptly, and written reports must be accurate
Access to hearings and all relevant information	Written reports must include the following: • Identification of the alleged victim and conditions of the evaluation • A detailed account of allegations including torture methods and physical and psychological symptoms • A record of physical and psychological findings • Interpretation of all findings, an opinion on the possibility of torture and/or ill treatment, and clinical recommendations • Identification and the signature of the medical expert(s)
Impartial investigations by independent commission	
Prompt, accurate public written reports	
Strict confidentiality	

evidence, sometimes relying exclusively on physical findings. This is erroneous and must be addressed at all levels of the investigation process. Medical experts correlate the degree of consistency between individual allegations of both physical and mental abuse and the physical and psychological evidence. They must also provide an opinion on the possibility of torture and/or ill-treatment based on their interpretations of physical and psychological evidence and communicate their opinions to judges and courts. It is important to understand that, ideally, IP medical evaluations typically take 2–4 hours and often longer when there are no time constraints. However, it must be recognized that there may be many pressures depending on the circumstances and setting of the evaluation that may limit the time for an assessment, perhaps to a few minutes. Comprehensive medical affidavits, reports, or statements are often many pages in length, but may be only several pages in other settings such as first encounters with nonforensic, medical personnel. While lengthy, comprehensive reports may not be usual practice in nontorture work, a detailed, consistent, and rigorous approach to reporting is crucial to a proper medicolegal assessment. Also, it takes considerable time for clinicians to become proficient in conducting these evaluations. It may take several years for medical experts to achieve high-quality IP medical evaluations, and prior training is essential.

The IP states that the following subject headings should be considered for the purpose of an individual forensic medical evaluation:

1. Relevant case information
2. Clinician's qualifications
3. Statement regarding veracity of testimony
4. Background information
5. Allegations of torture and ill-treatment
6. Physical symptoms and disabilities
7. Physical examination
8. Psychological history/examination
9. Photographs
10. Diagnostic test results
11. Consultations
12. Interpretation of physical and psychological findings
13. Conclusions and recommendations
14. Statement of truthfulness (for judicial testimonies)
15. Statement of restrictions on the medical evaluation/investigation (for subjects in custody)
16. Clinician's signature, date, place
17. Relevant appendices

As the IP makes clear, the absence of physical and/or psychological evidence in a medical evaluation does not rule out the possibility that torture or ill-treatment was inflicted. This is crucial, since as stated earlier, legal professionals and courts often inappropriately rely wholly on the presence of physical sequelae (particularly scars) as reliable proof of torture.

Brief History of the Istanbul Protocol

The IP—a consensus document—was the result of 3 years of analysis, research, and drafting undertaken by more than 75 forensic doctors, physicians, psychologists, human rights monitors, and lawyers who represented 40 organizations and institutions from 15 countries. The development of the IP was initiated and coordinated by PHR–USA, the Human Rights Foundation of Turkey (HRFT), and Action for Torture Survivors (HRFT–Geneva).

The IP was developed in Turkey in response to police coercion of physicians to produce false medical reports of detainee abuse and the exclusion of nongovernmental medical evaluations in legal proceedings. As one who initially conceived of the idea of the IP, the author believes that it is appropriate to say that the IP would not have been conceived or realized without the strong professional friendships and working relationships that were its true foundations.

The project was conceived in March 1996, after an international symposium on *Medicine and Human Rights* held at the Department of Forensic Medicine, Cukurova University Medical Faculty, in Adana, Turkey, by the Turkish Medical Association. Participants included Drs. Ümit Biçer, Necmi Çekin, Lis Danielsen, Sebnem Korur Fincanci, Mete Gülmen, Vincent Iacopino, Önder Özkalıpcı, Garry Peterson, Serpil Salaçin, Zigfrids T. Stelmachers, and Mark Williams. In the course of discussing potential research collaborations, the author proposed developing a series of guidelines on the effective investigation and documentation of torture, much like the guidelines in the Minnesota Protocol on death investigations. This would be a means of holding official forensic experts accountable to recognizable international standards and also enabling nongovernmental forensic, medical, and mental health experts to have their evaluations accepted in judicial proceedings.

The first draft of the IP was based on the assessment form that the author used in a PHR torture investigation in Turkey in 1996 (Iacopino et al. 1996). Dr. Robert Kirschner, then director of PHR's International Forensic Program, also provided editorial comments. PHR's initial draft was sent to Turkish colleagues in May 1996, and additional content was added by the HRFT, the Turkish Medical Association, and the Society of Forensic Medicine Specialists, Istanbul, by June 1998 as well as colleagues from Amnesty International, London, and Survivors International in November 1998. The drafting process concluded at a meeting in Istanbul in March 1999, when the manual reached its final form and was subsequently submitted to the UN Office of the High Commissioner for Human Rights (OHCHR) on August 9, 1999. In 2001, the OHCHR published the IP in its Professional Training Series in the six official UN languages (see http://www.ohchr.org/Documents /Publications/training8Rev1en.pdf for these and other translations).

International Recognition of the Istanbul Protocol

The Istanbul Principles have been recognized as a point of reference for assessing the effectiveness of torture investigations by a number of human rights bodies including the UN General Assembly, the UN Commission on Human Rights (since 2006, the UN Human Rights Council), the UN Committee Against Torture, and the UN SRT. In addition to recognition by the UN system, the IP has also been recognized by regional bodies including the African Commission on Human and Peoples' Rights and the European Union and a number of national human rights institutions. Such recognition represents a significant factor in the widespread use and acceptance of IP standards in medical legal contexts. IP guidelines and principles are now routinely used by medical experts in court cases in which torture and/or ill-treatment is alleged.

Practical Application of the Istanbul Protocol

One of the earliest examples of the application of the IP was in the case of Baki Erdoğan, a 29 year-old man who was detained in Aydin, in western Turkey, on August 10, 1993 and interrogated incommunicado in the Aydin Police Headquarters for 11 days (Amnesty International 1993). On August 21, he was taken to a hospital where he died the same day. In June 2000, six Aydin police officers, including the deputy security director and the anti-terrorism department director, were convicted of torturing Baki Erdoğan to death in police custody. They were sentenced to 5 1/? years in prison and barred from public service for life (Ocalan 2000). The conviction was largely based on the courageous efforts of Turkish forensic doctors who submitted an alternative medical report that revealed numerous flaws in the autopsy and medical assessment made by the official medical experts (McColl et al. 2012).

PHR Istanbul Protocol Implementation Experience

Since the development of the IP, human rights organizations and forensic experts around the world have routinely applied IP standards in their medical assessments of individuals alleging torture and ill-treatment. PHR has more than 25 years of experience in the medical documentation of torture and ill-treatment. It has investigated and documented medical evidence of torture and ill-treatment in dozens of countries and has extensive experience in the implementation of IP standards (PHR 2011a). PHR's IP implementation activities are designed to establish and transform government policies on torture and ill-treatment into action through coordinated and sustained capacity building, policy reform, forensic medical documentation activities, and research. In addition, through media and advocacy efforts, we also seek to engage civil societies in ending torture and ill-treatment in their countries. PHR's IP implementation efforts have been primarily supported by private foundations with additional support from local, nongovernmental organizations, and international human rights organizations such as the OHCHR and the Organizations for Security and Cooperation in Europe.

Examples of how IP evaluations may be used in practices are referred to in the following, particularly in relation to the work of one organization, PHR, in the context of the United States. Other organizations such as the HRFT, the International Rehabilitation Council for Torture Victims, and RCT/Empathy have considerable experience in applying IP standards in torture documentation and capacity-building activities. Readers are advised to identify similar organizations within their own jurisdictions or countries to identify local practice and initiatives.

Efforts by PHR to apply IP standards can be summarized as follows:

Forensic Medical Evaluations of Asylum Applicants in the United States

A well-founded fear of persecution, which includes being subjected to torture in their home country, is a cornerstone of refugee law and central to being granted asylum in a third country (UN Convention Relating to the Status of Refugees 1951). For survivors who make it to the United States, we use our forensic expertise to document their physical and psychological injuries for use in their applications for asylum. Every year, more than 40,000 people flee serious persecution in their home country and seek safety in the United States. These are survivors of some of the most egregious human rights violations in the world today. To gain asylum, they must prove they were abused or have a well-founded fear of future abuse. PHR's network of more than 400 health professionals throughout the United States assess claims of abuse and have been providing approximately 500 evaluations per year for more than 20 years (PHR 2011b). These clinicians are identified through PHR trainings in the United States. They learn to apply IP standards in their clinical evaluations, which are crucial in corroborating legitimate claims for asylum. A study by Lustig et al. (2008) demonstrated that asylum grant rates for asylum seekers with medical evaluations by the PHR Asylum Network clinicians was 89% compared to 38% among asylum seekers without medical evaluations.

Expert Forensic Medical Testimony

PHR forensic medical experts have conducted medical evaluations using the IP standards in a number of prominent individual cases of alleged torture around the world. In many of these cases, the forensic medical testimony was critical in supporting claims of torture and ill-treatment and subsequent judicial outcomes, including, for example, in a number of detainees held in the US detention facility at Guantánamo Bay.

On February 5, 2013, the author provided expert testimony in the case of *United States v. Abd al-Rahim al-Nashiri*. Al-Nashiri was charged with helping to plot Al Qaeda's attack on the *USS Cole* warship, in which 17 sailors were killed. In a U.S. Military Commission court hearing, the author testified on the relevance of IP standards for forensic medical evaluations of alleged torture and the importance of medical experts having access to all relevant medical and legal documents based on a recent statement by the International Forensic Expert Group (2013). On February 7, 2013, the judge ruled that all the medical and legal records in the case must be made available to the defense team (Savage 2013)—an important victory in institutionalizing the value of the IP within the United States.

The IP was also instrumental in a recent opinion provided by the Independent Forensic Expert Group on the use of hooding (International Forensic Expert Group 2011) in the case of Al Bazzouni v. The Prime Minister and others in the United Kingdom. The court subsequently ruled that hooding constituted cruel, inhumane, and degrading treatment, and the practice was banned in subsequent guidance to British troops and intelligence officers (Prime Minister 2011).

Human Rights Investigations

PHR routinely applies IP standards not only in individual forensic medical evaluations, but in population-based assessments in which torture and ill-treatment are alleged (Iacopino et al. 2001b; Rubenstein et al. 2001; Hirschfeld et al. 2009; Sollom et al. 2011; Tsai et al. 2012). The application of IP standards has been critical in PHR's documentation of the systematic use of torture by the US government against national security detainees (Hashemian et al. 2008), in documenting the neglect of medical evidence of torture in Guantanamo Bay by Department of Defense medical personnel (Iacopino and Xenakis 2011a), and complicity of medical personnel in the authorization and use of torture in the United States (Iacopino 2011a).

Resource Development

PHR's IP implementation activities have required the development of a number of related resources. All of PHR's medical evaluations, capacity-building trainings, and policy reform activities are based on the IP. The content of the IP has been adapted for medical evaluations of asylum applicants (PHR 2012), domestic and international human rights investigations, capacity-building initiatives, and policy reform activities on torture prevention, accountability, and redress.

In 2009, PHR developed the Model Curriculum on the Effective Medical Documentation of Torture and Ill-treatment (Iacopino et al. 2009) in conjunction with the International Rehabilitation Council for Torture Victims. The purpose of the model curriculum is to provide health professional students with essential knowledge and skills to prevent torture and ill-treatment through effective investigation and documentation of these practices using IP standards. The model curriculum consists of a 228-page, 9-module curriculum, PowerPoint presentations, and self-assessment quizzes for each module. The model curriculum has served as the basis for country-specific training materials in a number of countries including Turkey, Mexico, Georgia, Morocco, Sri Lanka, Uganda, Ecuador, Egypt, Kenya, the Philippines, Serbia, Sudan, Thailand, Chile, Colombia, Syria, Tunisia, Bahrain, Egypt, Iraq, Jordan, Lebanon, Libya, Kyrgyzstan, Tajikistan, Kazakhstan, and the United States.

A number of additional IP related resources are in the process of being developed including an *IP Short Form* and guidelines for judges and prosecutors (see the following).

Capacity Building

Since the development of the IP, the PHR and other organizations such as the HRFT, the International Rehabilitation Council for Torture Victims, REDRESS, and RCT/Empathy have worked to implement IP standards in more than 30 countries and often work in collaboration. A brief summary of PHR's capacity-building initiatives are described here to provide some insight into such capacity-building efforts.

The primary purpose of PHR's capacity building initiatives is to enable medical and legal experts, including judges and prosecutors, to effectively investigate, document, and adjudicate torture and ill-treatment. PHR works with representatives of civil society to hold state actors accountable for human rights violations, and under appropriate circumstances, we also work with state actors to institutionalize human rights protections and effective investigation and documentation practices. PHR's international efforts to implement IP standards consist of three primary activities: (1) an assessment of torture and ill-treatment practices, (2) capacity-building training for medical and legal experts on the effective investigation and documentation of torture and ill-treatment, and (3) policy reform activities (PHR 2011a). In general, we undertake a wide range of complementary and sustained activities and implement them in sequential, interdependent phases.

In the first phase, our primary goals are to (1) assess prevailing country-specific conditions and challenges, (2) raise awareness among relevant civil society and government stakeholders to IP standards, and (3) develop partnerships with civil society and government stakeholders as well as international human rights organizations. In the second phase, PHR's work transitions to developing systematic and sustained capacity building on IP investigation and documentation standards as well as critical policy reform activities to enable conditions for effective torture investigation and documentation practices. The third phase of our work focuses on (1) transferring capacity building and policy reform activities to PHR's national IP trainers, (2) integrating best practices into government institutions, (3) enhancing regional networking and collaboration, and (4) monitoring the IP implementation process including the quality and accuracy of forensic and medical evaluations of alleged torture and ill-treatment.

PHR's implementation projects often begin with research activities to inform subsequent capacity building efforts, recommendations for policy reform, and advocacy, including (1) individual forensic medical evaluations, (2) pre- and posttraining surveys of medical and legal experts, and (3) interviews with governmental and civil society stakeholders. PHR trainers develop country-specific training materials as well as standardized documentation forms and guidelines for medical, legal, and judicial target groups. Initial trainings for nongovernmental medical and legal experts typically include lectures, workshops, open panel discussions, and practical case applications, including mock trials. In the course of IP trainings, PHR seeks to identify medical experts who demonstrate the capacity for and interest in participating in additional training to become IP trainers themselves. These national IP trainers subsequently participate in individual mentoring activities, including conducting individual case evaluations with the supervision of PHR forensic medical experts and the planning and implementation of subsequent IP trainings.

In some cases where state officials demonstrate a serious commitment to the implementation of IP standards, we undertake multiyear projects to train official forensic medical experts, prosecutors, and judges. The continuation of such initiatives depends on the progressive and successful implementation of IP standards and fulfilling basic terms of reference for PHR's independence, access to relevant information, transparency, and control over the content of the project.

In order to assess the outcome of the IP trainings, participants complete an evaluation for each day of the training. In addition, we conduct pre- and posttraining surveys of health and legal professionals to assess the participants' attitudes on the investigation and documentation of torture and ill-treatment and the effectiveness of the IP training in improving the participants' capacity to document medical evidence of such abuses. In some countries, we have analyzed the quality and accuracy of medical evaluations conducted by IP trainees and published our findings (Heisler et al. 2003; Moreno et al. 2003; Moreno and Iacopino 2008a).

PHR also facilitates policy reform for torture and ill-treatment prevention, accountability, and redress based on PHR's research and analysis of torture practices. We engage in policy reform activities with stakeholders in government and civil society to develop and implement a national plan of action for effective torture investigation and documentation. Such national plans typically include (1) official recognition of IP standards, (2) legal and administrative reforms, (3) compulsory capacity building for relevant target groups, (4) structural independence of forensic institutions, and (5) national monitoring and accountability measures. In our 7-year experience of working with the federal attorney general's office of Mexico, PHR led the development of a quasi-independent monitoring committee to ensure the quality and accuracy of medical and legal investigation and documentation of torture and ill-treatment (Moreno and Iacopino 2008b). The monitoring committee had oversight over all investigation and documentation activities, supervised the design and implementation of all training programs, and established a medical advisory committee to assess the quality and accuracy of all medical evaluations and a legal advisory committee to review and assess the quality of legal proceedings and judicial outcomes. The monitoring committee was also charged with the duty of providing recommendations for remedial education of medical and legal experts.

PHR engages in media-related activities to raise awareness about individual cases of torture and patterns of abuse and to provide specific recommendations for reform. PHR's media interactions also serve to establish a public record of government intention for the implementation of IP standards.

TABLE 14.2

Facilitating Factors for Torture and Ill-Treatment

- Inadequate safeguards during arrest and detention
- Inadequate complaints procedures
- Inadequate investigations by prosecutors and law enforcement, which perpetuates a judicial system that depends on torture and ill-treatment for forced confessions
- Inadequate legal investigations
- Inadequate legal defense
- Inadequate forensic medical evaluations and assessments of alleged abuse in custody by other medical personnel
- Inadequate sanctions against perpetrators and those who are complicit
- Lack of systematic monitoring of torture and ill-treatment practices
- Fear of reprisals by law enforcement officials
- Inadequate redress for victims of torture and ill-treatment
- Corruption of government officials

Limitations and Misuse of the Istanbul Protocol

It is important to recognize limitations and potential misuse of the IP. IP guidelines aid medical experts in their efforts to correlate specific allegations of abuse with physical and/or psychological evidence. As the IP makes clear, the absence of physical and/or psychological evidence in a medical evaluation does not rule out the possibility that torture or ill-treatment was inflicted. Many factors may account for the absence of physical and psychological findings, and these factors can be documented in support of specific claims (for example, witness statements and physical evidence such as video recordings of the crime). Unfortunately, in some instances, the IP has been misused to exonerate police who are accused of abuses on the basis of the absence of medical findings (Moreno and Iacopino 2008a,b). For example, in Mexico, the absence of physical and/or psychological evidence of torture has been used by government officials to claim that torture allegations were false in a number of cases (Moreno and Iacopino 2008b). Such misuse of the IP should never be tolerated. The IP was developed to prevent torture and ill-treatment and to promote accountability. Governments must ensure that its official representatives do not engage in misuse or misrepresentation of the IP to exonerate police who are accused of abuses or for any other purpose.

Furthermore, it is important to recognize that torture and ill-treatment are facilitated by many factors (see Table 14.2). These factors must be addressed, including ensuring effective medical and legal investigation and documentation practices, in order to achieve torture prevention, accountability, and redress.

Future Directions for the Istanbul Protocol

Istanbul Protocol Plan of Action

The ultimate goal of the IP is to end the practice of torture in our time. Realizing the goal will require a wide range of remedial measures over time. The many factors that facilitate torture must be simultaneously addressed and without retrogression. During the past 14 years, the IP has been employed largely by nongovernmental organizations. As the responsible party for torture and ill-treatment, it is not surprising that states have resisted the implementation of IP standards. Although the IP provides states guidelines and principles on the effective investigation and documentation of torture and ill-treatment, it does not compel them or inform them how to do so. The author recently realized this in the context of implementing IP standards in Kyrgyzstan and Tajikistan. The realization has led to an ongoing project to develop an IP plan of action, a roadmap for states to achieve effective investigation and documentation of torture and ill-treatment and a means of accountability for states that fail to undertake necessary steps to effectively investigate and document torture and ill-treatment. The IP plan of action is a crucial element in the fight to end the practice of torture, but, as previously stated, it must be implemented together with other remedial actions such as establishing effective investigation and prosecution practices, establishing an independent judicial system, and addressing the corruption within law enforcement and legal systems, to name a few.

Thus far, five partner organizations, PHR, the International Council for the Rehabilitation of Torture Victims, the HRFT, REDRESS, and the APT, are working in collaboration with the UN OHCHR. The then UN High Commissioner for Human Rights expressed her strong support for the IP plan of action and for the ongoing implementation of IP standards (Iacopino and Moreno 2012; UN SRT 2014).

The content of the first draft of the IP plan of action addresses the following topics:

- State recognition of IP standards
- Legal provisions to ensure effective criminalization of torture, safeguards for persons deprived of their liberty, complaints procedures, investigation and prosecution, judicial proceedings, and redress
- Medical provisions to ensure that forensic and medical evaluations of alleged torture and ill-treatment are conducted promptly and objectively by qualified, independent, governmental and nongovernmental experts to assess physical and psychological evidence in accordance with IP standards
- Monitoring of the IP plan of action, including compliance with preconditions, development of standards, procedures and structures for legal and health profession, and training of relevant legal and health professionals
- Cooperation, coordination, and technical assistance to coordinate IP plan of action activities in cooperation with the assistance of multilateral institutions, regional human rights bodies, experienced nongovernmental organizations, and other states

We anticipate that the IP plan of action will require a 2- to 3-year effort to develop international consensus and will likely involve some 200 stakeholders, including representatives of nongovernmental human rights organizations, national human rights institutions, national preventive mechanism, UN agencies, forensic institutions, and victims' groups. The IP plan of action will consist of three main parts:

1. A statement of principles for effective torture investigation and documentation as they apply to the different stakeholders, in particular policy makers, politicians, legislators, legal experts (including prosecutors and judges), health professionals as well as other actors in the criminal justice system

2. A set of detailed actions providing a comprehensive step by step guide for specific state target users to establish and maintain a system of effective and independent torture investigations and documentation

3. A collection of resource materials for the different target users who will be involved in torture investigations and documentation

Implementation efforts will be undertaken in close collaboration with relevant international and regional organizations (including the UN OHCHR), nongovernmental organizations, national human rights institutions, and NPMs under the Optional Protocol to the UN Convention Against Torture. In addition, PHR's ongoing efforts to develop national IP plans of action in Kyrgyzstan and Tajikistan have served as the foundation for the development of the IP plan of action. Similarly, the international effort to develop the IP plan of action has informed PHR's efforts to draft national IP plans of action in Kyrgyzstan and Tajikistan.

Training and Resources

A number of IP-related resources are in the process of being developed in the context of PHR's IP implementation activities in Central Asia, the Middle East, and North Africa.

Istanbul Protocol Short Form

A comprehensive forensic medical evaluation of physical and psychological evidence requires considerable time to conduct, often 2–4 hours, and subsequent medicolegal reports may be quite long, not uncommonly 10–20 pages. There are some situations in which a comprehensive forensic medical examination may not be possible or practical, for example, during routine medical evaluations of pretrial detainees and prisoners. The risk of developing less than comprehensive assessment tools is obvious; some clinicians will fail to conduct thorough forensic medical evaluations when they are indicated, particularly evaluations of psychological evidence by clinicians lacking in mental health training. PHR has developed an IP medical assessment form that was adapted from the IP for use by nonforensic clinicians who conduct assessments of alleged abuse in custody (pretrial detention and/or penitentiary systems). This short form is currently being evaluated in several implementation field settings, including use by several NPMs, and may be included as a resource in the IP plan of action.

Guidelines for Judges, Prosecutors, and Law Enforcement Officials

Effective investigation and documentation of torture and ill-treatment will not result in effective adjudication unless prosecutors, judges, and law enforcement officials are aware of and apply IP standards. PHR has developed a judicial pretrial checklist to aid judges in assessing whether detainees have been subjected to torture and ill-treatment during the arrest, interrogation, and detention phases preceding trial. Furthermore, the checklist will help judges identify instances where confessions may have been obtained through the use of torture and or ill-treatment by law enforcement. PHR has also developed a judicial checklist for medical testimony designed to help judges assess the quality of forensic medical evaluations of torture and adjudicate claims of torture and ill-treatment by applying IP standards. Similar guidelines are being developed for prosecutors and law enforcement officials. Such aids will be considered as potential resources for the IP plan of action.

Istanbul Protocol App

PHR is undertaking the adaptation of Istanbul Protocol standardized forms for forensic medical experts as well as guidelines for judges, prosecutors, and law enforcement officials for use in portable electronic device applications or "apps." PHR is currently in the process of pilot-testing an app known as "MediCapt" (PHR 2017) for the medical documentation of sexual violence. Once finalized, the MediCapt app will serve as the basis for an Istanbul Protocol app. Such information collected by forensic medical experts in the field will be uploaded to secure servers for medicolegal purposes.

Procedures for Timely Documentation and Accountability of Torture

Currently in most conflict situations, it takes a great deal of time for national and international courts to act on medical evidence of torture and ill-treatment. In the International Criminal Court (ICC), many years may elapse between the time of alleged torture and the ICC's subsequent prosecution of the alleged crime. PHR is working with the ICC and training medical and mental health clinicians in conflict situations, such as Syria and Bahrain, to use IP standards to evaluate allegations of torture in field settings and to forward this information via a secure network for timely documentation and accountability of torture.

Monitoring Practices

Although the IP is considered the gold standard for the effective investigation and documentation of torture and ill-treatment, these standards have not been uniformly applied within international human rights bodies such as the Committee Against Torture, the Subcommittee for the Prevention of Torture, National Preventive Mechanisms, the CPT, national human rights institutions, official state forensic services, and human rights nongovernmental organizations. In our efforts to develop the IP plan of action, we seek to improve the uniformity of investigation and documentation practices in accordance with the IP.

The implementation of IP standards should also be monitored by individual countries, reported annually (e.g., U.S. Department of State Country Reports on Human Rights Practices), and considered in bilateral country relationships to progressively achieve torture prevention, accountability, and redress.

Recent ratification of the Optional Protocol to the UN Convention Against Torture (OHCHR 2006) has resulted in the unrestricted monitoring of places of detention by the Subcommittee for the Prevention of Torture and NPMs. While these are critical steps toward prevention, there has been little change in torture and ill-treatment practices in most countries. Unfortunately, such monitoring has not effectively addressed the problem of impunity, which sends a signal to perpetrators of torture and ill-treatment that there will be no consequences to their actions. Ending impunity is imperative and cannot be achieved without effective medical and legal investigation, documentation, and adjudication of torture and ill-treatment.

A Culture of Human Rights

The most significant challenge in achieving effective investigation and documentation of torture and ill-treatment and ending torture in our time is developing the will among state actors and civil society. A BBC World Service poll (2006) of more than 27,000 people in 25 different countries found that 30% of those surveyed think governments should be allowed to use some degree of torture in order to combat terrorism. The percentage of Americans favoring the use of torture in certain cases is one of the highest among the 25 countries, 36%.

Ending torture and ill-treatment is not simply a matter of having more effective medical and legal practices and procedures; it also requires the development of a global culture of human rights:

> One evening in Istanbul in 1998 just after completing our final meeting on the development of the Istanbul Protocol, Sir Nigel Rodley, then U.N. Special Rapporteur on Torture, and I sat down for a dinner celebration with our Istanbul Protocol colleagues. At some point, we began discussing what it would take to end torture. Nigel argued, "Ending impunity through legal prosecutions is the only way." I countered that, "There is no way that torture and its many cousins will end in the absence of a culture of human rights." We argued and smiled as we each knew the other was right.

Vincent Iacopino

FIGURE 14.2 Vincent Iacopino, MD, PhD (*left*), PHR, and Önder Özkalıpcı, MD (*right*), HRFT, presenting the IP to UN High Commissioner for Human Rights, Mary Robinson (*center*). Photo taken by Caroline Schlar, MS on August 9, 1999.

References

Amnesty International 1993, *News, worldwide appeals, Turkey*, Amnesty International, London. Available from http://www.amnesty.org/en/library/asset/NWS21/009/1993/fr/cd8cfe7d-f8c8 -11dd-b40d-7b25bb27e189/nws210091993en.pdf. [August 3, 2013].

Amnesty International 2008, *The state of the world's human rights: Annual report 2008*, Amnesty International, London. Available from: http://thereport.amnesty.org/eng/facts-and-figures. [August 3, 2013].

BBC 2006, World citizens reject torture, global poll suggests, *BBC World Service Online*, October 19. Available from: http://www.bbc.co.uk/pressoffice/pressreleases/stories/2006/10_october/19 /poll.shtml. [August 3, 2013].

Hashemian, F., Crosby, S., Iacopino, V. et. al. 2008, *Broken laws, broken lives: Medical evidence of torture by US personnel and its impact*, PHR, New York, pp. 1–130.

Heisler, M., Moreno, A., DeMonner, S., Keller, A., and Iacopino, V. 2003, Assessment of torture and ill treatment of detainees in Mexico: Attitudes and experiences of forensic physicians, *Journal of the American Medical Association*, vol. 289, pp. 2135–2143.

Hirschfeld, K., Leaning, J., Crosby, S. et al. 2009, *Nowhere to Turn: Failure to Protect, Support, and Assure Justice for Darfuri Women*. PHR, New York, pp. 1–65. Available from: https://s3.amazonaws .com/PHR_Reports/nowhere-to-turn.pdf. [August 3, 2013].

Iacopino, V., Heisler, M., and Rosoff, R. 1996, *Torture in Turkey and its Unwilling Accomplices*, PHR, New York, pp. 221–241.

Iacopino, V., Ozkalipci, O., and Schlar, C. 1999, The Istanbul protocol: International standards for the effective investigation and documentation of torture and ill treatment, *The Lancet*, vol. 354, p. 1117.

Iacopino, V., Frank, M. W., Bauer, H. M. et al. 2001a, A population-based assessment of human rights abuses against ethnic Albanian refugees from Kosovo, *American Journal of Public Health*, vol. 91, pp. 2013–2018.

Iacopino, V., Ozkalipci, O., Schlar, C. et al. 2001b, *Manual on the effective investigation and documentation of torture and other cruel, inhuman or degrading treatment or punishment (the Istanbul protocol)*, United Nations Publications, New York and Geneva. Available from: http://www.ohchr.org /Documents/Publications/training8Rev1en.pdf. [August 3, 2013].

Iacopino, V., Dandu, M., Wong, G., Ozkalipci, O., and Moreno, A. 2009, *Model curriculum on the effective medical documentation of torture and ill-treatment: Educational resources for health professional students*, International Rehabilitation Council for Torture Victims, Copenhagen, pp. 1–228. Available from: http://istanbulprotocolmodelcurriculum.org. [August 3, 2013].

Iacopino, V., and Xenakis, S. N. 2011a, Neglect of medical evidence of torture in Guantánamo Bay: A case series, *Public Library of Science Medicine*, vol. 8, p. e1001027. Available from: http:// www.plosmedicine.org/article/info%3Adoi%2F10.1371%2Fjournal.pmed.1001027. [August 3, 2013].

Iacopino, V., Allen, S. A., and Keller, A. S. 2011b, Bad science used to support torture and human experimentation, *Science*, vol. 331, pp. 34–35.

Iacopino, V. 2011a, U.S. torture and national security: The imperative of accountability. *Zeitschrift für Psychologie/Journal of Psychology*, vol. 219, pp. 190–192.

Iacopino, V. 2011b, A memo on torture to John Yoo, *The Guardian*, June 2. Available from: http://www.guardian.co.uk/commentisfree/cifamerica/2011/jun/02/john-yoo-torture -waterboarding?INTCMP=SRCH. [August 3, 2013].

Iacopino, V., and Moreno, A. 2012, *Ending impunity: The use of forensic medical evaluations to document torture and ill treatment in Kyrgyzstan*, pp. 50–51. Available at: https://s3.amazonaws.com /PHR_Reports/2012-kyrgystan-ending-impunity.pdf. [August 3, 2013].

International Forensic Expert Group 2011, Statement on hooding, *Torture: Journal on Rehabilitation of Torture Victims and Prevention of Torture*, vol. 3, pp. 1–3.

International Forensic Expert Group 2013, Statement on access to relevant medical and other health records and relevant legal records for forensic medical evaluations of alleged torture and other cruel, inhuman or degrading treatment or punishment, *Journal of Forensic and Legal Medicine*, April 2013. Vol. 20, Issue 3, p158–163. Available at: http://www.jflmjournal.org/article /S1752-928X(12)00175-8/pdf.

Lustig, S. L., Kureshi, S., Delucchi, K., Iacopino, V., and Morse, S. 2008, Asylum grant rates following medical evaluations of maltreatment among political asylum applicants in the United States, *Journal of Immigrant and Minority Health*, vol. 10, pp. 7–15. Available from: http://www .springerlink.com/content/r0g61557tn547086/?p=d7336632765841f2b8103fbe6d98e9b8&pi=0. [August 3, 2013].

McColl, H., Bhui, K., and Jones, E. 2012, The role of doctors in investigation, prevention and treatment of torture. *Journal of the Royal Society of Medicine*, vol. 105, pp. 464–471. Available at: https://www.ncbi.nlm.nih.gov/pmc/articles/PMC3526851/.

Moreno, A., Heisler, M., Keller, A., and Iacopino, V. 2003, Documentation of torture and ill treatment in Mexico: A review of medical forensic investigations, 2000–2002, *Health and Human Rights*, vol. 7, pp. 29–50.

Moreno, A., and Iacopino, V. 2008a, Forensic investigations of torture and ill-treatment in Mexico: A follow-up study after the implementation of the Istanbul Protocol, *Journal of Forensic and Legal Medicine*, vol. 29, 443–478.

Moreno, A., and Iacopino, V. 2008b, *Forensic Documentation of Torture and Ill Treatment in Mexico: An Assessment of the Implementation Process of the Istanbul Protocol Standards*, PHR, New York, pp. 1–117. Available from: http://www2.ohchr.org/english/bodies/cat/docs/ngos/PHR_via _IRCT_Report_Mexico_CAT49.pdf. [August 3, 2013].

Ocalan, J. 2000, *Zoominfo*. Available from: http://www.zoominfo.com/#!search/profile/person?pers onId=33166315&targetid=profile. [August 3, 2013].

OHCHR (Office of the High Commissioner for Human Rights) 2006, *Optional protocol to the convention against torture and other cruel, inhuman and degrading treatment or punishment*, UN, Geneva. Available from: http://www.ohchr.org/EN/ProfessionalInterest/Pages/OPCAT.aspx. [August 3, 2013].

PHR (Physicians for Human Rights) 2011a, *Effective training tool: The Istanbul protocol*, PHR, New York. Available from: http://physiciansforhumanrights.org/issues/torture/international -torture/istanbul-protocol.html. [August 3, 2013].

PHR 2011b, *Asylum network*, PHR, New York. Available from: http://physiciansforhumanrights.org /asylum/asylum-network.html. [August 3, 2013].

PHR 2012, *Examining asylum seekers: A clinician's guide to physical and psychological evaluations of torture and ill-treatment*, PHR, New York, Available from: http://physiciansforhumanrights .org/library/reports/examining-asylum-seekers-manual-2012.html#sthash.6wiqPj4J.dpuf. [August 3, 2013].

PHR 2017, *MediCapt*, PHR, New York. Available from: http://physiciansforhumanrights.org/medicap. [April 23, 2017].

Prime Minster Cameron, D. 2011, *Consolidated guidance on detainees (update)*, Prime Minister, London, Column 26WS. Available from: http://www.publications.parliament.uk/pa/cm201011/cmhansrd /cm111110/wmstext/111110m0001.htm#11111066000107. [August 3, 2013].

Rubenstein, L. S., Ford, D., Mach, O. et al. 2001, *Endless Brutality: War Crimes in Chechnya*, PHR, New York, pp. 1–143.

Savage, C. 2013, Mental tests are ordered for Cole bombing suspect, *New York Times*, February 4. Available from: http://www.nytimes.com/2013/02/05/us/mental-examination-ordered-for-cole -bombing-suspect.html. [August 3, 2013].

Sollom, R., Richards, A., Parmar, P. et al. 2011, A population-based assessment of health and human rights in Chin State, Burma: Evidence for crimes against humanity, *Public Library of Science Medicine*, vol. 8, p. e1001007. Available from: http://www.plosmedicine.org/article /info:doi/10.1371/journal.pmed.1001007#aff7. [August 3, 2013].

266

Tsai, A. C., Eisa, M. A., Crosby, S. et al. 2012, Medical evidence of torture and other human rights viola-tions in Darfur, *Public Library of Science Medicine*, vol. 9, pp. e1001198. Available from: http://www .plosmedicine.org/article/info%3Adoi%2F10.1371%2Fjournal.pmed.1001198. [August 3, 2013].
UN 1951, UN convention relating to the status of refugees, *Treaty Series*, vol. 189, p. 137, UN, Geneva. Available at: http://www.refworld.org/docid/3be01b964.html. [Accessed October 18, 2015].
UN SRT (2014). Interim report of the Special Rapporteur on torture and other cruel, inhuman or degrading treatment or punishment, 23 September 2014, UN Document: A/69/387. Available at: http://daccess-ods.un.org/TMP/6064724.92218018.html. [October 16, 2015].

15

Dilemmas for Healthcare Professionals Involved in the Care of Detainees

Máximo Alberto Duque Piedrahíta

CONTENTS

Introduction

Provision of medical care to detainees is a challenging responsibility for healthcare professionals including physicians, nurses, and dentists and for the hospitals and public or private companies involved in such activities. Particular tensions exist within the patient–healthcare provider relationship, which are not present in other settings, specifically the relationship of the physician with his/her employer, the prison service, and the general culture and attitude of society to prisoners (World Medical Association [WMA] 2012).

The health of a detainee is the responsibility of the detaining authority. For this chapter the meaning of the word *authority* will be used to speak about the institution, state or prison service, or other organization in charge of detention facilities and management of inmates. However, the detaining authority delegates this task to a healthcare professional or health institution. But in the case of detainees, the circumstances of the relationship between health professional and the patient are very different compared with when the patient is not a detainee.

Examples of these differences include that patients generally do not have a choice of physician or healthcare institution (such as clinic, hospital, insurance company), and normally they have to accept the healthcare professionals chosen by the authorities. However, the right to choose a physician can be understood as the same right to choose a lawyer, but in practice, it depends on how developed the prison healthcare system is in each country.

In most of the cases, and depending further on the security classification of the detainee, health professionals have restrictions on direct access to the patients and often conduct their work outside of the usual community health system, commonly in detention hospitals or clinics or in the prison physician's offices. Medical records contain sensitive information related to the health conditions of each patient and should be confidential files (and this may be protected by law in many jurisdictions). Unfortunately in practice, in some places of detention, the healthcare facilities and sometimes even the medical files are under the ultimate control of the detaining authority, and health professionals may have difficulty in preserving the confidentiality of their consultations and of the medical records.

TABLE 15.1

Principles of Medical Ethics Relevant to the Role of Health Personnel, Particularly Physicians, in the Protection of Prisoners and Detainees against Torture and Other Cruel, Inhuman, or Degrading Treatment or Punishment

Principle 1
Health personnel, particularly physicians, charged with the medical care of prisoners and detainees have a duty to provide them with protection of their physical and mental health and treatment of disease of the same quality and standard as is afforded to those who are not imprisoned or detained.

Principle 2
It is a gross contravention of medical ethics, as well as an offence under applicable international instruments, for health personnel, particularly physicians, to engage, actively or passively, in acts which constitute participation in, complicity in, incitement to or attempts to commit torture or other cruel, inhuman or degrading treatment or punishment.

Principle 3
It is a contravention of medical ethics for health personnel, particularly physicians, to be involved in any professional relationship with prisoners or detainees the purpose of which is not solely to evaluate, protect, or improve their physical and mental health.

Principle 4
It is a contravention of medical ethics for health personnel, particularly physicians:
  a. To apply their knowledge and skills in order to assist in the interrogation of prisoners and detainees in a manner that may adversely affect the physical or mental health or condition of such prisoners or detainees and which is not in accordance with the relevant international instruments;
  b. To certify, or to participate in the certification of, the fitness of prisoners or detainees for any form of treatment or punishment that may adversely affect their physical or mental health and which is not in accordance with the relevant international instruments, or to participate in any way in the infliction of any such treatment or punishment which is not in accordance with the relevant international instruments.

Principle 5
It is a contravention of medical ethics for health personnel, particularly physicians, to participate in any procedure for restraining a prisoner or detainee unless such a procedure is determined in accordance with purely medical criteria as being necessary for the protection of the physical or mental health or the safety of the prisoner or detainee himself, of his fellow prisoners or detainees, or of his guardians, and presents no hazard to his physical or mental health.

Principle 6
There may be no derogation from the foregoing principles on any ground whatsoever, including public emergency.

Source: UN, *Principles of Medical Ethics Relevant to the Role of Health Personnel, Particularly Physicians, in the Protection of Prisoners and Detainees against Torture and Other Cruel, Inhuman or Degrading Treatment or Punishment*. UN, Geneva, 1982.

This chapter identifies 10 common dilemmas for healthcare professionals involved in the care of detainees, in order to explain the difficulties and to offer practical solutions to the most common situations.

In 1982, the UN adopted the principles shown in Table 15.1, which are the basis of the ethical approach required by healthcare providers in charge of detainees.

First Dilemma: Rights of the Patient to the Confidentiality of Their Medical Files versus the Regulations of the Detaining Authority

The issues of confidentiality and privacy in healthcare are undoubtedly central in maintaining the healthcare provider–healthcare receiver (patient) relationship (Sheikh Asim 2008). Most patients expect that their medical information can be given in confidence to a healthcare provider and maintained securely and confidentially by that person or institution without any unauthorized access to this information by other people.

The doctor–patient relationship can only operate and succeed in such circumstances of trust that result in a full and frank exchange of medical information between the parties (Sheikh Asim 2008). Thus, a patient normally provides their medical information to the physician, who utilizes, records, and maintains this information only for the purposes of treatment and diagnosis. This is the normal mechanism of the doctor–patient data flow and is the primary objective of the data collection during medical consultations. A normal patient, not in detention, has a reasonable expectation that their information will not be used for any other purpose without being informed and consenting to those other purposes. A detainee should expect the same standard for the treatment of their health information, but in practice, it is possible that confidential medical information may be passed on to a third person or authority without their knowledge or consent.

The right of detainees to confidentiality of the consultation and their medical records has been recognized in the updated UN Standard Minimum Rules for the treatment of prisoners (the Mandela Rules) of 2015. This means that the detaining authorities should not be present during consultations, except in exceptional circumstances, and should not ask for medical information, and the healthcare provider must not deliver that information without consent from the patient (UN Human Rights, Office of the High Commissioner for Human Rights, Subcommittee on Prevention of Torture and Other Cruel, Inhuman or Degrading Treatment or Punishment 2011).

There is a specific instruction on medical confidentiality for women prisoners in the UN Bangkok Rules: "Rule 8. The right of women prisoners to medical confidentiality, including specifically the right not to share information and not to undergo screening in relation to their reproductive health history, shall be respected at all times" (UN 2010).

The only exception may be when the safety of other detainees, staff, or the patients themselves is in danger because of a disease or condition. In such cases, the healthcare provider should explain to the patients the need to inform others about their condition and ideally obtain consent (Wilson and Halperin 2008). Examples of this are infectious diseases such as tuberculosis (TB) and some mental health conditions, in particular where there may be a risk of suicide, self-harm, or injury to other people. In such situations, the information delivered should be only the minimum necessary to preserve the health and safety of all concerned. Furthermore, the authorities involved have the responsibility to keep the information as confidential as may be possible. The healthcare professionals should fully document the reasons for their decision to ensure that they have an appropriate explanation should a complaint arise.

Second Dilemma: Personal Rights of the Patient versus Collective Rights of the Detainee Community

The second dilemma is specifically related to those cases in which one detainee has a transmissible disease, which may present a risk for the community where they are living. The prevention of diseases is a very important part of healthcare (Organización Panamerica De La Salud 2003), and in places of detention, the risk of epidemics is even greater than that of schools, military bases, or other closed communities (Organización Panamerica De La Salud 2003). In places of detention in many countries, the risks of the spread of disease is significantly increased by poor hygiene, overcrowding, and a lack of preventive measures. Examples of serious outbreaks in prisons in particular are typhus, cholera, and scabies each of which can spread rapidly among closely confined populations.

At any given time, there are over 10 million people (King's College 2008) held in detention centers worldwide, and more than half are in pretrial or preventive detention. Considering the high turnover in the prison population, over 30 million people are imprisoned annually.

The rates of diseases such as HIV, TB, and hepatitis (both C and B) infections among prisoners in most countries are significantly higher than those in the general population. HIV/AIDS, hepatitis, TB, and sexually transmitted infections are significant health threats to prisoners, prison staff, and their families. Outbreaks of HIV infection have occurred in a number of prison systems, mostly related to drug use among detainees, demonstrating how rapidly HIV can spread in prison unless effective action is taken to prevent transmission (UN Office on Drugs and Crime 2013).

These diseases present significant challenges for prison and public health authorities and governments. Among prisoners, the burden of HIV infection, viral hepatitis, TB and sexually transmitted infections is high due to risk behaviors prior to and during incarceration. Risk behaviors can include sexual coercion, continuation and initiation of injecting drug use, unsafe medical practices, and, in the case of TB, environmental factors including overcrowding and poor ventilation (UN Office on Drugs and Crime 2013).

In light of this, the WMA has published the Declaration of Edinburgh on Prison Conditions and the Spread of Tuberculosis and Other Communicable Diseases (WMA 2011). That document addresses 13 basic topics that can help the healthcare provider to solve the dilemma, and key issues from the document are shown in Table 15.2.

Third Dilemma: Medical Ethical Principles and Needs of Detainees

In the context of detention, the healthcare providers can often experience pressures to adapt their professional behavior, both from the detaining authority and from the detainees themselves. They may also be confronted by their own personal prejudices in working with detainees. The primary concern of the authorities is usually the security of

TABLE 15.2

Basic Topics That Can Help the Healthcare Provider to Solve the Dilemma "Personal Rights of the Patient versus Collective Rights of the Detainee Community"

1. Prisoners should enjoy the same rights as other patients, as outlined in the WMA Declaration of Lisbon (WMA 2015).
2. The rights of prisoners should not be ignored or invalidated because they have an infectious illness.
3. The conditions in which detainees and prisoners are kept, whether they are held during the investigation of a crime, while waiting for trial, or as punishment once sentenced, should not contribute to the development, worsening, or transmission of disease.
4. Persons being held while going through immigration procedures must be kept in conditions which do not encourage the spread of disease, although prisons should not normally be used to house such persons.
5. The coordination of health services within and outside prisons should facilitate continuity of care and epidemiological monitoring of inmate patients when they are released.
6. Prisoners can't be isolated, or placed in solitary confinement, as a response to their infected status without adequate access to health care and the appropriate medical treatment of their infected status.
7. Upon admission to or transfer to a different prison, inmates' health status should be reviewed within 24 hours of arrival to assure continuity of care.
8. The authorities have to ensure the provision of follow-up treatment for prisoners who, on their release, are still ill, particularly with tuberculosis or any other infectious disease. Because erratic treatments or interruptions of treatment may be particularly hazardous epidemiologically and to the individual, planning for and providing continuing care are essential elements of prison health care provisions.
9. The authorities have to recognize that the public health mechanisms, which may in the rarest and most exceptional cases involve the compulsory detention of individuals who pose a serious risk of infection to the wider community, must be efficacious, necessary and justified, and proportional to the risks posed. Such steps should be exceptional and must follow careful and critical questioning of the need for such constraints and the absence of any effective alternative. In such circumstances detention should be for as short a time as possible and be as limited in restrictions as feasible. There must also be a system of independent appraisal and periodic review of any such measures, including a mechanism for appeal by the patients themselves. Wherever possible alternatives to such detention should be used.
10. The model proposed by WMA should be used in considering all steps to prevent cross infection and to treat existing infected persons within the prison environment.
11. Physicians working in prisons have a duty to report, to the health authorities and professional organizations of their country, any deficiency in health care provided to the inmates and any situation involving high epidemiological risk.
12. Physicians working in prisons have a duty to follow national public health guidelines, where these are ethically appropriate, particularly concerning the mandatory reporting of infectious and communicable diseases.
13. The WMA calls upon member associations to work with national and local governments and prison authorities to address health promotion and health care in their institutions, and to adopt programs that ensure a safe and healthy prison environment.

Note: Based on WMA Declaration of Edinburgh on Prison Conditions and the Spread of Tuberculosis and Other Communicable Diseases.

the institution, and there may therefore be pressure to take healthcare decisions based more on a security than a healthcare rationale. The empathy and professional confidence demonstrated by healthcare providers can also sometimes be misunderstood or even manipulated by detainees in order to seek privileges or other gains. Thus, the healthcare professionals must seek professional and ethical guidance in the management of these various opposing factors.

To address this issue, it is appropriate to refer to Principle 3 of the UN Resolution No 37/194 of 18 December 1982: "It is a contravention of medical ethics for health personnel, particularly physicians, to be involved in any professional relationship with prisoners or detainees the purpose of which is not solely to evaluate, protect or improve their physical and mental health."

It is important to inform the detainees in advance about this rule, making it clear that the healthcare professionals and the patients will have a fruitful relationship only in terms of health protection. The physicians and any other health professionals or institution should refuse any departure from this rule, since to do so may contravene ethical and professional codes and may breach other applicable laws.

Examples of this kind of situations are as follows: a detainee may ask the healthcare professional to bring something from outside for him/her; the detainee asks for privileged information regarding other inmates or even detention staff; the detainee offers money or other goods or services to the healthcare professional in exchange for something. These situations must be avoided by being clear about the extent and limitations of the physician–patient relationship, but if confronted by them, the healthcare provider must make their professional duties and obligations clear and refuse any acts or omissions that may compromise this relationship.

Fourth Dilemma: Lack of Resources for the Healthcare of Detainees

There is no perfect public healthcare system. Resources are invariably limited because of budget, lack of space, overcrowding, or the available technology. But it is expected and intended that detainees should have access to healthcare at the same level of the population outside of the place of detention (WHO [World Health Organization] 2007, WHO Regional Office for Europe 2003, UN Standard Minimum Rules for the Treatment of Prisoners, rule 24). This is the principle of equity of care.

According to the CPT (APT 2009; CPT 2002), an inadequate level of healthcare can rapidly lead to situations falling within the scope of the term *inhumane and degrading treatment*. Because of that, the healthcare service in a given establishment, prison, or place of detention can potentially play an important role in combating ill-treatment, both in those establishments and elsewhere (in particular in police stations or places of transitory detention). Moreover, it is well placed to make a positive impact on the overall quality of life in the establishment within which it operates.

Table 15.3 shows the checklist utilized by CPT, as part of the routine of its visits to evaluate prisons or places of detention (CPT 2002):

The first Principle of the Declaration of Lisbon (WMA 2005) talks about discrimination of patients in a very simple sentence: "Every person is entitled without discrimination to appropriate medical care." Detainees are no exception, but unfortunately, sometimes, cultural perception (Visher et al. 2007), combined with social and political pressures lowering their priority, is misunderstood as a form of discrimination.

In addition, a detained population presents special risks and vulnerabilities (WHO 2007), and they need specific healthcare solutions. One such example is vaccination for the prevention of disease. The threat of communicable diseases, including influenza, may be especially severe for detainees because infection control measures are often limited or inefficient. Arslanian et al. (2009) described the first such reported vaccination campaign in a county jail system in the United States. The Los Angeles Sheriff's Department's medical services staff vaccinated underserved individuals, particularly those at risk for severe complications from influenza. This is a good example of a proactive approach to detainee healthcare.

TABLE 15.3

Checklist Utilized by CPT, As Part of the Routine of Its Visits to Evaluate Prisons or Places of Detention

1. Access to a doctor: Access to a doctor includes a medical examination when the detainee enters the prison.
2. Equivalence of care: A prison healthcare service should be comparable to those enjoyed by patients in the outside community.
3. Patient's consent and confidentiality: Every patient capable of discernment is free to refuse treatment or any other medical intervention. They also have the right to consult with their family or lawyer before accepting medical treatment. Any derogation from this fundamental principle should be based upon law and only relate to clearly and strictly defined exceptional circumstances which are applicable to the population as a whole (CPT 2002).
4. Preventive health care: The task of prison healthcare services should also be entrusted with responsibility for social and preventive medicine including hygiene and suicide and violence prevention and the limit of disruption of family ties.
5. Humanitarian assistance: Certain categories of particularly vulnerable prisoners can be identified, such as mothers with children, adolescents, prisoners with personality disorders, and prisoners unsuited for continued detention such as those with end-stage terminal illnesses, e.g., cancer, respiratory or heart failure.
6. Professional independence: The healthcare staff in any prison are potentially staff at risk. Their duty to care for their patients may often enter into conflict with considerations of prison management and security. In order to guarantee their independence in healthcare matters, such personnel should be aligned as closely as possible with the mainstream of healthcare provision in the community at large (CPT 2002).
7. Professional competence: Prison healthcare professionals should possess specialist knowledge (APT 2002) enabling them to deal with, and adapt their approach and treatment to, the constraints and particular aspects of health in places of detention.

Fifth Dilemma: Rights of Noninmate Persons Living in Jails with Inmates

In some countries and depending on their own personal circumstances, especially in poor resources countries or cities, some people prefer to reside in a jail instead of outside. This may appear bizarre, but in practice, it happens because of, among others, the following reasons:

1. The economical provider of a family is in jail, and the partner or children do not have alternatives other than to go with him/her to the detention facility.
2. Mothers who go to jail do not want to, or cannot leave their children alone, and they prefer to take them with them.
3. Some prison services allow the mother to have their children with them, and it can prevent futures problems and improve the social rehabilitation of inmates (Crawford 2003).
4. Exceptionally, there are inmates who have been in jail for long periods and have become institutionalized, with no close family waiting for them outside, and they prefer to stay in the place they have been living for years.
5. Some inmates think that it is safer to be in jail instead of out the jail, for example, they may have received death threats on their release.

Such situations should not happen if the prison and social services of the country can achieve the accepted aim of imprisonment, which is the rehabilitation and reintegration of all detainees into society, and if the social services of a country can provide an appropriate safety net for the family, including children, of imprisoned persons. On the other hand, if the imprisonment of a mother will generate more problems than benefits to the society by separating her from her children, there may be reasons to seek alternatives to imprisonment, such as house arrest, electronic tagging, community service, etc. However, if a mother is imprisoned, the decision as to whether to allow her child to remain with her must be taken in the best interests of the child, and the duty of the authorities is to do everything possible to protect and promote the normal health (APT 2002), growth, social, emotional and intellectual development of the child and to support the mother and relatives as far as possible. Those children who stay with their imprisoned parents must never be treated as prisoners themselves (UN Standard Minimum Rules for the Treatment of Prisoners, rule 29).

Healthcare providers have the responsibility to inform the detaining authorities about circumstances in which the health and well-being of the mother and/or child is at risk. The state also has a responsibility to the broader social issues commonly associated with detained persons (e.g., the use of illicit drugs, problems with alcohol, mental health issues).

Sixth Dilemma: Babies Born in Places of Detention

UN General Assembly, in its resolution 58/183 of December 22, 2003, entitled "Human rights in the administration of justice," called for increased attention to be devoted to the issue of women in prison, including the children of women in prison, with a view to identifying the key problems and ways in which they could be addressed (UN 2010).

Around the world, there are babies living in jails (Women's Prison Association 2009). The rights of those babies are the same of those living in any other place. One of the rights is to have a mother (Dwyer 2009), but if the mother is in jail for any reason, the rights of the babies have to be respected, and one solution is to allow babies to live with their mothers; it also means that the mothers will enjoy special privileges to cope with their role.

The Universal Declaration of Human Rights (1948) was drafted by the UN Commission on Human Rights in 1947 and 1948. The declaration was adopted by the United Nations General Assembly on December 10, 1948. It contains three articles particularly relevant to this subject and is shown in Table 15.4.

The previous rights should be applied everywhere. But in practice, there are limitations and difficulties that may be addressed by states themselves, or by regional human rights bodies. The European Prison Rules make specific recommendations at paragraph 28 (Council of Europe 1987):

> **28.** 1. Arrangements shall be made wherever practicable for children to be born in a hospital outside the institution. However, unless special arrangements are made, there shall in penal institutions be the necessary staff and accommodation for the confinement and post-natal care of pregnant women. If a child is born in prison, this fact shall not be mentioned in the birth certificate.
>
> 2. Where infants are allowed to remain in the institution with their mothers, special provision shall be made for a nursery staffed by qualified persons, where the infants shall be placed when they are not in the care of their mothers.

The UN Bangkok Rules specifically mentions issues applicable to women prisoners, including those relating to parental responsibilities. However, as the focus includes the children of imprisoned mothers, there is a need to recognize the central role of both

TABLE 15.4

Universal Declaration of Human Rights (1948), Articles Particularly Relevant with Babies Living in Jails

Article 1. All human beings are born free and equal in dignity and rights. They are endowed with reason and conscience and should act towards one another in a spirit of brotherhood.

Article 7. All are equal before the law and are entitled without any discrimination to equal protection of the law. All are entitled to equal protection against any discrimination in violation of this Declaration and against any incitement to such discrimination.

Article 25. (2) Motherhood and childhood are entitled to special care and assistance. All children, whether born in or out of wedlock, shall enjoy the same social protection.

parents in the lives of children. Accordingly, some of these rules would equally apply to male prisoners and offenders who are fathers (UN 2010).

The Council of Europe has commented that there is no agreement regarding the duration and age ranges of the essential location of mother and child together. In many cases, the position will be constrained by resources. In others, the medical condition of the mother or child will be the determining factor. Whether or not the resources and other considerations allow an exercise of choice, the basic principle should be that which is concerned with the immediate and ultimate well-being of the child and his/her mother (UN 2010).

The recommendation from the Council of Europe is to make efforts to devise an environment for the accommodation of mother and child, as similar as possible to those good average conditions outside the prison, but the medical oversight and staff supervision will need to be more intensive than that which can be provided in the community (UN 2010).

Rule 28, paragraph 2 of UN (2010) goes on to consider the situation that arises when women are imprisoned with their children. In such cases, it is essential to bear in mind that experience has demonstrated that a continuous caring relationship between the mother and her child, particularly in the earliest months after birth, is important to the development and future welfare of the child.

The Bangkok Rules states

> *Rule 2*
>
> 1. Adequate attention shall be paid to the admission procedures for women and children, due to their particular vulnerability at this time. Newly arrived women prisoners shall be provided with facilities to contact their relatives; access to legal advice; information about prison rules and regulations, the prison regime and where to seek help when in need in a language that they understand; and, in the case of foreign nationals, access to consular representatives as well.
> 2. Prior to or on admission, women with caretaking responsibilities for children shall be permitted to make arrangements for those children, including the possibility of a reasonable suspension of detention, taking into account the best interests of the children (UN 2010).

Seventh Dilemma: Confidentiality versus Identification

Very often, healthcare providers have privileged access to information which can be used to identify either illegal activities or if the detention facility's rules have been broken. One example is when the physician knows that a particular detainee is using illegal substances in the jail.

Healthcare providers have to be independent to exert their duties. The fact is that health professionals do not have a choice in determining their loyalties: medical ethics clearly state that they are unequivocally always obligated to act in the best interests of their patients (MedicineNet.com 2002). It means that the healthcare providers must keep the information as part of the professional activity, and the authorities in charge of the jail should not oblige them to break that ethical principle. To do so would breach the trust that is fundamental to the physician–patient professional relationship.

Certain relationships are very special because the confidence and confidentiality they need to exist, deserving special recognition, treatment, and protection under the law; such concept is also inherent in the cultural norms, ethical considerations, and legal principles. Among those relationships are, for example, those between lawyer and client, priest and confessor, and doctor and patient. Society gives particular deference and respect to these relationships because doing so serves a variety of critical functions and supports values that its citizens hold dear. Because of the right to confidentiality between parties in these privileged relationships, the priest is able to give clear spiritual guidance to the confessor, the lawyer can protect the interests of their client, and the doctor can provide care for the patient (Physicians for Human Rights 2011). To prevent abuse of this relationship, the healthcare professional should advise the patient that the professional relationship depends on mutual openness and trust and that the information exchanged will be used only as part of the medical care.

The reporting of a patient by his/her doctor should be a very exceptional event. It may happen, for example, when the patient has physically attacked or threatened the physician or other healthcare worker. If an attack or threat is not directly related to healthcare issues, then it is not usually governed by the rules of medical ethics.

There are other situations when doctors have to report dangerous situations: (1) The negligent behavior of the detainee about his/her own healthcare endangers other inmates or prison staff; one example is the person who knows he/she has an infectious disease (HIV, TB, etc.) but does not take the prescribed treatment and yet remains in close personal contact with the surrounding people or even wants to infect other people. (2) When the doctor knows the patient is a victim of continuous violence from other inmates or prison staff, he/she may try to get consent from the patient to inform and to address the situation; however, the doctor should report the problem in order to protect the patient from future injuries or even death. (3) Even when a detainee does not make an allegation of ill-treatment, but the healthcare staff has reasonable grounds to suspect the person has been the victim, they should document the findings and report the case to the competent authorities. The healthcare staff should endeavor to obtain the consent of the detainee, but in all cases must make every effort to safeguard the person from further ill-treatment and possible retribution.

Eighth Dilemma: Documentation of Torture or Healthcare—Can They Go Together?

Firstly, it is very important to recall that all healthcare professional are absolutely prohibited from participating in, advising on, or otherwise being complicit in any form of torture or other ill-treatment. It is their responsibility to medically document any such cases and to report them to the appropriate authorities, while at the same time being aware of the need to protect the victim and themselves from reprisals or further ill-treatment (UN 1982).

To identify and document torture, it is important for the healthcare professional to be familiar with the Istanbul Protocol (IP) (UN Office of the United Nations High Commissioner for Human Rights 1999) as well as the operational manual, *Forensic Examination Missions by Medical Teams Investigating and Documenting Alleged Cases of Torture* (International Rehabilitation Council for Torture Victims 2012). It is recommended, if the healthcare professional is not an expert in the diagnosis of torture, to ask for an expert to do a forensic evaluation of the patient if there are suspicious injuries or psychological symptoms and signs compatible with torture. The misdiagnosis of torture can create many problems for both the detainee and the healthcare professional. This is why those health-care professionals working in places of detention should be trained in the medical documentation of torture and should have access to other independent experts in this field.

Healthcare for presumed victims of torture is mandatory, and it is mandatory for the authorities to remove the victim to a place of protection so as to prevent reprisals or further harm. Thus, the health professionals should report the cases through the appropriate confidential channels and actively seek the transfer of the victims to a hospital or other safe place.

Ninth Dilemma: The Prisoner Requiring Specialist Treatment and the Terminally Ill Prisoner

The healthcare professional in places of detention may be faced with patients with serious or indeed terminal illness. If the risk that a detainee might either die or suffer irreparable harm is significantly increased because the person is in detention, then the role of the physician is to recommend access to specialist medical treatment, either through the visit to the place of detention by the appropriate specialists or by referral to an appropriate hospital in the community. In the case of an illness that cannot be properly managed in detention, the physician may recommend another legal alternative to detention, for example, treatment in a hospital or domiciliary detention (Grabosky et al. 1988). The UK Prison and Probation Ombudsman has issued guidance for those with terminal illness in prisons (Prisons and Probation Ombudsman for England and Wales 2013).

If the situation is reversible and later on the inmate recovers his/her health, the patient can go back to the place of detention, and there he/she can continue with ambulatory treatments. If not, the authorities should consider if there is a place of detention with more appropriate conditions or better access to healthcare to which the person can be transferred or whether continued treatment in a hospital or even under house arrest is advisable. Such changes are usually temporary, and the patient has to be reassessed frequently in order to know the evolution of his/her condition.

In cases of terminal illness in which the likelihood of death in the short term is high (for example, cancer or permanent heart failure or stroke), the authorities should consider the release of the patient on compassionate grounds. The physician should seek the opinion and confirmation from independent colleagues on the best place to which to transfer the patient. This may be to a hospital, to a hospice, or, in some cases, to the person's home. The physician should present these findings to the appropriate authorities.

One example of this kind of situation is the case of Abdelbaset Ali Mohmed Al Megrahi, a Libyan citizen who was convicted for the terrorist attack against an airplane on Lockerby (UK), sentenced to life in prison (Scottish Criminal Cases Review Commission Statement of Reasons under Section 194D (4) of the Criminal Procedure [Scotland] Act 1995). This person was in jail and freed on compassionate grounds by the Scottish Government on August 20, 2009 following doctors reporting on August 10, 2009 that he had terminal prostate cancer. He returned to Libya, where he was initially hospitalized but was then allowed to live in his residence in Tripoli. He died on May 2, 2012, 2 years and 9 months after his release (BBC Press Files 2012).

Tenth Dilemma: Detainee Version versus Guards' Explanations: Who's Right; Who's Wrong?

Sometimes the detainees may ask for healthcare because they say they are sick. But the guards or the authorities have a different version, for example, they say the person is faking illness (Scharff Smith 2008). Also, there are very common situations when detainees harm themselves (e.g., by cutting or overdosing) in order to push for a transfer or some privilege.

First of all, the authorities should not deny medical attention to those cases. Whatever the situation, the patient must be examined by a health professional. The authorities should initiate an investigation about the circumstances of the event, in order to learn lessons and take disciplinary actions if needed.

One of the most important principles in the patient/healthcare professional relationship is mutual confidence and trust. The patients must be open and frank about their health condition, and the physician must make an independent and unbiased diagnosis purely based upon medical criteria (that is to say, without the influence of the detaining authorities or security requirements of the institution). If, after all the correct steps have been followed, the physician finds no illness, trauma, or other need for medical attention, then they must inform the patient and attempt to understand if there are other underlying reasons for the person to seek attention from the medical service. It may be, for example, that the detainee is the victim of physical, psychological, or sexual violence and that they have used a fictitious reason to seek help from the physician so as not to explicitly state the problem to the guards or other detainees. These are the kinds of cases that the healthcare professionals working in places of detention must always be aware of.

Conclusions

Protecting and promoting the health of detainees is a key responsibility of the detaining authority. Provision of medical care to detainees is a challenging responsibility for healthcare professionals including physicians, nurses, and dentists and for the hospitals and public or private companies involved in such activities. They face numerous ethical and professional dilemmas when addressing the healthcare needs of detainees, in particular those of the most vulnerable groups, including women, children, those with mental illness, people requiring specialist treatment, and the terminally ill.

The authorities have to provide the minimum conditions to support the job of the healthcare staff. These include safety and respect for their mission and their ethical obligations and respect for the confidentiality of the patient–doctor relationship and of medical information.

In order to improve the healthcare of inmates, the UN and other international organizations have delivered recommendations and practical rules for those who have to provide health services directly (doctors, nurses, etc.) or indirectly (detaining authorities) to detainees.

All health providers should know and put in practice the *Principles of Medical Ethics relevant to the Role of Health Personnel, particularly Physicians, in the Protection of Prisoners and Detainees against Torture and Other Cruel, Inhuman or Degrading Treatment or Punishment* (UN 1982). This provides a fundamental ethical guidance for professional practice in the context of places of detention and healthcare for detainees.

References

Arslanian, H., Carter, A., Kamara, F., Malek Mark, A., Miranda A., Namjoshi, S., Tadrous, M. 2009, Flu vaccination among general population inmates in a large urban jail system—Los Angeles, 2007–2008, *American Correctional Association, Correctional Health Today Journal*, vol. 1, pp. 21–28.

APT (Association for the Prevention of Torture) 2002, *Monitoring places of detention: A practical guide for NGOs*, APT, Geneva, p. 143.

APT 2009, *Visiting places of detention: What role for physicians and other health professionals?* APT, Geneva, p. 12.

BBC Press Files 2012, *Lockerbie bomber "should go free."* Available from: http://www.bbc.com/news/world-africa-18137896.

Council of Europe 1987, European Prison Rules. Recommendation No. R(87)3 adopted by the Committee of Ministers of the Council of Europe on February 12, 1987 and Explanatory memorandum, Council of Europe, Strasbourg. Available from: http://www.uncjin.org/Laws/prisrul.htm.

CPT (European Committee for the Prevention of Torture and Inhuman or Degrading Treatment or Punishment) 2002, CPT standards, CPT/Inf/E (2002) 1, Rev. 2010, English version, CPT, Strasbourg, p. 27.

Crawford, J. 2003, Alternative sentencing necessary for female inmates with children, American Correctional Association. *Corrections Today*, vol. 65, issue 3, p. 8. Available from: https://www.thefreelibrary.com/Alternative+sentencing+necessary+for+female+inmates+with+children.-a0123688020.

Dwyer, J. G. 2009, *Constitutional birthright: The state, parentage, and the rights of newborn persons*, Faculty Publications, Paper 26.56, L. Rev. 756 2008–2009, University of California Los Angeles, Los Angeles, CA.

Grabosky, P., Scandia, A., Hazlehurst, K., Wilson, P. (compiled) 1988, Aboriginal deaths in custody. *Australian Institute of Criminology Trends and Issues in Crime and Criminal Justice, Canberra ACT 2601*. Available from: http://www.aic.gov.au/media_library/publications/tandi_pdf/tandi012.pdf.

International Rehabilitation Council for Torture Victims 2012, Forensic examination missions by medical teams investigating and documenting alleged cases of torture, in *Operational Manual*, First edn, International Rehabilitation Council for Torture Victims, Copenhagen.

King's College 2008, *World prison population list*, Seventh edn, King's College, London. Available from: http://www.kcl.ac.uk/depsta/law/research/icps/downloads/worldprison-pop-seventh.pdf. [June 22, 2010].

MedicineNet.com 2002, *Definition of the Hippocratic Oath*. Available from: http://www.medterms.com/script/main/art.asp?articlekey=20909.

Organización Panamerica De La Salud 2003, *World Health Organization representation in Argentina*, Cárceles Saludables Promoviendo la Salud para Todos. Buenos Aires, p. 14.

Physicians for Human Rights 2011, Dual loyalties: The challenges of providing professional health care to immigration detainees, Physicians for Human Rights, Washington, DC.

Prisons and Probation Ombudsman for England and Wales. Annual Report 2012–2013. Presented to Parliament by the Lord Chancellor and Secretary of State for Justice by Command of Her Majesty September 2013. London 2013.

Scharff Smith, P. 2008, Degenerate criminals: Mental health and psychiatric studies of Danish prisoners in solitary confinement, 1870–1920, *Criminal Justice and Behavior*, vol. 35, p. 1056. Available from: http://cjb.sagepub.com/cgi/content/abstract/35/8/1048.

Scottish Criminal Cases Review Commission Statement of Reasons Under Section 194d (4) of The Criminal Procedure (Scotland) Act 1995. Available from: http://cryptocomb.org/SCCRC-Statement-of-Reasons-red.pdf. [September 2, 2013].

Sheikh Asim, A. 2008, *The Data Protection Acts 1988 and 2003: Some implications for public health and medical research*, Health Research Board, Dublin. p. 7. Available from: http://www.hrb.ie/uploads/tx_hrbpublications/Data_Protection_Opinion.pdf.

UN 1982, *Principles of medical ethics relevant to the role of health personnel, particularly physicians, in the protection of prisoners and detainees against torture and other cruel, inhuman or degrading treatment or punishment*, Resolution 37/194 of December 18, 1982, UN, Geneva. Available from: http://www.un.org/documents/ga/res/37/a37r194.htm.

UN 2010, *UN rules for the treatment of women prisoners and non-custodial measures for women offenders (the Bangkok Rules)*, UN, Geneva. Available from: http://www.un.org/en/ecosoc/docs/2010/res%202010-16.pdf. [July 22, 2010].

UN, *United Nations standard minimum rules for the treatment of prisoners (the Mandela rules)*, Rule 24, UN, Geneva. Available from: http://www.ohchr.org/EN/ProfessionalInterest/Pages/TreatmentOfPrisoners.aspx.

UN, *United Nations standard minimum rules for the treatment of prisoners (the Mandela rules)*, Rule 29, UN, Geneva.

UN Human Rights, Office of the High Commissioner for Human Rights, Subcommittee on Prevention of Torture and Other Cruel, Inhuman or Degrading Treatment or Punishment 2011, *Report on the visit of the Subcommittee on Prevention of Torture and Other Cruel, Inhuman or Degrading Treatment or Punishment to Benin*, UN, Geneva, p. 19. Available from: http://www2.ohchr.org/english/bodies/cat/opcat/docs/ReportVisitBenin-AdvanceCopy.pdf. [March 9, 2001].

UN Office on Drugs and Crime 2013, *HIV in prisons: Situation and needs assessment toolkit*, Advance copy, UN, Geneva, p. 8. Available from: http://www2.ohchr.org/english/issues/women/docs/WRGS/UN%20Agencies/UNODC2.pdf. [July 2010].

UN Office of the United Nations High Commissioner for Human Rights 1999, *Manual on the Effective Investigation and Documentation of Torture and other Cruel, Inhuman or Degrading Treatment and Punishment*. UN Office of the United Nations High Commissioner for Human Rights, New York and Geneva.

Visher, C., Palmer, T., Gouvis Roman, C. 2007, Cleveland stakeholders' perceptions of prisoner reentry, *Urban Institute Justice Policy Center, Policy Brief*, p. 3. Available from: http://www.urban.org/sites/default/files/alfresco/publication-pdfs/411515-Cleveland-Stakeholders-Perceptions-of-Prisoner-Reentry.PDF.

WHO 2007, *Health in prisons: A WHO guide to the essentials in prison health*, WHO, Copenhagen. Available from: http://www.euro.who.int/document/e90174.pdf. [April 10, 2017].

WHO Regional Office for Europe 2003, *Declaration on Prison Health as a Part of Public Health*. Adopted in Moscow on October 24, 2003. Available from: http://www.euro.who.int/__data/assets/pdf _file/0007/98971/E94242.pdf. [April 10, 2017].

Wilson, D., Halperin, D. T. 2008, "Know your epidemic, know your response": A useful approach, if we get it right, *The Lancet*, vol. 372, pp. 423–426.

WMA Declaration of Lisbon on the Rights of the Patient. Adopted by the 34th World Medical Assembly, Lisbon, Portugal, September/October 1981 and amended by the 47th WMA General Assembly, Bali, Indonesia, September 1995 and editorially revised by the 171st WMA Council Session, Santiago, Chile, October 2005. Available from: http://www.wma.net/en/30publications /10policies/l4/index.html.pdf?print-media-type&footer-right=[page]/[toPage].

WMA Declaration of Edinburgh on Prison Conditions and the Spread of Tuberculosis and Other Communicable Diseases: Adopted by the 52nd WMA General Assembly, Edinburgh, Scotland, October 2000, and revised by the 62nd WMA General Assembly, Montevideo, Uruguay, October 2011. Available from: http://www.wma.net/en/30publications/10policies/p28/index .html.pdf?print-media-type&footer-right=[page]/[toPage].

Women's Prison Association 2009, *Mothers, infants and imprisonment: A national look at prison nurseries and community-based alternatives*, Women's Prison Association, Institute On Women & Criminal Justice, New York. Available from: http://wpaonline.org/pdf/Mothers%20Infants%20and%20 Imprisonment%202009.pdf.

World Medical Association (WMA). Declaration of Lisbon on the Rights of the Patient. Adopted by the 34th World Medical Assembly, Lisbon, Portugal, September/October 1981 and amended by the 47th WMA General Assembly, Bali, Indonesia, September 1995; editorially revised by the 171st WMA Council Session, Santiago, Chile, October 2005; and reaffirmed by the 200th WMA Council Session, Oslo, Norway, April 2015.

16

Solitary Confinement: Current Concerns and Proposed Protections

Sharon Shalev and Jonathan Beynon

CONTENTS

Introduction

Solitary confinement is an extreme form of incarceration, arguably second in its severity only to the death penalty (Shalev 2008) and a practice which, in some circumstances, constitutes a form of torture or inhumane or degrading treatment (UN Special Rapporteur 2011; CPT [European Committee for the Prevention of Torture] 2011a, 2011b; *Ensslin, Baader and Raspe v. Federal Republic of Germany* [1978]; *Babar Ahmad and Others v. the United Kingdom* [2012]).

Despite this, solitary confinement is considered to be a legitimate practice in many prison systems around the world. Moreover, in the last two decades, entire new prisons have been constructed, centered on the near total isolation of the prisoner, not only from his/her fellow prisoners, but also from prison staff. In many countries solitary confinement also continues to exist as a tool for the prison administration to discipline those who break the rules and to segregate those viewed as disruptive for other, less well-defined, reasons. This is the case despite clear evidence that the negative health effects of solitary confinement can be of rapid onset and of prolonged duration, persisting in some cases long after the end of the period in isolation and sometimes even following the individual's release from prison.

This chapter defines basic terms and examines when and why solitary confinement is used, including some case studies from across the world. It also examines research findings on the health effects of solitary confinement and how those are affected by the circumstances of its use and the vulnerability of the individual. Guidance on how to assess the use and effects of solitary confinement when monitoring places of detention will be summarized. The chapter concludes by looking at recent developments in international efforts to limit the use of solitary confinement and proposing a number of safeguards to restrict its use in all but the most necessary cases for as short a time as possible.

What Is Solitary Confinement?

For the purpose of this chapter, the term *solitary confinement* means the physical confinement of an individual to a cell, typically for 22 to 24 hours or more a day without meaningful human contact (Rule 44, UN Nelson Mandela Rules [2015]) (see also Istanbul Statement 2007; Shalev 2008; UN Special Rapporteur 2011). This definition does not preclude cases where the individual spends a little less than 22 hours locked in their cell, cases where longer stretches of time spent out of their cell are spent undergoing questioning, cases where the individual can associate with others during a short exercise period, or cases where the individual has more than one cell at their disposal (but are nonetheless confined alone). The term *solitary confinement* is commonly used interchangeably with *segregation*, *isolation*, *closed confinement*, *23/7 regime*, and *supermax*. Each of these terms may represent something slightly different in each jurisdiction, but the basic premise of them all is that the suspect, detainee, or prisoner is held in strict physical and social isolation from everyone else and that they are subject to almost complete control of every aspect of their daily routine.

It is important to understand the various factors that aggravate the reality of being held alone in a cell. These factors can widely vary from one country and from one prison system to another. The cell itself may be of a small size with little possibility to move about; in some countries, the hygiene may be deplorable, while in others, units and cells are kept clean; there may be no window and no natural light (some such cells being underground); the cell may be dark, or it may be constantly illuminated by artificial light. In some jurisdictions, cells may contain a toilet and wash basin while in some countries, particularly when solitary confinement is used as a punishment or as a form of ill-treatment, cells may have no facilities, meaning that the individual must relieve themselves into a bucket or even onto the floor. The cell may be completely bare of any furniture, even a bed; whereas in some prisons, the cells do contain basic furniture, usually fixed to the floor or walls.

While in the cell, the person may have absolutely no means of occupying themselves, or they may have some access to books, newspapers, a radio, and even a television in the cell. Food is eaten alone in the cell, or the person may be allowed out to a food servery to collect it, but again with minimal contact with other prisoners. Contact with the prison staff is reduced to a minimum, and it can be of an abusive nature. When the person is allowed out of their cell, they may have their wrists and ankles cuffed, and in some situations, they may be hooded. For the 1–2 hours that the person is not confined to the cell, they may be permitted some exercise, but also without contact with other prisoners and typically in an outdoor cage or in a barren concrete yard.

In some countries, the person may virtually never be permitted to leave their cell. In others, the person in solitary confinement may be completely barred from any social, educational, or recreational activities in the prison, if indeed they exist, and where they are permitted access to some activities, they may be alone or with only a handful of other prisoners. Correspondence, if actually possible, may be restricted to a small number of letters, and family visits or even visits from lawyers may be infrequent or prohibited altogether. Where such visits are allowed, they are often held through a separating glass, meaning that there is no direct contact between the individual and their visitor.

Each of these factors, alone and in combination with others, can have an impact on how any one individual experiences their confinement and on how it affects their health and well-being.

What Are the Origins of Solitary Confinement?

> Solitary has changed over the years. From having nothing, I now have a TV in my cell, a radio, books, cell activities. I keep my mattress. Along with my 1 hour daily exercise, I also get to use a gym for one hour, if I want, Monday–Friday. Things have moved on. But it's still solitary. It's still 23 or 22 hour bang-up. And when you're banged up you're in a cell alone.
> "D", writing during his fourteenth year in solitary confinement.

Sharon Shalev
Personal communication

Solitary confinement has a long and unproud history: it predates the birth of the modern prison in the eighteenth century and was the principal form of imprisonment on both sides of the Atlantic in the large penitentiaries of the nineteenth century, used for reforming prisoners into law-abiding citizens. The complete isolation of convicts from each other and from the outside world was viewed as a crucial element for successful reformation, and great care was taken to ensure that the prisoner was isolated from the corrupting influences of others, in and outside of the prison. Prisoners were kept alone in their small cell, where they ate, slept, and worked. On the few occasions they left their cell, they were hooded to ensure that they never saw their fellow prisoners or their keepers. Elsewhere, prisoners spent their nights confined to their solitary cells and their days working alongside their fellow prisoners while observing strict rules requiring them to maintain complete silence. These so-called silent and separate penitentiaries were abandoned when it became clear that, rather than being reformed, prisoners were losing their minds (for an account of the rise and fall of these penitentiaries see the study by Evans [1982]). The practice of solitary confinement, however, remained part and parcel of most prison systems, being used among other things as a short-term but severe form of punishment for prison offenses, for holding a handful of high-profile prisoners (particularly those charged with crimes against the state) in separation from others, as a tool for managing challenging prisoners, and as a means of coercion during interrogation.

Over the centuries of its use in prisons and other places of detention across the world, health professionals and researchers alike have documented the potentially devastating effects that solitary confinement has on the health and well-being of those subjected to it. The practice of solitary confinement also attracts ongoing criticism by human rights and monitoring bodies, some calling for the prohibition of solitary confinement in punishment cells (Inter-American Commission on Human Rights 2008) and some going as far as calling for its complete abolition (UN 1990). Yet despite such criticisms, its severity and its documented negative impact on health, well-being, and chances of successful reintegration back into society, the practice has proven to be extremely resilient to change. To date, solitary confinement is widely used in prisons and detention centers across the world, in some cases for very prolonged periods. Even the most overcrowded prison systems—and many are—and even the most humane ones have some space reserved for isolating prisoners and detainees.

When Is Solitary Confinement Used and for What Purpose?

Solitary confinement is used throughout the different stages of criminal and other detention processes: immediately following arrest while a suspect is being questioned; when the suspect has been charged and is awaiting trial; during the trial and immediately after it; prior to placement in a penal institution; and during imprisonment, either as a part of the sentence or as a tool for maintaining prison discipline or as an administrative prison management tool and, in some cases, for the protection of certain vulnerable individuals. (For a detailed discussion of these different uses of solitary confinement in England and Wales, see Shalev and Edgar [2015].) In some countries, asylum seekers and immigration detainees may be held in solitary confinement, despite the fact that they are neither charged nor convicted of any criminal offence.

Perversely, the well-documented deleterious effects of solitary confinement have also been employed directly against detainees as a form of coercion and for breaking the will to resist during interrogation, in particular of those suspected of committing acts against state security and, those suspected of terrorist activities (FBI [Federal Bureau of Investigation] 2011).

Each of the different uses of solitary confinement entails slightly different arrangements and has a slightly different rationale, while maintaining the principle of isolation. And although at its base, the practice is identical, each type of solitary confinement has its own peculiarities, as discussed in the following passages.

Precharge and Pretrial

In the context of criminal investigation, the key (official) rationale for isolating suspects is to prevent collusion between suspects and between them and people on the outside and to prevent them from intimidating potential witnesses.

Such a rationale may be justified in particularly very high profile cases and only in jurisdictions where isolation before someone is charged would be limited to a maximum of a few hours (typically 48–72 hours). When isolation is used for longer periods before an individual is charged, and when it is then continued in the pretrial (remand) phase which may last for many months, it is likely that, at least in part, the isolation is intended to exert psychological and physical pressure on the suspect to cooperate and to confess. Despite ongoing criticisms by international and regional bodies (CPT 2011a,b), the Nordic countries routinely hold pretrial detainees in prolonged (minimum of 1 month and up to a year) court-ordered isolation with restricted access to visits, telephone privileges, correspondence, and newspapers—or a variety of such restrictions. In Sweden, for example, as of July 2011, as many as 47% of a total remand population of 4807 detainees were subjected to isolation and various other court-ordered restrictions (Swedish Prison and Probation Service 2012).

Researchers found that the risk of developing mental illness substantially increased for remand detainees held in isolation (Andersen et al. 2000; Holmgren et al. 2011). The authors of one study (Holmgren et al. 2011) note, rightly, that these findings also raise a legal question, as mental health problems including anxiety or depression could impair the detainee's ability to participate in and understand proceedings against them and, by extension, their ability to defend themselves.

Death Row and "Lifers"

In countries that still practice capital punishment, prisoners on death row will usually be held in solitary confinement while awaiting execution. The rationale is both to further punish those who committed the most serious transgressions against society and to ensure that those sentenced to death and who thus have little to lose by attempting escape or otherwise acting violently in prison do not have the opportunity to harm others or, indeed, themselves. Where the death penalty has been abolished, it has, in many cases, been replaced with life imprisonment, often under conditions of solitary confinement for the entire duration of the sentence or for its initial part. In some countries, the courts may even sentence prisoners to spend the initial part of their imprisonment in solitary confinement. In Japan, death row prisoners (numbering 107 in 2010) are held in strict solitary confinement in 50 sq. ft. (approximately 4.6 sq. m.) cells from the time of their sentence until their execution—on average of 6 years, but in some cases, more than 20 years and, in at least one reported case, 42 years (Tabuchi 2010).

In Russia, prisoners sentenced to life imprisonment may be subjected to a special regime that includes strict solitary confinement, solitary walking exercise for up to 1 hour and 45 minutes daily and two visits of up to 4 hours a year. Similar conditions of prolonged solitary confinement and/or semi-isolation for lifers can be found in Armenia, Azerbaijan, Kazakhstan, and Tajikistan (PRI 2012a,b).

Rwanda's Organic Law No. 31/2007 Relating to the Abolition of the Death Penalty substituted capital punishment with "life imprisonment with special provisions," which include the following:

- A convicted person is not entitled to any kind of mercy, conditional release, or rehabilitation, unless he/she has served at least 20 years of imprisonment
- A convicted person is kept in isolation (Article 4)

Maintaining Prison Discipline

Solitary confinement is commonly used as short-term but severe punishment for an infraction of prison rules. In such cases, the punishment is usually imposed for a limited and predefined time and be subject to some due process protections, such as a disciplinary hearing, information on the length of the punishment, and the right to appeal the decision.

Typically, solitary confinement would be imposed for somewhere between 7 and 28 days, but there are significant variations in the maximum permissible duration for its imposition as punishment: for example, 14 days in Finland, 45 days in France and Estonia, 28 days in Poland and in England and Wales, and 60 days in Ireland (CPT country reports. For a detailed discussion of the use of segregation as punishment in England and Wales, see Shalev and

Edgar [2015]). In some jurisdictions, however, even when safeguards appear to be in place, prisoners will be held in punitive isolation cells for the maximum duration allowed by law, released for 1 day, and then placed in isolation again. This can go on for months and even years. Furthermore, in some jurisdictions, prisoners committing only minor infractions may be sent to solitary confinement for prolonged periods purely on the basis of a decision taken by a prison officer, without any due process. Punitive segregation units are typically small and cramped and, in some case, windowless and or without internal sanitation. While subject to this form of prison discipline, the prisoner is often also punished further by the loss of most other privileges, which may include, for example, the right to correspondence or visits with their family, access to reading or educational material, exercise, and work.

Japan is an example of a jurisdiction in which minor rule infractions—such as looking a guard in the eye or sleeping on one's stomach—may result in very strict solitary confinement for several months (Human Rights Watch 1995). In California, one of the avenues into a state supermax for a period of up to 2 years is by committing a "serious rule violation" which may include offenses such as possession of USD 5 or more without authorization, acts of disobedience, gambling, and self-mutilation (Shalev 2009, pp. 71–75).

Segregation can thus be used by prison authorities to isolate individuals whom they see as nuisance prisoners. Tragically, this group often includes prisoners famously described by Hans Toch (1987) as "disturbed and disruptive," who simultaneously pose a mental health and disciplinary problem. These prisoners get caught up in a vicious circle: they behave in certain ways because of their mental illness, are placed in segregation, and are made worse because of it, leading to further "disturbed and disruptive" behaviors. As a former supermax prisoner aptly put it: "And once you lose your mind, you don't know right from wrong. You don't know that you're breaking a rule. You don't know what to do exactly" (cited in Shalev 2009, p. 192).

Prisoner's Own Protection

In many jurisdictions, prisoners can be isolated to protect them from others or indeed from themselves, sometimes for the duration of their prison sentence. This can be initiated by the prisoner himself/herself or, more frequently, by the prison authorities. Those who require protection may include, for example, former prison or police officers, sex offenders (in particular pedophiles who are often targeted by both other prisoners and prison staff), and other vulnerable individuals, for example, those who are very young or physically weak, transgendered individuals, and others who may be preyed on by other prisoners. In many cases, the length of stay in protective isolation is indeterminate, meaning that the prisoner will not know how long he or she might expect to spend in solitary confinement.

The Supermaximum Security Prison (Supermax)

Alongside these more traditional uses, the last two decades of the twentieth century saw an explosion in the use of large-scale and prolonged solitary confinement, led by the United States and its supermax prisons. These are large, purpose-built solitary confinement prisons, where prisoners spend years—and in some cases decades—in strict separation from one another and from the world at large and subjected to a variety of additional restrictions and restraints, governing each and every aspect of their lives. In 2011 to 2012, as many as 20% of the total prison and jail population in the United States, or some 430,790 individuals, have spent time in segregation or solitary confinement in a supermax or other "restrictive housing unit" (Bureau of Justice Statistics 2015).

Supermax prisoners can expect to spend 22.5–24 hours a day locked up in a small, often windowless cell, with few personal belongings and little to do. The little time they will spend outside the cell will be spent during an hour-long outdoor exercise (required by law) which would typically be held in a cage or barren concrete yard, known by prisoners as the *dog run*. On the few occasions that prisoners leave the cell area, typically for a family visit or an infrequent medical examination, they will be put in body restraints. Family visits are limited in number and duration and would typically be held through a glass barrier, eliminating any physical contact between the prisoners and his/her family members, despite which the prisoner would usually remain in restraints. In many cases, prisoners will even remain restrained throughout the medical examination, in blatant violation of basic medical ethics. Prisoners will typically spend anywhere from two years to life in these conditions (Shalev 2009).

State Security and Coercive Interrogation

Lastly, solitary confinement has been used for decades for those suspected or convicted of offenses against the state. Varying degrees of additional restrictions may be placed on their daily routine and upon their contact with the outside world both as punishment and as a means of preventing the spread of dissent or political opposition. This is particularly common in dictatorial or oppressive regimes, where imprisonment of the opposition is used as a means of control of, and spreading fear among, the population at large.

The adverse health effects of solitary confinement, especially the psychological effects, were manipulated by certain regimes in order to break the will of individuals, gain information, and induce cooperation. The use of isolation was central to creating the conditions of debility, dread, and dependency, or DDD (Farber et al. 1957), used in brainwashing and conditioning by, for example, the Stalinist regime, North Korea, and the former East Germany.

The rationale for isolating detainees in this context is clearly laid out in an FBI training manual for interrogators working overseas:

> Isolation of the detainee not only ensures the safety of other detainees but also prevents the individual detainee from drawing strength from the support and companionship of other detainees. It also prevents collusion on cover stories between detainees. A large part of the Interrogators advantage is the natural fear of the unknown that the detainee will be experiencing. Exposure to other detainees will mitigate that fear.
>
> …Having your subject return to communal cell between sessions is completely counterproductive. A subject returning to communal cell will feel pressure from fellow detainees based on the duration of his absence from the cell and the knowledge that he will be questioned by his peers upon his return. Isolation of your subject removes this intangible but extremely powerful influence from your subject. (FBI 2011, pp. 7–8)

In line with this rationale, in recent years, the severe psychological disturbances produced by solitary confinement were deliberately employed in the so-called war on terror to mentally and physically break down individuals as a part of what were euphemistically termed *enhanced interrogation* techniques (Physicians for Human Rights 2005).

Detainees were held in solitary confinement for months on end in secret locations and in prisons in Afghanistan, Iraq, and Guantanamo Bay and repeatedly subjected to numerous additional methods of interrogation including exposure to extremes of hot and cold temperatures, forced positions, sexual humiliation, threats, sleep deprivation, sensory overload, and waterboarding (suffocation by use of water), as well as other physical and psychological assaults (Table 16.1).

TABLE 16.1

Checklist for the Use of Solitary Confinement

Is Isolation Used for	
Arrested and pretrial detainees?	
As a part of the judicial sentence, including death row or a death sentence commuted to life imprisonment?	
Punishment/Prison discipline?	
Protective custody—for vulnerable groups?	Children; lesbian, gay, or transgendered individuals; sex offenders; former prison and police officers
For mentally ill prisoners or for suicide watch?	
Patients with HIV/AIDS?	
As a major part of the prison system in general?	
As part of interrogation procedures?	In combination with what other measures or methods of interrogation

What Are the Conditions of the Cell	
Size (sq. m. or sq. ft.)	
Light—Windows/natural light/artificial light	
Bedding/Furniture	
Hygiene and general condition of the cell	
Access to water and sanitation—in the cell/out of the cell	
Is the person restrained while in the cell?	Handcuffs; ankle cuffs; chains; body belt; other restraints?

What Is the	
Law/Regulation/Discipline code that governs the use of isolation?	
Maximum length of time that is permitted?	
Amount of time permitted out of the cell and for what purpose(s)?	
Level of contact with guards/staff or other prisoners?	
Access to medical care like?	
Access to other prison facilities?	

The Health Effects of Solitary Confinement

If "the degree of civilisation in a society can be judged by entering its prisons," as Fyodor Dostoyevsky wrote, then it is reasonable to suggest that the state of a prison can be judged by entering that prison's segregation or solitary confinement unit. Is it a dark, windowless, dirty, and claustrophobic space? Or is at a well-ventilated and clean, if austere, environment? Is there complete separation between the prisoners and between them and prison guards? Or is there a degree of meaningful human contact? Do prison staff and prisoners communicate with each other? And if so, what is the nature of their communication? What is the purpose of placing prisoners there? Who decides which prisoners should be isolated and for how long? Do prisoners know why they have been segregated? And how long they will remain in segregation? What in-cell provisions do they have access to? And how long do they spend in segregation on average? How long do prisoners spend outside their cells every day? And what degree of contact do they have with family and friends? What are the ethos and the atmosphere in the unit?

These factors are crucial for determining the health of the prison in general and its segregation unit in particular and for assessing their potential impact on the health and well-being of those confined in them. In addition to such environmental and institutional factors, of course, the physical and psychological effects of being isolated will also be determined by personal factors, including the individual's personal circumstances, history, habits, and health, including mental health, and the existence of previous trauma. Research also indicates that prior knowledge as to the expected duration of confinement is an important factor in how well the individual would be able to endure it.

Each of these institutional, environmental, and personal factors—in itself and in combination—can affect how any one individual would experience being confined in separation from others, how it would impact on them, and for how long.

And yet, research on the health effects of solitary confinement over the decades of its use consistently finds physiological, psychological, and social adjustment problems in those held in isolation from others. All studies of solitary confinement lasting longer than 10 days have demonstrated some negative effects (Haney 2003), with the risk of adverse effects increasing substantially after 4 weeks in isolation (Sestoft et al. 1998; Shalev 2008, pp. 21–22). One study found a decline in brain activity following 7 days in solitary confinement noting that if isolation lasts for a longer period, this decline may be irreversible (Scott and Gendreau 1969). Even studies suggesting that the effects of solitary confinement are minimal and/or reversible have found some negative effects (O'Keefe et al. 2010).

In 1861, George Attfield, a surgeon, the physician at the Convict Establishment Fremantle, in Western Australia, informed his superiors (letter to A. E. Kennedy, governor of Western Australia, April 30, 1861) that

> In a medical point of view I think there can be no question but that separate or solitary confinement acts injuriously, from first to last, in the health and constitution of anybody subjected to it…the symptoms of its pernicious constitutional influence being consecutively pallor, depression, debility, infirmity of intellect, and bodily decay. (Attfield 1861)

Three decades later, in what remains an eerily accurate observation and an excellent summary of the literature on the health effects of solitary confinement to date, the US Supreme Court noted that

> Solitary confinement at best failed to reform prisoners, and at worst caused serious mental problems… A considerable number of the prisoners fell, after even a short confinement, into a semi-fatuous condition, from which it was next to impossible to rouse them, and others became violently insane; others still, committed suicide; while those who stood the ordeal better, were not generally reformed and in most cases did not recover sufficient mental activity to be of any subsequent service to the community. (Re Medley 1890, p. 164)

With a few exceptions (notably O'Keefe et al. 2010, but see criticism of the study by Grassian [2010] and Casella [2010], among others), there is general consensus among health practitioners and researchers alike that solitary confinement adversely affects health and well-being and that it adversely affects prisoners' chances of successful reintegration into society.

These adverse effects, as previously noted, will vary with the premorbid adjustment of the individual and the context, length, and conditions of confinement. The experience of previous trauma will render the individual more vulnerable, as will the involuntary nature of his/her solitary confinement and confinement that persists over a sustained period. Initial acute reactions may be followed by chronic symptoms if the regime of solitary confinement persists. Despite any such differences, observations on the effects of solitary confinement are remarkably consistent. Indeed, Harvard psychiatrist Stuart Grassian—a long-time researcher and commentator on solitary confinement—contends that the constellation of these effects forms a unique syndrome which he termed the *isolation syndrome*:

> ...while this syndrome is strikingly atypical for the functional psychiatric illnesses, it is quite characteristic of an acute organic brain syndrome: delirium, characterised by a decreased level of alertness, EEG abnormalities...perceptual and cognitive disturbances, fearfulness, paranoia, and agitation; and random, impulsive and self-destructive behaviour.... (Grassian 2006, p. 338)

Research findings from the large body of literature examining the health effects of solitary confinement, and some of their reported signs and symptoms, are shown in Tables 16.2 and 16.3.

Some of the physiological symptoms may be manifestations of psychological stress, but the prolonged period of inactivity, lack of light and fresh air, lack of view to the outside world, and so on are also likely to have physical consequences. The most widely reported symptoms of solitary confinement, however, are psychological. These have been observed also in individuals with no prior history of mental health issues. As described in a US judgment, isolation units were "virtual incubators of psychoses—seeding illness in otherwise healthy inmates" (*Ruiz v. Johnson* [1999], p. 37).

If solitary confinement can lead to mental health problems in those with no prior history of mental illness, those with preexisting mental illness are at a particularly high risk of worsening psychiatric problems as a result of their isolation. There is wide agreement among experts (Kupers 1999; Haney 2003; Rhodes 2004; Grassian 2006; Kaba et al. 2014) that solitary confinement exacerbates mental illness, and this is increasingly recognized also by the courts.

In a class action lawsuit involving the Security Housing Unit (SHU) at Pelican Bay, California, for example, Federal Judge Thelton Henderson observed that conditions there may well "hover on the edge of what is humanly tolerable for those with normal

TABLE 16.2

Physiological Health Effects of Solitary Confinement

Physiological signs and symptoms	
• Gastrointestinal and genitourinary problems	• Heart palpitations
• Diaphoresis	• Migraine headaches
• Insomnia	• Back and other joint pains
• Deterioration of eyesight	• Poor appetite, weight loss, diarrhea
• Lethargy, weakness, profound fatigue	• Tremulousness
• Feeling cold	• Aggravation of preexisting medical problems

Source: Shalev, S. *A Sourcebook on Solitary Confinement*, Mannheim Centre for Criminology, LSE, London, 2008.

TABLE 16.3

Psychological Effects of Solitary Confinement

These can occur in the following areas and range from acute to chronic:

Anxiety, ranging from feelings of tension to full-blown panic attacks
- Persistent low level of stress
- Irritability or anxiousness
- Fear of impending death
- Panic attacks

Depression, varying from low mood to clinical depression
- Emotional flatness/blunting (loss of ability to have any feelings)
- Emotional lability (mood swings)
- Hopelessness
- Social withdrawal; loss of initiation of activity or ideas; apathy; lethargy
- Major depression

Anger, ranging from irritability to full-blown rage
- Irritability and hostility
- Poor impulse control
- Outbursts of physical and verbal violence against others, self, and objects
- Unprovoked anger, sometimes manifesting as rage

Cognitive disturbances, ranging from lack of concentration to confused states
- Short attention span
- Poor concentration
- Poor memory
- Confused thought processes; disorientation

Perceptual distortions, ranging from hypersensitivity to hallucinations
- Hypersensitivity to noises and smells
- Distortions of sensation (e.g., walls closing in)
- Disorientation in time and space
- Depersonalization/derealization
- Hallucinations affecting all five senses; visual, auditory, tactile, olfactory, and gustatory (e.g., hallucinations of objects or people appearing in the cell, hearing voices)

Paranoia and psychosis, ranging from obsessional thoughts to full-blown psychosis
- Recurrent and persistent thoughts (ruminations) often of a violent and vengeful character (e.g., directed against prison staff)
- Paranoid ideas, often persecutory
- Psychotic episodes or states: psychotic depression, schizophrenia

Self-harm and suicide
- Increased risk of self harm and suicide (see also Kaba et al. 2014).

Source: Shalev, S. *A Sourcebook on Solitary Confinement*, Mannheim Centre for Criminology, LSE, London, 2008.

resilience, particularly when endured for extended periods of time" (*Madrid v. Gomez* [1995], p. 1279). However,

> The already mentally ill, as well as persons with borderline personality disorders, brain damage or mental retardation, impulse-ridden personalities, or a history of prior psychiatric problems or chronic depression. For these inmates, placing them in the SHU is the mental equivalent of putting an asthmatic in a place with little air to breath. (*Madrid v. Gomez* 1995, p. 1265)

Twenty years later, the U.S. Court of Appeals noted:

> Of course, prison officials must have discretion to decide that in some instances tempo-
> rary, solitary confinement is a useful or necessary means to impose discipline and to
> protect prison employees and other inmates. But research still confirms what this Court
> suggested over a century ago: Years on end of near-total isolation exacts a terrible price.
> (*David v. Ayala* [2015] Judge Kennedy Concurring Opinion)

Solitary confinement has another possible implication for the mentally ill who, it is important to remember, are grossly overrepresented in prison in general and in segregation units
in particular. They may behave in ways that, in the context of high-security confinement, are
interpreted as rule violations rather than a manifestation of their illness. Where the prisoner's progression through the system is dependent on their behavior and perceived adherence
to prison rules, this may create a vicious cycle which results in a prolonged stay in isolation,
whose very conditions make him worse, and less able to abide by the rules and regulations
(see also Human Rights Watch [2003]). Levels of self-harm and suicide, which are anyway
much higher in prison, increase even further in segregation units (Fazel et al. 2011).

Children and young adults are another group which is particularly vulnerable to the effects
of solitary confinement, as they are still in the process of developing—physically, mentally, and
socially (ACLU 2013). Their placement in prolonged solitary confinement had been described
by psychologist Craig Haney (2003) as being equivalent to "putting them in a deep freeze."

Lastly, research shows that detainees held on remand are also particularly vulnerable to the
effects of solitary confinement. One study of detainees held on remand in Denmark found
that where detainees were isolated for 4 weeks, "the probability of being admitted to hospital
for a psychiatric reason was about 20 times as high as for a person remanded in nonsolitary
confinement for the same period of time." (Sestoft et al. 1998). A more recent longitudinal
study commissioned by the Swedish Prisons and Probation Service to examine the health
effects of restricted detention of those held on remand (including solitary confinement) found
that such detention poses a "significant risk of mental illness" (Holmgren et al. 2011, p. 22) even
when controlling for other factors (previous psychiatric contact, substance abuse, gender, par-
enting). One in four of those detained with restrictions suffered mental illness, compared to
one in five among those held without restrictions. A qualitative study carried out in parallel
to the main study found that three factors are particularly harmful to the mental well-being
and behavior in prison: passivity, uncertainty, and feeling impotent. These factors—present
to some degree in any form of confinement—are of course magnified in isolation.

A more subtle and lingering effect of solitary confinement is that it impairs the individual's social skills and abilities.

D., a prisoner serving his fourteenth year in solitary confinement at the time, describes
having experienced over the years many negative health effects including anger, cognitive disturbances, depression, confused thought process, and self-harm. He also describes
irreversible social effects:

> Talking, forming verbal sentences, drains me of energy. It takes too much effort at times.
> Very little interests me. "Small talk" bores the shit out of me. I struggle to find things to say
> to maintain what most people would regard as normal social interaction, chit-chat. And if I
> do have something to say but it involves too many words, it's like my mind gets overloaded
> with the seeming complexity of expressing it verbally. The words/thoughts basically get
> muddled up in my head. It's like I'm only good for short sentences for short periods... I
> wasn't the greatest of talkers before this stint in solitary. I always preferred my own com-
> pany, but I wasn't like I am now. (Sharon Shalev, personal communication, August 2011)

Many former prisoners also report similar difficulties, some many years following their release from prison. In the context of efforts to rehabilitate and reintegrate former prisoners back into free society, and considering that the key aim of prison systems, as reflected in numerous international instruments, is to rehabilitate offenders, this is a worrying problem.

Is Solitary Confinement Legal under International Law?

Despite a clear condemnation of the use of isolation in the 1990 UN Basic Principles for the Treatment of Prisoners, until recent years which called for an abolition of solitary confinement, there have been few if any concerted international efforts to achieve this aim. However, in addressing the issue, the growing jurisprudence of regional human right courts and UN treaty bodies repeatedly acknowledges the harmful physical and mental effects of SC.

Whether or not solitary confinement constitutes a legitimate, if extreme, prison practice or prohibited treatment in any given case, would depend on a number of factors. The European Court of Human Rights (ECtHR) identified determining factors to include the stringency of the measure, its duration, the objective pursued, and its effects on the person concerned (*Ensslin, Badder, Raspe v. Federal Republic of Germany* [1978]; *Babar Ahmad and others v. UK*, p. 209 [2012]). Any such effects, in turn, will depend on the individual's personal makeup, history, and circumstances and on institutional and environmental (or situational) factors. While the European Court considers that strict isolation with severe restrictions on contact with others may violate Article 3 of the European Convention on Human Rights (the prohibition of torture, inhumane or degrading treatment, or punishment), it appeared to ignore the fundamental need of every person to properly socialize with other people, since in cases where there was some contact with lawyers and family and access to television, books, and newspapers in a small cell, the court found that this did not violate Article 3 (see, for example, *Ramirez Sanchez v. France* [2006] and Öcalan v. Turkey [2005]). The Inter-American Court of Human Rights has more clearly judged in several cases that the psychological and physical suffering from strict solitary confinement with severely restricted family visits can amount to CIDT or torture (see, for example, *Velázquez-Rodríguez v. Honduras* [1988] and *Cantoral-Benavides v. Peru* [2000]).

The UN SRT (2011) considers that each case of isolation must be individually examined to determine if it constitutes CIDT or torture, in particular the reasons for being placed in isolation, the duration, the conditions, and the particular vulnerabilities of the individual. Where the psychological effects of solitary confinement are employed on pretrial prisoners to extort information or a confession, the special rapporteur considers this to be torture or cruel, inhumane, or degrading treatment of punishment. By extension, the use of the same methods during the interrogation of terrorist suspects to intimidate, break the will, gain information or cooperation (Physicians for Human Rights 2007) must also constitute torture or cruel, inhuman, or degrading treatment of punishment.

What Constitutes Prolonged Solitary Confinement?

There is no universally agreed definition of what constitutes prolonged solitary confinement. Noting the potential for serious adverse health effects and that all studies of solitary confinement lasting longer than 10 days have demonstrated some negative effects, the UN Special Rapporteur (2011) defined *prolonged solitary confinement* as a period lasting longer than 15 days. The updated UN Standard Minimum Rules (The "Nelson Mandela Rules") have incorporated the maximum limit of 15 days for solitary confinement. While stating that no disciplinary sanctions may amount to torture or other cruel, inhumane, or degrading treatment or punishment, the updated rules clearly stipulate that indefinite or prolonged solitary confinement are prohibited at any time, thereby implying that they would constitute torture or ill-treatment (UN Standard Minimum Rules 2015).

Provided that the decision to place a prisoner in solitary confinement is taken by the competent authority, in accordance with the law and subject to due process safeguards; that the prisoner is held in decent conditions and afforded outdoor exercise and a degree of human contact; and in the absence of additional deprivations and cruelties, we contend that in some cases, the upper limit may be set slightly higher. However, any decision must be taken on an individual basis, fully taking into account the individual's particular needs and circumstances. Experience has shown that in some cases isolation can lead to serious problems after a very short period—days and even hours—and that problems developed during isolation do not always subside after its termination.

Safeguards for the Use of Solitary Confinement

While working toward a ban or extreme restriction of the use of isolation for any reason and in any form, there are various safeguards that should be put in place to attempt to mitigate its arbitrary use and its negative health effects.

Procedural Safeguards

The use of isolation in any detention setting must be tightly regulated by laws, regulations, and codes of practice. No one should be allowed to be punished or coerced by isolation in an arbitrary fashion, that is, on the sole discretion of a prison officer, a police officer, or an interrogator. Due process procedures must be in place. In particular the individual must be informed, in writing, of the reason and length of their segregation; there must be a right to a hearing, the right to a defense, and the right to appeal (UN Standard Minimum Rules 2015). Once in isolation, there must be regular and frequent reviews of the decision by decision-makers, who are different to, and independent of, those who made the initial placement.

Placement in Solitary Confinement

Prison systems that are constructed around prolonged solitary confinement as a tool for managing prison populations cannot be justified, and indefinite solitary confinement is now expressly prohibited by the updated UN Standard Minimum Rules. The UN SRT considers that the use of isolation as a means of prison discipline can constitute torture, CIDT, or punishment, and therefore, it should only be used as a last resort and for no longer than a few days. The updated UN Standard Minimum Rules place an upper limit of 15 days on the use of solitary confinement. Using solitary confinement to apply psychological pressure on individuals for the purpose of extorting information or a confession during interrogation in any form, and for pretrial detainees, may constitute torture, CIDT, or punishment and must be prohibited. If shown on a case-by-case basis to be exceptionally necessary in such cases, it must be used with judicial oversight and only for a matter of a few days.

The use of solitary confinement for anyone with a mental illness or physical disability is prohibited where the condition would be exacerbated by the conditions of isolation. Prison authorities are further required not to punish any offense that may be the direct result of any mental illness or developmental disability. The use of solitary confinement is prohibited for pregnant women, women with infants, and breastfeeding mothers (UN Bangkok Rules, UN Standard Minimum Rules 2015) and is prohibited under any circumstances for children (United Nations Rules for the Protection of Juveniles Deprived of their Liberty, UN Standard Minimum Rules 2015).

Physical Conditions and Regime

The updated UN Standard Minimum Rules make clear that the minimum standards set out for all the general living conditions apply to all prisoners at all times, whether or not they are subjected to disciplinary sanctions (UN Standard Minimum Rules 2015). Because a prisoner in isolation will, by definition, spend over 22 hours per day in the cell, it is particularly important that they are not further deprived of these minimum conditions. There must be access to the open air and regular exercise, as well as reading and recreational material. The person should be allowed a degree of autonomy and control over their environment. There should be access to educational, recreational, and vocational training, and where possible, this should be in association with other prisoners. There must be regular and meaningful human contact including family visits as for the regular prison population. Prison authorities are further required to take measures to mitigate the potentially detrimental effects of solitary confinement prior to the person's release from prison (UN Standard Minimum Rules 2015).

Table 16.4 summarizes the checklist of safeguards for the use of solitary confinement.

TABLE 16.4

Checklist on the Safeguards for the Use of Solitary Confinement

Is the use of isolation governed by specific laws/regulations/rules?	What are the specific references to these rules and regulations?
What is the precise mechanism for deciding on the application of isolation?	Are there due process safeguards (disciplinary hearing, right of defense, right of appeal, etc.) or can it be decided arbitrarily by any staff?
Are particular vulnerable groups excluded from isolation?	Including children, mentally ill, people with disabilities, pregnant women, women with infants or who are breastfeeding, etc?
Is protective custody in isolation voluntary?	
Is there a health check before someone is sent to isolation?	By a nurse or a doctor? What are the criteria for excluding someone?
Is there a health check once in isolation?	How often and how does the person get access to the health system?
How much time can the prisoner spend out of the cell?	What activities are available?
What activities are available to the person in the cell?	
What form of contact is there with staff or other prisoners while in solitary?	
How much contact with family and legal representatives is permitted?	
Do prison staff have training in mental health issues?	

What Does the Future Hold for Solitary Confinement?

Solitary confinement is unlikely to ever completely disappear from prisons, jails, police stations, and military facilities. However, there are some early signs that its more extended use, especially in the United States, may finally be coming to a halt, as both national and international bodies have stepped up efforts in this area.

In 2007, a group of international experts adopted the Istanbul Statement on the Use and Effects of Solitary Confinement (2007), calling on states to limit the use of solitary confinement to very exceptional cases, for as short a time as possible and only as a last resort. In August 2011, international efforts received a further boost when the UN SRT focused his periodic report to the UN General Assembly on the practice of solitary confinement, stating that it is a "harsh measure which may cause serious psychological and physiological adverse effects on individuals" and which can violate the international prohibition against torture and CIDT. Importantly, the report called for the absolute prohibition of prolonged solitary confinement, which it defined as a period in excess of 15 days. Soon thereafter, in November, the CPT also focused its annual report on solitary confinement, calling on states to reduce its use to the absolute minimum and ensure that its use in any case is proportionate, lawful, accountable, necessary, and nondiscriminatory. More recently, the revised UN Standard Minimum Rules (Mandela Rules) have expressly prohibited indefinite and prolonged solitary confinement and indicate that such uses would constitute torture or other forms of cruel, inhumane, or degrading treatment or punishment.

While efforts continue to abolish or heavily restrict the use of solitary confinement, the implementation of the safeguards described earlier can help mitigate the severe nature of this practice. Only then can we have confidence that in the meantime, the human rights of prisoners are being respected and that, as Principle 1 of the UN Basic Principles for the Treatment of Prisoners requires, "all prisoners shall be treated with the respect due to their inherent dignity and value as human beings."

References

American Civil Liberties Union (ACLU) 2013, *Alone and Afraid: Children Held in Solitary Confinement and Isolation in Juvenile Detention and Correctional Facilities.* ACLU: Washington DC.

Andersen, H. S., Sestoft, D., Lillebaek, T., Gabrielsen, G., Hemmingsen, R., and Kramp, P. 2000, A longitudinal study of prisoners on remand: Psychiatric prevalence, incidence and psychopathology in solitary vs. non-solitary confinement, *Acta Psychiatrica Scandinavica*, vol. 102, issue 1, pp. 19–25.

Attfield, G. C. 1861, Surgeon at the Convict Establishment Fremantle, Letter to A. E. Kennedy, Governor of Western Australia, April 30, 1861.

Bureau of Justice Statistics 2015, *Use of restrictive housing in U.S. prisons and jails, 2011-12*, US Department of Justice, Washington, DC.

Casella, J. 2010, ACLU and experts slam findings of Colorado DOC report on solitary confinement, *Solitary Watch*, December 4. Available from: http://solitarywatch.com/2010/12/04/aclu-and-experts-slam-findings-of-colorado-doc-report-on-solitary-confinement/. [December 19, 2012].

CPT (European Committee for the Prevention of Torture) 2011a, *Report to the Norwegian government on the visit to Norway carried out by the European Committee for the Prevention of Torture and Inhuman or Degrading Treatment or Punishment (CPT) from May 18–27, 2011*, CPT/Inf (2011) 33, CPT, Strasbourg.

CPT 2011b, *21st general report*, CPT/Inf (2011), CPT, Strasbourg.

Evans, R. 1982, *The Fabrication Of Virtue: English Prison Architecture 1750–1840*, Cambridge University Press, Cambridge.

Farber, I. E., Harlow, H. F., and West, L. J. 1957, Brainwashing, conditioning, and DDD (debility, dependency, and dread), *Sociometry*, vol. 23, pp. 120–147.

Fazel, S., Grann, M., Kling, B., and Hawton, K. 2011, Prison suicides in 12 countries: An ecological study of 861 suicides during 2003–2007, *Social Psychiatry and Psychiatric Epidemiology*, vol. 46, pp. 191–195.

Federal Bureau of Investigations (FBI) 2011, *Interrogation primer: Cross cultural, rapport-based interrogation* (version 5), FBI, Washington, DC.

Grassian, S. 2006, Psychiatric effects of solitary confinement, *Journal of Law and Policy*, vol. 22, pp. 325–383.

Grassian, S. 2010, "Fatal flaws" in the Colorado Solitary Confinement study, *Guest Post for Solitary Watch*, November 15. Available from http://solitarywatch.com/2010/11/15/fatal-flaws-in-the-colorado-solitary-confinement-study/. [December 10, 2012].

Haney, C. 2003, Mental health issues in long-term solitary and 'supermax' confinement, *Crime & Delinquency*, vol. 49, pp. 124–156.

Holmgren, B., Frisell, T., and Runeson, B. 2011, *Psykisk hälsa hos häktade med restriktioner* (Mental Health of Detainees with Restrictions), Swedish Prison and Probation Service, Norrköping.

Human Rights Watch 1995, *Prison conditions in Japan*, Human Rights Watch, New York.

Human Rights Watch 2003, *Ill-equipped: U.S. prisons and offenders with mental illness*, Human Rights Watch, New York.

Inter-American Commission of Human Rights 2008, *Resolution 1/08 Principles and Best Practices on the Protection of Persons Deprived of Liberty in the Americas*, Principal XXII 3 (Measures of Solitary Confinement), Inter-American Commission of Human Rights, Washington, DC.

Istanbul statement on the use and effects of solitary confinement 2007, adopted at the International Psychological Trauma Symposium, Istanbul. Available from: http://www.solitaryconfinement.org/Istanbul.

Kaba, F., Lewis, A., Glowa-Kollisch, S., Hadler, J., Lee, D., Alper, H., Selling, D., MacDonald, R., Solimo, A., Parsons, A., and Venters, H. 2014, Solitary confinement and risk of self-harm among jail inmates, *American Journal of Public Health*, vol. 104, issue 3, 442–447. doi: 10.2105/AJPH.2013.301742.

Kupers, T. 1999, *Prison Madness: The Mental Health Crisis Behind Bars And What We Must Do About It*, Jossey-Bass, San Francisco, CA.

O'Keefe, M. L., Klebe, K. J., Stucker, A., Sturm, K., and Leggett, W. 2010, *One year longitudinal study of the psychological effects of administrative segregation*, Colorado Department of Corrections, Colorado Springs, CO. Available from: http://www.doc.state.co.us/sites/default/files/opa/AdSegReport_2010.pdf. [December 20, 2012].

Physicians for Human Rights 2005, *Break them down: Systematic use of psychological torture by US forces*, Physicians for Human Rights, Boston, NJ.

Physicians for Human Rights 2007, *Leave no marks: Enhanced interrogation techniques and the risk of criminality*, Physicians for Human Rights, Boston, NJ.

PRI (Penal Reform International) 2012a, *The abolition of the death penalty and its alternative sanction in Central Asia: Kazakhstan, Kyrgyzstan and Tajikistan*, PRI, London.

PRI 2012b, *The abolition of the death penalty and its alternative sanction in Eastern Europe: Belarus, Russia and Ukraine*, PRI, London.

Rhodes, L. A. 2004, *Total Confinement: Madness and Reason in the Maximum Security Prison*, University of California Press, Berkley and Los Angeles, CA.

Scott, G. D., and Gendreau, P. 1969, Psychiatric implications of sensory deprivation in a maximum security prison, *Canadian Psychiatric Association Journal*, vol. 14, pp. 337–341.

Sestoft, D. M., Andersen, H. S., Lillebaek, T., and Gabrielsen, G. 1998, Impact of solitary confinement on hospitalisation among Danish prisoners in custody, *International Journal of Law and Psychiatry*, vol. 21, pp. 99–108.

Shalev, S. 2008, *A sourcebook on solitary confinement*, Mannheim Centre for Criminology, LSE, London. Available from: http://www.solitaryconfinement.org.

Shalev, S. 2009, *Supermax: Controlling risk through solitary confinement*, Willan Publishing, Devon, England.

Shalev, S. and Edgar, K. 2015, *Deep custody: Segregation units and close supervision centres in England and Wales*, Prison Reform Trust, London. Available from: http://solitaryconfinement.org/UK-solitary -confinement [February 5, 2016].

Swedish Prison and Probation Service 2012, *Detainees with Restrictions*. Online at: http://www.kvv .se/sv/Publikationer/ (Accessed 20 December 2012).

Tabuchi, H. 2010, Japanese officials reveal execution chambers, *The New York Times*, August 27. Available from Japanese Officials Reveal Execution Chambers—NYTimes.com [December 2, 2012].

Toch, H. 1987, The disturbed and disruptive inmate: Where does the buck stop?, *Journal of Psychiatry and the Law*, vol. 10, pp. 321–349.

UN 1990, *Basic principles for the treatment of prisoners*, Principle 7, UN, Geneva.

UN Special Rapporteur 2011, *Interim report to the Human Rights Council on torture and other cruel, inhuman or degrading treatment or punishment*, UN DOC A/66/268, UN, Geneva.

UN Standard Minimum Rules for the Treatment of Prisoners (the Nelson Mandela Rules). Resolution adopted by the General Assembly on 17 December 2015 A/RES/70/175

United Nations Rules for the Protection of Juveniles Deprived of their Liberty. Adopted by General Assembly resolution 45/113 of 14 December 1990.

Court Cases Cited

U.S.
David v. Ayala, 576 U.S. (2015)
Madrid v. Gomez, 889 F.Supp. 1146, 1249 (N.D. Cal. 1995)
Re Medley, 134 US 160 (1890)
Ruiz v. Johnson, 37 F. Supp. 2d 855,909 (S.D. Tex 1999)

European Court of Human Rights
Babar Ahmad and Others v. the United Kingdom, Applications nos. 24027/07, 11949/08, 36742/08, 66911/09 and 67354/09, Judgment of April 10, 2012.
Ensslin, Baader and Raspe v. Federal Republic of Germany, Application No. 7572/76, 14 D.R.91, 109 (1978).
Öcalan v. Turkey, Application no. 46221/99, Judgment of May 12, 2005 [GC].
Ramirez Sanchez v. France, Application no. 59450/00, ECHR 2006-IX [GC].

Inter-American Court of Human Rights
Velázquez-Rodríguez v. Honduras, Inter-American Court of Human Rights, Series C, No. 4, para. 156 (1988).
Cantoral-Benavides v. Peru, Inter-American Court of Human Rights, Series C, No. 69, paras. 62 and 104 (2000).

Index

Printed and bound by CPI Group (UK) Ltd, Croydon, CR0 4YY

23/10/2024

01777682-0008